P9-CQP-742

"In an age in which conventional wisdom is confused with being wise, political correctness has replaced intellectual rigor, politicians speak of virtue but practice vice, and being accused of insensitivity is considered far more damning than being irrational, *The New Absolutes* resists the spirit of this age with clear and insightful analysis."

Francis J. Beckwith, Ph.D.
Assistant Professor of Philosophy, Whittier College
Author, *Politically Correct Death*

" 'It's all just relative!' That's what most Americans believe, right? Not so, says social critic, Bill Watkins. American behavior betrays this pop-belief. What Americans demonstrate in their fervent commitment to 'political correctness,' 'multiculturalism,' and 'universal tolerance' is an allegiance to an even greater absolute moral code. In the face of the 'New Absolutes,' Christians need to rationally show how the old absolutes are more capable of benefiting the national common good. An 'absolutely' superb treatment of where America is today by one of its best thinkers."

Dr. Robert Hicks
Educator, Author

"This book is a penetrating analysis of the hidden absolutes cloaked in the deceptive garb of cultural relativity. It unmasks the popular politically correct moral relativism for what it is—a new form of absolutism, attempting to replace the time-honored Judeo-Christian values with the absolutistic agenda of the cultural and moral left. Its insightful critique, lucid style, and clear exposé place it in the forefront of recent cultural apologetics."

Dr. Norm Geisler
Dean, Southern Evangelical Seminary
Author of more than 40 books

"Clear, cogent, compelling and concise, William Watkins' *The New Absolutes* is a highly readable and reliable road map for the modern age. Indeed, it is a veritable handbook of Christian cultural criticism, full of wisdom and insight."

Dr. Michael Bauman
Professor of Theology and Culture
Director of Christian Studies at Hillsdale College

"William D. Watkins has exposed the hypocrisy of the relativists and in so doing has made a major contribution to the critical struggle of our age. What is right? What is wrong? What is good? What is true? Those who claim not to know the answers to these big questions invariably substitute their own absolutes for the ones they have abandoned."

Dr. Michael Jones
Editor, *Culture Wars*
Author, *Degenerate Moderns*

"*The New Absolutes* is an interesting, well written analysis of modern culture which provides practical, well-reasonsed solutions to the difficulties surfaced in that analysis. In possession of a wide ranging grasp of the issues, Watkins dispenses with that old bromide that modern culture is relativistic and provides insights into the nature of the new absolutism infecting our society. No Christian activist can afford to ignore this book."

J. P. Moreland
Professor of Philosophy
Talbot School of Theology
Biola University

"I believe we stand in a 'millennial moment.' It is time for a new generation of leaders, apologists, scholars, and writers to re-present a message of hope for the third millennium. Bill Watkins is one of those men. His insights into the emptiness of the age and brillant presentation of its only hope-filled alternative, the classical Judeo-Christian message is a must read! As a lawyer, public policy analyst, and dedicated Roman Catholic, I heartily recommend *The New Absolutes* to all who seek to understand the currect cultural challenges we face and to be a part of the solution."

Keith A. Fournier, Esq.
Executive Director
American Center for Law and Justice

"Few works illumine the public debate about cultural values with such clarifying light and good sense as William D. Watkins' *The New Absolutes.* Watkins exposes the postmodern foundations of shifting sand upon which 'new' relative standards of belief and morality are based, and contrasts them with the solid wisdom of a biblical moral tradition. A compelling and persuasive apologetic for the twenty-first century."

Terry Lindvall, Ph.D.
President
Regent University

THE NEW ABSOLUTES

WILLIAM D. WATKINS

THE NEW ABSOLUTES

BETHANY HOUSE PUBLISHERS
MINNEAPOLIS, MINNESOTA 55438

Published by Bethany House Publishers
A Ministry of Bethany Fellowship, Inc.
11300 Hampshire Avenue South
Minneapolis, Minnesota 55438

Printed in the United States of America.

Library of Congress Cataloging-in-Publication Data

Watkins, William D.
The new absolutes and how they are eroding moral character, families, and society / William D. Watkins.
p. cm.
Includes bibliographical references and index.
ISBN 1–55661–721–6 (cloth)
1. Apologetics. 2. Skepticism—Controversial literature. 3. Relativity—Controversial literature. 4. Moral conditions. 5. Civilization, Modern—20th century. 6. Watkins, William D. I. Title.
BT1211.W38 1996
239—dc20 96–45783
CIP

To Dr. James Slinger

The first person to give me sound philosophical reasons
to believe in absolute truth
and universal moral prescriptions.

Acknowledgments

Several people have contributed significantly to the development of this book either through conversations, their own writings, or simply their moral support. Among these individuals I would like to mention especially David Clark, J. P. Moreland, Frank Beckwith, Norman Geisler, Gary Habermas, Kerby Anderson, Lanier Burns, E. Michael Jones, Thomas "Pat" Monaghan, Keith Fournier, and Michael Bauman.

I would also like to thank the Evangelical Philosophical Society, which in 1994 gave me the opportunity to present an early version of this book's thesis for peer review.

Of course, many thanks go to Bethany House Publishers for believing in this project. In particular I extend my appreciation to Steve Laube for seeing value in this book from the very start and for providing enthusiasm and helpful criticisms; to Gary and Carol Johnson for getting behind me and this book in ways most authors only dream about; to Kevin Johnson for being such an understanding advocate and go-between; and to Jeanne Mikkelson for her timely and creative marketing work.

Finally, my deepest sense of appreciation goes to my lifelong partner, Pamela. Her insight, love, patience, and perseverance give my being refreshment, my becoming enrichment, and my doing clarification.

Contents

PART ONE

Reality in the Balance

Chapter 1

"God" in Fresno

In his bestselling book *The Closing of the American Mind*, the University of Chicago professor Allan Bloom claimed, "There is one thing a professor can be absolutely certain of: almost every student entering the university believes, or says he believes, that truth is relative."[1] What Bloom wrote about in 1987, I experienced for the first time in 1976.

I had returned to college as a student after almost a three-year hiatus. I had changed my major from music to philosophy in hopes of exploring the central issues about reality, truth, and ethics that had begun to haunt me. One course was called Comparative Religions, and it was there I finally encountered a full-bodied relativist—someone who really believed that each person could determine their own truth. He was not the kind of self-avowed relativist who simply uses his position to avoid critical dialogue or excuse his behavior. I had met many who matched that description. Ed was a relativist of a different order. He was striving to carry out his position to one of its logical conclusions. Ed and I were attending the California State University at Fresno, which at the time boasted about fifteen thousand students.

Fresno's summers are blistering hot. Daylight temperatures ranging between 100 and 115 degrees are all too common. Aside from air-conditioners, the only relief comes after the sun sets, when the temperature can drop as much as forty degrees. It was on one of these 100-plus degree days around 1:00 P.M. when I met Ed.

Oppressed by the heat, I entered the building that housed the comparative religions class, hoping for some cool air. I stepped inside and dropped onto a desk near the door. No cold air. The air-conditioner was on the fritz again.

Hot and frustrated, I turned to look out the windows until class began. As a few more students anxiously entered the classroom, I saw the same expectancy of relief fall from their faces as it had from mine.

Just as I got about as comfortable I could, a heavy stomp announced the arrival of Ed. Those old army boots of his pulverized the dirt and sent little puffs of dust into the air. Dirt never had a chance with Ed around.

Every time I saw him, he reminded me of a husky mountaineer who must have moonlighted as a junk-hoarding hermit. He wore old faded blue jeans that had given out at the knees, and a long-sleeve shirt with thin mustard-colored stripes crisscrossing all over it.

Before sitting in the desk next to me, he brought his backpack around in front of him, dropped it to the floor, and kicked it into an upright position against the side of his chair. Slumping down, he let nearly half his body slip under his desk.

"Is it ever hot!" he exclaimed, adding an expletive as he wiped his limp, sweat-saturated hair out of his eyes. He pulled his front shirttail up to his face and dried his beard.

"Yeah, it's not much better in here either," I said. "The air-conditioner must be out. Uh, your name is . . ."

"Ed," he replied, shifting his head toward my desk. "And yours is Bill, right?"

"Yeah, that's right. So how do you like the class?" This was a favorite question of mine. It usually kept discussions from degenerating into trivial babble about the weather or something else banal.

Slumping still farther into his chair, he folded his hands and placed them on his head. "I think it's pretty good," he replied. "Carol, the prof, makes it interesting. That's more than I can say for some other profs I've had."

"I know what you mean." I turned around in my seat to look out the windows again.

"I'm glad Carol isn't hung up on whether something is true or false, or right or wrong. I don't go for labels like that."

"What?" I asked, turning back toward Ed. "What did you say?"

"I said, I'm glad Carol doesn't label different religions and ideas as true or false. Besides, it doesn't make sense to try, anyway, because no one knows what's true and what's false. Without absolutes, everything is relative to what one thinks."

That's not true, I thought. *What a ridiculous claim to make anyway. In effect he's claiming that it is absolutely true that no truths are absolute. That's contradictory.*

It was too hot to hassle with him, so I decided to listen to what he had to say until class began. I was hoping I could just ride him out without getting into a heavy philosophical discussion.

"Why, for all I know," Ed continued, "I could be God."

I abruptly shifted my full attention to Ed's sweat-beaded face. *He can't be serious,* I said to myself. *Of course not. He's just trying to get my ear, and he succeeded.*

"Sure you could," I said jokingly.

"Well, why not?" he retorted. "I'm just as good a candidate as any," he boastfully asserted.

I couldn't believe how easily his idea of being God rolled off his tongue. He had to be kidding.

"Come on, Ed. You don't really think you're God. That's . . ."

"Sure I do!" he said, sharply raising his voice. "What's so strange about that?"

I leaned back against my chair and looked straight into his pale blue eyes. *This guy must be nuts,* I thought.

The room was quickly filling up with students now, but I didn't pay much attention to them. Instead, I focused on Ed and tried to think of what to say.

"You really do believe you're God," I finally squeezed out. "Do you think you're the Creator also?" I quickly asked.

"What do you mean?" Ed queried.

"You know—the sun, the planets, the stars, human beings, the natural materials that went into the construction of this building—everything. Did you create it all?"

"I could have," he replied with less than an authoritative tone.

"I didn't ask whether you could have or not, but whether in fact you did create all that exists."

"Yes . . . yes, I did," Ed haltingly claimed.

"You're sure now?" I said.

"Sure I am! I created all things." He appeared a bit smug now.

"Well, then," I began, "if you really are God, and you really did create all these things, then why weren't you sure you were God when we first started talking about it? At first you only said that you *could* have been God, not that you were. It seems to me, Ed, that if you were intelligent and powerful enough to create and shape the entire universe, you could recall who you were rather quickly. But you couldn't."

Ed looked down at the desktop and deliberately folded his arms across his broad chest. Slowly, he turned only his head toward me until we were facing each other again. Then, in a soft yet unyielding tone, he said, "I could have created all things, then afterward fallen asleep. You and this class may just all be part of a dream I'm having. I really could be God, but in my dream I'm just a confused finite man."

I sat silent and motionless for a moment, wrestling for a reply. Finally, I looked up into Ed's solemn face and said, "Ed, that's crazy! If you really are God, and you're powerful and intelligent enough to have created the entire universe, then don't you think you would know whether you were dreaming? And don't you think you would be powerful and intelligent enough to snap yourself out of your dream at will? Couldn't you do it right now?"

Unfortunately, I never received an answer from Ed. Before he could respond, the professor began her lecture.

From that day on, Ed avoided me. I found that perplexing, even amusing. Why would "God" fear a mere mortal who supposedly existed only in His dream?

While I'm confident Ed's claim to deity was mistaken, I am also sure that Ed was right to carry relativism to that conclusion. If relativism is true, and I will show that it is not, the individual must eventually reign supreme. Self must put itself in the place of deity and become not the discoverer of truth but the determiner of truth. The relativist does not have to claim tremendous power or knowledge as Ed attempted to do, nor proclaim himself the Creator of the universe. But he will have to fashion his own world with beliefs of his choosing. Ed came to understand this and finally, though somewhat tenaciously, drew the appropriate conclusion—that he was divine. As it turned out, he was unprepared for the role. He couldn't even handle the questions of a fellow student.

I will show that Ed is not alone. No relativist is equal to the task of deity no matter how stripped down a version of god he is. No one adheres to relativism consistently; no one ever could. Out of necessity all relativists are closet absolutists.

This is a radical claim to make in our allegedly relativistic world. Cultural observers tell us that the notion that truth and morality are mere conventions created by groups or individuals supposedly pervades every facet of Western society. We are, most pundits claim, believers in the dictum that no truths or moral laws are universally binding. In *The New Absolutes* I contend that these pundits are wrong. Not only is relativism false and impossible to embrace, but it is not held in the West or the world at large. Many people claim to be relativists, but they are not.

Cultural commentators are correct concerning the West's cultural crisis. Western society is crumbling. Relativism, however, is not the culprit. The real causes lie elsewhere. One cause—the one I will focus on in Part II—is America's growing acceptance of a new set of alleged truths that we are being persuaded and sometimes forced to accept as absolutes. References to these absolutes are carefully avoided; nonetheless, the new "truths" and the behavior of those who accept (and oppose) them demonstrate that absolutism is alive and well.

I realize many critics will condemn this viewpoint as elitist and intolerant—the two worst sins of our "enlightened, progressive" age. I readily accept both charges, but, as you will see, not in the vein they are usually understood. I certainly believe that some truth claims are true and others false, and that some behaviors are moral and others immoral. I also believe that whatever is true is absolutely true and that whatever is moral is absolutely moral. I will demonstrate, in fact, that absolutism not only exists but must be true, and that even self-avowed relativists illustrate this reality.

On the other hand, I will also argue that much of what passes for universal truth today is nothing of the kind. The new absolutes and their foundational assumptions are false. Moreover, they are undermining the very building blocks of Western civilization, including basic principles of liberty, the institutions of marriage and the family, and our understanding of human nature, reason, ethics, and ultimately reality itself.

Just a few years after World War II, Richard Weaver, an English professor at the University of Chicago, wrote a profound treatise called *Ideas Have Consequences.* In it he stated, "There is ground for declaring that modern man has become a moral idiot."[2] He went on to show that the "dissolution of the West" he had witnessed was "the product not of biological or other necessity but of unintelligent choice." We have no one or nothing other than ourselves and our choices to blame for it. In Weaver's words, "For four centuries every man has been not only his own priest but his own professor of ethics, and the consequence is an anarchy which threatens even that minimum consensus of value necessary to the political state."[3] From his standpoint in history, he could tell that modern society was self-destructing. To those who thought he was wrong, he answered, "If you seek the monument to our folly, look about you." He writes:

> In our own day we have seen cities obliterated and ancient faiths stricken. We may well ask, in the words of Matthew, whether we are not faced with "great tribulation, such as was not since the beginning of the world." We have for many years moved with a brash confidence that man had achieved a position of independence which rendered the ancient restraints needless. Now, in the first half of the twentieth century, at the height of modern progress, we behold un-

> precedented outbreaks of hatred and violence; we have seen whole nations desolated by war and turned into penal camps by their conquerors; we find half of mankind looking upon the other half as criminal. Everywhere occur symptoms of mass psychosis. Most portentous of all, there appear diverging bases of value, so that our single planetary globe is mocked by worlds of different understanding. These signs of disintegration arouse fear, and fear leads to desperate unilateral efforts toward survival, which only forward the process.[4]

Standing on the threshold of a new century and a new millennium, I think it is accurate to say that moral idiocy has reached new heights in our world, especially in Western civilization. The "diverging bases of value" Weaver saw appearing fifty years ago have flowered under the banners of relativism, multiculturalism, pluralism, postmodernism, and the new tolerance. What he feared as a foreboding sign of social disintegration, we have embraced as emblems of social progress and maturity. The "worlds of different understanding" he believed would mire us in facts at the expense of knowledge and wisdom are today heralded as signs of our openness to exciting and enriching vistas of intellectual and moral awareness. Where Weaver saw perversity, we see lifestyle differences. Where he saw disintegration, we see pluralism. Where he saw the destructive influence of egotism, we see the celebration of individual liberty.

The rest of this book is about the very real possibility that Weaver's sight was virtually 20/20, while that of many Westerners verges on blindness. To see this, we must look at what afflicts us culturally, or at least what many people say is our malady. Like a doctor who arrives in the middle of an operation that should be succeeding but is failing, we need to reevaluate the patient's condition to see if a misdiagnosis is contributing to his slow demise.

The Rule of Relativism

- "What's true for you may not be true for me."
- "One person's art is another person's pornography."
- "No culture is better or worse than another."
- "There are no objective morals, just differing opinions."
- "Just go with the flow."
- "If it feels right, do it."
- "Anything goes."
- "Beauty is in the eye of the beholder."

Each of these statements reflects a relativist view of reality. "What's true for you may not be true for me" makes truth "person-dependent." What you and I believe may differ, may even be contradictory. For instance, I might believe that human beings can live beyond the grave, whereas you might believe that the grave is a dead end. That does not matter. You can believe whatever you want, just as I can. What matters is that you respect my truth and I respect yours.

Or take the statement "One person's art is another person's pornography." On one level, this is a statement of fact. It is true that people have conflicting views over photographs and paintings that depict individuals in sexually explicit poses or activities. However, this statement goes beyond this simple factual observation and makes an assertion about our ability to decide what is art and what is pornography. In effect it claims that we have no objective criteria by which we can make such a determination. People have honest differences of opinion, including informed art critics. These various interpretations, says the relativist, show that what constitutes art is subjective. How can we come up with objective standards for good art or bad art if we can't even say objectively what art is? It is best, therefore, to give free rein to artistic expression in the public arena and leave pejorative labels, such as pornography, at home. Besides, who can really say what is pornographic anyway?

Of course, people, including art critics, make decisions about works of art all the time. Sometimes these decisions impact an artist's reputation or pocketbook. At times they even lead to important cultural clashes over issues such as freedom of speech and community standards. As sociologist James Hunter observes in his book *Culture Wars:*

> One side claims that a work is "art"; the other claims it is not. One claims that a work has enduring aesthetic or literary appeal; the other claims it only appeals to the eccentric interests of a deviant subculture. At least on the face of it, one is tempted to agree with Justice Marshall Harlan who concluded that "one man's vulgarity is another's lyric." Such relativism may not be desirable but it seems to be the necessary outcome of the present cultural conflict. In this light, it is entirely predictable that each side would claim that the other side is not committed to free speech but to a systematic imposition of its values and perspectives on everyone else. Alas, one person's act of "censorship" has become another's "commitment to community standards."[1]

According to the relativist, we cannot adjudicate between these conflicting interpretations because there are no absolute standards by which to judge. Beauty is in the eye of the beholder, and there are as many "standards" of beauty as there are beholders. What you may find beautiful, I may see as offensive, and someone else may find boring or simply not worth bothering about. Why, then, should my view or yours be accepted as the standard? Better not to pass judgment at all, at least not a judgment that would keep other people from encountering the "art" and coming to their own conclusions.

Let's take one more of these claims: "No culture is better or worse than another." This is an expression of *cultural* relativism. Its focus shifts away from the individual and zeros in on the society in which the individual belongs and lives. It grows out of the conviction that there are no universal standards of good or bad, right or wrong, normal or abnormal, that we can apply cross-culturally. In fact, cultural relativists maintain that a society's beliefs and behaviors must be understood and judged within the context of that society. Whatever a society believes is right is right within that society; whatever beliefs and behaviors it condemns as wrong are, therefore, wrong for that group. We, from our culture, cannot impose our standards on any other culture, just as other cultures cannot judge us by their standards. No culture's code of conduct has special status; it is simply one code among many, no better or worse than any other.

In short, relativism is the belief that truth and error, right and wrong, beautiful and ugly, normal and abnormal, and a host of other judgments are determined by the individual, her circumstances, or her culture. Reality and morality are personal or social constructions or both. What we say we believe about the "real world" says more about us and our group than it does about something beyond us or our culture. Psychology and sociology have replaced philosophy, science, and theology. There is no transcendent God or universal natural law we can point to that can inform us about who we are, what our world is like, and how we should get along in it. We do not even have a neutral, objective referent point on which we can stand so we can get beyond our particular situations and discover universal truths. We are forever locked up in our mental constructions and emotional ebbs and flows. All we have are our interpretations of the text we call the world. We cannot get at the world itself. As one leading anthropologist put it, "life is translation, and we are all lost in it."[2] So we best learn to get along with one another, to accept one another's different interpretations, and learn what we can from them. This is the world of relativism, and this is the worldview the opening statements assume and convey.

A Personal Report

I have heard these statements in hundreds of variations since the mid-sixties. When they first started circulating, they were revolutionary. Most people thought it preposterous, arrogant, foolish, not to mention defiant of all reason, for individuals to act as if they were the sole determiners of right and wrong, true and false. That they controlled their destiny and no one else had any say in the matter. That a person's subjective feelings and desires took center stage over objective thought and time-honored, proven traditions.

No more. Today assertions such as these are part of our everyday vocabulary. In some quarters they are still controversial, but an ever-growing number of people accept them as if their truth were beyond question. We have come a long way in three decades, but the distance traveled has nothing to do with progress.

When I reentered the university setting as a philosophy student in the mid 1970s, relativism was occasionally discussed in courses, but it did not appear to dominate the beliefs of any of my professors. Regardless the discipline of study, the professors I had generally agreed that if something was genuinely true or right, it was true or right for all people no matter where or when they lived and despite their knowledge of or belief in the proposition. In other words, my professors and the many others I knew were largely absolutists. They believed that cross-cultural and transpersonal judgments could be made based on universal truths, moral and aesthetic standards, and the like.

For example, no teacher believed that the Earth suddenly became round during the time of Galileo. People in and outside university walls agreed that the Earth had always been round. Galileo simply discovered what had always been true and by that disproved the flat-earth theory.

What was true in the natural sciences was also true in most of the other disciplines, including history, philosophy, ethics, mathematics, and music. Historians accepted universal truths about the past and its knowability. Chemists taught absolute truths about chemical interactions and the basic constituents of the periodic table. Most biologists, along with the vast majority of anthropologists and physicists, embraced some form of naturalistic evolution to explain the natural order. If relativism had a foothold in the academy, it was largely confined to a handful of professors in the departments of English, religion, sociology, and art. Even there, of course, one could find many advocates for universal truths.

I recall taking a philosophy course in epistemology (the study of how we know). Dr. James Slinger, the philosopher who taught the class, began the course by handing out a paper called "Is Truth Relative?" When I first saw the paper's title, I thought I would soon hear a philosophical argument for relativism. Instead, Dr. Slinger presented a fascinating case against relativism and for absolutism. I soon realized why. Not only did the issue apply directly to the course's subject matter, but the professor knew that most students in the course would uncritically assume the validity of relativism. You see, even in the '70s, long before Bloom commented on the relativistic beliefs of university students in the '80s, relativism had a stranglehold on many students' minds. It did not yet have the same overpowering influence on many professors. Dr. Slinger realized this and determined to loosen relativism's grip early in the course.

Dr. Slinger also knew from experience that students would use the alleged relative nature of truth to evade serious discussions, especially if those discussions were critical of their viewpoints. So he met the challenge and sent the blind obedience to relativism scurrying with sound reasons.

When students later tried to raise the standard of relativism—"That may be your opinion but it's not mine"; "That truth doesn't work for me"; "One culture's fact is another culture's myth"—Slinger simply replied, "Remember, I refuted relativism. If you think my arguments are invalid or unsound, then you must make your case against mine. Just asserting your belief in relativism does not make it true. I would be happy to consider your arguments for relativism. But if you cannot make any, then the discussion will continue on the demonstrated assumption that all truth is absolute."

Within a few weeks, students stopped appealing to relativism. No one could refute professor Slinger's case. At times this exasperated them. Nonetheless, it also led them to think about the issues raised in the field of epistemology instead of constantly falling back on their opinions, many of which were held because they were personally expedient or fashionable—to put it in more contemporary parlance, what felt good or what was politically correct.

Ironically, today it is not only the students but often the professors espousing relativism and other politically correct views. In fact, as we'll see in later chapters, sometimes it's the students railing against political correctness while professors and administrators uphold it as the *sine qua non* of knowledge and wisdom.

Today you can hardly read a book, see a film, or listen to a lecture in the halls of academia without concluding that the new orthodoxy is that claims about truth and morality are relative to individuals, groups, or cultures. According to the new priests, historical time periods and geography, secular and religious leaders and institutions, and a host of other variables virtualy determine what people believe. Whatever humans perceive to be true or right, their perceptions tell us more about them and their times than about the "real world," whatever that is. Today's relativists tell us we are no longer knowers but myth-makers. Fiction is the new vehicle for the varied and conflicting worlds in which we have constructed to live. There is no one Truth, no one Reality, no one Right or Wrong. As a popular rock song of the late '70s expressed, "There's only you and me, and we just disagree."

What all this means is that a relativistic mind-set now appears to permeate American society, especially its educational centers. Students come from every facet of our nation. They represent families from every level of income and all types of blue-collar and white-collar jobs. They have aspirations that span the gamut from art to architecture, music to machinery, biology to business, animal husbandry to computer science. And they arrive on campuses nationwide with a belief many, perhaps most, of their professors share: truth and morals are relative. All these people did not arrive at relativism on their own. They must be picking it up from the larger culture. Indeed, that is the finding of some recent studies.

The Barna Survey

George Barna, a longtime, highly respected pollster, conducted three nationwide surveys—one in 1991, one in 1993, and another in 1994—that reveal a great deal about the American acceptance of relativism. The surveys, at least the latter two, each involved about 1,200 adults (eighteen years of age and older) who were interviewed for about twenty-five minutes. Respondents were picked at random, and further steps were taken to ensure that the surveys reflected "the true geographic distribution of the population" as well as "an accurate balance of people according to ethnic character and gender."[3]

Among the many issues addressed in these surveys was the matter of absolute versus relative truth and morals. The results were telling and disturbing.

Fluctuating Truth

According to Barna's surveys, the vast majority of Americans are adopting a relativistic view of truth in larger numbers that cut across age, gender, and racial differences. In 1991, Barna found that 28 percent of all adult respondents strongly agreed with the statement "There is no such thing as absolute truth; two people could define truth in totally conflicting ways, but both could still be correct." An additional 39 percent agreed less strongly with that statement. In other words, 67 percent rejected the reality of absolute truth to varying degrees.

When the same statement was posed to adults in 1994, the number who strongly agreed with it rose to 32 percent, and the number who somewhat agreed also rose slightly to 40 percent. This meant that relative truth now had a 72 percent acceptance rate. Roughly three out of four Americans claimed they embraced relativism and opposed absolutism.[4]

The acceptance of relative truth crossed gender lines just about equally. A person's age, on the other hand, did affect the results but not dramatically. In Barna's 1991 survey, 59 percent of the Builder generation (those born between 1927 and 1945) accepted the idea that truth is relative. This placed them eight points behind the 1991 national average. By 1994, however, their acceptance of relative truth had risen twelve percentage points, bringing them in line with the 1994 national average of 72 percent. The generation leading the way toward relativism is the Baby Busters. Born between 1965 and 1983, the adults in this generation rejected absolute truth by a staggering 78 percent.[5] It seems that the younger the Americans, the greater the percentage who believe in relative truth.

Those adults most out of sync with the rush toward relativism were certain kinds of Christians. For instance, many respondents claimed they had "made a personal commitment to Christ that is still important in their lives today." They also said they believed "that when they die they will go to heaven because they have confessed their sins and accepted Jesus Christ as their Savior."[6] Among this group, which Barna labeled born-again Christians, more than half (52 percent) surveyed in 1991 "sided with the national majority [of 67 percent] in accepting relative truth as the standard."[7] As of 1994, this percentage had risen ten points to 62 percent, which was close to the number of adults in the general population who scored on the side of relative truth just a few years before.

Evangelical Christians were less likely to reject absolute truth. According to Barna, respondents labeled evangelical Christians were those who met eight specific criteria. Two were the ones mentioned above under the category of born-again Christians. The other six criteria were (1) saying that "religion is important in their lives"; (2) believing that "God is the all-powerful, all-knowing Creator of the universe who rules the world today"; (3) rejecting the idea that "if a person is good enough, or does enough good things during life, he or she will earn a place in heaven"; (4) believing that "the Bible is accurate in all that it teaches"; (5) rejecting the claim that "Satan is a symbol of evil rather than a living force"; and (6) acknowledging that they have a personal "responsibility to tell other people their religious beliefs."[8] Yet even with these professed beliefs in place, 42 percent of evangelical Christians surveyed in 1994 voiced their rejection of absolute truth.[9]

If Americans stay true to form, we can predict that as the 1990s come to a close, belief in absolute truth will exist among an even smaller minority. Perhaps as few as two out of every ten Americans will confess to a belief that truth is absolute. Among religiously conservative Christians, the belief in relativism will also likely continue to grow but at a slower rate. Maybe by the year 2000 seven out of every ten Christians will reject the reality of absolute truth.

Convenient Ethics

As truth goes, so goes morality. Fewer Americans than ever before still believe that ethical norms are universal. Many more say they believe that what is right for me may be wrong for you, and that no individual, group, or governing body has the right to set the ethical standard for anyone else.

When Barna asked adults if they agreed with the statement "there are no absolute standards for morals and ethics," seven out of every ten (71 percent) said that they agreed with it. African Americans assented to the proposition more than any other group tested—83 percent—with Caucasians lagging eleven points behind. The lowest groups on the acceptance scale were born-again Christians (64 percent) and evangelicals (40 percent). Among those who fell under the broader religious classifications of Protestant and Catholic, the acceptance percentage was almost equal—67 percent for Protestants and 70 percent for Catholics. Seventy-seven percent of non-Christians said they rejected absolute moral standards.

When it came to the issue of morality, a person's gender did not matter. Both sexes voiced opposition to moral absolutes in equal numbers (72 percent), just as they had on the issue of absolute versus relative truth. Age played no appreciable role either, except among the youngest polled. Baby Boomers fell right in with the national norm of 71 percent. The oldest polled—Builders and Seniors (those born before 1926)—were divided by just four percentage points (71 percent and 67 percent respectively) as they too hovered around the norm. Baby Busters, the youngest adults surveyed, were the ones leading the pack at 80 percent.[10]

In short, on average almost three quarters of American adults, despite their age, sex, or basic religious orientation (except among the most religiously conservative Christians), said they had turned away from ethical absolutism and embraced moral relativism. In fact, one out of every three adults believes that "it is impossible to be a moral person these days."[11]

The Patterson/Kim Report

Barna's findings were even more conservative than those of two marketing and advertising specialists, James Patterson and Peter Kim.

In their 1991 book and national bestseller *The Day America Told the Truth*, they reported their findings to a national survey they had developed. This survey contained eighteen hundred questions, and it was given to two thousand Americans in fifty locations nationwide during a one-week period. A shorter version of the questionnaire was also given to thousands more Americans in telephone interviews. The anonymity of the respondents was guaranteed in an attempt to get heartfelt answers about what the respondents really believed.

Authorities Everyone

Among all the startling answers Patterson and Kim received, one stood out with stark relevance to the question of relativism's influence. As Patterson and Kim expressed it, "Americans are making up their own rules, their own laws. In effect, we're all making up our own moral codes. Only 13 percent of us believe in all of the Ten Commandments. Forty percent of us believe in five of the Ten Commandments. We choose which laws of God we believe in. There is absolutely no moral consensus in this country as there was in the 1950s, when all our institutions commanded more respect. Today, there is very little respect for the law—for any kind of law."[12] When Americans "want to answer a question of right and wrong, we ask ourselves.... We are the law unto ourselves. We have made ourselves the authority over church and God. We have made ourselves the clear authority over the government. We have made ourselves the authority over laws and the police."[13]

Patterson and Kim discovered that a whopping 93 percent of those surveyed declared that "they—and nobody else—determine what is and what isn't moral in their lives. They base their decisions on their own experience, even on their daily whims. In addition, almost as large a majority confessed that they would violate the established rules of their religion (84 percent), or that they had actually violated a law because they thought that it was wrong in their view (81 percent)."[14]

The result of this moral crisis, they claim, is that Americans "no longer can tell right from wrong."[15] Americans have found themselves in "a moral vacuum. The religious figures and scriptures that gave us rules for so many centuries, the political system that gave us our laws, all have lost their meaning in our moral imagination."[16] As historian Arthur Schlesinger, Jr., quipped, "Relativism is the American way."[17] Or at least in recent history, it has apparently become America's way.

Psychologist Paul Vitz decries this situation. As he writes, "One of the major characteristics of moral decline in the United States in recent decades has been the rapid growth of moral relativism. The idea is now widespread that each individual has some kind of a sovereign right to create, develop, and express whatever values he or she happens to prefer. This kind of personal relativism is far more serious and extreme than even cultural relativism. . . . Unfortunately, America has now reached the point where it permits almost everything and stands for almost nothing—except a flabby relativism."[18]

Academian S. D. Gaede agrees. In his book *When Tolerance Is No Virtue*, he argues that Americans "live in a culture that is riddled with moral and ontological relativism." One indication of this is that "most of us would have a hard time articulating what we believe." In a society where there are no fixed truths anymore, we do not have to think through what we believe because we do not have to defend it to anyone. My beliefs require no justification, just as yours do not. All that matters is that you and I believe them. Our sincerity counts, not our reasons.

"Moreover," professor Gaede adds, "what we believe today is easily displaced by something else tomorrow. Our beliefs are more a matter of feelings than anything, and thus our confidence in them varies with our hormones, our situation, and our friends. Most important, our beliefs are *our* beliefs, and that, we think, makes them worthy and beyond dispute."[19]

Time on America

This wholesale reliance on ourselves as the ultimate authority figures also manifests itself in a growing belief that success and security are best achieved through self-reliance and self-initiative. In a national survey reported in *Time* magazine and conducted each year since 1971, 75 percent of four thousand respondents indicated in 1989 that they agreed that "people have to realize that they can only count on their own skills and abilities if they're going to win in this world." By 1994, the percentage of people who agreed with this statement was up to 86 percent, an eleven-point jump. Commenting on these statistics, Jon D. Hull said, "Americans now put more trust in themselves than in authority figures. . . . For better and for worse, that renewed self-reliance is reshaping the way Americans educate their children, protect their families, invest their savings, run their communities, maintain their health, and view their government."[20]

This renewed dependence on self is not the outgrowth of a new optimism over individual ability. Rather, it appears to be the result of a growing pessimism, an emerging discontent and despair over America's cultural decline. In January 1995, *Time* and CNN conducted a poll in which they asked, "Which comes closest to your own feelings about America?" Forty-two percent of respondents threw their lot in with the assessment that America's current problems are no worse than they have been at other times in its history. However, 53 percent said they believed that America "is in deep and serious trouble." Just ten years ago only 40 percent of respondents shared this dire assessment of the American situation. Clearly people are feeling a deep discontent that they reflect in a deepening distrust of those authority figures they used to look to for answers and help. Among the authorities who have fallen in the eyes of the populace are "doctors, religious leaders, big companies, schools, and especially the Federal Government."[21]

An example of this solution of frustration is Vin Thomlin. According to the *Time* correspondent, Mr. Thomlin was so outraged over the state of the American Union that he broke a ten-year absence from the voting booth and voted a straight Republican ticket in the November 1994 elections. (The election results brought Republicans into political office in droves, while ousting many incumbent Democrats.) He left his apartment for just an hour to cast his vote. When he returned, he discovered that he had been burglarized. "My stereo, TV, money, everything was gone," he said. Slamming his fist on the nearest piece of wood, this forty-six-year-old handyman bitterly added, "You know what really kills me? . . . The whole [expletive] reason I voted was because I'm so sick of crime and the lack of values in this country." He has resolved this problem his own way. Now "he keeps a tire iron in his bedroom for protection."[22]

At times the American embrace of relativism seems less the result of a thought-out philosophical stance and more the consequence of political and social frustration. Times are desperate. Authority figures once respected are now seen as hypocrites and liars. In fact, more than half the Americans surveyed said that what made them "very angry" were "people in positions of power who 'say one thing and do another.' "[23] So people are buying more guns and locks. They are working to relax or repeal concealed weapons laws to protect themselves better. They are educating their children at home or switching them from public to private institutions that more closely correspond to their family's convictions. They are investing in their own retirement programs, beginning their own businesses, organizing their own community associations, patrolling their own streets, and doing their own home repairs. They are even creating their own religious movements.

J. Gordon Melton, a longtime student of religious movements in the

United States, lists 1,600 religious groups in the newest version of his book *Encyclopedia of American Religions.* Forty-four percent of these groups are non-Christian. Half the total listed "blossomed since 1960; some are homegrown, others imported by immigrants." While Christian groups are still the most numerous, Melton observes that America "now has a greater diversity of religious groups than any country in recorded history."[24] So while 96 percent of Americans profess belief in God, one must ask, Which God? The answer is more pluralistic than it has ever been before.

In short, whether as individuals or in group associations, Americans are increasingly preoccupied with caring for themselves—materially and spiritually, relationally and emotionally. "Self-centeredness," laments ethicist Harold O. J. Brown, has become our "normal orientation in life. . . . Nothing external matters, only . . . our own fancy or will. Thus we increasingly act on the assumption that whatever we desire to do or to have must be right. This self-centeredness extends to society as a whole, both individually and collectively: most of us think first . . . solely of ourselves, and as a nation we think so singly of ourselves that we are very ignorant of the impression we make on the surrounding world and the legacy we leave to history."[25]

Critical Conclusions

When many cultural critics look at such evidence for the ever-increasing rise of relativism, they conclude that relativism must be a major player in America's social decline. Without mentioning relativism by name but certainly describing the concept, former U.S. Secretary of Education William Bennett contends that the current "battle over culture . . . has to do with a growing realization that over the last twenty years or so the traditional values of the American people have come under steady fire, with the heavy artillery supplied by intellectuals." The fallout of this "all-out assault," argues Bennett, is that "too many Americans became either embarrassed, unwilling, or unable to explain with assurance to our children and to one another the difference between right and wrong, between what is helpful and what is destructive, what is ennobling and what is degrading." Consequently, "The fabric of support that the American people—families especially—could traditionally find in the culture at large became worn, torn, and unraveled."

Continuing, he writes, "We ceased being clear about the standards which we hold and the principles by which we judge, or, if we were clear in our own minds, we somehow abdicated the area of public discussion and institutional decision making to those who challenged our traditional values. As a result, we suffered a cultural breakdown of sorts—in areas like education, family life, crime, and drug use, as well as in our attitudes toward sex, individual responsibility, civic duty, and public service."[26]

If Bennett is right, what led us to grow quiet about our true beliefs? Why didn't we speak up earlier and say why we believed that certain acts were wrong and others right? One reason, suggests Gaede, is that relativism makes it "inappropriate to try to change someone else's mind.... These days it is a scary thing to stand face-to-face with another person and suggest that their ideas may be wrong." We don't want to violate "one of our culture's deepest values," which is "tolerance, and that value is embedded in a relativistic worldview. To assert truth in such an environment is blasphemy."[27] Who wants to be ostracized as a heretic?

Another critic, Jim Nelson Black, attributes "the suicide of society" at least, in part, to relativism. He states, "We should not be surprised when children who have been denied moral guidance act out behaviors that are dishonest and destructive. If morality is merely relative, it cannot easily be enforced. And if we excuse the most outrageous violations of decency, we should not be surprised when our nation is turned into urban jungles by the immature and irresponsible behavior of its sons and daughters."[28]

Charles Colson—former aide to President Nixon, winner of the Templeton Prize for Progress in Religion, and chairman of Prison Fellowship—agrees. "We live," he writes, "in a society in which all transcendent values have been removed and thus there is no moral standard by which anyone can say right is right and wrong is wrong." While this "value-free society" may sound "liberal, progressive, and enlightened" to some, it is actually reaping a whirlwind of socially destructive consequences—consequences that shock us but should not.

> Why are we surprised that crime soars steadily among juveniles when parents fail to set standards of right behavior in the home, when schoolteachers will not offer a moral opinion in the classroom, either out of fear of litigation or because they cannot "come from a position of what is right and wrong," as one New Jersey teacher put it?
>
> Why are we horrified at the growing consequences of sexual promiscuity—including a life-threatening epidemic—when sex is treated as casually as going out for a Frosty at Wendy's?
>
> Why are we shocked at disclosures of religious leaders bilking

> their ministries of millions when they've been preaching a get-rich-quick gospel all along?
>
> Why the wonderment over the fact that, for enough dollars or sexual favors, government employees and military personnel sell out their nation's secrets?
>
> Why is it so surprising that Wall Street yuppies make fast millions on insider information or tax fraud? Without objective values, the community or one's neighbor has no superior claim over one's own desires.
>
> Whether we like to hear it or not, we are reaping the consequences of the decades since World War II when we have, in Solzhenitsyn's words, "forgotten God." What we have left is the reign of relativism.[29]

There's no question that the majority of Americans today say they believe that truth and morality are relative. It's also true that Americans commonly appeal to relativism to rationalize their misbehavior and disarm their critics. But are Americans really relativists? Are they operating without any sense of objective values? Do they live as if right and wrong, truth and error, are up for grabs? Do they act as if people can do whatever they want and that's okay? Does relativism really rule the American conscience? The answers lie not so much in stated belief as in actual behavior. That difference makes all the difference in the world.

Chapter 3

The Betrayal of Behavior

I remember when the first Wendy's fast-food restaurant opened in my hometown of Fresno. McDonald's had already been around for some time, and I liked going there. The only thing that perturbed me about the Golden Arches was how quickly preparing fast food slowed down when I made that dreaded "special order." If you ordered from their menu without requesting any exceptions, you got your fast food fast. But make a special request—"hold the onions," "keep the pickles," "add an extra slice of cheese"—then you best take along that novel you had always wanted to read, because you would get ample time to enjoy it before your food arrived.

Wendy's changed all that. When the first Wendy's opened, their advertisements capitalized on what McDonald's couldn't do—deliver those special orders quickly. "Come to Wendy's, where you can have your food *your* way." Did they deliver on their promise!

"I'll take my hamburger with cheese, mayonnaise, and ketchup only."

"No problem."

"I'd like mine with pickles, lettuce, mustard, tomato but no mayonnaise or cheese."

"You got it!"

Whatever the request, Wendy's workers could fill it. Why? Because unlike McDonald's, the Wendy's chain sought to serve individuals and their different tastes first and foremost. So rather than precook and prepackage their sandwiches as McDonald's did, Wendy's cooked and prepared the food according to each person's order. And they found a way to do it with speed.

When I think of relativism, Wendy's comes to mind. Just as Wendy's found an effective way to reach the I-want-it-my-way fast-food longings of human beings, relativism strives to serve up human wants according to individual preferences.

"I want my reality with a morality that celebrates homosexuality, bisexuality, bestiality, and any other sexual desires I have."

"If that's what you want, you shall have it."

"I want all cultures treated as if they were all equal. I don't like evaluations that call some societies civilized and advanced and others primitive and backward."

"Okay, relativism can accommodate that desire too."

"What about the matter of truth? I want to believe in anything I want and not have anyone seriously question the validity of my beliefs."

"Not a problem. Relativism gives you that option."

What Wendy's did for hamburgers, relativism says it can do with a universe of choices. Relativism promises us that each of us can have reality *our* way: with or without deities and demons, virtues and vices, truth and error, holiness and depravity, progress and regress. The world is ours to shape, reshape, and reshape again to our heart's content.

If the critics and surveys are right, the overwhelming majority of Americans have accepted relativism's promise and ways. They have denied the existence—or at least knowability—of universal truths and morals, and they are living in Wendy's-like worlds of their own creation. They order what they want, when they want, and how much they want. They even decide what will be on the menu and how it will be served.

Will the Real Relativists Please Stand Up?

From all appearances, relativism has won the battle over absolutism. All that seems left to do is to carry out some mop-up operations to purge any stubborn absolutists from positions of power while marginalizing and converting the few remaining believers in absolute truth.

If this is true, if it is an accurate depiction of contemporary America, then we should see clear, undeniable signs of its presence nationwide. The problem is, we do not. What we see is the opposite of what we would rightly expect to find. The behavior of Americans betrays their real commitments, and *relativism is not one of them.* We can see this in a variety of areas.

No New Tolerance Here

The foundational virtue of relativism is what I call the *new* tolerance. (In a later chapter, I'll explain how this understanding of tolerance differs from the kind of tolerance that flows from an absolutist worldview.)

The new tolerance is a natural corollary of the relativistic perspective. Since all truth and morals are up for grabs, the relativist must be a person committed to living out the new tolerance. This means she must be broad-minded, open to other beliefs, claims to truth, moral convictions, and different lifestyles. The tolerant person must make room for others to do as they wish, even if their behavior contradicts or even mocks her own. The authentic relativist would not become upset when facing opposition to her views, and she would never try to push her personal convictions on other people. Declaring anything right or wrong, true or false for anyone but herself would be unacceptable—dare I say, a moral evil? Everyone must be left to live as they see fit. Live and let live—that is the summary maxim of the new virtue of tolerance.

Is this live-and-let-live attitude characteristic of contemporary America? Not at all. In fact, the very groups that claim to be advocates of the new tolerance are not. The political correctness movement seeks to squelch what various groups view as offensive language, behavior, and perspectives (see chapter 13). Multiculturalists seem bent on upholding the beliefs and practices of every other culture except those commended by Western civilization (see chapter 12). Secularists are determined to keep religious expression out of the public arena (see chapter 4). Pro-abortion and same-sex-rights activists march on city halls, run for political office, and lobby to change or enact laws in order to gain legal and social sanction for their personal views (see chapters 5, 9, and 13).

Then there are, of course, the many groups who oppose those just mentioned, such as the Christian Coalition, Concerned Women of America, the American Center for Law and Justice, Feminists for Life, the Rockford Institute Center on Religion and Society, Focus on the Family, and the Acton Institute. Most of them do not even regard the new tolerance as a virtue but see it as a vice.

Moreover, we see opposing groups charging one another with intolerance. Here's just one example among dozens: to many secularists, religious activists are rigid fundamentalists who want to force their ignorant, authoritarian ways on everyone else. To many religious activists, secularists are militantly antireligious, interested only in trivializing religion and barring it from having any influence in public debate and policy.[1] Millions of people support such groups with their time and dollars. I get mail every week from organizations that want my financial support so they can reach out and oppose someone. This is not the behavior of relativist-oriented people.

Look where you will. The live-and-let-live mentality does not mark the American landscape.

Law and Order

It is common in American politics to hear citizens calling for stronger laws and other civic measures that will more effectively curb criminal activity. It is also quite usual to see politicians practically fall over each other as they posture themselves as the hard-on-crime politician of choice. This is bizarre behavior if we are really a nation of relativists. Politicians should be chastising citizens for having such a low threshold of tolerance for lawbreakers. Likewise, voters should be electing political candidates who are "soft" on crime. After all, criminals are only living according to their code of conduct. What could be wrong with that? Nothing, if relativism is true.

To their credit, Americans do not believe such nonsense, which is why politicians consistently present themselves as tough on crime, despite the truth of their voting record. This is another telltale fact in support of my contention that America is not a nation of relativists.

Lawsuits Galore

America is an extremely litigious society, perhaps the most litigious nation ever. According to the Republican Party's 1994 *Contract with America*, "In 1989 alone, 18 million civil lawsuits were filed in state and federal courts—amounting to one lawsuit for every ten adults."[2] Does this sound like a people committed to the live-and-let-live attitude of relativism? Is a nation drawing on the talents of 800,000 practicing attorneys, judges, and law professors[3] a sign of its commitment to the new tolerance? I don't think so.

Moral Outrage

A young child is beaten to death by her drug-addicted mother. An alcoholic loses control of his car and spins into an elderly couple taking a leisurely walk and kills them both. A financier makes a number of reckless investments that cause many of his clients to go broke. A trusted adult takes sexual advantage of several children under his care before he's caught. Countless incidents such as these provoke moral outrage in Americans every day. We hear about them and get upset. We wonder what can be done. We contact the families of the victims and offer our help. We write letters and make phone calls to our civic leaders and demand more preventive and punitive action. Sometimes we even start organizations and head campaigns to combat these terrible crimes: Mothers Against Drunk Driving, the Just Say No drug campaign, Alcoholics Anonymous, Narcotics Anonymous, domestic violence programs, The Society for the Prevention of Child Abuse, and the list goes on.

Why would we do all this if we were relativists? A live-and-let-live approach to life would lead us to respond much differently. We would want to help people carry out their desires, not try to squelch, condemn, or counteract them. For pedophiles, we might decide to supply them with children with whom they could satisfy their longings. Abusive parents could receive training on how to hit, burn, and kill their children more effectively. We could establish driving classes for addicts that would show them how to run people over without damaging their cars in the process. We would permit, even endorse, organizations such as Alcoholics for Drunk Driving, The Society for the Promotion of Child Abuse, Financiers for Fraud, Clean and Sober Anonymous, and Just Say Let's Party. Ludicrous thoughts, I agree, but if we were a nation of relativists, these are ideas that could—in fact, should—find widespread support.

Missionary Zeal

If relativism were pervasive, we would also expect to find people eager to listen to the views of others and learn from them without trying to convert them. People would be allowed to believe and behave as they wished; indeed, they would be encouraged to do so. The public educational system would be particularly conducive to promoting just such an open, nonjudgmental perspective throughout its curriculum. All ideas would be welcomed and none disdained. No one would try to convince anyone else of their own view. We would be a nation of people saying to each other, "I'm personally opposed to that, but you can believe and practice it if you wish."

That, of course, is not what we find. Americans often show a missionary zeal for their views, seeking to win converts whenever they can. Homosexual advocates, for example, write books, articles, editorials, and movie scripts to convince others of their viewpoint. They teach courses in schools, speak at various civic gatherings, and engage in a range of other activities designed to either win people over to their position or at least get them to sympathize with it enough so they will not resist it. Opponents of homosexuality do the same to win converts or sympathizers to their view. The same phenomenon occurs over a wide spectrum of cultural debates, indicating how unrelativistic each group regards its own perspective.

The public school system is no harbinger of complete openness either. If it were, one would find creationist views taught alongside evolutionist theories . . . sexual abstinence presented as strongly as sexual activeness . . . homosexuality as a disorder taught beside homosexuality as an alternative lifestyle. One would also find public schools giving unbiased and balanced presentations of environmental care versus environmental exploitation, egalitarianism versus elitism, universal virtues versus relative values versus no values at all, belief in God versus unbelief in God, multiculturalism versus eurocentrism, public education versus private education and home schooling. But this is not what public schools are doing. They are, instead, actively taking sides, promoting one side of many debates as the only viable, responsible, and intelligent choice. They are trying to move minds in one direction and away from the other. They are anything but neutral.

Human Rights

Yet another indication that Americans are not relativistic is their pervasive use of human-rights language to support their views. Today it seems that every want is declared a human right by someone, which has led to a clash of so-called human rights. For example, proabortionists say that I have a right to have my offspring eliminated before their birth, while pro-lifers argue that no such right exists and that abortion is murder of the innocents who have a right to life. Many people believe I have the right to have sex with any consenting party I wish, while other people believe that at least some forms of sexual activity (such as homosexual sex) should be outlawed and other forms (such as premarital and extramarital sex) should be discouraged through moral instruction. People often use human-rights language to back up their case.

The problem with all this for relativists is that appeals to human rights conflict with relativism. If truth and morality are really relative, on what grounds could a relativist appeal to human rights? An individual's right, perhaps; or maybe even a culture's right. But *human* rights? No way. We can see this by exploring what a human right is.

A human right, if our choice of words means anything, must be a right grounded in the kind of beings we are. If we were vegetables or rocks, these rights would not be ours to claim. There is something about our humanness, our shared nature as human beings, that allows us to claim some rights as distinctively human rights.

Furthermore, if such rights exist, then they must differ from civil rights. Human rights cannot be the kind of rights granted by governments or their laws or constitutions. Human rights must be natural rights, not man-made creations. Governments may acknowledge and protect them, or reject and trample them. That does not make human rights any less real or valid. Their authenticity and justification lie within us, not in our institutions. This is why we can hold nations accountable for violating human rights. These rights are a moral standard that transcends political borders and ideologies. Without them, we could not put anyone on trial for crimes against humanity. Under the rule of relativism, the Nuremberg trials for Nazi war crimes could not have taken place. Neither would we be able to judge Croatians, Serbs, or Bosnians for acts of atrocity they committed against one another.

Moreover, rights to be *human* rights must apply to all human beings, not just to some. Their reality is not dependent on our level of intelligence, the color of our skin, our religious beliefs, our psychological condition, our alma mater, our political affiliations, our nationality, our family lineage, or anything else unessential to our humanness. To have these rights, all we must be is homo sapiens.

Finally, if these rights exist, they must apply to all human beings at all times and in all places. Ancient Aztecs, Egyptian Pharaohs, medieval shopkeepers, Chinese communists, Bolivian drug dealers, American slave traders, Australian bushmen, Roman gladiators, computer hackers . . . all possess these rights simply because they are human beings.

In his essay "What Are Human Rights?" political scientist Maurice Cranston answers the question well: "A human right is something that pertains to all men at all times. . . . [H]uman rights are not bought, nor are they created by any other specific contractual undertaking. They are not exclusive, they do not 'go with the job.' They belong to a man simply because he is a man. . . . In speaking of human rights, we are claiming that there is something about man's nature that entitles him to a particular respect. . . . They are not rights that are conferred exclusively on its members by a particular society. They are universal. And they are inherited, so to speak, with men's humanity itself."[4]

Given all this, seeing why a relativist could not accept human rights is obvious. Human rights belong to the world of absolutists, not relativists (although absolutists would readily grant that even relativists have human rights whether they believed in them or not). True relativists cannot appeal to human rights. At best, they must try to ground their rights beliefs in culture or the individual, but even then the best they can do is say rights are conventional—we simply decide what we will consider a right, then agree to act accordingly. If we change our mind about that right being a right, then it will not be a right any longer.

A few among the intellectual elite may reject human rights and their universal nature,[5] but the overwhelming majority of Americans do not.

Americans believe human rights are real and transcultural, and they are astounded and outraged when people violate those rights anywhere in the world. Their rhetoric and behavior exhibits their commitment to universal human rights and therefore to absolutes.

Over the Border

Furthermore, if Americans really accepted relativism, they would not seek to export their beliefs and values across their nation's borders. Yet they not only do that, they also demand that other countries embrace their views, often tying trade agreements and diplomatic relations to a nation's adherence to those demands.

We promote American democratic ideals to and in other countries. But it must be our understanding of democracy; no other variation is approved. For example, at the 1994 Cairo Conference on population control, our government representatives and several private U.S. citizens tried to get a provision for "reproductive rights" into the document that almost two hundred nations were expected to sign. At that same conference, we presented many other "women's rights" issues concerning education, employment, equality with men, and the like, contending these were transcultural rights. Our government, along with many outspoken U.S. citizens and social activist groups, even opposed the Vatican, Islamic countries, and most Asian and African nations on the alleged "women's rights" issue of abortion.[6] Jacqueline Kasun, an economics professor and author who attended the Cairo conference, concluded her eyewitness report with these telling comments: "The [Cairo] conference that I saw was not the one described in *The New York Times*, with an aging pope hopelessly opposing the liberation of the world's women. At the conference I attended I saw the Clinton administration, flanked by the World Bank, Planned Parenthood, Bela Abzug, and the Sierra Club, trying—a bit unsteadily at times—to stand against the world."[7]

On what grounds can we take such stands if we are genuinely a relativistic nation? These are not the actions of relativists but of absolutists who see their view of truth and morals as the one everyone else *globally* should embrace.

Culture War

In America and dozens of other countries worldwide, we see individuals and groups fighting with one another over what is really right and true, each person and group vying to persuade others to come alongside them in the fight. Many cultural observers have labeled this activity a culture war. But how could this be happening if we were truly relativists? Wouldn't we be tolerant of one another's viewpoint? Wouldn't we want to be left alone to live as we see fit? Wouldn't we want to leave others alone to do as they please as well? Why would we be challenging one another if we were relativists? Relativism simply cannot account for a culture war.

As I look over the American landscape, what I see is a culture war of opposing moral and social visions carried on by people convinced that their views are absolutely true and the views of their adversaries are absolutely false. *Relativism does not characterize the culture war in the United States. Absolutism does.*

Worlds in Collision

For the above reasons and many others, I think a more accurate interpretation of the cultural conflicts in contemporary America is this: we are a pluralistic nation, more pluralistic than we have ever been. Not only are more ethnic groups present in larger numbers, but so are more belief systems and behavioral patterns. And the vast majority of groups who have their own beliefs and lifestyles really believe that their views are true and other perspectives are false. Many groups are so adamant about this that they want local, state, and even federal laws passed to protect the practice of their views and, if possible, to stop other people from practicing their differing beliefs. These people do not believe what is vital to a relativistic perspective, namely, that individuals should be left to embrace and live out their own understanding of truth and morality. From what I see, Americans really do not live as if morality or truth is relative. Instead, they behave as if morality and truth are actually absolute. Later I will argue that they are right (see chapter 15). Absolutism is true.

I do not want to be misunderstood here. It is certainly true that many people wiggle out of confrontations claiming truth and morals are relative. Some cheat on their taxes and steal from their employers, asserting wrong is sometimes right. Others live promiscuously, take and sell drugs, and make legally questionable business decisions waving relativity as their justification banner. But they are not genuine relativists. They always cry foul when someone steals from them, destroys their kids with drugs, sleeps around on them, or does anything that violates their own well-being or their loved ones'. They want the perpetrators punished. They want the wrong righted. When moral relativism benefits them, they will use it. Yet when it works against them, how quickly they become absolutists!

In this way we are like the student who wrote a paper defending moral relativism. When his paper was returned, the student saw that he had been given a grade of F because the professor did not like the color of the folder holding the paper. The student, rightly outraged, stormed into the professor's office protesting, "The grade you gave me is unfair."

The professor calmly responded, "Unfair to you, perhaps, but completely justifiable to me based on moral relativism."

The student got the point, and the professor changed the grade to an A.

Commenting on this episode, philosopher Norman Geisler writes, "The student's reaction to the injustice done to him revealed, contrary to what he wrote, that deep down inside he really did believe in an objective moral principle of justice. . . . What he really believed was right manifested itself when he was wronged."[8]

We Americans are absolutists, despite any rhetoric to the contrary. Over the years, we have certainly changed what we believe and how we live, but we have not embraced relativism. Many of the clashes of values and lifestyles among us testify to our belief that our moral convictions and practices should be accepted by others as legitimate, if not outright fully embraced by them as well. The American people may say they accept the notion that a truth claim or moral claim is relative, but they do not behave as if this is true. Their behavior exposes what they really accept—that what they believe is true or right for them should be (and actually is) true or right for everyone else.

This brings me to the heart of my argument. Since we are a nation of absolutists at odds with one another, our differences must be over different understandings of what we believe is absolutely true. And since we have not always been at odds with one another to the heightened degree we are experiencing today, the culture war must be over the introduction of new ideas which some people believe everyone should accept. I believe this is precisely what is going on. The conflicts raging throughout America on such issues as abortion, euthanasia, homosexuality, feminism, race, and the public role of religion are over the emergence of new absolutes seeking to replace the old ones which used to dominate our country. These emerging absolutes are not simply slight modifications of the ones in decline. In many cases they directly oppose the old truths. They introduce foreign notions of freedom, religion, human nature, justice, sexuality, gender roles, and a host of other ideas the old order rejects. We are witnessing worlds of ideas in collision, and like any major crash, the wreckage is flying everywhere, and the number of injured and dead is rising to shocking levels.

The conflicting truth claims cover a wide range of subjects and issues. In Part II of this book, I have chosen to focus on ten arenas of conflict:

- religion and its place in the public square;
- pro-life versus pro-death beliefs;
- marriage;
- family;
- sexual liberty versus sexual license;
- same-sex rights;
- feminism;
- racial policies;
- multiculturalism;
- political correctness and the new tolerance.

In each of these areas, a truth Americans once held as an absolute is being challenged by a new truth that a growing number of Americans also accept as an absolute. These ten pairs of competing absolutes are the following:

The *Old* Absolutes	The *New* Absolutes
(1) Religion is the backbone of American culture, providing the moral and spiritual light needed for public and private life.	(1a) Religion is the bane of public life, so for the public good it should be banned from the public square.
(2) Human life from conception to natural death is sacred and worthy of protection.	(2a) Human life, which begins and ends when certain individuals or groups decide it does, is valuable as long as it is wanted.
(3) The institution of marriage is God-ordained and occurs between a man and a woman until death severs the bond.	(3a) Marriage is a human contract made between any two people, and either party can terminate it for any reason.
(4) The normative family is a married father and mother who raise one or more children.	(4a) Family is any grouping of two or more people with or without children.
(5) Sexual intercourse should be reserved for marriage.	(5a) Sexual intercourse is permissible regardless of marital status.
(6) Same-sex and bisexual intercourse are immoral.	(6a) All forms and combinations of sexual activity are moral as long as they occur between consenting parties.

(7) Women should be protected and nurtured but not granted social equality.

(7a) Women are oppressed by men and must liberate themselves by controlling their own bodies and therefore their destinies.

(8) All white people are created equal and should be treated with dignity and respect.

(8a) All human beings are created equal and should be treated with dignity and respect, but people of color should receive preferential treatment.

(9) Western civilization and its heritage should be studied and valued above others.

(9a) Non-Western societies and other oppressed peoples and their heritage should be studied and valued above Western civilization.

(10) Different perspectives should be heard and tolerated, but only the true and right ones should prevail.

(10a) Only those viewpoints deemed politically correct should be tolerated and encouraged to prevail.

I will argue that Americans should not accept either side of this divide in toto. Both sides have strengths and weaknesses in their applications, and truth and error in their affirmations, as I intend to show. On the other hand, I will also maintain that the new absolutes are socially destructive and should be abandoned with haste. My thoughts are offered in the classical spirit of dialogue and debate, not in the closed-minded spirit of the new tolerance.

PART TWO

The New Absolutes

Chapter 4

Freedom From Religion

The *Old* Absolute	The *New* Absolute
(1) Religion is the backbone of American culture, providing the moral and spiritual light needed for public and private life.	(1a) Religion is the bane of public life, so for the public good it should be banned from the public square.

One of the finest commentaries on the current state of religious liberty in America appeared in Johnny Hart's comic strip "B.C." Hart depicts an inquisitive caveman standing on the beach. He picks up a wood tablet and inscribes a question on it: "Is it true that, over there, you have freedom of religion?" Then he throws the tablet into the ocean and watches the tide take it away. The rest of the day and all night long he waits on the beach for the reply. Finally it comes floating back. Expectantly he lifts the tablet from the water and reads the unexpected answer: "Yes—and if the hotshots in the black robes have their way, we'll soon be free of it altogether."[1] All too true. Through their judicial decisions, black-robed judges have put religion in serious trouble in the land of the free.

They have had help, though. Between the American Civil Liberties Union (ACLU), People for the American Way, Americans United for Separation of Church and State, and other like organizations, religious freedom has taken a real beating over the last several decades. Let us consider the ACLU's record for a moment.

In his book *The Politics of the American Civil Liberties Union*, sociologist William Donohue observes that "removing religion from the womb of culture has become the practiced virtue of the ACLU over the past several decades."[2] Donohue cites a stream of examples that support his point, including these:

- fighting civic authorities who wanted to honor Pope John Paul's visit to the United States by extending to him the honor usually accorded a foreign dignitary;
- opposing the appointment of chaplains in prisons and military bases;
- eliminating chaplains from congressional service;
- working to remove the motto "In God We Trust" from U.S. coins and postage stamps;
- getting the words "under God" out of the pledge of allegiance;
- challenging "blue law" legislation intended to reduce commercial activity on Sundays;
- stripping the tax-exempt status from places of worship;
- sweeping public property clean of religious symbolism, even during holiday seasons such as Channukah, Easter, and Christmas.[3]

Alongside these activities, Donohue notes, "Most conspicuous of all, however, is the ACLU's annual ritual of filing suit in a federal court enjoining public school students from singing 'Silent Night.' It has also gone so far as to try to stop a city employees' Christmas pageant at the local zoo."[4]

Why such antagonism toward religious expression, especially from an organization that claims to be the protector of American civil rights? There are several reasons, but one will serve as our focus here because it has been repeatedly used by governmental and nongovernmental groups to purge religion from the public life of Americans. I'm referring to the First Amendment and the so-called separation-of-church-and-state requirement supposedly embedded in that amendment.

The Separation Distortion

The First Amendment of the U.S. Constitution begins like this: "Congress shall make no law respecting an establishment of religion, or prohibiting the free exercise thereof." According to Ira Glasser, the ACLU's executive director, "The First Amendment was meant to bar all government endorsement of religion." Glasser claims that the motivation behind this provision was to keep the government from meddling in the affairs of religion so religious liberty could "flourish." The original "proponents of separation" allegedly reasoned their way to adopt the provision on the following grounds:

> If a legislature were empowered to favor *any* religious practice, it was argued, its decision about *which* religious practice to support would have to be made by majority vote. Inevitably, minority religious beliefs would suffer. Some would be tolerated, others would not, and therefore the process of deciding which is which should not be made by the government. The uniquely American idea of religious liberty protected by a high wall of separation between church and state was forged during the time of the Revolution and ultimately codified in the Bill of Rights in 1791.[5]

This is an oft-told story, and activist lawyers and judges have used it to strip the public arena of religious expression, symbols, and practice. Rather than guaranteeing freedom *for* religion, this interpretation of the First Amendment has led to freedom *from* religion. It has not protected religious liberty from governmental intrusion but allowed the government to purge it from public life. It has certainly erected a "high wall between church and state," but it is a wall with a steel door covered with locks, and all the locks are on the state's side of the door. When the state unlocks the door and enters the church's domain, it almost always further restricts the church's freedoms. The state is definitely not a protector of religion.

Here are several examples (out of literally thousands one could list) of how well this "wall of separation" has "benefited" the exercise of religious liberty in recent years. The cases range from the ridiculous to the frightening. You be the judge on which is which.

- In Michigan, a federal court ordered the removal of a portrait of Jesus Christ that had been hanging in a public school for thirty years.[6]
- After several court battles, San Diego's popular Balboa Park ended up with two Christmas displays: eight scenes of Jesus Christ's life, which were sponsored by Christians, and five panels honoring the Bill of Rights, which the ACLU sponsored.[7]
- Twenty-four pro-life Christians were arrested and imprisoned in Atlanta, Georgia, because they were praying on a public sidewalk near an abortion facility.[8]
- The U.S. Supreme Court struck down New York's creation of a public school district that benefited a Hasidic Jewish community's attempt to provide quality education for two hundred handicapped and learning disabled children.[9]
- In Texas, officials denied a Christian woman's request to use an annex to the county courthouse for a local chapter meeting of the

Christian Coalition. The county clerk gave her this explanation for the action: "If a religious group would begin their meeting with a prayer, that would be violating the separation of church and state."[10]

- Also in Texas, a fifty-seven-year-old grandmother "was handcuffed, strip-searched, and thrown in an unheated jail cell for the 'crime' of passing out religious tracts on the public roadway across from a high school."[11]
- The California State Supreme Court ruled against a Presbyterian landlady whom a man and woman had sued. The couple wanted to live together, and they told the landlady they were married when they were not. When the landlady discovered the lie, she explained to the couple that her religious convictions would not permit her to rent an apartment to them. The couple sued, and the court ruled in their favor, arguing that the landlady had "violated the couple's right to 'freedom from discrimination based on personal characteristics.' " The attorney who won the case said about the decision, " 'We're not precluding [the landlady] from exercising her religion. We're just saying she can't bring it with her into the business world.' "[12]
- In the case *Brandon v. Board of Education of Guiderland Central School District*, a "federal court saw that 'nothing could be more dangerous' than an adolescent seeing the football captain, the student body president or 'the leading actress in a dramatic production participating in communal prayer meetings in the captive audience setting of a school.' "[13]
- In Florida, a male religious group leader who had been convicted of having sexual relations with an adolescent girl "won a new trial because a juror read a Bible passage about circumcision aloud during deliberations." The man's accuser had testified that he was circumcised, while his wife said he was not. The Bible-quoting juror read Genesis 17:10 to fellow jurors. The passage says, "Every male among you shall be circumcised." Apparently the argument was that the religious group's leader would have obeyed this text, and therefore would have been circumcised. Ergo: His accuser was telling the truth and his wife was lying. The judge threw out the case because of this incident. He held that " 'consulting a Bible during jury deliberations breaches the separation of church and state guaranteed by the U.S. Constitution.' "[14]
- A child in Kentucky was told she could not submit her chosen drawing for an independent school project. She had drawn a cross.[15]
- In Arizona, a teacher disciplined a second-grader in class for typing the word *Jesus* on her school computer during a computer lab.[16]

- In the case *Bankruptcy Trustee Christians v. Crystal Evangelical Free Church*, the Eighth Circuit Court of Appeals agreed with a lower court ruling that a married couple who regularly gave 10 percent of their gross income to their church engaged in a fraudulent transfer of funds. The couple had filed for bankruptcy, but had also donated about $13,500 to the church. The couple said that their practice of giving was as important to their beliefs as life's other necessities. The federal court disagreed, contending that the couple had received nothing of value in exchange for their financial contributions to the church.[17]
- School administrators refused to allow the Intercessors Christian Club at a local high school to display signs on the school bulletin board that advertised the club's activities. Other clubs could use the bulletin board, but the ICC could not because its signs used words like *God* and *Jesus*.[18]
- The Oregon Department of Motor Vehicles had no problem allowing a personalized license plate to read "Witches." It also permitted "Hot Dam," "2Sexy," and "2Hot4U." But when an Oregon citizen wanted "Pray" on her license plate, the department said no. The reason? Something about the state endorsing religion, and the matter of the separation of church and state, and all that.[19]
- In a similar case in Virginia, the state's Department of Motor Vehicles refused a pastor's request to have "4GOD-SO" on his license plate. For the pastor, the message was a reference to John 3:16. For Virginia, the plate was a violation of the wall dividing church and state because it displayed the word *God*. The DMV also denied another citizen's desire to have his plate read "ATHEIST." The grounds? The word referred to a deity by expressing unbelief in one.[20]
- In Wisconsin, a school threatened to censor a student's salutatorian speech if it contained a prayer or any other expression of religious sentiment.[21]
- Several proabortion protesters blocked worshipers from entering their church in New York City. When the church tried to get an injunction against the demonstrators, their request was denied, even though the state routinely granted proabortion groups injunctions against pro-life demonstrators.[22]
- School administrators suspended a Florida high school student for distributing religious literature on campus.[23]
- The University of Virginia decided it would not help fund a magazine called *Wide Awake* because it constituted a " 'religious activity.' "

The university already provided money for more than a hundred student organizations, but this one was different. It was Christian. A federal appeals court ruled in the university's favor when the matter came to it for review. According to the court, any financial support of *Wide Awake* would " 'send an unmistakably clear signal that the University of Virginia supports Christian values and wishes to promote wide promulgation of such values.' " Apparently a bad thing. An interesting side note, though. The university had no problem underwriting the values of many other groups, including homosexuals, feminists, animal rights activists, and non-Christian religious groups. University officials saw no discrepancy in their discrimination. The non-Christian organizations, they said, were " 'cultural organizations, not proselytizing organizations.' " Are we really expected to believe that none of the other groups conveyed their beliefs or values to anyone? This is what the university wanted people to believe, and this despite the fact that the Muslim group on campus published a magazine explicitly designed to " 'promote better understanding of Islam.' "[24] The school's former president and current law professor supported the university's position. As he put it, " 'If it [the school's decision not to fund *Wide Awake*] is discriminatory, it is a discrimination that is required by our separation of church and state.' "[25]

- Six students in Illinois were arrested, detained in squad cars, and threatened with mace all because they prayed around their school's flag pole as part of an annual national event called "See You at the Pole." Voluntary student participation in this event has gone as high as two million in a given year. Students gather to pray before, not during, regular school hours.[26]
- A Jewish Christian was denied the right to evangelize and distribute literature in a public park in Stone Mountain Park outside Atlanta, Georgia.[27]
- For expressing his religious convictions on his own time, a North Carolina University student was dismissed from his job at the school.[28]
- A woman who wanted to place a poster on the city library's bulletin board to advertise a Christian concert and "revival" meeting was refused permission. A library official told her that the poster was "too religious." If she would remove the word *revival*, the official said the library might reverse its decision. Without any changes, the library said the separation of church and state forbade it to permit the poster's display on city property.[29]

- A case called *Lamb's Chapel v. Center Moriches Union Free School District* concerned a church that asked the local school district if it could use the district's facilities to show a James Dobson film series entitled "Turn Your Heart Toward Home." The New York school district had "voluntarily opened its facilities after school hours to civic, social, and recreational groups, and to other uses that contributed to the 'welfare of the community.'" But because this film series discussed family issues from a *Christian* perspective, the school district refused to let the church use its facilities. When this case was argued before the U.S. Supreme Court, "the attorney for the school board and the State of New York admitted that the board would allow communists, atheists, and agnostics in their school auditorium after school hours to address family issues and even to proselytize against religion but that they would not allow even a single minister to debate against a room full of atheists in front of an atheist audience." Jay Sekulow, the attorney arguing on behalf of the church, responded to this revealing admission in his closing remarks to the Court. His comments accurately sum up the current legal situation on the separation between church and state: " 'The way I understand it is the communists are in, the atheists are in, the agnostics are in, but religion is out."[30]

All of this, and so much more, has been done in the name of religious liberty. That's the party line, and for too long it has worked its mischief to the detriment of our entire society.

Ira Glasser's portrayal of the history and meaning of the First Amendment is first rate—a first-rate fiction, that is. It has just enough fact in it to sound plausible, but more than enough fiction in it to help undermine religious freedom in the lives of all people of faith, no matter their religious persuasion. A brief tour of American history is adequate to demonstrate this fact.

America's Religious Heritage

Except for the Native Americans who were already on the North American Continent, the first explorers of the New World from the Old World were Roman Catholic adventurers and missionaries from Spain. They crisscrossed sections of the new land from one shoreline to the next, evangelizing the Indians, establishing settlements, and making maps of the vast, uncharted territory. They began arriving just a generation before the Protestant Reformation began in 1517.[31]

More than a century after the Catholics' arrival, various Protestant groups began pouring in. These included Episcopalians, members of Holland's Reformed Church, Puritans, Baptists, English Quakers, Irish and Scottish Presbyterians, and Swedish Lutherans. The Protestants concentrated their settlements along the eastern seaboard, while the Catholics spent most of their energies on the west coast and in the southwest. The East's original thirteen colonies were largely Protestant, with a small but vital Catholic constituency residing mostly in Maryland and Pennsylvania.[32]

The vast majority of these Protestant pioneers and settlers were deeply committed to and shaped by a reformed Christian outlook. They believed that God was real. To them God was all-knowing, all-powerful, all-good, and sovereign over the affairs of his entire creation. He had created human beings and endowed them with his image, which made them special in the created order. He created them to know him, serve him, glorify him, and find their greatest happiness in him, but they disobeyed him and were now fallen creatures, lost in their sin, utterly corrupt, humanly unredeemable. So God sought to save them by sending his own Son into the world to die on a cross for their sins and rise from the dead as the first fruit of everlasting resurrection life. Through God's Son, Jesus Christ, anyone could receive this gracious gift of eternal life by placing their faith in him. However, even this faith could not be exercised apart from the work of God's Spirit in a person's life. Human beings were so blinded and entrapped by sin that they had no ability or desire to reach toward God and do his will on their own accord. Apart from God, people were helpless and doomed. Nature, human conscience, and the Bible collectively revealed and confirmed these realities.[33]

This reformed view dominated the Protestant American psyche well into the eighteenth century. It was also the single greatest influence on the content and interpretation of America's foremost founding documents: the Declaration of Independence (1776), the Constitution (1787), and the Bill of Rights (1789).

The Declaration of Independence

"We hold these truths to be self-evident, that all men are created equal; that they are endowed by their Creator with certain unalienable rights; that among these are life, liberty, and the pursuit of happiness. That to secure these rights, governments are instituted among men, deriving their just powers from the consent of the governed."

These words are foundational in the Declaration of Independence. They decree the early Americans' conviction that certain truths are "self-evident," by which they meant known directly or intuitively, known with certainty, and requiring no proof. These truths included human equality, which was due to one God creating all people. Therefore, these truths were universal, absolute, not relative at all. Even the practice of slavery was generally not viewed as an exception to this rule (see chapter 11).

This God had given his human creatures "certain unalienable rights." An "unalienable" right was a natural right embedded in the created order itself, which came from the hand of God. This means that no created entity, human or otherwise, can grant these rights or destroy them. Their existence and authority are dependent on God, not man. They are sacred, inviolable God-given human rights.

The only legitimate role human governments can play in relationship to these rights is to "secure" them. By this the Declaration of Independence means "protect." If a government becomes the adversary rather than the protector of these God-given natural human rights, the Declaration says "it is the right of the people to alter or to abolish it [i.e., the government], and to institute a new government" that builds on and protects these rights. Governments do not have the right to squelch these "unalienable rights"; their job is to secure them. If governments fail to carry out their responsibility, the people have the right to change or replace them.

In effect, then, the true sovereign of the founding Americans was God the Creator of nature and Giver of rights, not the will of the people or human governments. And so that no one could miss this fact, the Declaration ends with the signers "appealing to the Supreme Judge of the world for the rectitude of our intentions" and voicing their "firm reliance on the protection of Divine Providence" in their "support of this declaration."[34]

Historians are divided over whether the God of the Declaration should be identified with Christian theism or an Enlightenment form of deism.[35] But for the purposes of my argument here, it really does not matter. The fact is that the Declaration unequivocally regards the existence of a deity as a given. It appeals to this God and what he has provided humankind as the rational foundation upon which liberation from a tyrannical government is based. Thomas Jefferson asked, "Can the liberties of a nation be thought secure when we have removed their only firm basis, a conviction in the minds of the people that these liberties are of the gift of God?"[36] His answer and that of the rest of the founders was no. God was the source of the Declaration's self-evident truths and liberties. This makes the Declaration a document highly favorable to religious belief.

Furthermore, and most importantly, the American population understood the Declaration's references to God, nature, human rights, and so on in Judeo-Christian terms, not Enlightenment or deistic ones. Protestant reformed "Puritanism provided the moral and religious background of fully 75 percent of the people who declared their independence in 1776." The estimate may even be as high as 85 or 90 percent.[37] Out of three thousand congregations in 1775, only 15 percent were Episcopal. Almost all the rest were reformed Protestant.[38] A few remaining ones were Catholic and Jewish. In his autobiography, Benjamin Franklin reported that the Bible and John Bunyan's 1684 Puritan classic *The Pilgrim's Progress* were the two most commonly owned and read books of his day. Between the two books, historian Joyce Appleby says that the Bible was without doubt "the most important source of meaning for eighteenth-century Americans."[39] Mountains of historical evidence such as this abundantly make clear that Revolutionary-era Americans, like their forebears, were immersed in the Judeo-Christian worldview. Historian Donald J. D'Elia sums up the situation well:

> The consensus of the overwhelming majority of the American people in 1776 and 1789 [was] that the state indeed has an obligation to worship God or perish. The Declaration of Independence and the Federal Constitution, as well as the state constitutions ... were seen at the time as having meaning only within the much larger "oral constitution" of what was a Christian culture—not an Enlightenment culture! ... The point is, that for practically everyone in that generation, it was still their Christian culture that endowed documents with meaning.[40]

The U.S. Constitution

If the Declaration of Independence was the document of self-evident principles, the Constitution was the document of governing practice. What kind of government would best ensure human liberties? The Constitution was the Americans' answer. With its balance of powers between the executive, legislative, and judicial branches, the Constitution's drafters believed they could curb political and moral aggression. Not because people were naturally virtuous, but just the opposite: they could be expected to go wrong. Protestant theology led them to this conclusion. They believed people were corrupt and that their proneness to evil had to be kept in check at every turn. As one 1776 publication stated, man "is a poor, indigent, frail, and helpless being; his reason corrupt, his understanding full of ignorance and error, his will and desires bent upon evil."[41] The framers thought a balance of power would discourage attempts by any one person or group to gain unmitigated control over the country's citizens. For them, the absence of government by common consent was tantamount to slavery and tyranny. Thomas Paine declared in 1792: "There is *one* general principle that distinguishes freedom from slavery, which is, that *all hereditary Government over a people is to them a species of slavery, and representative Government is freedom.*"[42]

Despite such reasoning and the constitutional provision of the separation of powers, the states and the communities within them remained unconvinced that the Constitution was an adequate foundation to protect them from the potentially intrusive practices of a centralized government entity. This concern especially revolved around religious belief and practice, which led to the Bill of Rights and the First Amendment to the Constitution.

First Amendment Realities

The colonists were very familiar with religious oppression and persecution perpetuated by national governments. They had fled their European homes because they were denied the right to exercise their religious convictions. Oddly enough, these countries were not antireligious, rather they were strongly religious. The problem was not their attitude toward religion, but in their promotion of one particular religious orientation over all others. Religious groups throughout the American colonies wanted assurances that they would never be subject to the tyranny of a religious majority through the complicity of the national government. That assurance was granted them in the First Amendment to the Constitution, the opening amendment of ten known as the Bill of Rights.

James Madison, considered the architect of the Constitution, proposed the wording to address this religious liberty concern that the First Congress eventually shaped into the First Amendment. His proposal for the Establishment of Religion Clause was this: "The Civil rights of none shall be abridged on account of religious belief or worship, *nor shall any national religion be established,* nor shall the full and equal rights of Conscience be in any manner, or on any pretext, infringed."[43] His suggested wording was in line with what the other states proposed. For instance, Maryland submitted this wording: "That there be no national religion established by law; but that all persons be equally entitled to protection in their religious liberty."[44] Virginia introduced a similar measure: "That no particular religious sect or society ought to be favored or established, by law, in preference to others."[45] New York,

North Carolina, and Rhode Island passed comparable resolutions and sent them on to the First Congress. Everyone was worried about the same thing. No one wanted the central federal government to set up a national religion or raise one religious group above another.

Between the Senate and the House, they eventually pared Madison's proposal down to the Establishment Clause we have today: "Congress shall make no law respecting an establishment of religion, or prohibiting the free exercise thereof." What did Madison think this condensed version of his proposal meant? We don't have to guess. It is recorded in the *Annals of Congress*: "Mr. Madison said, he apprehended the meaning of the words to be, that Congress should not establish a religion, and enforce the legal observation of it by law, nor compel men to worship God in any manner contrary to their conscience." Madison and the rest of the American people wanted to be sure that Congress would not use its power to make laws that "might infringe the rights of conscience, and establish a national religion."[46] The First Amendment was intended as that constitutional guarantee.

Now we are prepared to make two very critical observations concerning the religious liberty understanding of the Constitution. First, *the Establishment Clause does not deny individual states or local communities the right to establish religious preferences or policies.* Both before and after the Constitution and the First Amendment became law, "State constitutions rang with religious language and proceeded to build on religious assumptions. Though accepting religious liberty as a given of the Revolution, these documents did not accept religious neutrality or indifference as an [sic] necessary consequence. They wished to affirm a faith, take a stand, make a statement."[47] And that's just what they did. Among the state-sanctioned and state-conducted practices one could find were these:

- taxes were collected for the support of Christianity, which included underwriting clergy, places of worship, and Christian schoolteachers who taught religion, morality, and piety to the public;
- in several states officeholders had to be Protestants; in other states officeholders did not have to accept a particular religious persuasion, but they had to affirm at least a belief in the existence of a deity and a future state of rewards and punishments for humanity;
- one state limited its guarantees of religious freedom to adherents of the Christian faith alone;
- another state informed its citizens that one of their civic duties was attending church;

- some states barred all clergy from legislative positions.[48]

What all this shows is that the issue of establishing a religion, while denied to the federal government, was left to the states and their constituencies to work out.

The second observation I want to make is this: *The Establishment Clause does not say anything about the federal government maintaining a neutral, much less a hostile, stance toward religion.* On the contrary, its drafters and ratifiers supported many actions of the federal government that backed religion in general but without promoting a particular religious group over another. A few examples will suffice:

- In 1789, Congress unanimously approved a resolution requesting then President George Washington to proclaim a national day of thanksgiving and prayer.
- In 1787, the Congress ratified the Northwest Ordinance, which was intended to guide the civil ordering of the settlements west of the thirteen states. Article III of the Ordinance states, "Religion, morality, and knowledge, being necessary to good government and the happiness of mankind, schools and the means of education shall forever be encouraged."[49]
- In the early 1800s, Congress ratified treaties with several Indian tribes, which included using federal tax money to help support Catholic and Protestant clergy and the construction of churches for the education of the Indians. This practice lasted nearly a hundred years. According to Supreme Court Justice William Rehnquist, "It was not until 1897, when aid to sectarian education for Indians had reached $500,000 annually, that Congress decided thereafter to cease appropriating money for education in sectarian schools."[50]

After considering evidence such as this, political scientist Robert Cord sets the matter straight about the Establishment Clause of the First Amendment. He says it was "intended to accomplish three purposes": (1) "to prevent the establishment of a national church or religion, or the giving of any religious sect or denomination a preferred status"; (2) "to safeguard the right of freedom of conscience in religious beliefs against invasion solely by the national Government"; and (3) "to allow the States, unimpeded, to deal with religious establishments and aid to religious institutions as they saw fit." He adds that the "historical evidence" does not support the contention that the federal government could not provide "aid to religion when it was provided on a nondiscriminatory basis. Nor does there appear to be any historical evidence that the First Amendment was intended to provide an *absolute separation or independence* of religion and the national state. The actions of the early Congresses and Presidents, in fact, suggest quite the opposite."[51] In the words of John Quincy Adams, Americans "connected in one indissoluble band the principles of civil government with the principles of Christianity."[52] Or, as John Quincy Adams's father, John Adams, said: "We have no government armed with power capable of contending with human passions unbridled by morality and religion. Avarice, ambition, revenge, or gallantry, would break the strongest cords of our Constitution as a whale goes through a net. Our Constitution was made only for a moral and religious people. It is wholly inadequate to the government of any other."[53]

America's Secularization

It is clear, then, that the old absolute was that religion was the backbone of American culture. It, and it alone, provided the moral and spiritual light necessary for the common good of the republic in its public and private spheres. As such, the Establishment Clause of the First Amendment could not have been passed, as the ACLU's Ira Glasser claims, "to bar all government endorsement of religion." It is this fallacious and fictitious interpretation that is fostering the emergence of the new absolute: *Religion is the bane of public life, so for the public good it should be banned from the public square.* Separationist groups such as the ACLU, People for the American Way, and Americans United for Separation of Church and State are doing all they can to sweep religion's influence out of every nook and cranny of Americans' public life. And the federal, state, and even many local governments have joined their ranks. The constitutionally protected exercise of religious faith is quickly disappearing.

Yale University professor and political liberal Stephen Carter wrote about the demise of religion in his bestselling book *The Culture of Disbelief: How American Law and Politics Trivialize Religious Devotion.* He exposed and challenged what he labeled the contemporary "intuition" that "encourages a tendency to say of religious belief, 'Yes, we cherish you—now go away and leave us alone.' "[54] Further commenting, he said:

> It is an intuition that makes religion something that should be believed in privacy, not something that should be paraded; and if religion is paraded, it is this same intuition that assures that it likely will be dismissed. This intuition says that anyone who believes that

> God can heal diseases is stupid or fanatical, and the same intuition makes sure that everyone understands that this belief is a kind of mystic flight from hard truths—it has nothing to do with the real world. The same intuition tells the religious that those things that they know to be true are wrong or irrelevant. . . . At its most extreme, it is an intuition that holds not only that religious beliefs cannot serve as the basis of policy; they cannot even be debated in the forum of public dialogue on which a liberal politics crucially depends.
>
> The intuition says, in short, that religion is like building model airplanes, just another hobby: something quiet, something private, something trivial—and not really a fit activity for intelligent, public-spirited adults. This intuition, then, is one that in the end must destroy either religion or the ideal of liberal democracy. That is a prospect that can please only those who hate one or the other or both.[55]

This secular intuition has led to what Keith Fournier, the executive director of the American Center for Law Justice, calls "religious cleansing":

> *Religious cleansing* is a term I use to describe the current hostility and bigotry toward religion and people of faith that are leading to covert and overt attempts to remove any religious influence from the public arena. Just as ethnic cleansing attempts to rid certain ethnic groups and their influence from public life, so religious cleansing attempts to do the same with religious groups, their beliefs, and their values. How? Not by physical extermination—at least not in the United States—but by political and legal containment. You see, if as Christians all of our views on contemporary major issues are seen as "religious"; if "religious" views are to be kept in church buildings or behind the front door of our homes lest we somehow violate certain contemporary notions of the separation of church and state; and if taking positions on the critical ideas—such as liberty, life, and family—that shape culture is somehow deemed "improper" for a religious person, then what are we left with? No voice in the marketplace of ideas. Sure, we can sit around in our homes and churches and discuss political, moral, and social issues. Yes, we can vote our conscience. But if we move beyond these borders and step into city hall or the courts or the public schools or federal offices or virtually any other public arena, then we become trespassers—violators who need to be pushed back to the private sphere where our ideas cannot impact, or even threaten to impact, anyone but ourselves.[56]

Undoubtedly believers of all faiths face an increasingly hostile culture in which religion can play a private role, much as a hobby might, but it dare not slip beyond into the public sphere. When it does, those who practice it are generally caricatured as extremists, fundamentalists, religious zealots, bigots, right-wing fanatics, enemies of genuine liberty, censors of free speech, ignorant antagonists of liberal education. Keep your faith at home. That is the resounding message of most of America's courts, political leaders, educators, liberal clergy, and a growing number of secular-minded common citizens.

Secularism is becoming religion's replacement. And it is bringing with it a breakdown of the moral, spiritual, and intellectual fiber that religion, especially Christianity, held together for centuries on the North American Continent. This secular spirit is even reshaping matters of life and death. We will turn to that subject next.

Chapter 5

Death, What a Beautiful Choice

The *Old* Absolute	The *New* Absolute
(2) Human life from conception to natural death is sacred and worthy of protection.	(2a) Human life, which begins and ends when certain individuals or groups decide it does, is valuable as long as it is wanted.

An anxious couple receives a telephone call. It's the adoption agency. They become all smiles when the agency tells them that their adopted child is a daughter. With the newborn now wrapped in her adoptive mother's arms, the narrator on the television advertisement says, "Last year, over 50,000 women found families to adopt their unexpected children. They decided instead of abortion to tough it out and bring their babies into the world. They held to their belief that nothing is more precious than human life. Life. What a beautiful choice."

When I first saw this ad air in 1992, I thought it was wonderfully done. Artistically, it was well crafted. Better than that, it put the focus of the so-called "pro-choice" debate where it belongs—on the beauty, wonderment, and inherent value of human life. I also felt the ad's appeal on a much more personal level. You see, I was adopted at birth, about twenty years before the 1973 U.S. Supreme Court ruling in *Roe v. Wade* legalized abortion on demand. I have often wondered if my biological mother would have denied me my inalienable right to life if she had conceived me just a couple of decades later under *Roe.* I was fortunate. I got to live. I was also adopted by a young couple who loved me as much as any child could be loved. Like the child in the ad, I too had come from the womb of a mother who nurtured me within her until my natural exit came due. After bringing me into the outside world, she helped assure my stay in the world through adoption. The ad was right. Life is a beautiful choice.

The creators of this ad—the Arthur S. DeMoss Foundation—followed it with another. The new one showed a wriggling newborn next to an ultrasound video of a ten-week-old unborn baby who was also squirming about. The narrator said, "The only difference is that the baby on the left is already born, and the baby on the right would very much like to be." Another powerful piece showing the preciousness of life, I thought.

Not everyone felt this way. Many people objected to the commercials. The abc affiliate in Philadelphia would not run them because they said they had a policy against airing "ads for controversial advertising."[1] Jacquelynn Brinkly, the director of public affairs for Planned Parenthood of Southern Pennsylvania, called the ads "simplistic." "They show children who are beautiful and well adjusted," she said. "That's not the true story for most children available for adoption."[2]

I wasn't quite sure what Ms. Brinkly meant by her comments. Was she suggesting that couples seeking to adopt are so shallow that all they will consider are the physically gorgeous and the psychologically approved? This is untrue, for I have met many couples who had adopted even severely deformed and disabled children, not out of desperation, but out of love for all human life. I also knew that Planned Parenthood, Ms. Brinkly's employer, had been directly responsible for dramatically reducing the number of children available for adoption and for contributing to higher rates of child abuse among the born.[3] If the pool of potential adoptees was not up to Ms. Brinkly's standards of quality, her employer was largely to blame.

Among all the criticisms the DeMoss ads received, my favorite came from Alex Sanger, the president of New York's Planned Parenthood office and grandson of the organization's founder, Margaret Sanger. Mr. Sanger claimed that the "Life. What a Beautiful Choice." ad campaign was "extremely deceptive." Such "advocacy" does not belong on television, he insisted. In response, Mr. Sanger warned that Planned Parenthood may launch a counteroffensive—a national campaign against these "pro-life advocacy ads." The piece that really riled him was the commercial with the ultrasound video of a wriggling ten-week-old preborn next to a fidgeting newborn. "This ad," he said, "only gives half the story. The baby on the left is big. The fetus on the right is only a few inches long. There's no comparison. It's deceptive."[4]

What is going on here? When did size become the criteria for determining who should live and who should die? When did celebrating life become controversial? Why is death becoming the only beautiful, acceptable choice? Before we can answer these questions, we first need to see how far we have traveled from being a culture committed to life.

The Sanctity of Life

America's Judeo-Christian heritage is rooted in an ancient belief in the sanctity of all human life, including preborn life. This is founded on the biblical idea of the *imago dei*, image of God. The Hebrew book of beginnings, Genesis, describes God creating Adam and Eve, the first human couple, as his image-bearers: "So God created man in his own image, in the image of God he created him; male and female he created them."[5] After Adam and Eve disobey God and are exiled from the Garden of Eden, Genesis reaffirms that they are still God's image-bearers and that the image is being passed on to their children through the procreative process.[6] Even following the great judgment on sin through the flooding of the earth, the biblical text records God telling Noah that "Whoever sheds the blood of man, by man shall his blood be shed; for in the image of God has God made man."[7] Human sin has not erased the divine image. The Christian Scriptures also confirm that human beings are God's image-bearers, and they add that when the Son of God joined himself with a human nature that he too was in the image of God.[8] The biblical view, then, is that the divine image is what sets human beings apart from the rest of creation. We are like the created order in many ways, but it's the divine imprint that constitutes our distinct humanness. We are human because we are divine image-bearers. No image, no human person. Therefore, each human being—no exceptions—bears this image from conception and into the afterlife.

The biblical doctrine of the divine image is multifaceted, much as an expertly cut diamond. The Hebrew word translated "image" in the key passages in Genesis (1:26–27; 5:1, 3; 9:6) and the Greek word used to translate it in the ancient Septuagint have the same basic meaning. The words refer to a likeness, form, or appearance of an original. In reference to God, an image is something that visibly represents, reflects, and reveals the invisible God. This is what human beings are. We are living, physical-spiritual, finite icons of the living, all-spiritual, infinite Creator. The image means we are related to God in a special, glorious way. We can commune with him in an intimacy not shared by other creatures. The image also includes our ability to reason, make moral judgments, and exercise caring sovereignty over the rest of the created order. Because it encompasses both male and female, the image further indicates the communal side of our nature. We are created as social beings. We are not designed to live as independent islands, cut off from all others. Our fulfillment comes in community with fellow human beings, especially in that most intimate man-woman union known as marriage.[9] In these ways and others, we are God's image-bearers, says the Bible and orthodox Jewish and Christian reflections on its teachings.[10]

Throughout history, practices that devalued human life were challenged and greatly curtailed among the peoples influenced by the church's activities. Religious leaders spoke out against abortion, infanticide, euthanasia, human sacrifice, cannibalism, and the amusements that turned killing into sport. They worked to change the social conditions that made these practices attractive and available, sometimes sacrificing their own lives in the process. For instance, through their efforts in fourth- and fifth-century Rome, "Licentiousness and cruel sports were checked; new legislation was ordered to protect the slave, the prisoner, the mutilated man, the outcast woman. Children were granted important legal rights. Infant exposure was abolished. Women were raised from a status of degradation to that of legal protection. Hospitals and orphanages were created to take care of foundlings. Personal feuds and private wars were put under restraint."[11] The bloody and gruesome gladiatorial games also came to an end.[12]

In their fight for life, Christians adopted and depaganized the Hippocratic Oath, which physicians today still swear to uphold. The Oath explicitly opposes abortion, suicide, and euthanasia, and it calls on those who swear by it to "never use" their medical knowledge and abilities "to injure or wrong" their patients.[13]

This is the understanding of human nature and the high regard for human life that permeated the American psyche and America's founding documents. Based on it our forebears held that *human life from conception to natural death is sacred and worthy of protection.* That was their absolute conviction. They immortalized it in the Declaration of Independence, which lists life as the first God-given inalienable right. The Fifth and Fourteenth Amendments, which declare that no "person" shall be "deprived" of "life, liberty, or property, without due process of law," continued this tradition, as did the addition of the Thirteenth Amendment, which abolished slavery and overturned the infamous U.S. Supreme Court decision in the *Dred Scott* case. (I'll have more to say about the slavery issue in chapter 11.) Law scholar Joseph Witherspoon confirmed this view in his testimony before the House Subcommittee on Civil and Constitutional Rights:

> Careful research of the history of the Thirteenth and Fourteenth Amendments will demonstrate to any impartial investigator that the principal, actual purpose of their framers was to prevent any court, and especially the Supreme Court of the United States because of its earlier performance in the *Dred Scott* case ... from ever again defining the concept of person so as to exclude any class of human beings from the protection of the Constitution and the safeguards it established for the fundamental rights of human beings, including ... the unborn from the time of their conception.[14]

The American religious heritage, founding documents, subsequent amendments, and, if we had the space to review it, vast majority of the judicial decisions prior to the 1960s all witness to the conviction that life is the most fundamental, the most basic, foundational right any person has.[15] Without it, no other rights are possible. We cannot exercise any other freedoms or pursue any opportunities unless we are alive. Rob us of that and all our other rights disintegrate.

The Emerging Culture of Death

Despite this pro-life heritage, today we are witnessing the removal of the right to life from various classes of people. The dislodging tools usually used are abortion, infanticide, euthanasia, population control, and certain practices associated with genetic engineering. Death is becoming the solution of choice for our problems, our panacea for our personal and social woes. All around us we see a new absolute emerging—namely, that *human life, which begins and ends when certain individuals or groups decide it does, is valuable as long as it is wanted.* To show this, I want to introduce you to three individuals and their legacy. They are not the only reasons death is replacing life in contemporary America, but they have contributed their fair share to this disturbing trend. The individuals I'm referring to are Thomas Malthus, Charles Darwin, and Margaret Sanger. Their ideas have radically reshaped the world, including yours, and the adjustments have been nothing short of disastrous.

Malthus and Population Control

Thomas Robert Malthus (1766–1834) was an ordained Protestant minister, and a professor of economics and history in England. He wrote several works, but the one history remembers him by the most is his *An Essay on the Principle of Population.*[16]

Malthus's central thesis was simple and apocalyptic. In his day, the dominant view was that the world needed more people to help create better economies, more resources, and stronger societies. Malthus argued that just the opposite was the case. The more people, the greater stress there is on the world's food supply. The greater the scarcity of food, the more poverty, sickness, crime, wars, and mass starvations will occur to bring the population back in line with the available resources. He used his mathematics background to support his thesis. He claimed that the food supply increases in an arithmetical ratio—1, 2, 3, 4, 5, 6, 7, 8, 9, etc. The population, however, increases geometrically—1, 2, 4, 8, 16, 32, 64, 128, 256, etc. The increases occur every twenty-five years, so that in two hundred years the ratio between food and population would be 9 to 259, and in three hundred years the ratio would be 13 to 4,096. If the population's growth was not adequately controlled, the human race would face an abysmal future. This would be particularly true for the working class, he argued. As E. Michael Jones explains Malthus's reasoning:

> If we have a situation in which the wealth of a nation increases as a whole, but the working classes receive none of the benefits of that increase in wealth, increased production will always seem to mean simultaneously an increase in population and a decrease in the amount of resources available to that population. This is simply because the increase in productivity is not shared equitably. The increase in wealth will go to the expansion of industry, which will involve the hiring of more workers, but the wages of the workers will be fixed and low. Thus the population of the workers will increase while their purchasing power will not. As a result, farm prices will remain low and that will cause farm production to level out or decrease. Before long the wealth will become so concentrated in the hands of so few people that economic exchange will collapse, as it did periodically throughout the nineteenth century and well into the twentieth century.[17]

Malthus said there were three forces that could keep populations in check so they would not outrun the food supply: all causes of premature death; all checks on the birth rate; and moral restraint, by which he meant remaining single and chaste, or marrying a woman nearing the end of her child-bearing ability. The first two forces brought misery and vice. As historian Gertrude Himmelfarb explains, misery would come "when sickness, starvation, and death carried off the excess population; and vice when the immoral practices of men—war, infanticide, and the resources of promiscuity—either prevented procreation or disposed of the unfortunates who could not be fed." To this Himmelfarb adds:

> This misery and vice were as much of the essence of the human condition as the need for food and the instinct for cohabitation, which reacted together in such catastrophic fashion. The evils of overpopulation were not . . . in the remote future, when every inch of the earth would have been cultivated and inhabited. Population was always and everywhere, in some measure, pressing against the available food supply. If the means of subsistence should suddenly become abundant, either because of the opening up of new food resources or because of a plague carrying off large numbers of people, the remaining population, enjoying relative affluence, would be apt to marry earlier than otherwise, have more children, and die later. In a short period of time, population would thus have adjusted to the means of subsistence—and more than adjusted, population reproducing at so much more rapid a rate than the food supply that numbers would soon once again be in excess of available food. The oscillation created by the permanent imbalance between food and people was a feature of every country, county, and hamlet, in every period of its history.[18]

To Malthus, this population problem was man's struggle for existence. But the picture was not totally bleak. The virtue of moral restraint was the most powerful force of the three mentioned, and Malthus believed it showed the most promise. He thought this virtue was founded in nature and reason, and confirmed in revealed religion, which to him was Christianity. He thought that the best way to address the population problem was by people restraining "the excessive or irregular gratification of the human passions." "Each individual has, to a great degree, the power of avoiding the evil consequences to himself and society resulting from it [the population problem], by the practice of a virtue [moral restraint] dictated to him by the light of nature, and sanctioned by revealed religion." To this he added, "There can be no question that this virtue tends greatly to improve the condition, and increase the comforts, both of the individuals who practice it, and, through them, of the whole society."[19]

Malthus did not believe that birth control was the means to keep the population's growth in check. He was opposed to the use of mechanical devices to prevent procreation, even in marriage. As far as he was concerned, contraceptive use was immoral. He would not have been a card-carrying member of Planned Parenthood.

While Malthus's argument had its critics, it quickly gained widespread support among the populace and politicians of his day. Some people even moved to different countries to escape becoming victims of Malthusian predictions.[20] Despite the popularity of his work, Malthus's forecasts failed, even in his native England. The population grew, and none of the events he foretold occurred as a consequence of the rising population. In fact, the economy improved and the prosperity of the poor increased under social reforms.[21] But Malthus's thesis lived on anyway, even into the twentieth century.

In 1968, a scholar at Stanford University named Paul Ehrlich wrote a book called *The Population Bomb.* It was a runaway bestseller built on Malthusian ideas. It predicted frightening regional and worldwide disasters even if the population's growth rate was quickly stopped. He opened his book with a startling prophecy: "The battle to feed all of humanity is over. In the 1970s the world will undergo famines—hundreds of millions of people will starve to death in spite of any crash programs embarked upon now."[22] He predicted that 65 million Americans would starve to death in the 1980s and that by 1999 America's population would decline to 22.6 million. He suggested that England would cease to exist by the year 2000, and that it was too late to prevent widespread starvation in India. To save our future, Ehrlich urged a worldwide program of population control and resource conservation that would reduce the global population to 1.5 billion.

Well, according to 1995 estimates, the world's population has risen to more than 5.6 billion.[23] None of Ehrlich's worldwide catastrophes have occurred. Nor did the United States suffer mass starvations. England is doing well, and India never did experience a great famine. As Tim Stafford reports, contrary to Ehrlich's dire forecasts, "there is considerably *less* hunger" in the world today than ever before.

> Famines have come—in Africa, not India—but they have been caused primarily by war, secondarily by poverty (people who can't afford food can't eat it), and by poor distribution. In fact, some famine-stricken countries increased their net exports of food, even during famine.
>
> Meanwhile, farmers managed to grow more food than ever. While global population was growing at an unprecedented rate, hunger was *falling* at an unprecedented rate. Food production in the developing world more than doubled between 1965 and 1990.... Caloric intake per person in developing countries increased an extraordinary 21 percent. The number of chronically malnourished people fell 7 percent in the 11 years from 1979 to 1990.[24]

Moreover, a recent study conducted "by Paul Waggoner of the Connecticut Agricultural Experiment Station in New Haven," showed that the "gross productive potential of the Earth—set by available land, climate, and sunlight for photosynthesis—is sufficient to produce food for a staggering 1,000 billion people. Even without irrigation, available water is sufficient to grow food for 400 billion, and a conservative estimate of sustainable fertilizer production implies ample supplies to produce food for 80 billion."[25]

Facts and statistics such as these whiz right past population control advocates. Convinced the world is overpopulated and that we will not survive unless we reduce our numbers, they continue to fight for the establishment of "family-planning policies" in every country. To them, the most fundamental answer to our alleged population problem is birth control, which really amounts to people control. Inimical to Malthus who urged voluntary moral restraint and opposed artificial means of birth control, today's Malthusians make no appeals to personal moral restraint if it involves sex. They think people should be free to have sex with anyone, anytime. Of course uninhibited sex would breed far too many children to the liking of the population controllers. More mouths requires more food and drains other natural resources. So, to guarantee unhindered sex while putting a lid on population growth, the new social engineers push to make artificial forms of contraception, abortifacient drugs, and abortion available to people worldwide. Think of it: achieving a world of unrestrained sexual activity completely divorced from its life-giving consequence. This is the utopian dream they are striving to attain.[26]

The next major player is a naturalist who, with a lot of help from his friends, revolutionized the way we see ourselves and the rest of the world.

Darwin, Death, and Dehumanization

In 1859 a new revolution began in England with the publication of a single book. Its title was *On the Origin of Species by Means of Natural Selection, or the Preservation of Favoured Races in the Struggle for Life.* It was followed in 1871 by an even more controversial work: *The Descent of Man, and Selection in Relation to Sex.* The author of both books was Charles Darwin (1809–1882), a well-to-do, reclusive naturalist who had been developing and sitting on his new ideas for two decades.

Darwin set forth the theory of natural evolution. Scientist Robert Jastrow summarizes Darwin's theory and his reasoning this way:

> (1) A population grows until it approaches the limit of its resources; (2) in the struggle for existence that results, individuals with traits that help them to overcome the adverse forces of the environment—famine, disease, a harsh climate, and the attacks of the predator—are more likely to survive and produce offspring; (3) the offspring tend to inherit the favorable traits from their parents, and carry them on into future generations; (4) on the other hand, individuals with traits that handicap them in the struggle against adverse forces are less likely to reach maturity and therefore less likely to produce offspring, and their traits will tend to disappear from the population; (5) over the course of many generations, this process, which preserves and strengthens some traits while it prunes away others, gradually transforms the species.[27]

All the world's life forms, including human beings, are the products of this evolutionary process.

One of the central ideas behind Darwin's theory is Malthus's theory of the geometrical growth of populations working against the arithmetical growth of the food supply. As Darwin applied it in the *Origin of Species:*

> A struggle for existence inevitably follows from the high rate at which all organic beings tend to increase.... Hence, as more individuals are produced than can possibly survive, there must in every case be a struggle for existence, either one individual with another of the same species, or with the individuals of distinct species, or with the physical conditions of life. It is the doctrine of Malthus applied with manifold force to the whole animal and vegetable kingdoms; for in this case there can be no artificial increase of food, and no prudential restraint from marriage. Although some species may be now increasing, more or less rapidly, in numbers, all cannot do so, for the world would not hold them. There is no exception to the rule that every organic being naturally increases at so high a rate, that if not destroyed, the earth would soon be covered by the progeny of a single pair. Even slow-breeding man has doubled in twenty-five years [*Malthus's hypothetical figure!*], and at this rate, in a few thousand years, there would literally not be standing room for his progeny.[28]

In other works, Darwin readily admitted the tremendous influence Malthus's population theory played in his understanding of the struggle for existence and in his development of the theory of natural selection.[29] He said that no one conveyed "the warring of the species" as strongly as Malthus did.[30]

With Malthusian principles at his side, Darwin turned nature into "a seething slum, with everyone scrambling to get out, rushing to break from the rat-pack. Only the few survived, bettering themselves by creating new dynasties. Most remained trapped on the breadline, destined to struggle futilely, neighbors elbowing one another aside to get ahead, the weak trampled underfoot. Sacrifice and waste were endemic, indeed necessary. Nature was abortive, squandering, profligate. Her failures were discarded like the breeder's runts to rot on some domestic dump."[31]

Darwin also turned the image of God into a product of nature. Man was no longer a special work of the divine Creator but a successful mutation of lower life forms that adapted and won its struggle to survive. This also meant that nothing else in man's life had a divine origin. As Darwin saw it, "The 'feeling of religious devotion' was not basically different from a monkey's affection for its keeper.... Nor was the 'ennobling belief in God' innate and universal, merely the highest sanction for keeping society in order. All beliefs and mores had originated in animal instincts and savage superstitions."[32] Whatever man was or believed, it all had a natural origin stemming from the brutal Malthusian struggle for existence.

If man's life was due to natural causes alone, then his death must be completely natural as well. There must not be an afterlife of reward or punishment. With the extinguishing of natural life all ceases. The philosopher Bertrand Russell, himself a believer in naturalistic evolution, could not have put it better: "I believe that when I die I shall rot, and nothing of my ego will survive."[33] In his 1993 bestselling book *How We Die*, respected surgeon and professor Sherwin Nuland agreed. Death is "permanent unconsciousness in which there is neither void nor vacuum—in which there is simply nothing."[34]

This end should not discourage us, though. At least that is what we are told. For death is nature's way of providing for the new, the healthier, the better, the stronger. Death is a good fact about life. We could not live without it. Life thrives on the litter of the deceased. The organic decompose and replenish the earth so more organisms can have life and enjoy their day in the sun. Death is life's fertilizer. If it were not for the deaths of others, we would not have the chance at life that we do. How could animals live without killing other animals and plants? How could we survive without killing what we need to eat? How could we conquer new lands, find new cures, invent new machines or products unless some of us make sacrifices, even to the point of giving up our lives? How could the stronger have the food and space they need without the demise of the weaker? The earth's resources are not infinite. Therefore, when death is viewed from the larger vantage point, one can see that death, each of ours included, is essential to life.

We are told to accept death and make the best of it. Even use it to cut suffering short, or to keep the unwanted from neglect and hatred, or to make room for the better, the stronger, the genuinely desired among us. Survival goes to the fittest. The rest become fodder or refuse.

Evolutionary theory swept through nineteenth-century America. Educators, scientists, moralists, politicians, ministers, journalists . . . people from every walk of life drank from naturalistic evolution's well. And it didn't take long for it to poison our daily lives. For instance, American industrialists often ruthlessly crushed competitors, citing natural selection as the law by which they operated. "Evolution," writes Robert Clark, "gave the doer of evil a respite from his conscience. The most unscrupulous behavior toward a competitor could now be rationalized: evil could be called good. [W. G.] Sumner, who came to be called the Darwin of the Social Sciences, put the new doctrine very well when he claimed that 'while men were fighting for glory and greed, for revenge and superstition, they were building human society.' "[35]

Of course, English and American societies were not the only places polluted by naturalistic evolutionary theory. Darwin's influence can be traced to the communist theories of Karl Marx and Friedrich Engels, to the Russian socialist tyrants Joseph Stalin and Lenin, to the Nazi ideology of Adolf Hitler, and to China's communist revolutionary Mao Tse-tung. Between the ideologies, policies, and practices of these men alone, conservative estimates reported in 1972 put the human-caused death toll anywhere between 100 million and 150 million.[36]

Darwin's impact in the United States has been no less significant. His ideas permeate our public and many of our private educational institutions at all grade levels. Nearly all curriculum and instruction have been filtered through naturalistic glasses. Because of this, naturalism has invaded our every social stratum and profession. Nothing has been untouched, including our religious and legal institutions and our sources for news and other types of information. California law professor Phillip Johnson even understates the situation when he says, "Naturalistic thinking rules the intellectual world, including the National Academy of Sciences, the public schools, the universities and the elite of the legal profession." It "underlies not only natural science but intellectual work of all kinds."[37] Naturalism is so pervasive in our culture that many of us think in naturalistic categories without even realizing it. It has become like the air we breathe—invisible, omnipresent, and oh so natural.

In reality, though, Darwinian-spawned naturalism is choking us to death. When Darwin made us in the image of nature rather than leaving us in the image of God, we were dehumanized. No longer are we heaven-sent; now we are earth-produced. Our most ancient forebears were not humans but chemicals sloshing about in some prebiotic soup. Our next of kin were apes, and our worth no greater than the rest of the animal world. In fact, even that has come into question. In college, I had an anthropology professor who took an entire week of class lectures to demonstrate that man was not the height of evolutionary progress but a sign of de-evolution. "After all," he theorized, "apes were better foragers, and they could get around much better in trees. People were definitely lower on the evolutionary ladder than apes. Perhaps we are mutations that will not long survive the struggle for existence."

What began with utopian theory had become supported by the scientific community. Next came the social and practical implementation of these concepts. Human dignity finally gave way to inhumane indignities.

Sanger and Birth Control

The eugenics movement (a science that deals with the improvement of the hereditary qualities of a race or breed) was introduced by a man named Francis Galton. He was a cousin of Darwin, and he belonged to the same elite club in England—the Royal Society. Galton wrote a book called *Hereditary Genius* that Darwin praised. In fact, it led Darwin to modify his understanding of natural selection.[38]

In his history of the eugenics movement, California Institute of Technology professor Daniel Kevles described Galton's mid-nineteenth-century world and views: "It was well known that by careful selection farmers and flower fanciers could obtain permanent breeds of plants and animals strong in particular characters. 'Could not the race of men be similarly improved?' Galton wondered. 'Could not the undesirables be got rid of and the desirables multiplied?' Could not man actually take charge of his own evolution?" His answer was yes. Galton argued that, by selectively breeding human beings, one could control a family line's physical features, talent, and character. To achieve this end, Galton suggested that the state publicly award people who have the finest "hereditary merit ... foster wedded unions among them ... and encourage by postnatal grants the spawning of numerous eugenically golden offspring. (Some years later, he would urge that the state rank people by ability and authorize more children to the higher- than to the lower-ranking unions.) The unworthy, Galton hoped, would be comfortably segregated in monasteries and convents, where they would be unable to propagate their kind."[39] For those "unfit" individuals not dedicated to the celibate or chaste life, he advocated sterilization to keep them from producing more undesirable progeny.[40]

Who were the unfit among the eugenicists? Anyone who wasn't like them. They were white supremacists, promoting white European upper-class society as the model to achieve. In other words, they wanted to create what Hitler later popularized as the pure Aryan race. By getting the fit to reproduce prolifically and containing the unfit through segregation, sterilization, birth control, and abortion, they believed they could help nature evolve a purer and hardier race.

Margaret Sanger (1883–1966) is the mother of the modern-day birth-control movement and the founder of Planned Parenthood. She took Malthusian ideas and racial eugenics, which had already been linked to the survival-of-the-fittest views of Darwin, and added large helpings of socialism. Then she tied them all to birth control,[41] offering it as a critical part of the solution to a host of problems in the areas of personal health, family life, economic and social stability, biological freedom, and world peace.

Highlights of Sanger's views follow. All the quoted material is from her, unless I have noted otherwise. As you read this material, keep in mind that these are not isolated thoughts. They accurately depict Sanger's positions—positions she repeatedly explained and defended with religious zeal. Like a fiery pastor pounding his pulpit as he reaches the crux of his sermon, Sanger pounded her message home in article after article, issue after issue, book after book, speech after speech, never letting up and never backing down. Her strategy would change occasionally, but her persistence never waned. Here's a sampling of what she said:

- Birth control is not the same as abortion. Birth control methods prevent pregnancy, whereas abortion ends pregnancy.[42]
- Birth control is much better than abortion. Birth control is "normal" and "scientific." It brings "health and happiness." Abortion is "repulsive," "cruel, wicked, and heartless," "abnormal, often dangerous," and "always a very serious risk to the health and often to the life of the patient." It frequently leads to "disease, suffering, [and] death." If a woman survives an abortion physically, she "is not therefore safe." Her "womb may not return to its natural size," she may become barren and experience "serious, painful pelvic ailments," and suffer the "ruin" of her "general health."[43] Sanger even calls "abortion . . . the great indictment against a civilization that tries to enslave motherhood."[44] Abortion, she says, "is an alternative that I

cannot too strongly condemn." Yet she quickly adds that "abortion may be resorted to in order to save the life of the mother."[45]

- On the status of the fetus, Sanger wrote, "No new life begins unless there is conception. From this beginning grows the embryo which in time becomes a child." Abortion kills life. Birth control "prevents the beginning of life."[46]
- The key to stopping abortions and "the long trail of disease, suffering, and death which so often follows" is repealing the laws against birth control and educating women on how to use contraceptive methods effectively.[47]
- While abortion poses severe problems, it should not be outlawed. The mother's reproductive liberty should be preserved. It should be up to "the parent and relatives in general, to decide, even at the end of the third month, whether the child should be born or not." On the other hand, "A knowledge of Birth Control . . . would, of course, wipe out the practice of abortion."[48] This "disgraceful custom of abortion" is a "practice that must be combated with all the weapons at our command," the greatest weapon of which is birth control.[49]
- Sanger said that birth control "should combine the following conditions: (1) It should depend exclusively upon the woman; (2) it should cause neither the man nor the woman any inconvenience; (3) it should be absolutely certain and dependable; (4) it should cost very little."[50]
- Women are "enslaved through [their] reproductive powers" by men. The "man dictates and controls the standards of sex morality," and as long as this situation remains this way, men will continue to "control the world."[51] Therefore, women must take charge of their reproductive functions to find freedom: "No woman can call herself free who does not own and control her body. No woman can call herself free until she can choose consciously whether she will or will not be a mother."[52]
- When women are biologically free, the rest of the world will be too. "The basic freedom of the world is woman's freedom. A free race cannot be born of slave mothers."[53]
- The way to reproductive freedom is through birth control. Women must face this matter squarely. The "quicker" women address this issue as their "problem . . . alone, the quicker will society respect motherhood. The quicker, too, will the world be made a fit place for children to live."[54]
- Birth control is the key to achieving the eugenic goal of the improvement of the race: "Birth Control . . . not only opens the way to the

eugenist, but it preserves his work.... Eugenics without Birth Control seems to us a house builded upon the sands. It is at the mercy of the rising stream of the unfit.... Only upon a free, self-determining motherhood can rest any unshakable structure of racial betterment."[55] In another article Sanger wrote, "The campaign for Birth Control is not merely of eugenic value, but is practically identical in ideal with the final aims of Eugenics.... Birth Control propaganda is thus the entering wedge for the Eugenic educator."[56]

- Through birth control and eugenics, the "unfit" would be purged and the Aryan race purified. For Sanger, the unfit included "morons, [the] feebleminded, [the] insane and various criminal types" who add "to the already tremendous social burden" created by the "unfit" "majority of wage-workers who cannot provide for their children's "physical and mental health."[57]
- Parents should avoid having children under several conditions. One is when their kids are born *"physically or mentally defective."* No parent has "a right to bring into the world those who are sure to suffer from mental or physical affliction. It condemns the child to a life of misery and places upon the community the burden of caring for them, [and] probably [for] their defective descendants for many generations." Furthermore, parents should not reproduce when they lack the means to care properly for their children. That too places a terrible burden on the parents, the children, and society.[58] Indeed, it is a "crime" for a child to be born into a large family with an insufficient income.[59] Neither should parents have children when they suffer from *"such diseases as tuberculosis, gonorrhea, syphilis, cancer, epilepsy, insanity, drunkenness, or mental disorders"* or when the mother has *"heart disease, kidney trouble* [or] *pelvic deformites* [sic]." The "jails, hospitals for the insane, poorhouses, and houses of prostitution are filled with the children" of parents who have these disorders.[60]
- Certain people should just be sterilized outright. "I personally believe in the sterilization of the feebleminded, the insane, and the syphilitic," Sanger wrote.[61] She also suggested that the "United States government [offer] a bonus or a yearly pension to all obviously unfit parents who allow themselves to be sterilized by harmless and scientific means. In this way the moron and the diseased would have no posterity to inherit their unhappy condition. The number of the feebleminded would decrease and a heavy burden would be lifted from the shoulders of the fit. Such a bonus would be a wise and profitable investment for the nation. It would be the salvation of American civilization."[62] In yet another context she said,

"Parenthood should be forbidden to the insane, the feebleminded, the epileptic, and to all those suffering from transmissible diseases. Modern methods of sterilization make this possible."[63]

- Under certain conditions, infanticide is justifiable. For example, "When I was in Germany in 1920 and saw for myself more than 10,000 little starving infants, the results of the blockade and the war, I felt that it would be far kinder for Germany's future and for the future peace of the world to humanely allow these little victims to pass away rather than to keep them alive to perpetuate disease and misery."[64] In one of her major books, Sanger frankly said, "The most merciful thing a large family can do for one of its infant members is to kill it."[65]
- The struggle for the race's purity and existence is between the "healthy and intelligent" mothers and their physically and mentally fit offspring, who must defend themselves against the "less healthy, less intelligent, less discriminating mothers" and "the children of the feebleminded, the diseased, and the mentally dwarfed [who] drag down the standards of schools and society. It is one of the strange paradoxes of human existence that while health itself is not contagious or infectious, diseases—the great social scourges—are. So that health, so precious to the individual and the race, must continually defend itself, defend itself against the inroads of disease and its baneful train of evils and miseries.... Neither in the neighborhood nor the school should the progress of the normal, healthy, growing child be impeded by those poor little victims of hereditary disease whose bodies and brains are incurably subnormal from the start.... [E]verything must be done to right the wrong that was committed in bringing them with such tragic handicaps into this world."[66]
- A baby's "rights," which Sanger agreed with and attributed to a friend, includes these: "To be wanted. To be loved before birth as well as after birth. To be given a body untainted by a heritable disease, uncontaminated by any of the racial poisons." After listing these rights, Sanger said, "If intelligent and wide awake mothers of these United States would protect these rights not only for their own children but for all, motherhood would then be truly mobilized."[67] In an earlier article, Sanger stated emphatically, "The first right of the child is to be wanted—to be desired with an intensity of love that gives it its title to being and joyful impulse to life. It should be wanted by both parents, but especially by the mother, who is to carry it, nourish it, and perhaps influence its life by her thoughts, her passions, her loves, her hates, her yearnings."[68] As far as my studies have

confirmed, Sanger never regards life as a child's right. Instead, a child's "title to being"—meaning permission to live—is wrapped up in wantedness, particularly in the desires of the mother. When parental desire for the child is absent, Sanger believes the child's life should be terminated. This is best for the parents, society, and, ironically enough, the child.

- As Malthus argued, "A nation cannot go on indefinitely multiplying without eventually reaching the point when population presses upon [the] means of subsistence."[69] Neither "a nation nor a race can long survive in the world struggle" without checking its population growth[70]—a growth that left uncontrolled increases geometrically every twenty-five years.[71] This means "*we need not more of the fit, but fewer of the unfit.*" We must prevent the "propagation of the degenerate, the imbecile, the feebleminded," while also paring back the growth of the self-reliant, independent, and healthy.[72] We need to work for achieving a higher racial quality, not a greater quantity.[73]
- "When overpopulated countries learn that there is neither strength nor cohesive force in mere numbers, but in the development of a strong and healthy self-sustaining population, a new direction will be given to national aims; and much will be done toward the elimination of waste and war. The strength and wealth of a country are to be sought, not in mere numbers, but in the number of self-reliant and independent men and women who have physical, intellectual, and productive value. Is there any more truly patriotic doctrine? Put into effect the world over, Birth Control would make possible the growth and intensive development of happy nations. Without it, no League of Nations can ever eliminate contentions and war. Birth Control is the only true foundation of national strength and security.... Birth Control points, to all peoples under the sun, the one and only way which can lead all nations to well-being, independence, and dignity—to peace, justice and happiness."[74]

Sanger had more than just a professional or philosophical interest in promoting her agenda. She wanted it personally. By even the most favorable accounts of her life, she was brazenly promiscuous. Two authors offered this partial summary of her exploits:

> Sanger was something of a sexual adventurer and high society camp follower who, in today's vernacular, liked to party....
>
> One of Sanger's lovers was English sexologist Havelock Ellis. Other paramours included English writers Hugh de Selincourt, Harold Child, and H. G. Wells.... She had what is now called a

"trial marriage" with Corey Alberson and liaisons with her lawyer J. G. Goldstein, American architect Angus S. MacDonald, and several more. She had "crushes" on two female classmates, which drew comments. In 1922 she would marry Three-in-One oil magnate J. Noah Slee of South Africa. They agreed to have what would be called in modern terms "an open marriage."[75]

Sanger had two husbands, and she openly cheated on both of them. She also had children from her first marriage. While living a life of sexual indulgence mixed with drug abuse, Margaret abandoned Peggy, her third child and only daughter, who was stricken with polio. When Peggy died unexpectantly of pneumonia, Margaret mourned. Her mourning never really stopped. Peggy's death led Margaret into the occult to try to contact her daughter through seances. It also heightened her drive to see women liberated through birth control. "Both effects were related to guilt," Michael Jones says.[76] Sanger's biographer, Ellen Chesler, agrees: "The tragedy of Peggy's death may have tied Margaret emotionally to her daughter, but it left her little more attentive to the practical care of her surviving sons than she had been before. To the contrary, she could now satisfy a sense of maternal obligation without deviating from her chosen path, since Peggy remained with her—in effect, if not in reality—as the justification for her own professional preoccupations."[77] Reflecting on this, Jones draws a striking, and, I think, accurate conclusion: "In the absence of repentance, the most common way to assuage guilt feelings is by transmuting vice into a sacred cause. The birth control crusade seems to have fulfilled just this need in the lives of Margaret Sanger and the women she inspired."[78]

Deadly Consequences

The Malthus-Darwin-Sanger legacy is still very much with us. Through Sanger's efforts and the people who worked with her, contraception was finally legalized in the United States, women gained control over their bodies, birth control (much more broadly understood, though) is taught in public schools nationwide, abortion-on-demand is the law of the land, infanticide is becoming a more acceptable option, the viability of sterilizing at least certain types of criminals is becoming more popular, population control is on the national and international agendas, and euthanasia as a means of getting rid of more of the unwanted is gaining legal and popular sanction. As we close out this chapter, let's look at a few of these "victories" to see what they have brought us.

Abortion

On the abortion front, since *Roe v. Wade* and its companion case *Doe v. Bolton* became law in the early 1970s, the beginning of life has become a death sentence for about 33 million aborted babies. That's almost three times the number of people who died under the Nazis in the Holocaust during World War II.[79] Every fifteen seconds an abortion occurs in America.[80]

Three out of every ten pregnancies ends in abortion, and more than 40 percent of "women receiving an abortion have had one before."[81] Due to the baby dearth, adoptions are at an all-time low, and the U.S. population growth is below replacement levels. At this rate, the size of the older generation will outpace the younger, creating for both generations a medical and economic nightmare and straining personal, community, and government resources beyond the breaking point.[82]

The preborn have been robbed of their humanity. They are called fetuses, globs of cells, embryos, entities, uterine contents, fertilized ova, products of conception, potential persons . . . but only in rare instances granted the status of human person or baby or child. For example, have you ever noticed that when a "fetus" is operated on while still in its mother's womb, it is called a baby or a patient, even by doctors and the media? On the other hand, in a procedure popularly referred to as a partial-birth abortion, the preborn are still called fetuses, even though they are brought partially into the outside world. In this grisly procedure, a child is partially extracted through the birth canal feet first until all but the head is delivered. Then the doctor forces surgical scissors into the base of the child's skull, spreads them to enlarge the opening, then uses suction to evacuate the child's brain. The child, of course, feels all of this. It dies an excruciating, gruesome death. All of this occurs on a living, breathing, in most cases, full-term baby. And yet, because the procedure has been placed under the category of abortion, the baby is denied the status of human personhood. Even when the *American Medical News* described the procedure, it referred to the baby as "an intact fetus."[83]

In November 1995, Congress overwhelmingly passed legislation that would have banned partial-birth abortions, but President Clinton vetoed it, claiming partial-birth abortion was a "potentially lifesaving, certainly health-saving" procedure for mothers and their families.[84] So far, I have found few instances that even come close to supporting this claim.[85] Otherwise, my research has shown that the procedure is used overwhelmingly to get rid of unwanted children. One doctor who performs partial-birth abortions said that 80 percent of the time the procedure is requested by the parents because they do not want their child. Another doctor appeared before Congress and said that he performed nine partial-birth abortions solely because the children had cleft palates, a physical defect surgery can repair. A nurse told Congress that "she quit her job at one of the only clinics in the country where such abortions are performed after she saw the procedure done on six healthy fetuses and one with Down syndrome. 'It was the hardest thing in all the years I've been a nurse to see,'" she said.[86] The reality is that these children are killed because someone does not want them. It generally has nothing to do with saving lives or ensuring health, especially not that of the aborted.[87]

Let's suppose that the life of the mother may require such a drastic measure. The bill Clinton vetoed allowed for that exceptional circumstance. It appears that the real reason the bill did not become law is because the President, to curry political favor with proabortionists, sided with the Sangerian mentality: women must have complete control over their reproductive powers, even if that means destroying the human life growing within them.[88]

Infanticide

If we can kill children in the womb, why not outside the womb? Two proabortion and pro-infanticide advocates answer these questions with incredible candor:

> The pro-life groups are right about one thing: the location of the baby inside or outside the womb cannot make such a crucial moral difference. We cannot coherently hold that it is all right to kill a fetus a week before birth, but as soon as the baby is born everything must be done to keep it alive. The solution, however, is not to accept the pro-life view that the fetus is a human being with the same moral status as yours or mine. The solution is the very opposite: to abandon the idea that all human life is of equal worth.[89]

So the reasoning goes. Deny the right to life to one group and you will eventually add more groups to your hit list. As you do, you have to cover your tracks by changing the language and the focus. Children must be branded as humans of lesser worth, or as subhumans, or, better still, nonhumans. Procedures that kill must be relabeled to sound more positive. Abortion becomes family planning, planned parenthood, reproductive control, the termination of a pregnancy, the evacuation of uterine contents. I wonder how infanticide will be dressed up. One philosopher has called it a "post-natal abortion."[90] Perhaps that's the way to go, since abortion has made so much headway already. Why quibble with success?

Is infanticide occurring in America? Yes, and with growing frequency. More and more parents are having their children killed in the hospital or taking them home to do it, and often with physician support. In many cases, doctors are even terminating children *without* parental consent. These children are drugged, strangled, smothered, burned, shot, stabbed, drowned, pummeled, abandoned, even buried alive. In every instance, the children are killed because they are unwanted, and this for any number of reasons. As two researchers on this topic said, these children are killed because "their care will be expensive. They have survived an abortion. They will never walk. They will lead 'unproductive' lives. They might end up in an institution at state expense. Above all, children in the United States are likely to be unwanted if they will suffer some degree of mental impairment. When such children need something to keep them alive—a routine operation, antibiotic therapy, even food and water—they may not get it in American hospitals today."[91] Their parents may not even authorize the care.

Euthanasia—the Final Solution

If it's too late to abort or commit infanticide, then there's the option of euthanasia. This involves either allowing a person "to die by withholding or withdrawing life-sustaining treatment," or taking a more active role by directly and intentionally killing oneself (suicide) or another (assisted suicide or mercy killing).[92]

Polls show that nearly three out of four Americans support some form of euthanasia.[93] Americans show their interest by putting such pro-euthanasia books as Derek Humphrey's *Final Exit*, Betty Rollin's *Last Wish*, Timothy Quill's *Death and Dignity*, and Sherwin Nuland's *How We Die* on the *New York Times* bestseller list. We have refused to convict Dr. Jack Kevorkian of breaking Michigan's law against physician-assisted suicide, even though he assisted in the deaths of thirty-three people by July 1996.[94] We approved via popular vote a measure in Oregon that legalized physician-assisted euthanasia for the first time in American history.[95] And furthermore, there is rising support for such pro-euthanasia groups as EXIT, the Hemlock Society, Euthanasia Research and Guidance Organization, and Choice in Dying.

Americans are also increasingly buying into the rhetoric of the euthanasia activists. They are allowing terms such as *self-deliverance, assisted dying, planned death, death with dignity, mercy killing, death by choice, physician-assisted suicide,* and *gentle death* to put a happy face on killing off the ill, the dying, the mentally and physically disabled, the depressed, the elderly, the despairing. Anyone deemed not worthy of life, anyone who becomes unwanted, a burden to friends, family, or society, or is made to feel like an undesirable—these are the ones who become the targets. Rather than help people through their pain, we offer to end their lives. Rather than work through our own pain over a loved one's agony, we end our pain by eliminating its source.[96]

And why should we not do all these things? After all, the image of God is gone. We are not special anymore. We are merely biological beings, blips in nature's vast evolutionary history. Whatever dignity we have is wrapped up in our relational, vocational, or social value. We are valued for what we do, not for who we are. We are just chemicals and cells with a fleshy coat, nothing more. So when our usefulness enters its twilight years, when we become more of a burden than a gain, then it is time for us to step down—six feet down. This is nature's way.

How far we have come from the pro-life teaching of the Judeo-Christian worldview that served us so well for so long. We have gone from the procreation generation to the termination generation in just a few decades. We have rejected the inalienable right to life and put in its place the right to die. But this new right is not for all. It belongs only to the strong to exercise on the weak. And the strong convince themselves that their death sentence on the weak is for the benefit of all, including the weak who usually have no choice.

Pro-choice is pro-death. That is the real face of the new absolute.

Chapter 6

I Do, for Now

The *Old* Absolute	The *New* Absolute
(3) The institution of marriage is God-ordained and occurs between a man and a woman until death severs the bond.	(3a) Marriage is a human contract made between any two people, and either party can terminate it for any reason.

The junior high school teacher looked around the classroom. The almost forty children were seated, talking among themselves. No one was being obnoxious or rude. They were just talking shop: "Did you hear the newest song by. . . ?" "I didn't know Bobby was going with Teresa." "What she did was so uncool." "Wow, hot shoes." Everything was going as usual.

The teacher settled everyone down, went through some preliminary matters for the day, then sat on the edge of her desk. "Today I want to begin with a question. We're moving into an area of our social studies that may hit close to home to many of you. So rather than let you feel as outcasts, I want to assure you that you are not alone. Here's the question: How many of you have parents who have divorced? Please raise your hands."

All but two children raised their hands above their heads. One of them was one of my daughters. The other teenager was living with his mother; his father had been dead for little more than a year.

The teacher was not surprised. She had seen numbers like these for several years. I, on the other hand, was stunned. I knew divorce was a growing problem, but I had no idea how large it loomed.

This event occurred in a public school in the late '80s. I have heard it repeated a few times since in three different states: California, Texas, and Tennessee. On each occasion, all but two or three of the class's students have indicated they are from broken homes. Like the public school teacher, I no longer show surprise, just dismay. Marriage is just not what it used to be.

The Way It Was

Early Americans had the same view of marriage as they had of most other matters—a Judeo-Christian one. They viewed marriage as a God-ordained institution begun in the pristine world of the Garden of Eden after the creation of Adam and Eve.[1] They believed marriage was designed as a lifetime affair of love and devotion between one man and one woman. Annulments and divorces were permissible in certain situations, but the reasons had to be justifiable, and it was the dominant religious persuasion of each community that determined what those reasons were.[2] For the vast majority of Americans, however, once they got married, they stayed married. Declaring the marriage invalid or severed was a rare and unpopular option.

This was not strange anywhere Christianity found a home. Even political scientist Ferdinand Mount, no friend of the Christian faith, admits this when he contrasts the Christian view of marriage with others:

> The most regular and universal feature of non-Christian or pre-Christian marriage is the relative ease of divorce. Certainly in Western Europe, what marks out the Christian era from earlier and later times is the insistence that marriage should *invariably* be "till death us do part." It is this that makes the dramatic contrast with the marriage customs of virtually all the peoples who were to be Christianized over the centuries: the Romans no less than the Anglo-Saxons, the Celts in the Dark Ages no less than most of the inhabitants of Africa and Asia who were to be converted by missionaries a thousand years later. Only the Hindus seem to have maintained anything like the strictness of the Catholic Church toward divorce.[3]

"The right of divorce," Mount bemoans, "was gradually eroded by the Church in its long struggle to gain control of matrimony."[4]

According to historian Barry Shain, early Americans also saw marriage as "essential to human flourishing."[5] It was a relationship that served to condition and control the individuals within it. In the Christian view, especially as found in the reformed Protestant tradition that dominated early America, all people were sinners. They were sinful in their nature and behavior. Even in the best of circumstances, they tended to go bad. Due to man's rebellion against God, corruption and further corruptibility were the human norm. To help check these evil tendencies, early Americans looked to God, their communities, their churches, their families, and their marriage partners.

In respect to God, Americans found what they held was the basis of all their liberties—spiritual liberty. This kind of liberty could be found only through godly living, and that was impossible apart from trusting in Jesus Christ for one's salvation and obeying the Bible's dictates with the aid of divine grace. The Reverend Jonas Clark, who hid Sam Adams and John Hancock on the night of Paul Revere's famous ride, said that "the gospel of *Jesus Christ* is the source of liberty, the soul of government, and the life of a people."[6] Spiritual liberty was the voluntary submission of one's will to "an objective set of divine and universal ethical standards by which it and license could be carefully distinguished."[7] It was also liberty from sin, Satan, and death, and from being dominated by one's self-interests and passions. Put another way, spiritual liberty was freedom to live morally and the freedom from living immorally.

Moreover, early Protestant reformed Americans saw themselves establishing a new political and moral order under the auspices of God. They consecrated themselves and the land to serve and glorify him. Because of this national covenantal commitment, Americans believed "they were corporately responsible for the behavior of their fellow citizens.... Thus, fires, wars, earthquakes, thunderstorms, plagues, and other such disasters were believed to be expressions of God's displeasure with a community for the failure of its public officials to control sinful behavior that failed to honor God."[8]

Within this religious context, it was the job of the community, church, family, and even marriage partner to help regulate the behavior of individuals. In regard to marriage, Americans believed it served to enhance godliness and hinder licentiousness; marriage, in other words, promoted moral living. Hence, single individuals not looking to marry were viewed as suspect. They were often seen as rootless and immature. In fact, "Living alone, or even without children, frequently made one unworthy of acceptance as a full member of society." In many American communities, single adults were not permitted to live alone. They had to take up residence with a family.[9]

While strange to us, these types of controls and commitments provided a strong sense of stability and accountability. People knew their place and their roles. They knew what was expected of them and what they could expect from others. At times the environment could be quite intrusive into one's personal and family life. Nevertheless, it was also conducive to producing and assuring high standards of individual and corporate behavior. Within this soil, the vast majority of marriages held together for life and families were raised intact well into the twentieth century.

In his insightful book *Utopia Against the Family*, Bryce Christensen makes these observations about the viability of traditional views of marriage and family into the 1950s and even early 1960s:

> Lifelong marriages and intact families remained moral ideals for the vast majority of Americans well into this century.... Writing in the *New York Times* magazine in 1958, Dorothy Barclay acknowledged "family unity" as one of the nation's "unquestioned values," even as she urged her readers not wholly to sequester themselves in domestic isolation. The popular press of the period denounced divorce as "a social calamity" and "the disgrace of Hollywood," while illegitimacy was considered a scandalous offense. In 1957, 80 percent of Americans regarded a woman who deliberately chose not to marry as "neurotic" or "immoral." ... Actual behavior in the 1950s and early 1960s reflected this widespread support for family ideals. Sociologist Susan Cotts Watkins believes that during this period Americans "approached the full potential for family life" through "relatively early and widespread marriage, relatively low divorce rates, and relatively high fertility."[10]

I was a beneficiary of this traditional marriage-and-family perspective. I was a '50s kid and a '60s teenager. The '50s, at least for me, were a carefree time of playing and learning, while the '60s were full of transitions and turbulence. I was able to enjoy both eras. I could live in times of calm or upheaval—it didn't matter. The deciding factor for me was not my external circumstances but my homelife, particularly my parents' marriage. I could handle life's challenges with hope and courage because I had no doubt my parents would never divorce. They loved each other dearly and deeply. They had their share of disagreements, but I knew they were resolutely committed to each other no matter what. My mother made sure I understood this. She often told me, "Billy David, sometimes your father and I don't agree on things, but we always work them out. Don't let our disagreements ever lead you to think that we will get a divorce. That will never happen. Your father and I love each other very much. You can count on us always being together. Never worry about that." I never did. I simply reveled in the sense of security it gave me.

When it was time for me to marry, I never questioned I was making a commitment for life. Neither did my wife-to-be, who also came from an intact home. We dedicated ourselves to living and growing together till death do us part. We not only made that commitment during our wedding vows, but we decided that the word *divorce* would never enter our vocabulary as a solution to anything. For us it would be a four-letter word standing for an option deserving nothing less than an anathema. Like my mother did for me, we have told our five children many times that they can rest in the knowledge that they will never know divorce through us. They have mentioned to us on occasion how much that commitment has meant to them. It's a legacy we're delighted to pass on.

The Way It Is

Today marriage is regarded as a *human contract made between any two people, and either person can end it at any time and for any reason.* Marriage has gone from a covenant of promise to a contract of convenience. This is the new absolute. Evidence of this truth is all too easy to see.

The United States now has the highest divorce rate in the world.[11] Since 1960, the number of divorces has tripled. In 1960, around 393,000 marriages ended in divorce or annulment. In 1993, 1.2 million couples divorced, while 2.3 million couples married.[12] About sixty percent of all marriages now end in divorce. Although one usually hears the 50-percent figure cited, marriage advocate Michael McManus points out why the larger percentage is more accurate. He notes that the 50-percent calculation "does not include separations that dissolved 2.9 million marriages. For this reason, the *National Survey of Families and Households* [conducted by the University of Wisconsin] measures 'a marital dissolution rate,' which includes both divorce and separation. By that measure, *60 percent of new marriages are failing.*" To get a handle on how staggering this is, consider that just a century ago only seven percent of all married couples divorced.[13]

Statistics such as these don't seem to deter many people from remarrying. In fact, 45 percent of today's weddings involve at least one divorcee, and more than 75 percent of all marriages are remarriages.

Do remarriages fare any better than first marriages? No. First marriages that end in divorce average just eight years' longevity, whereas second marriages that end last only an average of six years.[14]

People give many reasons for walking away from their mates. In the study conducted by Patterson and Kim and reported in their 1991 book *The Day America Told the Truth,* the Americans surveyed said that communication problems were the number one reason for their divorce, with sexual infidelity and constant fighting tying for second place. The other top ten reasons cited were emotional abuse, falling out of love, unsatisfactory sex, insufficient finances, physical abuse, falling in love with someone else, and boredom. The latter two reasons tied at 22 percent.[15]

Today fewer couples are actually tying the knot. Instead, they are choosing to simply live together. The U.S. Census Bureau estimates that in 1970 about 523,000 couples were cohabiting. By 1980 that figure had tripled to almost 1.6 million. Within eleven more years, the number had doubled to three million. That's 700,000 more couples living together than the number of couples who married in 1993. Indeed, more than half of today's first marriages are preceded by cohabitation, and about two-thirds of remarriages are also.

Living Together

As more Americans experiment with live-in arrangements, the numbers show that the experiment is a colossal failure—that is, if marriage is the eventual goal. At least one partner in 90 percent of live-in arrangements wants to get married,[16] and about 60 percent eventually do.[17] But out of the ones who do marry, the marriage disruption rate is 50 percent higher among them than it is among couples who do not precede marriage with cohabitation.[18] Among the cohabitation arrangements that never reach the marriage stage, a third split apart within two years.[19]

Between the rise in cohabitation and divorce, the percentage of adults who actually marry is down to 55 percent, the lowest marriage rate in American history. Just a generation ago, the percentage was 64 percent.[20]

What was once abhorrent and rare in early America is now the national norm. Marital commitment through sickness and health, good times and bad, has almost vanished. Indeed, the very viability of the traditional view of marriage is shattering on rocky ground. According to Patterson and Kim, "Nearly half of us say that there is no reason to ever get married. And even when children are involved, only 32 percent of us believe that we should try to stick out a bad marriage for the sake of the kids." In fact, "forty-four percent of us agree that most marriages will end in divorce."[21] We have become so pessimistic about the longevity of marriage that "59 percent of all Americans believe that it's a smart idea to draw up a prenuptial agreement, just in case" the marriage does not last.[22]

Why do Americans still get married if the reality is so dismal? Patterson and Kim discovered that Americans have no good answer to that question. "The picture we got is that the majority of men and women aren't sure why they got married or whether they did the right thing. They're skeptical about the future of their marriages and even more so about the marriages of other people they know."[23]

Homosexual Marriage

So far I have been speaking about heterosexual marriages. But homosexual and lesbian unions are becoming increasingly acceptable in the United States as well. As of this writing, no state has legally sanctioned same-sex marriages, but they are occurring throughout America anyway. Many are sanctioned by churches and given as much legal clout as possible by attorneys.[24]

Despite the disintegration of traditional marriage nationwide, the issue of same-sex unions has created a groundswell of opposition on many local, state, and even federal levels. In May 1996, the Defense of Marriage Act (DOMA) was introduced in both houses of Congress. As of this writing, DOMA guarantees that, at least as far as the federal government is concerned, a civil marriage will be defined as "a legal union between one man and one woman as husband and wife." DOMA also frees states from having to recognize same-sex marriages performed in other states, and it precludes homosexual couples from receiving such federal benefits as pensions and health benefits.[25] The bill passed the House in July with a vote of 342 to 67, and the House rejected two amendments that would have weakened the bill. If the Senate passes DOMA, and it appears it will, President Clinton has said he will sign the legislation into law.

As important as such measures are, they will not restore what we have obviously lost. As Elizabeth Fox-Genovese has observed, "Marriage as the essential social unit—the glue that binds men and women to one another and, from infancy, binds children to society—has disintegrated."[26]

Why It Is

What has led to such a decline in the Judeo-Christian view of marriage? Once again, the reasons are many. We don't have the space to cover them all here. Some later chapters will deal with several contributing factors: feminism, homosexuality, declining sexual mores, sex education, and the new tolerance. Here we will zero in on just one: secularization.

As religion is moved out of the public arena and trivialized in our laws, media, politics, and educational establishments, we increasingly accept a kind of practical atheism. We may say we believe in God—and about 96 percent of Americans do say that[27]—but we live as if no God exists. The supernatural makes no real difference in our day-to-day lives. With God out of the picture practically, eternal verities pass away. The vertical dimension of our lives gives way to absorption in the horizontal. Nature supplants supernature. All things lose their sacredness and become profane. A person's worth is reduced to his or her usefulness: Does she make me feel good? Is her paycheck large enough? Can he love me as I want to be loved? Will this relationship fulfill me? Other-centeredness is lost to self-centeredness. We become like mere animals, driven by our cravings. Philosopher Laura Garcia brings out the implications of this view with clarity and force:

> If we see ourselves as nothing more than glorified animals, then the purpose of our lives must resemble that of other animals—maximizing pleasure and comfort, and minimizing pain and sacrifice. This in turn leads to an obsessive concern for personal freedom, where freedom means simply license to do as I please. Classical writers thought of freedom primarily as liberation from the dominion of one's lower desires and passions so that one could will what is genuinely good. Now the tendency is to accept, even embrace, our passions and desires as they are and seek to eliminate every obstacle to their fulfillment. In this hedonistic view, others play a mainly instrumental role in one's own happiness. As long as the benefits outweigh the costs, one can value the company of others. But if they become an obstacle to one's pleasure or comfort or freedom—if one should get bored—then the relationship has to go. In marrying, as in other human relationships, many persons are primarily seeking themselves.[28]

Marriage cannot survive this onslaught. It never has in human history, and it never will. As Ferdinand Mount observed, "The most regular and universal feature of non-Christian or pre-Christian marriage is the relative ease of divorce." There is a good reason for that. It is a false view of marriage.

Marriage is not a contract or a pact to gain property, heal divisions, seal treaties, fulfill self, find excitement, relieve boredom, or enjoy uninhibited sex. It is a deeply interpersonal covenantal relationship of unconditional promise designed to stretch us beyond our own means while promising to satisfy our deepest longings for community. It is like having a relationship with God, a relationship so demanding that it requires all we are. The world's religions testify to this fact. All of them, to one degree or another, make the demand revealed in the Jewish Scriptures and repeated in the Christian Scriptures: "Love the Lord your God with all your heart and with all your soul and with all your strength."[29] The commitment must be total.

Marriage makes the same demand. It is not a 50–50 arrangement built on egalitarian principles. Those marriages are the most frail; they rarely last. Writes Barbara Whitehead:

> Egalitarian marriage, the model most highly prized and increasingly pursued by many younger Americans is "frighteningly fragile." Married couples with demanding careers can be pulled apart by jealousy, competitiveness, loneliness, worries about children, or sheer sleep deprivation. Worse, their taut working lives leave little room for midcourse adjustments, let alone unscheduled crises with a child who doesn't play by the developmental rule book. Of all marriage types, therefore, this one requires the most constant vigilance and most heroic effort.[30]

The traditional view of marriage does not suffer from this inherent weakness. It sees "marriage as a school of virtue, a domain that requires tact and restraint along with open and honest communication, kindness and gratitude along with assertiveness and autonomy."[31] It is a model "based not on theories of exchange or self-interest but on notions of sacrifice and altruism."[32] Couples in this kind of relationship seek to protect and cherish it. They give each other their all, no effort withheld, no conditional commitments, no wishy-washy love that is really no love at all. Only this kind of marriage works its intended magic: restoring the luster of the image of God we are, and thereby bringing us into the heart of Love itself. Love is always other-centered. As the ancient love hymn says, "Love is patient, love is kind. It does not envy, it does not boast, it is not proud. It is not rude, it is not self-seeking, it is not easily angered, it keeps no record of wrongs. Love does not delight in evil but rejoices with the truth. It always protects, always trusts, always hopes, always perseveres. Love never fails."[33] Love cannot be otherwise. As soon as the self becomes the focus, love has gone, and in its absence rush in greed, envy, and lust.

In his classic treatment of marriage, Mike Mason tells about this side of marriage and brings out the bottom line:

> Marriage is a relationship far more engrossing than we want it to be. It always turns out to be more than we bargained for. It is

> disturbingly intense, disruptively involving, and that is exactly the way it was designed to be. It is supposed to be more, almost, than we can handle. It was meant to be a lifelong encounter that would be much more rigorous and demanding than anything human beings ever could have chosen, dreamed of, desired, or invented on their own. After all, we do not even choose to undergo such far-reaching encounters with our closest and dearest friends. Only marriage urges us into these deep and unknown waters. For that is its very purpose: to get us beyond our depth, out of the shallows of our own secure egocentricity and into the dangerous and unpredictable depths of a real interpersonal encounter.
>
> And that, incidentally, is also what true religion is supposed to do. It is supposed to remind us that God is not an idol of our own making, not a human invention, not a concept or a theory or a projection or extension of ourselves, not a tool (any more than a marriage partner is a tool)....
>
> Like God himself, then, marriage comes with a built-in abhorrence of self-centeredness. In the dream world of mankind's complacent separateness, amidst all our pleasant little fantasies of omnipotence and blamelessness and self-sufficiency, marriage explodes like a bomb. It runs an aggravating interference pattern, an unrelenting guerrilla warfare against selfishness. It attacks people's vanity and lonely pride in a way that few other things can, tirelessly exposing the necessity of giving and sharing, the absurdity of blame. Angering, humiliating, melting, chastening, purifying, it touches us where we hurt most, in the place of our lovelessness. Dragging us into lifelong encounters which at times may be full of boredom, tension, unpleasantness, or grief, marriage challenges us to abandon everything for the sake of love.[34]

The old absolute was built on love. The new absolute is based on lust. The old delivered security. The new brings only insecurity. The old provided a relational and moral foundation for society. The new undermines relationships and morals and ushers in social confusion. As we'll see in the next chapter, this is clearly evident in the breakdown of the family.

Chapter 7

Family Is Who You Come Home To

The *Old* Absolute	The *New* Absolute
(4) The normative family is a married father and mother who raise one or more children.	(4a) Family is any grouping of two or more people with or without children.

What is a family?

In 1992, a reporter in Sacramento, California, went to a street named Darwin and posed that question to Kelly Toller, a single mother living there. Here's how the reporter wrote up the response:

> "Let's see," says single mom Kelly Toller, her finger turreting from one squat ranch-style house to the next on her . . . street. "She's a single mother, and Terri, there's a single mother; the house on the end, they're living together, and the one down there is single."
>
> Many of the houses in this time-worn neighborhood once held "Ozzie and Harriet" families.
>
> Now, the home or apartment of every fourth family is presided over by a single parent.
>
> Three out of ten adults in the neighborhood around Darwin Street have never married, yet five dozen unmarried young women between the ages of sixteen and twenty-four already are mothers, census information shows.
>
> There are twenty-nine dads tending their children alone here, and, as Toller reviews the street's social makeup, a grandfather in a straw hat ambles to the store with a tiny girl in tow.

> This, census information tells us, is a family portrait of a common American neighborhood, where numerous homes hold a new definition of family.[1]

Today the "new definition of family" is even broader than this reporter indicated. Children now live with single never-married parents, single once-married parents, single more-than-once-married parents, stepparents, unmarried heterosexual couples, unmarried homosexual couples, "married" homosexual couples, and extended family members such as grandparents. Half of America's kids live apart from one or both of their parents, or they live with people outside their immediate family. Among those children living with just one of their parents, the parent is most likely to be their mother. "One in seven children lives with at least one stepparent, stepsibling, or half-sibling."[2] And nearly a third of America's children live in a home headed by a single parent.[3]

According to U.S. Census Bureau statistics, in 1970 single-parent households made up 13 percent of America's families. Ten years later that number had climbed to 22 percent. By 1994 it reached almost 31 percent. Figures in 1994 also show that nearly 10 million single mothers are heading households with children compared to 1.6 million single fathers. Out of the 11.4 million single parents, nine million own their own home or rent a house, 1.8 million live in a relative's home, and 650,000 live in the home of a nonrelative.[4]

The Census Bureau defines a nuclear family as a two-parent household in which all the children present are the "biological offspring of those parents and no other persons are present."[5] In light of this definition, the Census Bureau has found that only half of America's children live in a nuclear family household.[6]

This brief survey of America's family landscape shows how hard it is to answer the question, What is a family? However it's answered, someone will be unhappy with it. I, for one, do not agree with the Census Bureau's definition of a nuclear family. It excludes parents who have only adopted children. It also leaves out two-parent families that have one or more relatives living with them. So if a family had a grandparent living in their home rather than residing in a retirement home, that family would not count as a nuclear family. That seems too restrictive and a bit silly to me. Of course, the Bureau's nuclear family idea would not sit well with single parents, stepparents, or unmarried parents either.

Perhaps then we should accept the definition of family provided by the American Home Economics Association (AHEA): a family is "two or more persons who share resources, share responsibility for decisions, share values and goals, and have commitment to one another over time. The family is that climate that one 'comes home to' and it is this network of sharing and commitments that most accurately describes the family unit, regardless of blood, legal ties, adoption, or marriage."[7] This is certainly broad enough to cover all the variations of family I mentioned, and then some. In fact, in this group of "two or more persons," no children are mentioned, marriage is unnecessary, and same-sex unions are permissible. A family could be any combination of two or more people sharing some things and having a semblance of commitment to each other. This could include friends, business associates, and any combination of sexual partners—and none of these arrangements would have to include a child or a marital commitment. Is this what a family is?

Many feminists and homosexuals would like us to think so. After all, this definition would allow them to achieve their agendas, which encompass complete sexual freedom uncumbered by consequences.

The Feminist Ideology

In her case for abortion, feminist Ellen Willis argues against prolifers who say that "if a woman chooses to have sex, she should be willing to take the consequences." Willis fires back that "men have sex, without having to 'take the consequences.'" Doesn't it stand to reason, then, that "a woman has as much right as a man to enjoy sex? Without living in fear that one slip will transform her life?" Sex, Willis says, is "a basic human need, no less for women than for men." According to her, pro-lifers want women "to resort to the only perfectly reliable contraceptive, abstinence." This, of course, is unacceptable since everyone must have sex.[8] She disparages the idea that a woman should exercise control over her body before getting pregnant. Instead, she rants about the evils of "forced childbearing," which "does violence to a woman's body and spirit," and "contributes to other kinds of violence," such as "deaths from illegal abortion; the systematic oppression of mothers and women in general; the poverty, neglect, and battering of unwanted children; [and] sterilization abuse." Willis assures us that the solution to these problems is "to invent safer, more reliable contraceptives, ensure universal access to all birth control methods, eliminate sexual ignorance and guilt, and change the social and economic conditions that make motherhood a trap."[9] In other words, Willis wants us to ensure that she can have unrestricted sex divorced from any sense of self-responsibility. Society must accommodate her sexual appetites and remove all hindrances—especially babies—from her self-indulging behavior.

Margaret Sanger wanted this too. Sex without consequences is what she lived for. She had numerous lovers before, during, and after her marriages. She even left her children for months at a time, not just to crusade for birth control but to wallow in the lifestyle of a sexual libertine. She was a sexually driven woman, unwilling to control her own lustful appetites.

Instead of coming to grips with her perversity and taking steps to become a responsible wife and parent, Sanger rationalized her behavior and turned it into a defense for reproductive freedom. In her article "The Case for Birth Control," she wrote that "sex attraction is almost never accompanied by the wish to be a parent. Nor during the sex act itself is there often any desire to conceive. It's the exception rather than the rule even among the most primitive tribes." What I think she is really saying here is that she did not want her children. Her desire was for sexual abandon without the "threat" of parental responsibility. She goes on to say, "The sex urge is as old as life itself. . . . It is a force which cannot be swept back nor crushed down without damage to the individual. It should be accepted with reverence and pride, not connected with shame."[10] In other words, Sanger did not want to control her own sex drive, and she did not want anyone trying to make her feel as if she was doing something wrong.

So she handled her lust and guilt by working to disconnect sex and love from procreation. In 1924 she stated categorically that she had been challenging "this union of ideas" for "ten years."[11]

Even Ellen Chesler, in her biography of praise to Margaret Sanger, says that Sanger "saw nothing wrong in wanting [women] to have it all." Sanger "believed optimistically in the power to liberate human sexuality." She saw this liberation as "a tool for redistributing power fundamentally, in the bedroom, the home, and the larger community. Women would achieve personal freedom by experiencing their sexuality free of consequence, just as men have always done, but in taking control of the forces of reproduction they would also lower birthrates, alter the balance of supply and demand for labor, and therein accomplish the revolutionary goals of workers without the social upheaval of class warfare. . . . Not the dictates of Karl Marx, but the refusal of women to bear children indiscriminately, would alter the course of history."[12]

Sanger was right. The revolution she spawned through the legalization of contraception and abortion did change history. But it was a change for the worse for women, as well as for men and children and society in general. Already 33 million babies are dead, and, as I'll continue to show, the so-called liberation of sex from procreation has brought incalculable misery in many other ways also.

With sex taken out of the context of marriage and removed from the act of procreation, feminists must strive to redefine family so their revolution can continue. Remember, the revolution must move beyond the bedroom and get into the home—that is, the family. Take David Allen, for example. As the professor of women's studies at the University of Wisconsin, he claims that "an overly rigid definition of the family and its responsibilities can contribute to limiting women's participation in the work force, perpetuating constrictive gender identities, and sustaining a sense of entrapment." Therefore, he argues that we must advance "emancipatory interests" by "opening up a plurality of definitions" for family.[13]

Feminist writer Letty Cottin Pogrebin agrees. When family is "used prescriptively," she says, the term serves to "coerce people into roles" and "to create a national ethos out of a myth of domestic bliss." It is so much better, she argues, to admit that "*what* is family is a contradictory mess." Let us abandon designations such as "broken family" and "single-parent family" and instead embrace family with all its "different meanings." Let us do this with the understanding that this plethora of meanings will produce "different results in different contexts."[14] We should speak of families, not family. Familial pluralism, that is what we should embrace, and that is exactly what an increasing number of Americans are doing.

In a 1992 survey conducted by the Roper Organization, a thousand people received descriptions of a number of living arrangements and then were asked to indicate which ones they thought could be called a family. While 98 percent agreed that a married couple living with their children was a family, 87 percent thought that a married couple without children also constituted a family, and 53 percent called an unmarried childless couple a family. Other living arrangements accepted as family were an unmarried couple raising children together (77 percent), a "group of unrelated adults who live together and consider themselves a family" (28 percent), "two lesbian women living with children that they are raising" (27 percent), "two gay men living with children they are raising" (26 percent), "two lesbian women committed to each other and who are living together" (21 percent), and "two gay men committed" to their relationship and sharing living space (20 percent).[15]

Notice once again that for many people neither marriage nor children are central to family. It's also clear that same-sex unions are losing their stigma, and the idea of homosexuals raising children is gaining acceptance. It appears more likely than ever that the AHEA's definition of the family may soon be the nationally adopted norm.

If Webster's latest edition of its Collegiate Dictionary is any indication, perhaps AHEA's idea of family already is the normative view. Under *family*, Webster's 1993 tenth edition gives this as the first, most common definition: "a group of individuals living under one roof and usu. under one head." No reference to marriage, children, or specific sexual unions here. Everything is open. Definition two is "a group of persons of common ancestry," such as a clan; number three is "a group of people united by certain convictions or a common affiliation"; and number four is "a group of things related by common characteristics," such as a "closely related series of . . . chemical compounds." It's not until you reach definition five that you read this: a family is "the basic unit in society traditionally consisting of two parents rearing their own or adopted children." Webster's includes in this definition "any of various social units differing from but regarded as equivalent to the traditional family," such as a single parent with children. So, the two-parent family model doesn't even rank as high in English usage as the family of chemical compounds.

When we consider the history of the family in America, we can see how far away we are from the standard our country first universally accepted. In colonial America, you would have received strange looks if you asked what a family is. Everyone knew what a family was and how one began. A man and a woman married, built a home together, engaged in sexual intimacy with each other, and conceived and raised their children. This nuclear family had an extended family, too, that sometimes shared the same house, or lived in a house on or nearby the nuclear family's land. This extended family included grandparents, aunts, uncles, cousins, widows, even orphans. Many households also kept under their roof servants, apprentices, boarders, and lodgers. Regardless of how many people the family brought into its household, everyone knew that the central, nuclear family unit was a married heterosexual couple with at least one child, natural or adopted. This was the rule and the expectation.

For the early Americans, this concept of the nuclear family arose directly out of the soil of their Judeo-Christian heritage. And it was this heritage that depaganized ancient Rome and for the first time made the nuclear family the norm for Western civilization. In fact, the Judeo-Christian view of the family revolutionized the West, especially the lives of women, children, and the poor. A look back at this history will help us see how radical and stabilizing the nuclear family concept really is.

Pagan Pluralism

When the Christian movement was still young, pagan Rome held sway over people's lives. For the poor, women, and children especially, it was not a pleasant time.

The Romans promoted monogamy and regarded marriage as "a matter of agreement between partners, validated before suitable witnesses."[16]

They also considered husband and wife as equal partners when it came to running the household. Nonetheless, women had no legal standing. They could not bring law suits, own property, or hold public office. Legally, women were property, not persons, and their parents arranged their marriages.[17]

Not just anyone could marry legally. Roman citizens could enter into lawful marital unions with each other, but marriages involving slaves, foreigners, and close blood relatives were not legally recognized. This meant too that the children of these unions had no legitimate status before Roman law. While many slaves were not poor or ill-treated, many were. The Roman prohibition against marriage in these groups placed grave burdens on the poor.[18]

Family in Roman society was not anything like the modern idea of the nuclear family. Their word for *family* came from a term that meant "band of slaves." The Romans picked it up and applied it to authoritarian structures and hierarchical orders that included people or property or both. Eventually the word was expanded to cover wives and children, natural or adopted, as well as slaves—all headed by a single male authority figure. This man could be the biological father or simply the holder of authority. Whoever he was, his authority over his family was absolute. He headed the household, and he had the legal right to handle the family's affairs any way he chose. He could easily divorce his wife, but his wife could not divorce him. He could also legally kill any member of his family, including his spouse and children.

Abortion and infanticide were widely practiced among all classes of Romans in and outside family households. The poor killed their children out of desperation, and the wealthy did so to keep them from fragmenting their assets.[19] The destruction of children became so common toward the end of Rome's rule that legislation was passed in an attempt to curb the killing and increase the birthrate. Roman political leaders feared the demise of the empire through these methods of population control. Their efforts were ineffective, however. Families continued to limit their size so severely that by the mid-second century A.D., even the many great houses that had formed Rome's aristocracy were reduced to one.[20]

In this context, a second-century jurist named Ulpian said that Roman law designated a family as "several persons who by nature or law are placed under the authority of a single person."[21] This sounds awfully similar to Webster's first definition of a family as "a group of individuals living under one roof and usu. under one head."

Eventually upper-class women found ways of getting around some of the legal restrictions placed on them. Many ended up owning property and securing an education equal to that of men. Some ran businesses and influenced politics. Divorce finally became a matter of mutual consent, and that dramatically increased its practice. One Roman writer even talks about women who had as many as eight husbands in five years.[22] Another writer topped that one by mentioning "one man who had buried twenty wives" and then married "a woman who had buried twenty-two husbands."[23] For many Romans, marriage was a fragile bond often broken.

Husbands and wives also commonly practiced adultery. For wives, this often amounted to lesbian affairs, whereas men could legally choose to have sex with men or women, boys or girls. Some husbands even lived with their wife and concubine under the same roof.[24] Slaveholders frequently made their human property serve their sexual fancies.[25] Couples also often availed themselves of local prostitutes. They could even make liaisons with prostitutes a part of their religious devotion, since in some temples sexual relations with harlots played a role in worship. Prostitution became so widespread that the state finally legalized it in order to regulate it.[26]

The city of Corinth was one place where temple prostitutes flourished. There the temple of Aphrodite, goddess of love and beauty, provided a thousand female prostitutes for would-be worshipers. The city was so well known for its sex trade that it added two terms to Roman vocabulary: *Corinthianize*, which meant "sexual immorality," and *Corinthian girl*, which designated a prostitute. The ready availability of Corinth's sexual pleasures created headaches for Paul of Tarsus, a first-century Christian missionary and apostle. Some Christians in Corinth decided they could have sexual relations with the temple prostitutes under the guise of Christian liberty. Paul wrote them a stern letter to set them straight on the matter.[27]

Cohabitation was not unknown in the Roman Empire either. Many couples never married, especially if they were from different social classes that Roman law tried to keep apart. On the other hand, Roman law did recognize and allow for various forms of live-in arrangements. All forms of cohabitation were not outside the legal or social sphere of acceptability.[28]

Although the Romans were monogamous, they permitted local customs throughout their Empire that did not embrace this standard. In pagan Ireland and Germany, for example, men could have more than one wife at a time, although women were allowed only one husband. Called polygany, this practice led to two detrimental consequences in these locales. As historian Robert Shaffern explains:

> First, since only rich men could afford more than one wife, females tended to drift into the households of the wealthy. Poor men were much less likely to find a mate. Without a stake in established society, many single males became members of wandering bands of brigands, much like the gangs of modern American inner cities. These cutthroats, who lived in the forests on the edges of settled areas, destroyed and stole property and abducted and raped women. Even among the lawful members of society, sexual mores were lax in pagan Ireland and Germany. In both societies most people traced their lineage through their female ancestors, and many people did not know their father.[29]

In short, the inhabitants of the Roman Empire knew nothing about a nuclear family. For them marriage was tenuous and unnecessary. Cohabitation—what we used to call shacking up—was common. Children were little more than chattel. And no one idea of family was normative. In these ways, at least, the ancient Roman Empire and contemporary America have much in common.

The Nuclear Norm

This is the world Christianity faced and conquered. Through missionary efforts, social action, martyrdom, rising up the social and political ladders, and simply living out their faith day to day, Christians won Europe over to a single view of the family. They applied a single ethic to everyone, male and female, slave and free, young and old, wealthy and poor. This ethic included monogamy and sexual fidelity within the bonds of marriage. It also prohibited cohabitation, premarital and extramarital sex, and it severely restricted the justifiable reasons for divorce. It accorded equal dignity and worth to husband and wife and their offspring—indeed, to all human beings. But within this state of marital and familial equality, it also imposed an ordered hierarchy with mutual obligations. Children were to honor and respect their parents, and parents were to love and guide their children according to Christian instruction. Husbands and wives owed their deep and ever-abiding love to one another until death separated them. The church also called for moral and religious education in the home, and it rejected limiting families through sterilization, abortion, and infanticide.[30]

What impact did this new ethic have on Western Europe? Robert Shaffern tells us: "Christianity regularized the household . . . thereby making the nuclear family normative. . . . With the gradual imposition of monogamy, the number of marriageable women increased. More poor men could find mates and raise families. They were given a stake in settled society, and the numbers of wandering outlaws decreased. Christian Ireland and Germany became patrilineal in part because of the fidelity of marriage partners. The modern conception of family—consisting of parents and the children they rear—was a product of Christianity meeting the household."[31]

The new uniform ethic also removed the father's arbitrary control over his wife and children. It did this by placing the consent to marriage firmly in the hands of the couple contemplating marriage. This effectively removed that control from aristocratic fathers, political rulers, and even church officials. No earthly entity could now interfere with the right of a man and a woman to marry, and now no husband or father could legally terrorize any members of his household. Mutual love and service replaced dictatorial male control.[32] "The Christian family was not a patriarchal despotism, but evolved into a moral economy in which each member was called to service and grace."[33]

Furthermore, marriage itself took on greater significance. It was not simply the union of two people but the means to reunite society. Christian reflections on marriage went all the way back to the initial Creation to demonstrate this. Beginning with Genesis, Christians maintained that all human beings were descendants from one set of parents—Adam and Eve. Over time, however, their descendants grew apart, becoming cold, even hostile toward one another. The marital union heals this rift. Two blood lines come together—the lineage of the wife and that of the husband. Marriage binds these bloodlines; they become kin. Once they were separated, going their own ways. Now they are one, sharing the same path. Marriage became the blood that binds.[34]

Since husband and wife were now "authentic kin," women, not just men, enjoyed the rights of inheritance. What had been denied to Roman and pagan women was granted to all women with the rise of the nuclear family.[35]

Child-rearing became the focus of marriage. The Romans had recognized procreation and the proper education of children as purposes of marriage, but they also put children at grave risk through their low view of human life. Christianity changed that. For them, all human beings were God's image-bearers, and therefore had intrinsic value and worth. Moreover, the Christian view of love bound believers to love all people, including their enemies. For these reasons and others, abortion and infanticide, while not disappearing, became rare. Christians opened up their homes, churches, monasteries, and convents and founded orphanages to care for children who would have otherwise been killed or abandoned. Households became "oriented in significant measure toward children, to be aware of them and to delight in them." The Christian family even "idealized" childhood "as a time of life marked by innocence, openness, simplicity, and contentment."[36] Society finally valued children in their own right rather than regarding them as potentially disposable property.

Shaffern goes on to say, "Children spent more time with their mother, and when mothers died young, widowers often married another young bride. Widowers' remarriage maintained the children's close affiliation to the mother."[37]

Christianity also made sexual fidelity the norm rather than the exception. This included barring such practices as homosexuality, pedophilia, bestiality, and prostitution.[38] "Although the Christian Middle Ages were by no means puritanical, the more bizarre sexual practices of the pagan era diminished."[39]

Concluding, Shaffern states: "The spread of Christianity in the early Middle Ages radically altered European households and promoted the stability of the family. Not diversity, but uniformity characterized the medieval Christian household. . . . Christian teachings altered the legal underpinnings of the household and made normative the form of social organization in which husband, wife, and children were responsible to each other for survival, the fulfillment of obligations, mutual love and respect."[40]

Given the backdrop of pagan Rome, we can see how revolutionary the Judeo-Christian idea of the nuclear family really was. Through it the pluralism of families so prevalent in the Roman Empire went into the dustbin of Western history for more than a millennium.

Family, Early-American Style

When Christian Europeans immigrated to the New World, they brought the Judeo-Christian understanding of marriage and family with them. The ethic that conquered Rome would now settle America.

Families were large in colonial America. The first U.S. Census taken in 1790 showed that the average household had 5.8 people. But it was fairly common to find families with five to ten children, sometimes even fifteen children or more. Benjamin Franklin came from a family of seventeen.[41]

Parents carefully nurtured their children, treating them as precious in themselves. Parents also valued their children as economic assets. Families worked together. "Most productive activities—from furniture construction and candle-making through the raising and preparation of food—were family based."[42] Fathers, mothers, and children divided the labor and together built thriving businesses. When parents grew too old or ill to work, their children supported them. This arrangement was so effective that in 1776, the great American economist Adam Smith commented: "Labor [in North America] is . . . so well rewarded that a numerous family of children, instead of being a burden, is a source of opulence and prosperity to the parents. The value of children is the greatest of all encouragements to marriage."[43] Children were valued resources, not problems to purge.

On the legal side, "Husbands were responsible for the support of their wives and for any debts incurred by them. Women had inheritance rights with regard to their husband's property. Additionally, wives were legally protected against any abuse or maltreatment by their husbands. Strict discipline and parental respect were the hallmarks of child-rearing practices."[44]

Moreover, divorce was extremely rare. Plymouth, for example, was settled in 1620 and did not experience a single divorce until 1661. In some of the colonies, particularly southern ones, no provisions for divorce existed. Where divorce was allowed, the legal grounds were generally restricted to adultery or cruelty, and even then they were sometimes punishable as crimes. The courts in some colonies could grant divorces, whereas in others the authority fell to the legislatures.[45]

Early Americans saw the family as the basic building block of all larger units, be they religious, social, political, or economic. The family was the civilizing center of civilization. In the home American children received moral and religious instruction, learned about their country's heritage and its laws, and most importantly, perhaps, were taught that their lives did not belong to them. Their first duty was to God, their second to their country, their third to their family, and their fourth to themselves. The individual's happiness and aspirations were subordinate to these parties. "Service to the family was therefore a calling that was valued over that to the individual, and service to the larger public good was deemed superior to both." In this way "all corporate bodies, even ones as small as families, stood as barriers to heightened senses of the self and served to control the sinful and irrational wants of individuals."[46]

Rome Reborn

In comparison to the situation of families today, the families of yesteryear are aliens from another world. If we encountered such a family, we would likely catalog it along with other anomalies—UFOs, two-headed dogs, cars that never break down after their warranties expire, and pay increases commensurate with our financial needs. The Judeo-Christian understanding of the nuclear family is not only rare but discouraged and even disdained, especially if the number of children surpasses politically correct limits. The ethic America once embraced is now frequently spurned. Here are just a few choice quotes that illustrate what I mean:

> "People hold out the ideal of the mythical traditional family.... Fantasies die hard."[47] (Emily Brown, family therapist)
>
> "Very early in my childhood ... I associated poverty, toil, unemployment, drunkenness, cruelty, quarreling, fighting, debts, jails with large families."[48] (Margaret Sanger, founder of Planned Parenthood)
>
> "The family, historically, *was* a prison."[49] (Karen Lindsey, educator)
>
> "The tragedy of marriage is not that it fails to assure woman the promised happiness ... but that it mutilates her: it dooms her to repetition and routine.... At twenty or thereabouts mistress of a home, bound permanently to a man, a child in her arms, she stands with her life virtually finished forever."[50] (Simone de Beauvoir, feminist philosopher)
>
> "[We should] abandon the erroneous assumption that pregnancy is per se a normal and desirable state.... [Pregnancy] may be defined as an illness requiring medical supervision ...; may be treated by evacuation of the uterine contents; may be tolerated, sought, and/or valued for the purpose of reproduction; and has an excellent prognosis for complete, spontaneous recovery if managed under careful medical supervision."[51] (Warren M. Hern, medical doctor)

"The isolated nuclear family of the 1950s was a small blip on the radar.... We've been looking at it as normal, but in fact it was a fascinating anomaly."[52] (Leslie Wolfe, executive director of the Center for Women Policy Studies)

"Family sociologists should take the lead in *burying* the ideology of 'the [nuclear] family' and in rebuilding a social environment in which diverse family forms can sustain themselves with dignity and mutual respect."[53] (Judith Stacey, sociologist and educator)

"However much individuals in modern Western societies may want a child—and most men as well as women want at least one very much indeed—they certainly do not *need* children for any practical purpose and, practically speaking, would almost always be better off without any."[54] (Penelope Leach, author, psychologist, and mother of two)

"The family is an institution in transition. Fewer and fewer families resemble the traditional family popularized in 1950s television shows. With almost half of all marriages still ending in divorce and more single women choosing to have children, the number of single-parent families belies *right-wing, family-values extremists'* insistence on the traditional family as the only 'norm.' "[55] (Elizabeth Debold, consultant and member of the Harvard Project; Marie Wilson, mother, and the president of the Ms. Foundation for Women; Idelisse Malavé, mother, and the vice president of the Ms. Foundation)

This is what we've come to. These are the deceptions we're told.

The new American family is families. It doesn't need parents. It doesn't require children. Marriage is optional too. Family is whatever you want to call it, whatever you come home to. This is the norm we are supposed to accept. This is the emerging absolute. This is decadent Rome reborn.

Chapter 8

Love the One You're With

The *Old* Absolute	The *New* Absolute
(5) Sexual intercourse should be reserved for marriage.	(5a) Sexual intercourse is permissible regardless of marital status.

The talented foursome Crosby, Stills, Nash, and Young took the world of rock music by storm in the late '60s. They combined a folk-rock style of acoustic and electric instruments with soothing, four-part vocal harmonies to create a unique sound that became widely recognizable and highly profitable. The group formed in 1969 after David Crosby quit the Byrds, Stephen Stills and Neil Young left Buffalo Springfield, and Graham Nash walked away from the Hollies. Their second live performance together occurred before half a million people at the Woodstock Festival in August 1969. The next year, their recording of Joni Mitchell's song "Woodstock" memorialized the spirit of that event.

During their off-and-on career as a musical ensemble, different members of the group produced solo albums. In 1970, Stephen Stills' first solo release included a song that made it to number four on the pop charts. "Love the One You're With" featured two of the finest rock musicians who have ever played electric guitar—Eric Clapton and Jimi Hendrix. Its lyrics captured the youth culture's mind-set by advocating what was already the new sexual ethic: "free love." The song encouraged people to have sex with whoever was within arm's reach. If one's regular lover—wife, husband, live-in, steady date—was not around to enjoy a sexual liaison, then they should reach out and make love to someone else. People should not put their sexual urges on hold simply because their regular partner was absent. They should spread their love around, which meant have sex with whoever was handy. Sexual faithfulness was out; playing around was in.

Just the Facts

The message reflected the changes in contemporary culture. Among all women born between 1933 to 1942, 84 percent were either virgins or had had sexual intercourse with just one person by age twenty. And the person they had sex with, they usually married soon after.[1]

Within a very short time, this percentage dropped dramatically to only 50 percent of all women born after 1953.[2] Among those born between 1953 and 1962, just six percent of men and 3.6 percent of women were virgins by their twentieth birthday.[3] In this same age group, only about 47 percent of men and 57 percent of women married the first person with whom they had sex. This is a significant drop from those born between 1933 and 1942, where nearly 85 percent of men and 94 percent of women married their first sexual partner.[4] By the early 1970s, more than half of nineteen-year-old women and about two-thirds of nineteen-year-old men had had sex.[5] Loving the one you were with was becoming the norm.

As teenage promiscuity rose, so did out-of-wedlock births. In 1960, little more than 15 percent of births were to unmarried teenagers. By 1970, this figure had jumped to more than 22 percent.[6]

The total number of illegitimate births to teens and non-teens was 245,000 in 1962. This rose to 448,000 in 1975. During roughly this same period, the number of abortions also increased dramatically. In 1960, most of the estimated 100,000 abortions performed were illegal,[7] although abortions necessary to save the life of the mother were always legal in the United States and the vast majority of them were performed by qualified physicians.[8] As abortion restrictions were loosened, abortions increased considerably. In 1972, just prior to the *Roe v. Wade* decision, the abortion level had already reached an annual rate of almost 587,000. By the end of 1978, the annual number of abortions had soared to more than 1.4 million.[9] More than ever before, death was becoming sex's most prolific product.

While the sexual revolution altered teenage beliefs and behavior, it did not seem to impact older Americans, at least at first. According to family scholar Bryce Christensen, "As late as 1967, 85 percent of the parents of college-aged children judged premarital sex as immoral."[10] At least middle-aged Americans and those older believed that virginity was not an embarrassment but a gift to give one's loving mate upon marriage. The Judeo-Christian conviction of reserving sexual intercourse for marriage was still intact for most of America even during much of the sexual revolution of the '60s. It didn't take long, however, for this to change. Almost overnight, all of America went from a society accepting sex as something reserved for marriage to adopting a new sexual ethic: sex is permissible regardless of a person's marital status.

Living Together

Today, the majority of Americans believe it is better to live together in sexual intimacy with someone before committing to marrying that person. In the 1994 book *Sex in America*, which has been called the most comprehensive and definitive study to date on the sexual activities of Americans, the authors concluded that "within the past few decades, a form of sexual behavior, cohabitation, has gone from being almost unheard of to being a very common form of sexual partnership."[11] How common? Here is what they had to say:

> Since the 1960s, the route to the altar is no longer so predictable as it used to be. In the first half of the twentieth century, almost everyone who married followed the same course: dating, love, a little sexual experimentation with one partner, sometimes including intercourse, then marriage and children. . . .
>
> But a new and increasingly common pattern has emerged: affection or love and sex with a number of partners, followed by affection, love, and cohabitation. This cycles back to the sexual marketplace, if the cohabitation breaks up, or to marriage. Pregnancy can occur at any of these points, but often occurs before either cohabitation or marriage. . . .
>
> Like other recent studies, ours shows a marked shift toward living together rather than marriage as the first union of couples. . . . Our study shows that people who came of age before 1970 almost invariably got married without first living together, while the younger people seldom did. . . .
>
> In our study, we find that 93 percent of women born between 1933 and 1942 married without ever living with their partner. And 90 percent of these women were either virgins when they married or had premarital intercourse only with the man they wed. In contrast, just 36 percent of women born between 1963 and 1974 got married without living with their spouse first. But among the majority who lived with a man, 60 percent had no other sexual part-

ners or only one other before they moved in with their lover.

With the increase in cohabitation, people are marrying later, on average. The longer they wait, however, the more likely they are to live with a sexual partner in the meantime. Since many couples who live together break up within a short time and seek a new partner, the result has been an increase in the average number of partners that people have before they marry.[12]

The good news coming out of this study is that once a couple marries, they are most likely to remain sexually faithful to each other. "More than 80 percent of women and 65 to 85 percent of men of every age report that they had no partners other than their spouse while they were married."[13] But prior to marriage and between marriages, abstinence is not the rule. These statistics also mean that 20 percent of women and 15 to 35 percent of men, regardless of age, have cheated on their spouses. Another recent study confirms this. It found that 31 percent of "all married Americans . . . have had or are now having an affair. . . . The affairs aren't one-night stands either. American affairs last, on the average, almost a year. That shows more staying power than do many American marriages."[14]

Does this mean that Americans believe marital infidelity is all right? Yes. "Today, the majority of Americans (62 percent) think that there's nothing morally wrong with the affairs they're having." And the rationalization cited most often for adultery is "everybody else does it too."[15]

Anything Goes

In modern America, sex is not just a fact but an obsession. We think about it, fantasize about it, talk about it, hear about it, watch it, display it, read about it, pay for it, and engage in it with virtual moral abandon. Marriage still has its place, but it is losing ground to America's insatiable appetite for new sexual excursions.

While pedophiles (those who prefer sex with children) are still ostracized in American society, what adults do with other adults sexually, short of mutilation, is morally acceptable as long as the participating parties consent to it. Just about anything goes as long as the activity is not forced against one's will.[16] The Patterson-Kim study revealed some startling results:

Top 10 List of Sexual Fantasies

1. Oral sex

2. Sex with a famous person
3. Sex with multiple partners
4. Sex with someone of another race
5. Using sexual devices
6. Sex in a public place
7. Swapping partners
8. Sex with a much younger person
9. Sex with a fictional TV character
10. Sex with a teenager[17]

Many Americans are not just dreaming about these activities either. Below are the percentages of men and women who have actually engaged in specific sexual fantasies:[18]

Fantasies Fulfilled	*Men*	*Women*
Oral sex	79%	70%
Using sexual devices	32	31
Sex in a public place	37	25
Sex with someone of another race	42	18
Sex with a teenager	35	8
Sex with a much younger person	28	10
Sex with multiple partners	31	10
Sex with dominance/submission	22	14
Swapping partners	20	6
Sex with violence	12	7
Incest	8	4
Sex with an animal	7	3
Sex with defecation	5	2

Clearly, much of American culture is absolutely sex crazed. However, we want our sex without its procreative product—children. We have bought the Malthusian-Sangerian line that fewer and only wanted children is the road to personal happiness, social progress, and population control.

Barbara Ehrenreich, in an essay in *Time*, carried this reasoning to its logical conclusion. Accepting the idea that the world is overpopulated, she asks her readers to look on the bright side. We should pat ourselves on the back for doing such a great job populating the earth. It is truly a "stunning achievement" that women for millenniums have risked their health and lives to obtain. Women should be rewarded for finally hitting the population mark. They no longer have to listen to anyone, including the pope, tell them "they must hew to their traditional role or risk letting the human race die out." Women should take control of their reproductive power, seeing this step as their "overdue reward for filling the planet with humans." Moreover, "With more women freed from repeated childbearing, each child can potentially have a more generous share of attention and resources."[19]

While all this is fine and good, Ehrenreich claims, she adds that there's an even happier "consequence of overpopulation." Now "sex can finally, after all these centuries, be separated from the all-too-serious business of reproduction. Technology has made it possible to uncouple sex and babymaking; ecology has made it necessary. Now all that remains is for us to make the cultural leap to an ecologically responsible sexual ethic." What is this new ethic? That "sex, in our overpopulated world, is best seen as a source of fun."[20] Ehrenreich lets us in on how she arrived at this conclusion:

> If, after all, the essence of morality is respect for each life, and if, furthermore, all future life is threatened by rampant reproduction, then what could be more moral than teaching teenagers that homosexuality is a viable lifestyle? Or that masturbation is harmless and normal? Or that petting, under most circumstances, makes far more sense than begetting? The only ethic that can work in an overcrowded world is one that insists that women are free, children are loved, and sex—preferably among affectionate and consenting adults—belongs squarely in the realm of play.[21]

To put this ethic in practice requires at minimum that "contraception, with abortion as a backup," be available "to all who might need it."[22] This is already being done throughout the United States. Sex as play is the new standard. Sex may have other functions, such as making babies, but its purest, moral role is entertainment. Since sex is good and fun, we should encourage it for everyone no matter their age, sexual "orientation," or marital status.

Sex in Early America

This new standard clearly contradicts what our forebears believed about sex. Early Americans viewed sex as they did everything else, through Judeo-Christian glasses. To them, sex had a threefold purpose derived from the Bible and natural law. First and foremost, sex was *unitive.* It helped seal the bond between a man and a woman in holy matrimony. The physical act of intercourse made the two "one flesh"; it created a new, wondrous entity distinctly two yet mysteriously one.[23] For this reason, "Once singles chose their marriage partners, they were expected to stay together in marriage. Abandoning one's spouse was a crime, not an inalienable right as it is in today's society. Men who refused to support their wives and men and women who deserted their spouses or their children were subject to criminal prosecution."[24] One of the few grounds for divorce was adultery, and it was greeted with social stigma and legal sanctions. As one scholar states:

> Very possibly the most broadly enforced tenet of family law in the first three hundred years of American family life was the prohibition against adultery. In colonial days, adultery was prosecuted vigorously as a subversion of the promise of physical and emotional unity between the wedded couple. Punishments in various jurisdictions involved monetary penalties, floggings, public humiliation, and, in a number of cases, even the death penalty. State officials continued to vigilantly prosecute adultery throughout the 1800s. For example, of the first 26 cases docketed in the U.S. District Court in Rosell, Territory of New Mexico in 1890, 5 were for fornication and 17 were for adultery. Fidelity in marriage was so important that when states allowed but one ground for divorce, inevitably that ground was adultery.[25]

Americans also believed sex was *procreative.* It gave life to new human beings. It perpetuated the divine image throughout the world. It fulfilled the divine command to fill and subdue the earth.[26] The procreative purpose was so important that American law encouraged it.

> Traditionally, American legal policy fostered responsible childbearing within marriage. This policy was designed to ensure that the offspring of sexual union would receive the nurturance of a two-parent family. Furthermore, the physical perils inherent in childbearing and childrearing in frontier America were such that the central social problem was not how to *prevent* the conception or childbearing, but how to *promote* the conception and childbearing once a hopeful basis for family life was well established. For this reason, in the post-revolutionary period the nation adopted laws prohibiting the use of contraception and the dissemination of information about how to prevent pregnancy. These laws were reinforced in the post-Civil War period. . . .
>
> With families breaking up and the birthrate falling at an unprecedented rate after the Civil War, the federal government and the states acted. In 1873, Congress passed a federal law that pro-

> hibited the sale of contraceptives and abortion-inducing drugs, the distribution of birth control information, and advertising for abortion. . . .
>
> Between 1880 and 1900, state legislatures across the country sought to prop up the declining national birthrate by adopting laws prohibiting abortion. In over half of those states, the law permitted abortion only to save the life of the mother. In other states, abortion was permitted in other circumstances such as when it was deemed necessary to prevent serious or permanent bodily injury to the mother.[27]

Finally, our American forebears saw sex as *recreative.* Sex was good and fun as long as it was practiced in the context for which it was created—marriage.[28] The early Americans were not prudes. They enjoyed sex. Just look at the number of children they had! When you consider that a woman can only get pregnant about three days out of every month and put that next to the size of colonial families, which sometimes rose to more than fifteen children, you can safely conclude that sex was a natural part of the marriage relationship.

The Americans of yesteryear clearly believed that the most satisfactory and only moral sex was marital sex, and the finest fruit of marital sex was a strong marriage bond and children.

Today most Americans have abandoned this view. Sex has no unitive value. You can have as many sexual partners as you want and even have one-night stands without any sense of identity with or responsibility to your sexual partners. Sex has also been effectively divorced from procreation, so now you can have sex without getting pregnant or at least giving birth. Even the recreative side of sex is gone as traditionally understood. Married couples think singles are having the best sex, and they rarely equate good sex with pregnancy and babies. Sex American-style is now completely secularized. The Bible and natural law have been given the boot. Like family, sex is now pluralistic. Marital sex is okay, but the sexual menu has so many choices that more Americans are tasting the available dishes at earlier ages and then throughout the rest of their lives.

Teen Fallout

As you might expect, America's teens have accepted this new ethic and made it their lifestyle of choice. In a 1990 study conducted by the Centers for Disease Control and Prevention, "three out of four teenagers said that by the time they graduated from high school, they had engaged in sex. And 40 percent said they were not virgins by the ninth grade."[29]

It's not unusual anymore to hear about twelve-, thirteen-, and fourteen-year-olds who are no longer virgins.

This high level of adolescent sexual exploration has led to a rash of pregnancies, abortions, and births. Each year more than one million teens become pregnant. Many of these babies never make it to term. One out of every five abortions is performed on a woman under age twenty, and four of every ten teenage pregnancies ends in abortion.[30] In other words, about 400,000 of the 1.6 million abortions occurring annually are performed on adolescent mothers.[31] Of the babies who are allowed to live, more than two-thirds are born to unmarried teens, most of whom are between the ages of fifteen and nineteen. The United States has one of the highest adolescent birthrates of any country in the world. America's teens bear children almost twice as much as teens in the United Kingdom, nearly seven times more than France's adolescents, and about fifteen times more often than their counterparts in Japan. When it comes to teenage childbearing, the United States "looks more like a developing country than an industrialized one."[32]

These numbers are even more staggering when one realizes that they have occurred under years of sex education classes in the public schools and the widespread availability of contraceptives to teenagers. This could lead one to conclude that sex education does not work. On the contrary, it is working all too well. Sex education classes are not designed to prevent sex but to promote it. From kindergarten through high school, sex educators teach children to exercise their "right" to be the sexual beings they are—whether they are heterosexual, homosexual, or bisexual. They are encouraged to explore their sexuality and the great variety of sexual opportunities open to them. Educators tell American children that sexual fantasies and masturbation are normal, that they are free to choose the sexual life they desire, and that no kind of sex act is wrong as long as the persons involved agree to it and don't get hurt beyond their wishes. Some also tell kids that pornography is harmless and even useful for stimulation and to discover uncharted territory. Children learn about venereal diseases and how to prevent or terminate pregnancies. They are told that babies must be wanted to be born and that having an abortion to end an unwanted pregnancy is morally right. They get explicit instructions on how to use various methods of contraception, and they learn in detail about sexual play, arousal, and intercourse between male and male, and female and female, not just between male and female. Many sex education materials actually encourage children to embrace a homosexual lifestyle and to accept incest as a potentially pleasurable and fulfilling experience.

In a book for sex educators entitled *Sexuality Today and Tomorrow* (dedicated to Margaret Sanger), an essay appears called "Sex in the Year 2000." It is written by Professor David Mace, who is on the faculty of Wake Forest University and who is a founding member of Sex Information and Education Council of the United States (SIECUS). SIECUS is the most influential sex education organization in America, and it has been so since 1965. It has strong ties with Sanger's Planned Parenthood, sharing the same philosophy, public policy agenda, and even some of Planned Parenthood's personnel.[33] In his essay, Dr. Mace lays out the future possibilities of sex under two opposed perspectives. He calls them the "most liberal" view and the "extreme conservative" one. Mace makes it clear that he favors the "most liberal" option. The conservative one closely resembles the view Americans used to hold, though Mace caricatures it. The liberal view, on the other hand, the one he hopes will materialize, is summarized by two astute cultural observers this way:

> Children are encouraged to enjoy to the fullest all sensual libidinal experiences; the child would be exposed fully to adult sexual behavior, wherein it would be "commonplace for him to witness heterosexual and homosexual encounters" and other unspecified sexual experiences that, Mace says, cover the entire range of what is now considered normal and abnormal; no attempts would be made to restrain the "sexual play of children, including attempts to simulate intercourse"; at puberty, girls and boys would freely gratify any sexual urge, excluding only rape, as it arose; it would, he writes, "be entirely proper" to invite any person, of either sex or any age group, to participate in any kind of couple or group sex. Marriage would not exist; temporary or permanent relationships between any combination of two or more persons would be embarked upon and dissolved by mutual consent. Finally . . . Mace writes that "procreation would probably be controlled to some extent. Tests of health might be required of the intending parents." Children would be raised at home or by "specially selected and trained 'up-bringers' at state expense."[34]

This is where the leading sex educators want to lead our children. In their ideal world such horrible things as monogamous, lifetime marriage, sexual abstinence before marriage, sexual faithfulness within marriage, the procreative purpose of sex, and heterosexuality as normative and the only moral option would be notions left in a dusty corner of the Smithsonian Institute. They represent the Judeo-Christian view of sex, and that, to most of today's sex education advocates, is anathema. It represents to them oppression and ignorance, despite the fact that it helped civilize the Western world and shaped the American conscience, including its legal codes, for centuries.

In short, government-sponsored, Planned Parenthood-and-SIECUS-approved sex education turns America's traditional moral convictions on their head, calling what was once deemed good as evil and what was once considered evil as good. Today's sex education curricula is anything but value-neutral, and it is definitely anti-marriage and anti-family as historically understood in the American experience.[35] Is it any wonder that with instruction such as this America's children are sexually active and having children themselves?

Of course, many other factors have contributed to the incredible rise in teenage promiscuity and its consequences. But among all the factors, one constant stands out: adults. Eric Buehrer, the founding president of Gateways to Better Education, says it well:

> Adults are the ones making television shows and movies more sexually explicit. . . . Adults are the ones who are creating sexually alluring advertising. Adults are the ones writing the sex-education courses. Adults are the ones promoting homosexual "sensitivity" training in schools. . . .
>
> In short, it should come as no surprise that children are becoming more sexually aware and active. They are only responding to the messages the adults in our society give them. The problem is that while many parents recognize this problem, they are often unwilling to take responsibility for the healthy sexual education of their children, and too many educators want to wrench this responsibility from them. Their aim is to create a society whose views on sexuality are properly progressive and "liberating."[36]

The Elders Connection

Few sex educators epitomize the contemporary attitude toward sex and its acceptance on state and federal levels as clearly as Dr. Joycelyn Elders. An African-American, she is the daughter of poor rural Arkansas sharecroppers and the oldest of eight children. She worked her way through medical school on the G.I. Bill, became a pediatric endocrinologist,[37] and eventually joined the faculty at the University of Arkansas, where she has taught nearly thirty years. In a 1995 article, K. D. Whitehead, a former U.S. Assistant Secretary of Education, reported that Elders had about "150 scholarly research papers to her credit."[38] If she never did anything else, Elders would have been regarded as a very accomplished woman by professional measurements.

But she did more. She rose to the highest medical office in the land. Appointed by President Bill Clinton and confirmed in the U.S. Senate by a vote of 65 to 34, she became the Surgeon General of the United States in 1993. She had been one of Clinton's first appointments after he moved into the White House. Prior to that the two had had a long, mutually beneficial relationship in Arkansas.

When Clinton was Arkansas's governor, he chose Elders to serve as the State Health Director in 1987. In that position, she worked to establish her six-point plan that she believed would "secure an equal chance for our children, a chance that the children of today will be bright, energetic, and healthy adults of tomorrow."[39] Her plan included what she called comprehensive health, family life, and/or sex education, and school-based health services. Elders wanted the former objective geared for children from preschool through twelfth grade and the latter from kindergarten through twelfth grade. According to Elders, the first program would teach children what "they need to know about human reproductive biology and development and the risks of early and unprotected sexual activity." "We can no longer ignore or deny," she said, "that our children need this information. If we don't give it to them in an appropriate educational environment, someone else will, and the delivery of that information may be anything but appropriate."[40] Or, as she put it more memorably in another context, sex education is like drivers education: "We taught them what to do in the front seat of a car. Now it's time to teach them what to do in the backseat."[41] Her second program, the school health clinics, would provide "family life counseling and contraceptive services," along with a number of other so-called health-supporting items.[42] Elders wanted these clinics to provide a full range of "services," including prescribing and dispensing contraceptives, testing for pregnancy, counseling pregnant students, and handling sexually transmitted diseases.[43]

Arkansas Accomplishments

Elders got what she wanted in several of Arkansas's public schools. Sex education and school-based clinics were instituted. Between 1992 and 1993, twenty-four clinics were operating in the public schools, and twenty-eight more school districts were on the waiting list. One reporter observed that "the clinics are essentially doctors' offices inside the school, with regular visits by specialists in medicine, social work, psychiatry, and reproductive health."[44] Despite the full-service rhetoric, however, the primary goal of these clinics is to dispense free condoms, especially to high school students. These clinics also refer students to abortion providers without parental notification or approval. Elders wanted to end what she called "an epidemic of teenage pregnancy." In her opinion, that required abortion counseling and access to contraception "in those places [teenagers] frequent."[45]

Elders admitted that her plan faced "the most vocal opposition from right-to-life and right-wing groups, who claim the clinics promote abortion." Knowing her critics were right, she diverted the issue by calling her critics "very religious non-Christians [who] love little babies as long as they are in someone else's uterus."[46] She also ducked the charge by saying the clinics themselves did not perform abortions. She took Margaret Sanger's publicity tack and said her focus was on pregnancy prevention, not termination. "It is plainly obvious," Elders stated, "that if a child is not pregnant, she does not need an abortion. Furthermore, the need for an abortion by any child represents a personal failure for every citizen in this country."[47] Of course, if the counseling and contraceptives failed, Elders' clinics were ready to refer students to places where they could have their preborn infants killed privately and legally.[48] She was willing to do anything necessary to prevent the births of babies. And if the babies had birth defects, such as Down syndrome, she saw abortion as an especially effective antidote to the burden they would place on their mothers and society.[49]

Well, how did Elders' statewide plan do? Did it accomplish her goals? Not in the least. Under her watch, teen pregnancy didn't stabilize or slowdown; it rose 15 percent. Arkansas went from the fourth to the second highest teen pregnancy rate of any state in the United States. Sexually transmitted diseases (STDs) were not held in check either. In fact, they rose at a staggering rate. Syphilis cases among teens skyrocketed 130 percent, and HIV infection went up even higher to 150 percent.[50] In other words, adolescents became even more sexually active and paid the price for it. Armed with condoms and how-to instructions, teens explored the unforbidden territory with new abandon, all the while thinking they were practicing "safe sex." They were wrong. They had been deceived by their state's health director. Now they were having more babies out of wedlock, getting more abortions, and contracting harmful and painful diseases with the support of Elders' social experiment.

The situation of Arkansas's teens was worsened by the poorer than normal condom protection they received. Elders was so intent on getting a condom into the hands of every teenager that she "ordered the distribution in public schools of condoms with a defective rate ten times greater than what the federal government allows." Then she withheld information about the risk of the faulty condoms so the public would not lose "confidence" in what little value they had left. Through her spokesperson, Elders claimed that the "non-use of condoms would have been a greater risk to public health" than using the faulty ones.[51] Obviously, she was more motivated to stop even a few pregnancies than to discourage premarital sex or protect students from sexually transmitted diseases, including AIDS.

When confronted with her poor performance in Arkansas, Elders never questioned her own policies. Rather, she blamed "poverty and ignorance and the Bible-Belt mentality" as the real roadblocks to the success of her programs.[52] The victims were responsible, not the victimizer. If they had only been richer, smarter, and possessed her scruples instead of the Bible's, all would have gone well. In truth, none of these factors were the problem. STDs, pregnancies due to condom failure, and the many other real and documented side effects of the Elders sex program are no respecter of persons. They do not take into consideration one's financial status, knowledge base, or religious beliefs. They are a risk to all who decide to play by Elders' rules.

America's Doctor

In spite of such policy failures and irresponsible actions, President Clinton appointed her to the post of U.S. Surgeon General. He had always supported her, no matter how outrageous her views or activities became. When he, for instance, introduced Elders to the people of Arkansas in a 1987 press conference, he nodded his agreement when Elders said she planned to distribute condoms in public schools, but would not be putting them on the kids' "lunch trays."[53] When Elders endorsed the legalization of drugs, Clinton said he stood "foursquare" behind her.[54] Ken Lobel, lead organizer for the Arkansas Women's Project, watched the relationship between Clinton and Elders for several years. According to Lobel, "Clinton relies on Dr. Elders to say the things he cannot say for political reasons. . . . When he finally said that he was prochoice, we all said, 'Well, of course he's pro-choice,' but we really only knew that because she had been so outspoken and he would not have let her do that unless he agreed with her."[55] Elders herself confirmed this observation. After she became the U.S. Surgeon General, she told the *New York Times* magazine, "I worked for [Bill Clinton] for five and a half years. I served on commissions and task forces with him for thirteen years, so he couldn't say that he didn't know what I was about. There were times when even I was concerned that maybe some things I was doing were putting heat on him. So I'd go ask him and he'd say, 'No, no, keep it up. I like it. . . . ' "[56] According to Whitehead, when Clinton chose Elders for the surgeon general post, he told her, "Joycelyn, I want you to do for the whole country what you've done for Arkansas."[57] And he let her do it with carte blanche approval.

As the nation's leading health authority, Elders continued to make her case for sex education and condom distribution in the public schools. She even advocated that children as young as two should be taught about sex in daycare centers.[58] For her views on sexuality to reign freely, Elders decided that her critics must be trivialized or banished. As the appointed sex czar, she went after the enemies of her Clinton-approved plans with a vengeance.

She told pro-life advocates "to get over this love affair with the fetus and start worrying about children." She also advocated legalizing the abortifacient drug RU–486. If women used the drug, she claimed there would not be "identifiable clinics where people go just for abortions," therefore there would not be places pro-lifers could picket or abortionists pro-lifers could "stalk."[59] She charged that the Catholic Church hierarchy's pro-life stance against abortion is more vehement than its stand was against the Holocaust in Nazi Germany and "the 400 years in which black Americans had their freedom aborted."[60] "Look who's fighting [against] the pro-choice movement," she said, "a celibate, male-dominated church."[61] Elders claimed that denying "women an approved medical service [i.e., abortion] is absolutely wrong." People who disagreed with her, she asserted, were "narrow-minded."[62]

After the Traditional Values Coalition—an organization representing 31,000 churches—dubbed her the "condom queen," Elders said, "Coming from them, it doesn't bother me. If I could be the 'condom queen' and get every young person who is engaged in sex to use a condom in the United States, I would wear a crown on my head with a condom on it!"[63]

To those who advocated sex within the bonds of matrimony only, she said, "Get real." Since "an awful lot of our children are not being abstinent" and since "we can't legislate morals, we have to teach [children] how to take care of themselves."[64] In other words, since so many kids are acting irresponsibly in the sexual arena, Elders decided to show them how to do it with a condom—her version of protected sex. Forget about learning sexual responsibility or self-control. Disregard the time-honored moral axiom that sex outside of marriage is wrong and harmful. Ignore the facts about the failure rate of condoms to prevent pregnancy, which one study conducted by condom promoters placed anywhere between 13 and 22 percent.[65] Play down the truth that the virus that leads to AIDS and the germs that cause STDs are much smaller than sperm, so they're much more likely to escape a condom through a small hole or tear.[66] Simply assume that young people are like animals and cannot control their sexual appetite. Buy into the bogus claim that morals cannot be legislated, even though they are legislated all the time (murder is wrong and punishable, stealing is wrong and punishable, rape is wrong and punishable, etc.). Refuse to face the incredible rise in sexual activity, pregnancy rates, and STDs among teenagers who receive sex education and condoms in the public school system.[67] Facts and sound reasoning aside, Elders was bent on using America's children to carry out her sexual agenda, and Clinton stood at her side.

She also widened her vision to include homosexuality. Elders told her opponents to stop being judgmental, unfair, and ignorant, and to start being "more open about sex." She said, "Tell people that sex is good, sex is wonderful. It's a normal part and healthy part of our being, whether it is homosexual or heterosexual." Any kind of sex is wholesome in the Elders moral code. And if you retort that sex is at least partly for procreation and therefore only fulfilled through heterosexual sex, Elders responds, "The religious right at times thinks that the only reason for sex is procreation. Well, I feel that God meant sex for more than procreation. Sex is about pleasure as well as about responsibility."[68] She also exhorted homosexual activists to "take on those people who are selling our children out in the name of religion."[69] The religious right, of course, does not deny that sex is pleasurable, as well as procreative. They, however, reject Elders' suggestion that these two aspects of sex should be divorced from its responsible practice within a heterosexual marital union.

On such questionable grounds, Elders "endorsed gay and lesbian adoption, advocated suicide-prevention efforts aimed at gay and lesbian youths, termed the Boy Scouts of America's ban on gay scouts and scout leaders 'unfair,' [and] denounced anti-gay campaigns by conservative religious groups."[70] Americans need to learn, she said, that "gay people are not just out there wanting to have sex with anybody who walks down the street and that gay people have real loving, lasting relationships and families." She goes on, "I feel that good parents are good parents—regardless of their sexual orientation." Furthermore, "It's clear," she asserts, "that the sexual orientation of parents has nothing to do with the sexual orientation or outlook of their children. Many children in this society are born unwanted, and I feel that if gay or lesbian couples feel that they want children enough to adopt, well, then they are probably just as capable of being good parents as heterosexual parents who choose to adopt."[71]

She was adamant that she was right and her opponents were wrong. She said that "denying young people health education, denying them the availability of contraceptives," and thereby putting them at risk should they engage in "unprotected" sex, "is almost child abuse." Anyone who challenged her had, she claimed, a fear of sex.[72]

The End of Elders' Reign

After fifteen stormy months at her post, President Clinton fired Elders. The reason had nothing to do with the positions she had articulated; it had everything to do with politics. Before the 1994 elections sent so many Republicans to Capitol Hill, eighty-eight Republican congressional leaders signed a letter and sent it to Clinton calling on him to request Elders' resignation. Clinton turned them down. After the elections, however, a new conservative wind was blowing liberalism into retreat. The president had to shore up his defenses.

The opportunity came in the first week of December 1994, when Elders spoke during the World AIDS Day at the United Nations. After her speech, an AIDS activist asked her if masturbation should be taught in schools as a way of limiting the spread of the AIDS virus. Elders replied, "I think that [masturbation] is something that is a part of human sexuality and it's a part of something that perhaps should be taught."[73] Compared to her many other controversial statements and positions, this one seemed somewhat benign. And it certainly was not novel. Says Whitehead, "The kind of classroom sex education which Planned Parenthood and Joycelyn Elders alike favor and promote has always included telling children as young as five about masturbation; educators in the field are perfectly well aware of this and are apparently not generally alarmed by it."[74] Elders' statement, however, gave the opening the president needed to distance himself from her and thereby appear more conservative. He told the press that "his own convictions" varied from those of Elders on the masturbation issue.[75] Given his unswerving support of her in the past, it seems highly unlikely that he had finally found an ideological difference, particularly one that would lead him to dismiss his choice for surgeon general.

Elders resigned as requested, but she never apologized for any of her statements. She didn't have to. Shortly after leaving office, in an interview on TV's "Meet the Press," she said, "I don't really have any regrets.... I've always tried to speak what I knew to be a truth."[76]

The Newest Brutes

While Dr. Elders may no longer be in the national spotlight, her ideas continue to spread unabated. Hers are simply the logical conclusions that must be drawn from a society dedicated to unlimited sexual freedom. The "truth" accepted today is that sex is good, wholesome, and fun between consenting parties whoever they are and regardless of their marital status, gender, or even species. Man with man, woman with woman, man with woman, older with younger, human with animal, self with self, group sex—it doesn't matter. When it comes to sex, the command today is not "Thou shalt not" but "Just do it with contraception protection." And if our contraception fails or we choose not to use it, we don't have to worry. Abortion can wipe out the mistake.

Clare Boothe Luce, former congresswoman and former U.S. ambassador to Italy, points out that one of the distinguishing marks between man and beasts is that man "has made *conscious efforts* to control his lustful impulses, and to regulate and direct them into social channels. There is no primitive society known to anthropologists, no civilization known to historians, which has ever willingly consented to give its members full reign—bestial reign—of their sexual impulses. Sex morals, mores, and manners have varied enormously from age to age and culture to culture. But sexual taboos and no-nos, sex prohibitions (and consequently, of course, inhibitions) are common to all human societies."[77] She points out that in America, however, these prohibitions and inhibitions are rapidly disappearing.

America has done what no other society has: joined the animal kingdom in its sexual behavior, then declared it good and justified it in the name of moral progress. Perhaps my anthropology professor was right after all. Humans are a sign of de-evolution, not evolution. At least that seems true in the sexual mores of contemporary America. We don't have to turn on our televisions to watch the animal kingdom. We have become the new, more brutish animal kingdom: human lust unleashed from sea to shining sea.

Dial Deviant for Normal

The *Old* Absolute	The *New* Absolute
(6) Same-sex and bi-sexual intercourse are immoral.	(6a) All forms and combinations of sexual activity are moral as long as they occur between consenting parties.

What do you get when you cross a wasp collector with a sex-history collector? You get a revolution in deviance that is still stinging American society. The fountainhead of the insurrection was Alfred Charles Kinsey, a collector of four million gall wasps and eighteen thousand sex histories. More than any other person, he set the stage for the sexual revolution of the '60s. What Malthus did for population control, Darwin for evolution, and Sanger for birth control, Kinsey did for sex—and the fallout has been every bit as devastating.

Before we look at Kinsey's revolt, we need to place it in its historical context and against the backdrop of the societal precedents it transgressed and so quickly undermined.

Good and Bad Sex

As we have already seen, the Judeo-Christian worldview that shaped the beliefs and behaviors of Americans for centuries recognized heterosexual sex within marriage as the only moral option. Americans regarded all other sexual expressions as immoral, and some they spurned as unnatural. Practices that fell under both categories were homosexuality, bisexuality, and bestiality. Heterosexual sex acts outside of marriage were bad enough. But same-sex sex acts (which would include the homosexual side of bisexuality) and sex with animals were outright perversions of the God-ordained natural order of things. American and English jurisprudence sought to enshrine the laws of their understanding of this natural order and work out the implications. The result in respect to sexual relations was a blanket condemnation of non-heterosexual sex acts.

Consider Sir William Blackstone, for example. He was an eighteenth-century English jurist who was highly respected and influential throughout England and the colonies. In 1775, Blackstone published his multivolume authoritative work entitled *Commentaries on the Laws of England*, where he gave the background to English law in general and to its particular manifestations. This law, he argued, was based on the common law, which is nothing else but the universal natural law revealed by God. Stated Blackstone:

> As man depends absolutely upon his Maker for everything, it is necessary that he should, in all points conform to his Maker's will. This will of his Maker is called the law of nature. . . . This law of nature being coeval with mankind, and dictated by God himself, is, of course, superior in obligation to any other. It is binding over all the globe, in all countries, and at all times: no human laws are of any validity, if contrary to this; and such of them as are valid derive all of their force and all of their authority mediately or immediately from this original.[1]

A few years earlier, American patriot James Otis argued for this natural-law position in his tract "Rights of the British Colonies." He declared that parliaments should always seek to establish laws that are good for all peoples under their jurisdiction. This good, however, is not dependent on the declarations of parliaments but on "a higher authority, viz. GOD." Otis went on to say that "should an act of parliament be against any of *his* [God's] natural laws, which are *immutably* true, *their* declaration would be contrary to eternal truth, equity and justice, and consequently void."[2] Alexander Hamilton, who played a key role in the development of the U.S. Constitution, said that "no tribunal, no codes, no systems can repeal or impair this law of God, for by his eternal laws it is inherent in the nature of things."[3]

In regard to homosexuality and bestiality, the British and Americans shared the same understanding: natural law opposes both practices as disordered appetites. Using the word *sodomy* to cover same-sex, bi-sex, and human-with-animal sexual activities, English law and its American successor enacted laws against their practice. In his *Commentaries*, Blackstone summed up the state of the issue this way: sodomy is "the infamous crime against nature, committed either with man or beast . . . the very mention of which is a disgrace to human nature."[4] All the nations of Western Europe, England, the American colonies, the first thirteen U.S. States, and all states added to the Union outlawed sodomy and prosecuted and punished offenders. In the United States, sodomy remained an illegal activity until the early '60s, at which time individual states began quietly repealing these laws. Today nearly half the states in the Union have decriminalized sodomy. Several of these states, as well as county and local municipalities, are considering, or have already passed, legislation providing protections for bisexuals and homosexuals due to their alleged sexual orientation.[5]

Sodomy is considered less and less a transgression of God's established order. The long-held view of sodomy as an unnatural, disordered appetite is being replaced by the view that sodomy is a natural, immutable condition every bit as healthy and good as heterosexuality. Thousands of years of Jewish and Christian condemnation and 450 years of English and American criminalization are quickly coming to an end. Alfred Kinsey and his followers have played one of the most critical roles in bringing about this moral and legal shift. Here's a sketch of how they did it.

Kinsey's Kinks

Kinsey was a Darwinian evolutionist, a eugenicist, and possibly a homosexual,[6] who grew up fascinated with botany and the diversity he found there. He liked all sorts of animals, especially snakes, but early in his career he became particularly interested in insects. Gall wasps really struck his fancy. According to one of his biographers, Kinsey's attraction to the gall wasp had to do with the insect's reproductive quirks: the gall wasps' "curious life history sometimes includes alternating generations, a rather rare biological phenomenon, in which offspring do not resemble their parents. One generation may be agamic—that is, able to reproduce without sexual union."[7]

Kinsey claimed that in 1938 he was approached to teach a noncredit course on marriage at Indiana University. His biographers report that when he researched the subject, he was "appalled by the lack of 'scientific' material on sexuality," so he set out to conduct some research of his own and began collecting sex histories.[8]

Dr. Judith Reisman disputes this official version of Kinsey's venture into the study of human sexuality. Reisman is the president of the Institute for Media Education in Arlington, Virginia. She has concentrated a good deal of her time studying pornography in the media and researching Kinsey. In 1990 she coauthored a book entitled *Kinsey, Sex and Fraud: The Doctrination of a People.*[9] It created a firestorm of controversy that sent Kinsey advocates scrambling to defend their mentor. Reisman said that Kinsey "spent at least a decade preparing the groundwork" for the marriage course. "He planned every step of the way," she said. "There was nothing coincidental about it." It was a part of "a long carefully structured strategy."[10]

By the summer of 1939, Kinsey was spending just about every weekend in Chicago conducting interviews on sexual matters, building his log of sex histories. As variety tickled his fancy in the animal kingdom, so it did in the human sexual realm. Heterosexual sex among adults was not nearly as interesting to him as homosexuality, bisexuality, bestiality, and pedophilia. Variety, he thought, was the engine of life. As he told a campus chapter of Phi Beta Kappa in 1939, just a year into his sex history collecting, "Individual differences are the materials out of which nature achieves progress, evolution in the organic world."[11] And, "Variability," he claimed, "is universal in the living world.... [W]hat is one caterpillar's poison may be the next worm's meat."[12]

What is true in botany holds in anthropology. "Social forms, legal restrictions, and moral codes," Kinsey stated, "are of little significance when applied to particular individuals," for "what is right for one individual may be wrong for the next; and what is sin and abomination to one may be a worthwhile part of the next individual's life. The range of individual variation in any particular case is usually much greater than is generally understood." Kinsey further claimed that "continuous variation ... is the rule among men as well as among insects." From such assumptions Kinsey made the leap to moral relativism: "Our conceptions of right and wrong, normal and abnormal, are seriously challenged by the variation studies."[13] Kinsey was using Darwinian evolution to justify sexual deviance and through it subvert the moral order. His efforts would prove successful.

In 1948 he published his study of male sexuality, then five years later followed it up with a work on female sexuality.[14] The bulk of the histories came from homosexuals, prostitutes, and prisoners. In his study on male sexuality, Reisman claims "that one out of every four men interviewed ... was a prisoner. Many were convicted sex offenders" with "homosexual experiences."[15] Kinsey also recorded that he interviewed "pimps, bootleggers, thieves, hold-up men and 'ne'er-do-wells.'"[16] He was most fascinated by homosexual behavior. He called it "the most marvelous *evolutionary* series" with "a biologic basis that is so simple that it sounds impossible that everyone hasn't seen it before."[17] With sex histories drawn largely from these fringe groups, Kinsey made sweeping conclusions about the sexuality of all Americans.

For instance, he claimed that "half the women who married after World War I were not virgins on their wedding day." He also argued that biology did not support "the idea that virginity before marriage was natural."[18] He reported that extramarital sex was widespread too, occurring in about half of American marriages. This, he said, was a positive in many cases. As he wrote, "Some women who had difficulty in reaching orgasm with their husbands, find the novelty of the situation with another male stimulating to their first orgasm; and with this as a background they make better adjustments with their husbands."[19]

On the matter of homosexuality, Kinsey asserted that 37 percent of American males had a sexual experience with one man to the point of orgasm at least once in their lives, and 10 percent had sex with men exclusively for any three-year period between mid-adolescence and age fifty-five.[20] "Among males who remain unmarried until the age of thirty-five," Kinsey alleged, "almost exactly 50 percent have homosexual experiences between the beginning of adolescence and that age."[21] Of those adult men who are exclusively homosexual, Kinsey put the figure at four percent. He concluded that women had same-sex experiences too, but not nearly as many as men did. He estimated that about 13 percent of females had at least one homosexual experience leading to orgasm during their lifetime.[22]

In keeping with his commitment to evolution and variety, Kinsey claimed that many "variant types of behavior represent the basic mammalian patterns which have been so effectively suppressed by human culture that they persist and reappear only among those few individuals who ignore custom and deliberately follow their preferences in sexual techniques." To Kinsey, the suppressing agent was the Judeo-Christian ethic, and the few brave souls who willfully "ignore" it are not acting immorally but simply following their sexual "preferences." According to Kinsey, in "some instances" at least, those sexual behaviors that fall "outside the socially accepted pattern" are "the more natural" ones because they are "less affected by social restraints."[23] In other words, what Judeo-Christianity calls deviant, evolutionary science calls natural. Kinsey casts his vote on the side of science and suggests that true sexual, and therefore evolutionary, progress will come when society frees itself from religious restraints and lets nature have its way. Virtue must yield to the new morality of evolutionary variety. Science, not religion, must set the standard for human conduct.

When Kinsey's books came out, they made for great press coverage because of the fantastic nature of his claims. However, Kinsey carefully controlled this coverage. He would not allow journalists to hear his presentations at speaking events and required them to submit their articles to him before their publication. The press didn't seem to mind these restrictions. As Michael Jones observes, "The sweeping generalizations he made about sexual mores were guaranteed to stimulate reader interest." Kinsey "provided the perfect cover for the liberation from Christian mores and restraints."[24] He used the assured results of science to undermine America's moral base. The problem was that the results were not assured, nor were they the result of pure science.

Kinsey's Flaws

Kinsey's studies had three major flaws that severely skewed their conclusions. First, Kinsey interviewed mostly volunteers—people who he could persuade or who agreed on their own to tell him about their sexual lives. Most people are shy, even secretive, about the sexual aspect of their lives. They simply don't believe that that knowledge is anyone else's business. The people who tend to open up on this subject usually have what may be described as unconventional, even abnormal, sex lives. Just recall the volunteers who formed the basis of Kinsey's studies: prostitutes, homosexuals, and prison inmates. Certainly not your typical citizens, even by today's standards.

Humanist psychologist Abraham Maslow, who worked with Kinsey briefly in the 1940s, coauthored an essay with James Sakoda, in 1952 for *The Journal of Abnormal and Social Psychology.* They pointed out the problem with using volunteers: "The more timid and retiring individuals, evidently, are apt to be privately, as well as socially, conforming. They are likely, it seems, to refrain from volunteering for sex studies in which they are asked embarrassing questions." Volunteers, on the other hand, tend to report "unconventional or disapproved sexual behavior—such as masturbation, oral sexuality, petting to climax, premarital and extramarital intercourse, etc."[25]

Given such factors, the best we can conclude is that Kinsey's work tells us about the sex lives of his volunteers, most of whom were on the outskirts of American society, not in its mainstream. His studies don't tell us anything about the sex lives of Americans in general.[26]

This assumes, of course, that his volunteers told him the truth. We cannot know whether they did for sure, but it's likely many did. Kinsey himself said that many people volunteered because they wanted information about or help for their personal problems.[27] We also have good reason to believe that numerous people, in a sense, used Kinsey as a surrogate priest and his interviews as a confessional. Says Jones:

> Homosexuals in the 1940s were . . . almost exclusively "in the closet." They were part of a secret society, engaging in criminal activity. . . . Such a life causes a great deal of psychic strain. Homosexuals then, once they felt secure that their confidentiality wouldn't be breached, would find the type of interview Kinsey conducted deeply cathartic. In fact, many wrote and told him exactly this. Here one could tell one's deepest secrets, not to a confessor who would expect that person to change his life, but to a sympathetic, nonjudgmental scientist, whose refusal to entertain moral concerns would in itself be deeply soothing to a troubled conscience. It is no wonder then that once Kinsey penetrated their *monde* homosexuals would flock to Kinsey to tell their stories. Kinsey for his part reciprocated by being deeply interested in the homosexual world. . . .[28]

It is also apparent that some of Kinsey's volunteers lied to him. There was one woman interviewed by Kinsey while she was in prison who was paroled soon afterward. According to her parole officer, this female ex-con "refused to talk" to him during the first two months of her parole. "However," he recalls, "I tried to talk to her kindly. At the third month she opened up and this is what she told me about the Kinsey interviews. 'The gals had a wonderful time making up all sorts of stories to tell the people who talked to us.' " This was part of the " 'grand time had by the gals in Indiana State Prison for Women.' "[29] How many of Kinsey's interviewees may have played him for a fool, we'll never know. But that some did seems certain. Sexual deviance is not the outgrowth of good character. Perversion breeds perversion. That's not to say that immoral people never tell the truth. But we would be foolish, indeed, if we thought honesty pervades their lives.

This brings us to the second major flaw with Kinsey's studies: his reliance on a large number of prisoners. Aside from accidental or many one-time offenders, criminals tend to live by deceit and denial. There may be a code of honesty among thieves, but even they cheat one another when they think it's to their advantage. Like the woman parolee just mentioned, it stands to reason that many prisoners had fun with Kinsey, spinning tales and getting a kick out of his reaction. It's also fair to say that lawbreakers, especially career criminals, live different sorts of lives than law-abiding citizens. Deviance to many criminals is not a rarity but may even become common. This would also apply to their sex lives. Child molesters, prostitutes, pimps, rapists, and wife abusers are not the best interview candidates for discovering normal patterns of sexual behavior among the average American.

Kinsey's assistants pointed this problem out to him, but he ignored them. His critics chastised him for depending so heavily on criminals, but he rebuffed their objections and refused to deal with them in a scientifically respectable manner.[30] He rejected many of his critics out of hand as moralists and prudes, some of whom he believed betrayed him out of jealousy. Kinsey did not exhibit the signs of a disinterested scientist looking for the truth.[31] Instead, his demeanor fit better with that of the demagogue seeking to propagandize in order to subvert.

The third major problem with his conclusions is that they include a large number of homosexuals. Dannemeyer points out that "Kinsey sought out people he knew to be homosexuals, frequenting their bars, prowling their rooming houses, and even attending their club orgies, because he was so fascinated with their behavior. He gathered literally hundreds of such histories, thereby weighing his study heavily in favor of homosexuals."[32] One biographer who wrote a sympathetic account of Kinsey admits that "one of the chief complaints [of Kinsey's work] was that he compiled too large a portion of homosexual histories. There was some truth in this."[33]

Plagued with these problems, we can see that Kinsey's work was anything but scientifically objective. This is bad enough, but the situation gets worse. There's reason to believe that he used perverse and criminal ways to achieve his results. In his book on male sexual behavior, Kinsey documents incidents of orgasm in preteens, including infants. Some of this material is graphic. You may find it perverse and disgusting. I certainly did. I have chosen to mention it not to offend but to show how far Kinsey went to achieve his "scientific results." If you are soft of heart, you may want to skip the next paragraph.

Kinsey reported that an eleven-month-old child had fourteen "orgasms" over a thirty-eight-minute period. A four-year-old was "specifically manipulated" for twenty-four hours nonstop, resulting in twenty-six orgasms.[34] He also documented the "speed of pre-adolescent orgasm," noting some took up to ten seconds to achieve orgasm, while others took more than ten minutes.[35] Kinsey and his team also observed the responses of these children during these sexual manipulations and encounters. Some children exhibited "extreme tension with violent convulsion: often involving the sudden heaving and jerking of the whole body ... gasping, eyes staring or tightly closed, hands grasping, mouth distorted, sometimes with tongue protruding; whole body or parts of it spasmodically twitching ... violent jerking of the penis ... groaning, sobbing, or more violent cries, sometimes with an abundance of tears (especially among younger children)." Other children showed "extreme trembling, collapse, loss of color and sometimes fainting," while still others gave signs of pain or manifested fright as orgasm approached. Kinsey also observed that "some males suffer excruciating pain and may scream if movement is continued or the penis even touched. The males in the present group become similarly hypersensitive." They "will fight away from the [adult] partner and may make violent attempts to avoid climax."[36]

As Jones points out, the details Kinsey reports lead to just two alternatives on how he secured the data. "Either Kinsey got the material anecdotally from pedophiles ... or Kinsey and his researchers got their data from actual experiments involving child/adult sexual contact. In the first case, the Kinsey data is hearsay and scientifically bogus; in the second instance it was obtained by criminal activity. Either way it doesn't look good for sex research in general or for Kinsey and Co. in particular."[37] Jones also notes that a sexologist named John Gagnon, who worked for a decade with the Kinsey Institute for Research in Sex, Gender and Reproduction, confronted this issue in his book *Human Sexualities.* According to Gagnon, "A less neutral observer than Kinsey would have described these events as sex crimes, since they involved sexual contacts between adults and children."[38] That is an understatement. Paul Gebhard, a colleague of Kinsey, identified one of these "trained observers" in these experiments with children as "a man who had numerous sexual contacts with male and female infants and children, and being of a scientific bent, kept detailed records of each encounter."[39] To a neutral observer, this *is* child sexual abuse—pedophiliac perversity dressed up in a lab coat.

Kinsey's Sexual Orientation

After reviewing Kinsey's life history and work, Jones wonders what motivated Kinsey to delve so deeply into human sexuality, to plummet even the depths of human perversity. "Are we to believe," Jones asks, "that it was simply pure, dispassionate thirst for the truth? Or were there other personal factors at work here? Given Kinsey's bias in collecting data, given his preference for deviance, is it not possible that his project . . . was nothing more than the expression of deep-seated personal need if not compulsion?"[40] From the available evidence, the answer to this question certainly seems to be yes.

Those who knew Kinsey during his growing-up years said he never dated or showed any interest in the opposite sex. According to his biographer, Cornelia Christenson, in Kinsey's "senior year the South Orange High School yearbook placed under his picture a quotation from *Hamlet*: 'Man delights not me; no, nor woman either.' A classmate recalls that he was 'the shyest guy around girls you could think of.' "[41] Kinsey more than made up for lost time during his years of sexual studies. In fact, he had many sex acts filmed so he and his associates could view them "over and over again."[42]

One of the participants in these films wrote about his experiences with Kinsey in a pro-homosexual publication called *The Advocate*.[43] Samuel Steward said he was a university English teacher when he met Kinsey in 1949. He later became the owner of a tattoo parlor. Kinsey knew Steward experimented with sadomasochism, so he asked Steward to have sex before the camera with a male sadist. Steward agreed. The meeting began a collaborative relationship between Steward and Kinsey that lasted until Kinsey's death in 1956.

They had quite a relationship. Kinsey influenced Steward to give up his "phony 'bisexuality' " and pursue the pure homosexual lifestyle, which he did. The two men shared an avid interest in pornography, and both kept coded records of their sexual explorations. Steward writes that in "the eight years of our friendship, I logged (as a record keeper again) about 700 hours of his pleasant company, the most fascinating in the world because all of his shop talk was of sex."[44] Steward added that in Kinsey he saw "the ideal father—who was never shocked, who never criticized, who always approved, who listened and sympathized. I suppose I fell in love with him to a degree, even though he was a grandfather."

Steward denies that there was any "physical contact" between him and Kinsey, except for handshakes. But he says he told Kinsey that he was often asked if Kinsey was "queer." Kinsey asked him how he answered, and Steward told him: " 'Well,' I said slowly, 'I always say, Yes he is—but not in the same way we are. He is a *voyeur* and an *auditeur*. He likes to look and listen.' " Kinsey laughed, but a moment later I caught him observing me thoughtfully. I may have hit closer to the truth than I realized."[45]

Whether Kinsey was gay or not, we may never know. The Kinsey Institute, which houses his records, has so far refused to let anyone have free access to the material, even though the institute receives federal money each year to further its research. The institute has stated emphatically that it will never open all these records to scholars or the government, much less to the general public. One wonders what they have to hide.[46]

Kinsey's Legacy

Kinsey's perverse infatuations have greatly aided the radicalization of sexual morality in America. Kinsey strove to blur the lines of sexual identity and wrap sexual deviance in the cloak of evolutionary progress. For him, anything goes in human sexual expression, including premarital and extramarital sex, bisexual and strictly homosexual sex, sex between adults and children, and sex between humans and animals. While heterosexuality and monogamy are okay, they are socially restrictive of the wider, more pleasurable, and more natural expressions of human sexuality. One of Kinsey's associates even referred to heterosexual intercourse as an "addiction," as if it were a condition needing a cure rather than the truly normal and natural sexual expression between human beings.[47] These attitudes have permeated the warp and woof of contemporary America. Here are just a few examples to ponder.

Legitimizing Pornography

One of the most influential and visible figures in the sexual revolution has been Hugh Hefner. He has been almost omnipresent in his lobbying for the end of moral restraints on sex, and he openly defied America's Judeo-Christian sexual ethic by living a hedonistic lifestyle. He established two ventures that have become acceptable, even enviable, institutions in America: his slick, four-color magazine *Playboy* and his exclusive Playboy clubs. Particularly for American males, he gave new meaning to the words *centerfold* and *bunny*. He has even joined the elite ranks of subjects highlighted on A & E's award-winning television program *Biography*. When it came to providing justification for creating *Playboy* magazine, Hefner cited Kinsey's research. Kinsey became Hefner's rationale for producing and marketing pornography.

Compared to the levels of degradation available for one's viewing pleasure in the pornography industry today, *Playboy* is mere child's play. People can purchase smut in just about any kind of medium imaginable. They can call it up on the Internet through their computers or sit in their homes in front of their televisions and access it through cable. Showtime, Home Box Office, and Cinemax are three of the largest mainstream purveyors of "soft" pornography on cable today. You can go down to your local bookstore or mini-mart and get *Playboy*, *Playgirl*, *Penthouse*, *Forum*, and several other "soft porn" magazines. Many local video stores have an "adult" movie section where you can rent anything from R-rated films with strong sexual themes to XXX-rated movies showing one graphic sexual encounter after another with every kind of arrangement and behavior degeneracy can create.

Sexual deviance has become a big money-maker. The Kinsey-Hefner team have been quite successful.

Deviance Goes to School

The promotion of immorality as normality has taken an educational turn as well. Many sex education programs and materials draw on Kinsey's research and conclusions to teach moral subversion. Consider, for example, a program called *About Your Sexuality*. It was developed by Deryck Calderwood, who died in 1986 of either AIDS or cancer, depending on whom you talk to.[48] Calderwood was a disciple of Kinsey and the head of a graduate program in sexuality at New York University. Like Kinsey, he believed that "no type of sexual behavior is abnormal or pathological."[49] Anything goes. To disseminate his views, he created a sex education curriculum that one of his former students calls "a gay studies program for heterosexuals."[50]

In *About Your Sexuality*, the full range of human sexual behavior is presented as normal. Students also get to see on video what the written material and audio cassettes talk about. In the written portions of the course, Calderwood encourages students to get involved in supporting homosexual rights. A "sexual minorities" section discusses the social injustices homosexuals and bisexuals face and includes a "Homosexual Bill of Rights."[51] On one of the audio cassettes, students get to hear three bisexuals tell about the pleasures of having intercourse with people of both sexes, and they hear from four homosexuals (one male and three females) who share their sex lives in positive terms. The videocassette brings the course to life through a series of full-color still shots minus sound. With the help of Calderwood's university students, a wide variety of sexual experiences are clearly and graphically depicted, including vaginal, anal, and oral intercourse, oral-anal sex acts, and the use of artificial objects such as dildos. Course-viewers can see male-with-male, female-with-female, and male-with-female couples performing these activities.

This sex education program is not designed for adults or collegians, not even for high school students. It is geared for seventh and eighth graders, kids ages twelve to fourteen. It has even been used with fifth graders—ten- to eleven-year-olds.[52]

Has it come to a school near you? If it has, you may never know. While Calderwood stresses that parents should give their permission for their children to go through his program, he warns the program's teachers to keep a tight lid on the course's details. His words are clear about this: "*Caution:* Participants should not be given extra copies . . . to show to their parents or friends. Many of the materials of this program, shown to people outside the context of the program itself, can evoke misunderstanding and difficulty."[53] No kidding. Calderwood wants no interference from parents in accomplishing the goals of the course, which are to help children "explore the meaning and significance of lovemaking to the human being," to "provide accurate information to young people about heterosexual, bisexual, and homosexual lovemaking," and to "make clear that sexual relationships with the same sex during youth are normal and do not necessarily indicate one's future sexual orientation as an adult."[54]

I wish I could say this kind of program is rare in America's public schools, but it would not be true. A similar program produced by the National Center for Health Education in New York City is used in forty-five states and eight thousand schools. Comparable to *About Your Sexuality*, this sex-ed program promotes deviance—the politically correct term is *diversity*, a synonym for Kinsey's understanding of variety. The course says that "most people fall somewhere on a continuum between . . . homosexual and heterosexual orientation."[55] Just as many other sex-ed programs do, this one blurs the sexual lines of distinction and, in so doing, subverts morality in the name of science, education, and tolerance.

SIECUS—Sex Information and Education Council of the United States—also produces a sex education program used in many schools nationwide. Dr. Mary Calderone, co-founder of SIECUS and a past president of the organization, told students at a New Jersey prep school her enlightened understanding of sex. "What is sex for? It's for fun, that I know, for wonderful sensations. . . . Sex is not something you turn off like a faucet. If you do, it's unhealthy. We need new values to establish when and how we should have sexual experiences. You are moving beyond your parents. Not just economically or educationally, but sexually as well."[56] In Calderone's world, the only virtue is to let your sexuality express itself in any way that brings you pleasure; anything else is "unhealthy." Such old-fashioned and repressive notions as self-control, heterosexuality only, and sex within marriage alone must be left behind. Evolution wants to move us forward and experience sex in all its entertainment value. We should not let the old values hold us back any longer.

A student doesn't have to attend a class to receive the message that sexual diversity is in and sexual morality is out. In Portland, Oregon, high school counselors place magnets outside their offices that display pink triangles—a symbol used by homosexuals and bisexuals to identify their "orientation." Some of these magnets have messages on them like "Bigotry-Free Oregon" and "Equity for All." The magnets are supposed to indicate that these counselors are "safe" people with whom students can talk about their sexuality without facing any sense of condemnation.[57]

Many school counselors nationwide use materials provided by Project 10, an organization begun by Virginia Uribe, a lesbian high school science teacher in Los Angeles. The group takes its name from the 1948 Kinsey study that claimed 10 percent of American males had homosexual sex exclusively over any given three-year period. More recent scientific studies and surveys put this figure much lower, between one and four percent.[58] But that hasn't stopped homosexuals such as Uribe from reciting the fallacious Kinsey figure as beyond dispute.

From Project 10, counselors receive materials that present homosexuality as an alternative lifestyle. Many educators use these materials in their classes. One of these resources, *How to Come Out to Your Parents,* advises students not to discuss their sexual orientation with their parents until they are secure in their lifestyle. "Parents," the book says, "are part of a guilty society, a homophobic society," therefore one should not trust them until it's too late for them to do anything about one's sexual choice. Another Project 10 book—*One Project in 10: Testimony of Gay and Lesbian Youth*—contains "graphic descriptions of unnatural sexual behavior. A pornographic chapter describes how a twelve-year-old girl is seduced by her teacher into a three-year relationship. Another chapter tells how young people were 'brought out' of their oppressive heterosexuality into the 'blissful' gay lifestyle."[59]

In the Seattle area, "high schools invite gay and lesbian speakers to address school assemblies during homecoming week as a part of 'National Coming Out Day.' . . . Each speaker is accompanied at these assemblies by 'other alumni of the same high school, especially politicians, clergy, teachers, law enforcement personnel and others in classic role-model positions.' "[60]

A principal at an elementary school in New Hampshire invited a homosexual men's chorus to give a concert to the kids. The choral members "changed the words of familiar children's songs to sing about boys loving boys and girls loving girls ('Mister Sandman, bring me a dream/ Make him the cutest that I've ever seen'). During their concert they asked the children to raise their hands if they have two mommies or two daddies living with them." When parents heard about the concert after the fact, they confronted the principal, but she wrote them off, saying that the concert was "part of a multicultural emphasis at the school."[61]

The National Education Association passed a proposal to support the celebration of a Lesbian and Gay History Month in the public schools.

The NEA wants to raise the "awareness" and increase the "sensitivity of staff, students, parents and the community to sexual orientation in society."[62] While the proposal has encountered a good deal of flak from teachers and administrators nationwide, it shows how respectable deviance has become in America's leading educational organization and how far the NEA will go to promote it. In fact, the NEA has been at the forefront of "training teachers on how to offer 'equal opportunities' to gay and lesbian students."[63]

In San Francisco, lesbian couples read to kindergartners politically correct children's books supporting sexual diversity, and they share their experiences as a "family" with students. One of the books read is *Gloria Goes to Gay Pride*, which tells children, "Some women love women, some men love men, some women and men love each other. That's why we march in the parade, so everyone can have a choice."[64] In the summer of 1992, San Francisco adopted a curriculum that "requires formal lessons about same-sex families and homosexuality from seventh grade on and allows—but does not require—elementary-school teachers to talk about homosexuality."[65]

Two other children's books turning up in school classrooms and libraries across the country are *Heather Has Two Mommies* and *Daddy's Roommate*. The first book tells about a lesbian couple who have a child through artificial insemination.[66] The second one depicts a boy whose parents have divorced. He visits his father and his father's new male roommate, who is obviously the father's lover. In this book the youngster declares, "Being gay is just one more kind of love."[67]

In Boston, Massachusetts, some high schools give official recognition to students from their campuses who march in the annual Boston Gay Pride parade. Many schools have gay assemblies where they extol the alleged virtues of homosexuality. Among students it's becoming chic to tell others that you're bisexual or homosexual. It's even less rare to see same-sex couples holding hands and making out at school or attending school dances together.[68]

If you live in New York City and you are not a heterosexual-only teenager, you may be able to attend Harvey Milk High School, the brainchild of the Hetrick-Martin Institute that provides "support and services" for homosexual and bisexual youth. The high school is fully accredited, and the Hetrick-Martin Institute runs it "under the auspices of the school board's Alternative High Schools and programs division." The school provides "a safe and happy environment" for "bisexual, gay, and lesbian kids who couldn't function in traditional schools."[69] This puts a new twist on specialized education.

Neutering the Law

With regard to civil law, former congressman William Dannemeyer points to Kinsey and the social scientists he spawned as the philosophical forces largely responsible for "sweeping changes" in America's "sex laws."[70] Dannemeyer describes what happened:

> Essentially they argued as follows: everyone is committing adultery, and most men are having homosexual adventures, so how can we possibly outlaw this conduct? You can't have a law that no one obeys. It makes a mockery of law itself. Therefore, anyone prosecuted for sex acts is doing no more than what everyone else is doing. The only difference is, the others aren't getting caught.
>
> Eventually lobbyists for the liberalized sex laws began using this argument in quiet conversations with state legislators around the country, pointing to the widespread acceptance of Kinsey as evidence in courts at every level. The result: most states have modified their criminal codes to eliminate such acts as fornication, adultery, and sodomy, while leaving rape and child molestation on the books.[71]

For the states, counties, and cities who want to keep their sodomy laws intact, they have often had to go to court to do so. Homosexual legal advocacy groups have challenged sodomy laws throughout the country.

In 1986 they encountered what appeared to be a resounding defeat at the U.S. Supreme Court level. In the case of *Bowers v. Hardwick*, the Court upheld by a five to four margin a Georgian statute that made all forms of sodomy a criminal offense.[72] Writing the majority opinion, Justice Byron White said that "the respondent would have us announce . . . a fundamental right to engage in homosexual sodomy. This we are quite unwilling to do." The Court rejected the respondent's claim that "the Federal Constitution confers a fundamental right upon homosexuals to engage in sodomy and hence invalidates the laws of the many States that still make such conduct illegal and have done so for a very long time." Justice White also noted that the prohibitions against sodomy have "ancient roots." "Sodomy," he wrote, "was a criminal offense [in] common law and was forbidden by the laws of the original thirteen States when they ratified the Bill of Rights. . . . In fact, until 1961, all fifty States outlawed sodomy, and today, twenty-four States and the District of Columbia continue to provide criminal penalties for sodomy performed in private and between consenting adults. . . . Against this background, to claim that a right to engage in such conduct is 'deeply rooted in this Nation's history and tradition' or 'implicit in the concept of ordered liberty' is, at best, facetious."[73]

The Court's majority realized the implications of striking down sodomy laws as unconstitutional based on the idea that any private, "voluntary sexual conduct between consenting adults" should be legal. Such reasoning would make it impossible, except by an arbitrary judicial decision, to prosecute "adultery, incest, and other sexual crimes" since "they are committed in the home" as well. "We are unwilling to start down that road," White remarked.[74]

In his concurring opinion, Chief Justice Warren Burger echoed Justice White's contention that "proscriptions against sodomy" go way back. Stated Burger:

> Decisions of individuals relating to homosexual conduct have been subject to state intervention throughout the history of Western civilization. Condemnation of those practices is firmly rooted in Judeo-Christian moral and ethical standards. Homosexual sodomy was a capital crime under Roman law.... During the English Reformation when powers of the ecclesiastical courts were transferred to the King's Courts, the first English statute criminalizing sodomy was passed.... Blackstone described "the infamous crime against nature" as an offense of "deeper malignity" than rape, a heinous act "the very mention of which is a disgrace to human nature," and "a crime not fit to be named." ... The common law of England, including its prohibition of sodomy, became the received law of Georgia and the other Colonies.... To hold that the act of homosexual sodomy is somehow protected as a fundamental right would be to cast aside millennia of moral teaching.[75]

Unfortunately, in 1996, the U.S. Supreme Court may have undermined its *Bowers v. Hardwick* decision. (I will discuss the *Romer v. Evans* case in chapter 13.) For now, however, laws against sodomy are still legally defensible, although they are quickly becoming extinct.

Is Pedophilia Next?

If Kinsey and his fellow sexologists are right, not only must laws against sodomy be repealed, but laws against rape and child molestation will have to go too. Remember, variety—which is really just a synonym for deviance—is the driving force of life. Progress is wrapped up in what many people think is perversity. So if we are going to evolve higher, we must descend lower.

Feminism has made it politically incorrect to challenge existing rape laws. If anything, feminists are working to expand the definition of rape so it includes many acts not formerly covered. The matter of pedophilia, however, is a different story.

The move to normalize pedophilia is growing at an alarming rate.

Wardell Pomeroy, a former associate of Kinsey's and a founding board member of SIECUS, has publicly stated that incest "can sometimes be beneficial" to children.[76] "People seem to think," he says, "that any contact between children and adults . . . has a bad effect on the child. I say that this can be a loving and thoughtful, responsible sexual activity."[77] I would venture to guess that victims of incest might have a different opinion.

Listen to Larry Constantine, a family therapist at Tufts University who is also on the board of consultants for *Penthouse* and *Forum* magazines: "Children really are a disenfranchised minority. They should have the right to express themselves sexually which means that they may or may not have contact with people older than themselves."[78]

Dr. John Money is professor emeritus of medical psychology and pediatrics at Johns Hopkins University and an influential voice in sex research. In an interview with *Paidika*, a magazine that advocates civil rights for pedophiles, Dr. Money said: "[I]f I were to see the case of a boy aged ten or eleven who's intensely erotically attracted toward a man in his twenties or thirties, if the relationship is totally mutual, and the bonding is genuinely totally mutual, then I would not call it pathological in any way."[79] Money believes that pedophilia is "an orientation which cannot be changed or permanently suppressed."[80]

He also thinks that pedophilia advocates should attack age-of-consent laws. Taking his cue from the strategy of homosexual activists, Money states: "When the gay rights activists began being politically active, there wasn't a sufficient body of scientific information for them to base their gay rights activism on. So, you don't have to have a basic body of scientific information in order to decide to work actively for a particular ideology. As long as you're prepared to be put in jail. Isn't that how social change has always taken place, really?"[81]

The editors of *Paidika* state that the "starting point" of the magazine is "our consciousness of ourselves as paedophiles." They see the publication as helping fellow "paedophiles" to seek "a greater understanding of their own identity." The editors also want *Paidika* to convey information to "members of the academic community" who are "open to objective investigation of the phenomenon" of pedophilia. The editors claim that they "intend to demonstrate that paedophilia has been, and remains, a legitimate and productive part of the totality of human experience."[82]

Imagine a society in which sodomites and pedophiles have the civil right to express their sexuality freely and with anyone they claim gave his or her consent. No age barriers, no moral prohibitions, just the legal right and scientific respectability to be perverse—oops, I should have said sexually diverse. Imagine that their chosen partner is someone you love and cherish. Is this the culture we want? If we don't wake up and effectively fight back, it may very well be the culture we get—and deserve.

Chapter 10

I Am Woman, Hear Me Roar

The *Old* Absolute		The *New* Absolute	
(7)	Women should be protected and nurtured but not granted social equality.	(7a)	Women are oppressed by men and must liberate themselves by controlling their own bodies and therefore their destinies.

Have you ever done something nice for someone, only to have that person snub you for it? That has happened to all of us several times. For me, it marked one of my earliest encounters with feminism.

It was the mid 1970s, and I was a philosophy student at the local university. I was opening one of the front doors to the school's library to go inside when I noticed a female student walking just behind me. So, out of a sense of respect and good manners, I held the door open so she could enter first. (I usually did the same for men too.) As the student walked by me, she turned her head and spit in my face, then hurled a string of profanities, all modifying the kindest words she spoke to me, "you white chauvinist pig." She then continued into the library without looking back.

I was stunned. I had never seen this student before, and to my knowledge she didn't know me either. Still, she had already judged me as a despicable being worthy only of her venom. Her ideology saw men as evil, particularly white men. Since I matched that description, I became her target.

In an English literature class, I had a similar experience. We were discussing a novel. I believe it was *Moby Dick.* I remember going to the class prepared to explore story line, literary style, plot development, and the like. However, the professor had a different agenda. She began talking about the politics of male-female relationships. To her, all encounters between men and women were about power. Men were always working to subjugate women, and women unknowingly let them. Women were deceived by men and the social structures men had erected. Men wanted women barefoot and in the kitchen. The last thing they wanted was to have an educated woman competing against them in the academy or the marketplace. Men were therefore evil oppressors. Women needed to realize this and work toward their liberation. They would find their freedom by taking full control of their bodies and completely ridding themselves of any dependence upon men. In fact, she said, men were only good for sex, and even then women enjoying sex with other women was still a far better experience.

During the professor's diatribe, she occasionally asked leading questions of the largely female class. "How have you been put down by a man?" "When was the last time a man treated you as just a sex object?" "*Chick, baby, honey, sweetie-pie*—what other words have been applied to you that define you as an animal, food, or weakling?"

Since none of the questions were directed at any of the male students, we all sat quietly, listening to the male-bashing and watching the female students get more and more whipped up.

Fed up, I raised my hand and held it high in the air, determined to have the professor call on me. She didn't. She simply ignored me. The class lecture and intermittent discussion continued with my hand never lowering.

So, I did what I had never done before: I stood up next to my desk with my hand still held high. I felt like a living Statue of Liberty, even a bit foolish. But I was determined not to let all the comments pass by without a challenge.

The professor was still unmoved. She kept lecturing and posing questions as if I weren't there.

Finally, still standing, I interrupted her. "Excuse me . . . excuse me."

The professor stopped talking and just glared at me.

I waited a few moments for her to address me, but she didn't, so I pressed on. "You have spent almost all of this class period telling us a lot about your political beliefs but nothing about the assigned reading."

Her face was getting red.

"You have also addressed the class as if it were all female, which it isn't. About a quarter of this class is male, and yet you have systematically ignored us."

I saw her hands clench and lips tighten. I knew she was getting really mad, but I wasn't about to stop yet.

"I just want to know one thing: if this is a class on classic English literature, which the course description said it was, then I want to know when we are going to discuss literature rather than your politics. If it's a class on politics, then I want to drop the course. I've had a political science class already, and it was much fairer and open-minded than your class has been. If I want a class on political philosophy, I'd rather go to the political science department where all positions and genders are heard."

There, I had said my piece. Now I just stared back at her.

"Are you finished?" she managed to squeeze out of her almost twitching body.

I didn't answer. I simply sat down as I kept eye contact.

"Mr. Watkins."

I didn't know she knew my name.

"You have just demonstrated the point of my lecture. You have done your best to intimidate me, but I will not be intimidated."

My purpose had not been to bully her, just to be treated as a participating member of the class. Out of the corner of my eye, though, I noticed some female students nodding their heads in agreement with her.

"You are white male scum."

I wondered if the female student who had spit on me had taken one of this woman's courses.

"As far as I'm concerned, you're just taking up valuable space in my class. You are welcome to leave anytime you want."

Several female students chimed in, cussing at me and the other male students and telling us to leave. Some other female students looked embarrassed. The males started growing fidgety. I returned to making eye-contact with the professor. I said nothing. I just stared straight ahead, peering into the professor's eyes. I was angry, but I tried not to show it. I wanted to ride out the lynch mob without breaking my composure.

Then the buzzer sounded, indicating the end of the class period.

As I pulled my books together to leave, some female students passed by me and slipped in a few more verbal jabs. The male students quickly left without speaking a word to anyone. When I finally walked by the professor on my way out of the room, she once again acted as if I did not exist. *This isn't an English class,* I thought, *it's a feminist inquisition.*

Feminist Waves

All my experiences with feminists have not been this negative. I had some other feminist professors who encouraged intellectual curiosity and exploration and who respected men who respected them. I have also read feminist novelists, philosophers, ethicists, historians, sociologists, journalists, and theologians who challenged my thinking and sensitized my behavior. I have an abiding respect for the courage, tenacity, and vision of the feminist activists of the nineteenth and early twentieth centuries who fought so hard for the abolition of slavery, the right to vote, improvements in the conditions of the working class, child labor laws, opening doors to more educational opportunities for women, and many other social issues most of us take for granted. These were the accomplishments of the First Wave feminists, and, for the most part, I applaud the outcome of their efforts.

These feminists were challenging an absolute that had been informed and shaped by the Judeo-Christian worldview the pilgrims brought with them to North America. Then the accepted absolute was: *Women should be protected and nurtured but not granted social equality.* Women were treated as the "weaker" sex, not normally in terms of character, intellect, or moral stamina, but in terms of sheer physical strength.[1] Men were regarded as physically stronger and therefore better able to handle the rigors of the new land, which was beautiful and promising but also terribly hostile. Men were also held legally responsible for the welfare of their wives and children. Hence family property was in the name of men, not women, and the men were treated as the family's and society's primary authority figures.

There was no male chauvinism meant in this arrangement. Men needed women as much as women needed men. Everyone had to help each other just to survive. Women played a critical role in all this, assisting their husbands in such family trades as "butchering, smithing, upholstering, printing, [and] farming." Women also developed other usually home-based trades of their own, including "spinning, weaving, and sewing of apparel; furniture-making; gardening, preserving, and cooking of foodstuffs; manufacturing of soap, buttons, candles, and even herbal medicines."[2] There were no factories or corporate offices to go to. The home was the center of industry and trade well into the 1900s.

Throughout most of the last two hundred years, families worked together in a family business. "They operated stores, offices, or shops in their homes, reserving living quarters for the upstairs or rear part of the house."[3] Even when the industrial revolution began in 1780, whole families would leave home to work together in the factories. It wasn't Dad going off to the jobsite while Mom and the kids stayed home. Indeed, even their homes were built around the jobsite.

Those families who chose to stay out of the new factories frequently produced resources out of their homes for the factories. This practice of outworking—similar to what we today call outsourcing—lasted until 1938. It kept families together as they worked together to provide for their economic needs. Ironically, it was well-intentioned male and female activists who brought home-based outworking to an end. They claimed that the conditions were unsanitary, wages low, and hours long. They also asserted that outworking "competed with and undercut male wages in factories and caused a mother to 'exploit her own children and to neglect her home and her children.' " These activists, many of whom were First Wave feminists, finally brought home-based outworking to an end and with it "the opportunity for mothers to maintain close contact with their children while working for pay."[4]

In short, the old absolute was not intended to denigrate women, though sometimes that happened in its application. Nor was it designed to subjugate women or disadvantage them, though that sometimes happened too. It did, however, recognize the need for hierarchy at every level of society in order to achieve and maintain social harmony, order, and progress. However inadequately and unfairly it tried to fulfill that vision, I believe the vision itself was a good one.

Struggling largely with some of the misconceived applications of this regulating absolute, the First Wave feminists united to demand what society denied them. The changes for which they fought included the right to vote, to "negotiate their own contracts, run their own businesses, keep their own earnings," attend more institutions of higher learning, receive equal pay for equal work, and have the opportunity to succeed in careers men had dominated.[5] I certainly believe these were all just causes.

With the Second Wave of feminism, which erupted in the 1950s and 1960s, feminists called for a new absolute: *Women are oppressed by men and must liberate themselves by controlling ther own bodies and therefore their destinies.* This is the position championed by Betty Friedan, Gloria Steinem, Marilyn French, Andrea Dworkin, and Catherine MacKinnon. They represent what many now call gender feminism. Like their predecessors, Second Wavers have been socially engaged, largely striving for the government to fulfill the needs families once met for themselves. Their agenda has been, for the most part, a socially and politically liberal one.

Though Second Wave feminists have helped sensitize men to some of the needs and concerns of women, much of their movement is both disturbing and destructive. They generally show a bitter antagonism toward anything male and a callous disregard for the preborn. Their movement deifies women, distorts America's religious heritage, and undermines and even dismisses the value of marriage and the family. Overall they have displayed a spirit of utopian militancy, myopic and socially and personally destructive in vision and implementation. Journalist and author Sally Quinn sees Second Wave feminism as "anti-male, anti-child, anti-family, and anti-feminine."[6] It also tends to be anti-Christian, immoral, and frequently outright irrational.

Since the mid-1980s, some feminist voices have arisen challenging the more extreme positions of the Second Wave feminists. Some of these feminist critics are Second Wavers with second thoughts. Betty Friedan, the godmother of Second Wave feminism, is among them. Other new voices are more moderate still, often calling themselves equity feminists or the new Victorians. In this regard I'm thinking of such notables as Christina Sommers, Elizabeth Fox-Genovese, and Frederica Mathewes-Green. As one of its most articulate spokespersons, Sommers says that equity feminists are really akin to the First Wave feminists. Like them, the equity feminists have as their "main goal" what most American women want—"fair treatment, without discrimination." They do not subscribe to the male dominance and female victimization themes of the gender feminists (the sort I had some run-ins with while a university student). The more moderate feminists are instead looking to fully realize what they see as the goal of the First Wave feminists. According to Sommers, this is a goal that "by any reasonable measure" has already "turned out to be a great American success story."[7] For the most part, I must agree.

I dare not predict who will win the growing ideological tug-of-war among these contemporary feminists. However, as the situation now stands, most of the political clout and money are in the hands of the more radical Second Wavers. They have the ear of Congress, the president, the judiciary, and the academy. Because of this, the rest of this chapter will concentrate on Second Wave feminism and the new absolute they champion.

From the Womb to the World

Regardless of one's feminist colors, almost all feminists embrace reproductive freedom as the fundamental tenet of feminist ideology. That is, women must have complete control over their bodies without any interference from men, the state, or other women. Only when women control their reproductive processes will they control their destinies and achieve their liberation. This, of course, was Margaret Sanger's message.

Sanger did more than any other feminist to get women to view themselves and the world through their womb. As we saw in chapter 5, Sanger made the application quite clear and she made it often. Like a mantra, her panacea-like view of personal and social liberation through reproductive freedom has been repeated by feminists throughout the twentieth century. If women can just control the womb, they will liberate themselves from male dominance as well as cure a wide range of social ills. And the key to controlling the womb is contraception and, as a backup, abortion. Hence the movement's clarion call for reproductive rights for women worldwide.

Aborting Women Speak Out

When you look at the most common reasons why women abort their babies, however, they are nothing as grandiose as resolving society's ills or liberating humanity. Women make the abortion decision for a wide range of reasons. The reason could be as serious as the unborn child posing a life-threatening situation for the mother or as trivial as the child being the wrong sex. If you listen long enough to the rhetoric used by today's proabortion activists, you might begin to believe that most abortions occur because either the life of the mother or child is threatened, or the mother is the victim of rape or incest. These reasons are related to individual physical preservation or psychological trauma, not the typical Sangerian liberation themes of societal transformation. The fact is, several studies on this issue contradict the proabortion reproductive freedom message in virtually all its forms.

The Studies

According to the Abortion Case Study Project, the top five reasons women gave for electing to terminate their pregnancies were:

- Their husband or partner wanted the pregnancy ended (11.8 percent).
- They were confused, misinformed, or made the decision with inadequate information (11.7 percent).
- Their parents wanted them to abort (8.7 percent).
- They felt they lacked alternatives to abortion (8.7 percent).
- They felt too immature or too young to have a child (8 percent).

Less than two percent of respondents cited their health or their child's as the reason for choosing abortion, and less than one percent claimed they were victims of rape or incest.[8] No one mentioned saving the world or solving any social problems, nor did they cite their desire to control their reproductive functions. Instead, it appears that many women wanted to free themselves from outside pressure or the responsibility of raising a child. They didn't see themselves as empowered but as victims.

A post-abortion organization known as Open Arms has been gathering information since 1986 from women who made the abortion choice. Their surveys indicate that 82 percent cited social reasons for their choice, eight percent gave economic reasons, and five percent said health was the primary factor. The other three categories—life, rape, and incest—were each selected by one percent or less of those women surveyed.[9] Because the categories are so broad, it's hard to know what they include or exclude. One thing is certain, however: hardly any of the women faced a life-threatening pregnancy or claimed they had become pregnant against their will.

In the summer of 1988, the Alan Guttmacher Institute conducted a study to find out why women have abortions. Their findings are especially noteworthy since the institute is associated with Planned Parenthood, the largest abortion provider in America. According to the Guttmacher study, 21 percent of women gave two reasons as the most important decision-making factors: inadequate funds to care for a child, and a belief that they were unready for the responsibility a child brings. The other most important reasons cited were concern about how having a baby might change their lives (16 percent), and problems with relationships or a desire to avoid single parenthood (12 percent). Among the reasons women cited least were rape and incest (one percent) and health problems with them or their unborn child (three percent).[10] No world liberation rationales or eugenics messages here—just self-centeredness and perhaps feelings of victimization.

Feminist Frederica Mathewes-Green directed a project called "Real Choices." It was a research project conducted by the National Women's Coalition for Life, which, as of 1994, serves as an umbrella for fourteen groups and has a combined membership of more than 1.3 million people. The project had several dimensions to it, one of which was to compile as much as possible an exhaustive list of reasons women gave for choosing abortion. In her book *Real Choices*, Mathewes-Green reports the study's findings. The five most common reasons for abortion were:

1. Adoption appears too difficult (practically or emotionally).
2. Husband or partner [was] absent, undependable, or insufficiently supportive.
3. Woman says she can't afford [the] baby now.
4. Child-rearing will interfere with school or job situation.

5. Pregnancy will interfere with school or job situation.

Once again, the reasons occurring practically at the bottom of the list were health problems of the mother or unborn baby, and rape or incest.[11] Most of the reasons were selfish and some conveyed a sense of disempowerment.

In summary, then, the most common reasons for aborting a child generally revolve around personal relationships, personal convenience, and personal finances. Health, rape, and incest are almost nonexistent as decision-making factors. Overpopulation, social-conscience concerns, and issues of reproductive freedom never made the list. In other words, the vast majority of women who abort do so in an attempt to solve non-life-threatening problems. They are hoping to alleviate strains—real or perceived—on their personal finances, relationships, or life plans.

The Voices

Many women are quite frank about the self-interest that motivated their abortion decision:

- "There was no question about this pregnancy. I really don't want the hassle. I don't want to be bothered with a baby, and that's the cold, hard truth. I'm simply not interested in bringing one up. Four years ago, yes, but not now. I don't even like babies. Keep them away from me. They are a drag."[12]
- "I was going to school at night, and I have a garden, and I keep busy, and I just didn't want any more children. . . . We like to do outdoor things and this is impossible with a baby—canoeing and camping and things like that. So I just feel that it's better for me, and it's better for the children, and better for my husband."[13]
- "I couldn't have that baby. That baby would ruin my whole life. It would ruin my mother and father; it would ruin me; it would ruin everybody who had ever known me and loved me."[14]
- "I had three abortions in five years. . . . I have to say that I had my abortions for convenience. The reasons were selfish."[15]
- "To continue the pregnancy I would have had to be honest about who I was, and I hadn't hit rock bottom yet. I guess the bottom line was lifestyle—I wasn't ready to give up having *fun*."[16]

Guilt racks women who choose abortion, regardless of the justification they attach to their decision. Testimonial after testimonial confirms this. Sometimes the guilt leads to self-destructive behavior and alienation in what used to be close relationships. Many women try to assuage their guilt by casting blame on other people. At times women see the abortion itself as their punishment and hope having it will relieve their guilt. Here are just a few of the countless voices that illustrate this point:

- "[Following the abortion] my immediate response was relief—but that soon passed away and all that I have ever felt since is guilt. I knew that abortion is killing and I would give anything to have the child now."[17]
- "I didn't allow myself to feel the pain about all this [i.e., my abortion] until a couple of years ago. I didn't think I had the right to grieve because, after all, the abortion was my choice. But I spent those fifteen years trying to pay myself back, with drugs, alcohol, you name it."[18]
- "I chose to abort my baby in January of 1980. I was seventeen years old. The tremendous guilt and sense of loss that I have felt since then have, at times, been insurmountable. I tried, for nearly five years, to justify my decision to abort. 'I was too young,' 'I was going to college in the fall,' 'Where would I be now if I had a baby,' etc. I came up with all the *really good* excuses—but none of them eased the turmoil that was inside me."[19]
- "Those people at Planned Parenthood are so cold. . . . They deny that you have feelings, guilt about what you're doing to your baby. It's like you hit a child with your car and you feel devastated, but they're trying to pass it off, telling you you weren't responsible."[20]
- "At work I'd sit and cry [after my abortion]. I just couldn't handle routine things anymore. . . . I planned my death. I was going to drive to my peaceful cemetery, swallow a bottle of sleeping pills and cut my wrists. I wanted to make sure I'd die."[21]

From Guilt to Feminism

A revealing fact emerges from the stories many aborting women tell. While feminist ideology did not motivate them before their abortion, it frequently became a driving force in their post-abortion life. For example, in the "Real Choices" study, several women indicated that they became politically active in women's issues *after* their abortions. Their newfound feminist activism was an effort to resolve the personal guilt they felt for aborting their children.

During the discussion time of a post-abortion support group in Washington, D.C., a woman named Kelly spoke out: "The first two years after my abortion, I was probably the strongest pro-choice supporter you could find. It was my way of making sure that what I had done was right. I often wonder about some of the louder pro-choice voices out there, because I remember feeling like that. You have to keep telling everybody that you did the right thing."

In response to Kelly's confession, a woman named Elizabeth chimed in, echoing similar sentiments: "I was a big contributor to Planned Parenthood and NARAL [National Abortion Rights Action League]. . . . It was like: this must be the right position, because I have to be okay; if not . . . I'd have to look at what I've done."[22]

In a similar post-abortion support group in Phoenix, Arizona, another woman confessed: "Talk about getting angry after abortion—by the time I had my fourth one I was like, 'okay, now I'm *really* angry.' I was out to really hurt men, and I got very involved with feminist issues, feminist spirituality. It was funny how we said God had to be a she, but never said the Devil was a she!"[23]

The evidence suggests that in the lives of many women, their feminism is more closely related to resolving post-abortion guilt than justifying their original decision to abort. Rather than admit making a tragic mistake they defend the right for all women to feel as badly as they do. It is really the struggle to find a political substitute for personal penitence.

Many women (just like many men) are adept, however, at transferring their guilt to others, particularly to men. Even a Planned Parenthood counselor, Martha Mueller, made this observation after listening to untold numbers of women. Linda Francke, who also had an abortion, summarized Mueller's thoughts:

> When abortion was illegal, there was a common enemy in the form of the law. Now that abortion is primarily a matter of choice, the decision rests squarely on the shoulders of the woman, a decision many would rather not take the responsibility for. Some blame their husbands or boyfriends for "forcing" them to have the abortion. Others point the finger at their parents, who have insisted on the abortion or who, the patients maintain, would be furious if they found out their daughter was pregnant. Often it's the doctor who takes the blame for the abortion. "He did it to me" is a phrase heard often in clinic or hospital corridors when the doctor walks by. "That's just moving the responsibility," says Mueller. "Women are very good at that."[24]

I would be remiss if I did not also confirm that men are often accomplices in the abortion decision. As the surveys above indicate, many women feel pressure from fathers, husbands, and boyfriends to end their pregnancies.

Compounding this is the fact that studies show that anywhere from 50 to 70 percent of male-female relationships dissolve after an abortion, usually within thirty days.[25] In many cases, it's the men who walk away from the women. In others, it's the women who turn on the men. Sometimes it's just a mutual sense of alienation that leads couples to part.

Between the pressuring and the high dissolution rate of the relationships, women often become distrustful of and angry toward their mates and many times toward males in general. Here are some revealing and typical comments from women who have had abortions:

- "You have no idea how much I hated him. And I sure as [expletive] was not going to have that child. I had the abortion to hurt him primarily."[26]
- "This was a man who, besides everything else, was physically repulsive to me. It was a very sick relationship, and I was a very unhappy person. And at the time I got pregnant my immediate response was one of utter disgust. . . . I had no sense, really, of the fact that I was pregnant with a child. It was much more as if I had a growth, or a tumor that I just wanted to get rid of, and I didn't want anybody to know about it because it was so 'disgusting.' "[27]
- "They never tell you of the emotional trauma you go through after the abortion. I have attempted suicide twice, had numerous failed relationships because of *my deep hate I had for all men*, got involved with drugs and alcohol to help me forget."[28]

When the anger and guilt are channeled into the feminist cause, women often end up in a rage against men, marriage, family, and the Judeo-Christian religion that provided the foundation and structure for America's social institutions. Let us take Gloria Steinem for example.

The Case of Gloria Steinem

In a book in which longtime feminist activist Gloria Steinem writes the Foreword, several women who chose to abort tell their stories. In most instances, their coming out as women's rights advocates occurred after their abortions as well. Gloria Steinem herself is a prime example. In her Foreword, she says, "My own abortion was pivotal in my life; the worst and the best of it; a symbol of fear, but also the first time I stopped passively accepting whatever happened to me and took responsibility. Even disclosing it years later was a turning point." She says that she had her abortion after college when she was twenty-two, and that she had "gone through it totally alone, out of both humiliation and pride." She calls her decision "a first and long overdue effort to control my own destiny."[29] Steinem makes it sound like she was at least a latent feminist at the time, but that doesn't seem to be the case.

In her glowing biography *The Education of a Woman: The Life of Gloria Steinem*, Carolyn G. Heilbrun provides the pieces that fill out Steinem's more sketchy testimonial.[30] Reviewer John Reilly fits the pieces together from Heilbrun's account and gives us the fuller picture:

> Steinem's life does seem to have been strongly influenced by the search for mechanisms to cope with the guilt she experienced from an abortion she underwent in 1956, the year after she graduated from Smith College. The incident was a sad end to a romantic story. Steinem had been courted in college by a young man then serving in the air reserve, who used to do things like skywrite her name with his jet in order to get her attention. They became engaged. His family, however, disapproved of her, possibly because she was poor and insufficiently Jewish, and they pressured her fiancé to end the engagement.... While she was in England preparing to travel to India she discovered she was pregnant. Almost penniless in a foreign country and with her plans for her life apparently about to collapse, she discovered almost by accident how much easier it was to obtain a legal abortion in England than in the United States. With the signatures of two doctors, she was able to obtain one on psychological grounds. Then she went on her Indian adventure, keeping the abortion a dark secret for many years.
>
> You do not have to speculate about the importance of this incident for Steinem's later life; it was by her own account what made the Redstockings rally she attended in 1969 so important for her. [This was a proabortion rally sponsored by a New York City women's group.] It was the reason she became a feminist. Before her conversion, the abortion had been a shameful act, though one for which her hard circumstances went far to mitigate her blame. After her conversion, it was a brave, revolutionary act, a blow against patriarchy, even though at the time she was unaware of the existence of that evil.... She thereafter dedicated her life to transforming the world in such a way that her post-conversion assessment would be true for everybody.[31]

It wasn't until just before she published the first issue of the proabortion, profeminist magazine *Ms.* in December 1971 that she finally revealed her abortion experience to her mother. And she only did that because, as she said, "The first issue of *Ms.* magazine was going to include a list of many notable American women who admitted that they had had abortions and asked for a repeal of all anti-abortion laws. I couldn't ask others to be truthful if I was not, so before I signed, I had to tell my family. We became closer—thanks to feminism."[32]

Whether you accept Steinem's feminist spin on her past or not, it's clear that her feminism was a consequence of, not a rationale for, her abortion. It also seems clear that her activism became a political means for dealing with her inner turmoil over her abortion.

The "Evil" of Patriarchy

Steinem, like most other feminists, is a conspiratorialist. She sees male oppression behind virtually everything she thinks is evil. Her favorite word to describe this wickedness is *patriarchy.* She also calls it *male supremacy.* Andrea Dworkin, a feminist to whom Steinem dedicates one of her books, says more clearly what Steinem is driving at: "Men love death. In everything they make they hollow out a central place for death.... In male culture slow murder is the heart of eros, fast murder is the heart of action, and systemized murder is the heart of history."[33]

Language is important to Steinem and rightly so. She sees the power of words to define, limit, or expand one's perceptions about self, others, their relationships, social institutions, and dreams.[34] For instance, on the patriarchal side, she believes that words such as "*Man, mankind,* and *family of man* have made women feel left out." So she sides with the use of "more inclusive" words, such as *people, humanity,* and *humankind.*[35] Her appreciation of language, however, is two-edged. She uses it to include women where she thinks they have been excluded, and she uses it to exclude men and women who do not share her views. For example, she calls pro-life advocates "rightwing," "ultrarightists," "anti-abortion," "anti-choice," agents of "compulsory childbearing," "anti-equality," "overwhelmingly white," opposers of "most integration and civil rights efforts," "authoritarians," "religious fundamentalists," and "male supremacists" (would this make pro-life women female supremacists?).[36]

She says she wants this patriarchal system of dominance replaced with an egalitarian system within which both men and women have the power to control their own lives without trying to dominate one another.[37]

Reproductive Rights

Since her conversion to feminism, Steinem has advocated reproductive freedom passionately and relentlessly. By *reproductive freedom,*

Steinem means "the right of the individual to decide to have or not to have a child." The term includes "safe contraception and abortion, as well as freedom from coerced sterilization (of women or of men) and decent health care during pregnancy and birth." The opposite of reproductive freedom, of course, is reproductive slavery, what Steinem often refers to as "compulsory childbearing." In her world, sex should be unshackled from its natural product—children. If you can't stop them from coming with a condom, you can eliminate them with abortion. Sex without consequences, this is the freedom she wants. After all, as she says, "Individual women have the right to decide the use of our own bodies."[38]

The preborn have no such right to the use of their bodies. While they grow as dependent yet distinct human beings in the womb, they are open to execution in Steinem's world, and this under the banner of "reproductive freedom."

Of course, Steinem does not see the product of conception as human. To pro-lifers who compare the dehumanization of slaves in the nineteenth-century to the dehumanization of the preborn in the twentieth century, Steinem says balderdash. Denying "legal personhood to a slave and to a fetus" are not "the same thing," she asserts. A woman "has a logical right to decide whether or not a pregnancy will use her body and all its life-support systems."[39] Notice her choice of words. According to her, it's not the fetus who uses a woman's body but "a pregnancy." If she used the word *fetus* in this context, she would imply that it has a will and intelligence and other qualities of humanness and personhood. Since she can't do that, she uses the word *pregnancy* instead.

This word usage makes no sense in this context. Pregnancy is a condition of the woman; it describes her state when she is with child. A pregnancy does not use her body; it is part and parcel of what her body is like for an average of nine months. It is a temporary condition of her body brought on by the life conceived within. It is the life within that draws resources from her body. And that life is a separate individual, though dependent, life with all its human genetic characteristics from the moment of conception forward. This life is, therefore, fully human. It is not a fish, a dog, a dolphin, or anything else but human. As it grows, it undergoes change, but not in its humanity. Whether it lives and develops for thirty seconds or thirty years, it will remain a particular human individual different from its mother or its father its entire lifetime. The renowned French geneticist Jerome LeJeune made this point quite clear in testimony before the U.S. Congress: "To accept the fact that after fertilization has taken place a new human has come into being is no longer a matter of taste or opinion. The human nature of the human being from conception to old age is not a metaphysical contention, it is plain experimental evidence."[40]

Steinem declares that "this reproductive veto power on the part of women is exactly what male supremacists fear most."[41] Men, she believes, are dedicated to controlling the means of female reproduction in order to keep women under their thumb and add numbers to the workforce and military.[42] Steinem adopts a Marxist view of economics and uses it to explain the capitalist American male's so-called phobia of women using contraception and abortion to keep the birthrate low.

Furthermore, like her predecessor Margaret Sanger, Steinem sees contraception and abortion as a social remedy, particularly for the poor. She even strained her relationship with one of her heroes, Cesar Chavez, over this belief. Chavez once headed the United Farm Workers and through it strove to improve the compensation and work conditions of migrant farm workers in California. Steinem compared Chavez to India's Gandhi and spent a good deal of time with Chavez during his organizing efforts among the farm workers. Yet, she upset him when she insisted that "the most pressing medical need of women farm workers, people who often lack even the most rudimentary medical care, was contraceptives."[43] Vaccinations, dental care, physicals, affordable medicines, medical insurance, routine and emergency medical care for pregnant women and migrant children. . . . Steinem could have mentioned almost anything more critical than birth control measures. The fact that she and many other feminists place such a high premium on contraceptives speaks volumes about the low regard they have for families and children. The slogan "Every child a wanted child" always means the fewer children the better.

I've long been amazed at how elitist certain feminists can be on this matter of reproductive rights. By elitist I mean that most feminists only take into consideration women who can bear children when they defend this freedom. I have rarely heard a feminist urge pregnant women who don't want their children to carry them to term anyway and put them up for adoption so that women who can't bear children can love and raise them. Most feminists would rather see children aborted than adopted. This is because for many feminists childlessness is bliss; it is the favored state. In 1981, the liberal magazine the *Village Voice* even reported that some feminists "deliberately get pregnant so they can have abortions in order to show their fertility and commitment to feminist principles." The National Organization for Women, a leader in feminist causes, once put out a catalog that recommended a book entitled *Abortion*

Is a Blessing.[44] This die-hard commitment to abortion denies countless numbers of barren women the opportunity to become mothers. Apparently feminists don't care about seeing the desires of these women fulfilled.

The only real exception most feminists make to this obsession with abortion is when lesbians wish to adopt. Feminists have been quick to rush to the defense of lesbians who want to have children through either adoption or artificial insemination, but it's a rare feminist indeed who does the same for a heterosexual woman, especially if she is married. Blessed are the barren and the lesbian. If you're a heterosexual married woman who wants kids but can't, you won't find much support in the feminist community.

Feminists also show their elitism when they favor born females over preborn females. If you're a female living outside the womb, your feminist sisters will protect you. If you're still inside the womb, your life is in danger. In fact, according to the available evidence, wherever abortion is legal and the parents can choose whether to have the child based on its gender, most of the aborted children are female. In Bombay, India, alone, all but one of 8,000 abortions were female fetuses.[45] In Third World and Asian countries, at least tens of thousands, perhaps hundreds of thousands, have been aborted simply because of their female gender.[46] While the case might be made that in foreign countries gender-related abortions are due to cultural, not feminist, pressures, it is estimated that in the United States alone, around 16,000 abortions are performed each year for reasons of gender preference only.[47]

One would think feminists would be up in arms over such numbers. I have been waiting for them to include the body-count figures of these sex-selection abortions with their many other statistics concerning the so-called global undeclared war against women. Perhaps I missed it, but so far I have found no such response. Indeed, in Marilyn French's best-seller *The War Against Women,* she laments that due to female deaths worldwide, men are now "the majority of the world's population."[48] It doesn't seem to enter her mind that the millions aborted worldwide might be contributing to the decline in the female population.

Instead of feminists fighting for the women in the womb, they are defending the alleged inviolable right of women outside the womb to destroy the female offspring within. It seems to me that if pro-lifers have a love affair with the unborn regardless of its gender, most feminists simply have a love affair with their power over life and death.

Marriage and Family

Steinem refers to the traditional family as "patriarchal," which therefore makes it something all right-thinking people should avoid. She says "the patriarchal family is the basis and training ground for any authoritarianism." She argues that this family model was the "basic cell" of Nazi Germany's social order, therefore implying the traditional family structure is tyrannical. In her view, this family order means that "individuals are men, the family is their basic unit of security in which the state has no right to interfere, and women are nowhere. It's as if a basic right of men *is* to dominate women and the family."[49]

These comments tell us more about Ms. Steinem than they do about real husband-wife-with-children families. She simply doesn't understand how a man and woman can be loving and faithful to each other in a marital union and raise children together without everything between them being precisely equal. Order requires hierarchy. It does in a business, a marriage, a family, a military unit, or any other relationship between humans designed to accomplish anything of worth. This does not mean that the relationships must be dictatorial or oppressive. In fact, the best-working relationships are not that way at all. But Steinem cannot make these distinctions.

I do not want to be misunderstood here. I am not advocating ancient Rome's version of male dominance or male authoritarianism in or outside the home. Nor am I suggesting that we should return to a society in which women were often denied certain educational, vocational, and political opportunities simply because they were women. What I am saying is that while we should recognize the equality of persons, we should not join the feminists who see the slavery motif in every human relationship that does not fit a strict egalitarian model. Political leaders exercise authority over their country's citizens, commissioned officers over enlisted personnel, ministers over their congregations, employers over their employees, teachers over their students, parents over their children. If the authority figures are unselfishly fulfilling their roles, they are serving those under them, seeking to achieve what's best for those in their care. In turn, those being served well will generally reciprocate by supporting those over them. In time, many of the served will rise to positions of authority, sometimes even over those who once exercised authority over them. We see this happen often in families where adult children make decisions on behalf of aging parents who cannot function on their own anymore.

These kinds of hierarchial arrangements are good and necessary, and they have been practiced for thousands of years in societies worldwide. Yes, they can be abused, but abuse should not bar use. Steinem and many other Second Wave feminists see and frequently exaggerate the abuses and distort the history and wisdom behind these arrangements. I suggest we identify and correct the abuses as the First Wave feminists often did so well rather than abolish all hierarchy, whether the person in authority is a man or a woman. As a society, this will carry us much further toward the goal of achieving the common good.

Given Steinem's disparaging view of the nuclear family and hierarchy, you can guess that she is not a strong advocate for marriage. In fact, in her national bestseller *Outrageous Acts and Everyday Rebellions*, which was first released in 1984, then in a revised version in 1995, one will not find the words *wife* or *husband* in the index. These are terms she avoids. Under the topic of marriage the subcategories listed are "domestic violence and," "as gamble," "genital mutilation and," "new vocabulary of," "as ownership contract," and "work outside the home vs." Without even looking up the page references, one gets the impression that Steinem has little regard for the marriage institution.

When Steinem fought for passage of the now defunct Equal Rights Amendment, she spoke before the League of Women Voters and told them that one of the duties of a married woman was part-time prostitution.[50] On another occasion she said that "decently married bedrooms across America are settings for nightly rape."[51] Of course, Steinem is not alone in this attitude. Catharine MacKinnon, professor of law and one of today's most prominent feminists, has said, "Feminism stresses the indistinguishability of prostitution, marriage, and sexual harassment."[52]

For Steinem, naming is another powerful tool of domination. Hence she does not like the idea of a wife taking her husband's last name or combining her maiden name with her husband's. The former option is patriarchal, and that's bad. The latter option leaves "an unequal mark" on the marriage unless the husband adds his wife's maiden name to his.[53] Once again Steinem proves how absurd she can render equality in marriage. A lasting marital relationship is not built on such trivialities.

Steinem has frequently voiced anger over the fact that women homemakers receive short shrift when it comes to placing a monetary value on their social contribution. She referred to "the job of homemaking" as "poorly rewarded, low-security, [and] high-risk," while she described jobs outside the home as "more secure, independent, and salaried."[54] Equality will not take place "until men are encouraged, pressured, or otherwise forced, individually and collectively, to integrate themselves into the 'women's work' of raising children and homemaking."[55]

To be fair to Steinem, her remarks about women homemakers are tame in comparison with those of some of her compatriots. Betty Friedan, for example, compared homemakers to Holocaust victims: "The women who 'adjust' as housewives, who grow up wanting to be 'just a housewife,' are in as much danger as the millions who walked to their own death in the concentration camps—and the millions more who refused to believe that the concentration camps existed."[56] Simone de Beauvoir, one of the most influential feminist intellectuals of this century, wanted to deny women the choice of being full-time mothers: "No woman should be authorized to stay at home and raise her children ... one should not have the choice precisely because if there is such a choice, too many women will make that one."[57] So much for pro-choice feminism.

Perhaps Steinem's poor regard for marriage and family is due to her personal experience. Her parents separated when she was ten years old, and her father left the family to survive on its own. Her mother was mentally ill, so she ended up mothering her mother.[58] Steinem has never married, but she has had numerous lovers, what her biographer calls "mini-marriages."[59] She has admitted to seducing one of these men "by playing down the person she was and playing up the person he wanted her to be. When he did fall in love with her, she says, 'I had to *keep on* not being myself.' "[60] Even in her love affairs Steinem seems incapable of accepting responsibility for her actions. She's always the victim, never the victimizer. This victim mentality even influenced her feminist activism. As she told one reporter, "I was always driven by the need to help other women. ... I was always identifying with the victim without realizing it was part of me."[61]

Sexual Choice

Steinem believes the feminist movement has changed our language and perceptions of sexuality for the better.

> In sexuality, the assumption that a person must be either heterosexual or homosexual has begun to loosen up enough to honor both the ancient tradition of *bisexuality* and the new one of individuals who themselves are *transgender* and cross what once seemed an immutable line. Many groups within the lesbian and gay movement now add these two words to their descriptions. People in couples are also more likely to speak of each other as *partner* or *life partner*, a relationship that goes beyond the limited connotation of *lover*. *Homophobic* has been joined by *heterosexist*, a way of describing a person or entity that places heterosexuality at the center, or assumes

> that all other sexualities are peripheral or nonexistent. At the same time, *sexual preference* is frequently replaced by the term *sexual identity,* a way of including both those who feel they were born with a particular sexuality and those who feel they chose it.[62]

Steinem has long supported sexual choice. *Ms.*, the magazine she started and edited for fifteen years, has published scores of articles condoning what Betty Friedan has called "the lavender menace" of lesbianism.[63] Steinem has called "lesbianism an honorable choice."[64] She also opposes those "male supremacists" who set themselves up "against any sexuality not directed toward childbirth within the patriarchal family (that is, against extramarital sex, homosexuality, and lesbianism, as well as contraception and abortion)." She is proud to say that feminists and lesbians have stood together "on the side of any consenting, freely chosen sexuality as a rightful form of human expression."[65] In other words, Steinem has feminized the *Playboy* mentality and declared it good.

When you think about it, the coupling of lesbianism and hedonism with feminism makes sense, especially in light of the values now dominating American culture. With feminism's antagonism toward men, dehumanization of the preborn, and de-emphasis on childbearing, a homosexual union seems the ideal match. As one philosopher and mother of four explained it, in a same-sex relationship:

> There is no possibility that children will enter the picture unexpectedly to create burdens on the couple's time or money or freedom. Partners are free to leave whenever the relationship no longer suits them, with no repercussions on children and little financial impact. There are likely to be few financial difficulties, in fact, since both partners are likely to be working and in general handle their accounts separately. Sexual desires are gratified without risk of pregnancy. If children are seen as a desirable addition, perhaps they can be adopted or artificially produced—poster babies for Planned Parenthood's slogan "Every child a wanted child."[66]

A Chill in the Air

In the 1974 edition of her book *The Feminine Mystique,* Betty Friedan admitted, "It was easier for me to start the women's movement, which was needed to change society, than to change my own personal life."[67] It's always easier to change the outward rather than the inward. Internal changes can be painful. Making them forces us to face ourselves, the good and bad within. The process exposes our weaknesses, failings, guilt, humiliations, and shame. It calls on us to abandon our idols, especially to dethrone ourselves. As a priest in the movie *Rudy* said, "I'm sure of two things: there is a God and I am not He."

Friedan, Steinem, Sanger, and many of the other social activists we have covered in this book rationalized their misbehavior and worked to enshrine it as social policy. Rather than facing their errors and guilt, they changed society and remade it in their image. Too many have accepted their offer.

The exchange has given us more than we bargained for. We now have a disordered and disorientated society where the strong make life-and-death decisions over the weak . . . where marriages are terminated at will and families blow apart like straw in a gusty wind . . . where self-control is shunned and self-obsession praised . . . where license is confused with liberty . . . where barbarism is king and God the exile. We must ask ourselves, Has the price paid been too high?

Sometimes on still, warm southern nights, I step into my backyard and look into the night sky. I peer into the star-studded dark and wonder what America's fate will be. Will we gain the vision and the will to turn back the night enveloping us? Or will we continue to imbibe the new absolutes? At times I feel hopeful. On some nights, though, there's a chill in the air.

Chapter 11

Race Colors Everything

The *Old* Absolute	The *New* Absolute
(8) All white people are created equal and should be treated with dignity and respect.	(8a) All human beings are created equal and should be treated with dignity and respect, but people of color should receive preferential treatment.

Along with hundreds of other people, I was looking forward to hearing a spirited panel discussion on the present state and future prospects of America on the grounds of Regent University in Virginia Beach, Virginia. Among the panelists were leaders from such diverse organizations as the American Civil Liberties Union, the *Chicago Tribune*, the *Boston Herald*, the American Center for Law and Justice, People for the American Way, and Americans United for Separation of Church and State.[1] The moderator was Morton Kondracke, a noted political columnist who regularly appears on the television program *The McLaughlin Group*.

While the panelists were articulate and well received, none captured the attention of the audience as completely as Alan Keyes. A black Christian political conservative, Keyes is an author, public speaker, media personality, social activist, and career diplomat. In 1996 he made an unsuccessful bid for the Republican presidential nomination. No matter where the discussion traveled, Keyes kept bringing it back to the moral center with a philosophical grounding in the Judeo-Christian worldview.

During the panel discussion, Kondracke turned to Keyes and asked him to what extent he thought racism was "alive and well in America today." Alan Keyes' answer is instructive:

> I'm not entirely sure why this question would be directed at me. I suppose because I am a black person. If you are a black person in America, then everybody assumes that you're the one to comment about racism.
>
> I think that even based on the examples I can think of—Louis Farrakhan and others—there are other people sitting on this panel who could comment about racism. . . . Racism is an equal opportunity employer. . . . [C]olor is no bar or barrier to being a racist. This is a sad statement, but it is true.[2]

Keyes is right. Racism knows no color lines. It does not discriminate. Racism solicits anyone who will heed its call of accusing, blaming, hating, and dehumanizing other people because of their blood line, skin color, or some other innate or natural feature.

One way racism is perpetuated is through the manipulation of history. People of different colors reach into the past not so much to understand it but to politicize it so they can use it to shame others into accepting their assessments and agendas. They distort history for present gain. The tragedy in this is that when our past is muddied, our present is clouded, too.

However, there are no perfect people, no pure, guilt-free races. No oppressed people who have never oppressed others. No oppressors who have never been oppressed. Each person's heritage has its share of inhumane, immoral behavior.

In this chapter I want to trace the history of black and white relations in America. I do not have the space to deal with Native American Indians, Mexican Americans, Asian Americans, and the many other races and nationalities that also have unique and important contributions to make to the topic of race relations in the United States. I have chosen the black and white American story because it is the one that has most definitively shaped the nation's political landscape. It is also the story that best illustrates America's shift between competing absolutes—the old one being: *All white people are created equal and should be treated with dignity and respect*, and the more recent one: *All human beings are created equal and should be treated with dignity and respect, but people of color should receive preferential treatment.* I think *both* claims to truth are wrong, as are the reasons people have used to support each. I will appeal to the historical record to show that whites and blacks have often abused one another and their histories to get what they wanted. It is, indeed, a sad and troubling story.

Accounting for Difference

In the early 1600s white Europeans were coming to view the vast majority of blacks as "degraded beneath the standards of humanity, corrupt in religion to the point of being in league with the devil, [and] incorrigibly barbarian to the point where slavery seemed appropriate to their natures."[3] Europeans traveling throughout sub-Saharan Africa found, with few exceptions, very primitive peoples barely out of the Stone Age. There was no evidence of literacy and virtually no knowledge of the wheel. Many tribes practiced cannibalism, head-hunting, voodoo, and witchcraft. People worshiped and sacrificed to the spirits of trees, rocks, water, the sun, and moon. Polygamy was common as was slavery. Tribes conquered neighboring tribes, then killed the men and used the women and children as concubines, slaves, and religious sacrifices. Some African parents conceived children to sell them into slavery, viewing their offspring merely as economic assets. In the few areas that showed higher stages of civilization—such as Ethiopia and Timbuktu—the advancements in the black population were frequently attributable to the previous outside influence of Christians or Muslims.[4]

When Europeans compared the advances of their society with that of black Africans, they were struck by the tremendous chasm that lay between them. The civilization gap was huge, indeed.

> When the Portuguese sailed abroad [to places like Africa and South America] in the second half of the fifteenth century, they left an emerging modern European civilization which had almost a hundred universities; which had several hundred printing presses and some fifteen thousand book titles in circulation; which had cannons and body armor and gunpowder; which used modern business methods such as checks, bills of exchange, insurance, and double entry bookkeeping; which had mechanical clocks and precision instruments; which had harnessed the power of wind and water to grind grain, crush ore, mash pulp for paper, saw lumber and marble, and pump water; which had built Gothic cathedrals. This technical head start would soon produce a very large gap between Europe and the rest of the world. The enormous European lead is suggested by just a few European inventions and technological advances of the period, a list which could be vastly multiplied: the microscope (1590), the telescope (1608), the barometer (1643), the pendulum clock (1656), the thermometer (1714), the spinning jenny (1770), the steam engine (1781), vaccination (1796), the electric battery (1800).[5]

Europeans tried to account for the cultural differences between them and black Africans in a number of ways, but they found evidence debunking them all. Eventually, Europeans settled on a race-based theory, the only one that made any rational sense to them. They decided—albeit wrongly—there had to be a relationship between social progress and physical characteristics, such as skin color. Some people, in other words, were superior to others by nature and this accounted for their greater cultural advance. What accounted for this superiority was a matter of debate. Some people pointed to natural processes, others to the favors of history, and still others to God. But that some races had somehow developed unique advantages over others seemed unquestionable. To Europeans, the evidence pointed away from all other explanations but this one. So they concluded that since they were white and their culture was so advanced, they were the superior race. Since Africans were black and their progress so stunted, they must be inferior.[6]

Hence began European racism.

However, we cannot say that European racism led to the dehumanization of black Africans. That would be putting the effect before the cause. The truth is that the enslavement of blacks was in full swing long before Europeans had developed race-based explanations for the civilization gap. In fact, it existed long before there was a Europe. Slavery was a global phenomenon that predated Islam, Buddhism, and Christianity, as well as Rome, Athens, and Jerusalem. It knew no color lines or religious distinctions, and it required no supporting ideology. Whites enslaved whites, blacks enslaved blacks, Orientals enslaved Orientals, Indians enslaved Indians, Egyptians enslaved Hebrews, pirates enslaved Christians, Christians enslaved pagans, Muslims enslaved infidels, and on and on it went. Like prostitution, slavery was one of the oldest institutions on earth, and it needed no moral or racial justification to be practiced.[7]

Why did people enslave others? For the same reasons people commit other crimes: self-interest and opportunity. Wherever people were vulnerable, they were prime candidates for military conquest. Subjects were not chosen for conquest or servitude for racist reasons; they were simply selected because they were easy targets. Once they were enslaved, though, racial animus often followed. Black scholar Thomas Sowell supports this conclusion in his book *Race and Culture*: "Peoples regularly subjected to slave raids might indeed be despised, and treated with contempt both during their enslavement and after their emancipation, but that was not what caused them to be enslaved in the first place.... [R]acism was promoted by slavery, rather than vice versa."[8]

Slavery was part of the fabric of society. There were laws to regulate slavery but none to abolish it. It was simply there, and it was accepted.

America's Terrible Institution

The first black Africans to arrive in colonial America came in 1619. They likely arrived as indentured servants rather than slaves.[9] By the time the 1600s drew to a close, indentured servitude had evolved into slavery. That's not to say that until this point the colonists had treated black and white servants equally. They had not. In 1642 a Virginia judge sentenced two white servants to an additional year of service for running away from their master. The same judge locked a black servant into labor for the rest of his life for the same offense. In 1661 the Virginia Assembly decided that white servants running away with blacks was more of an offense than whites taking off by themselves, so the assembly passed a law making whites who escaped with blacks liable for the same life tenure blacks had to serve.[10]

Over the next two hundred years, the slave trade flourished. By 1790 one-fifth of the country's population were slaves (approximately 700,000 blacks). Just before The War between the States broke out in 1860, the number of black slaves had risen to more than four million.[11] Interestingly enough, the increased number in slaves did not indicate more white slave owners. "In 1790, the number of slave-owning families in America was as high as 25 percent, but by 1850, the number declined to 10 percent. Even in the South, less than one third of free white families owned slaves on the eve of the Civil War."[12]

All the slaves were not owned by whites either. Many Native American Indians were slave owners,[13] as were many free blacks. In 1830 more than 3,500 blacks collectively owned more than 10,000 members of their own race.[14] All the states in the Union, except for Delaware and Arkansas, allowed free blacks to own slaves. As D'Souza explains:

> Between the American Revolution and the Civil War free blacks made up approximately 10 percent of the total black population; in 1860, for example, there were almost half a million free blacks, 50 percent of whom lived in the South. Some free blacks were former slaves and, once manumitted, they could accumulate income and property by marketing skills they once used on the plantation. Many free blacks worked as blacksmiths, carpenters, brick masons, tailors, shoemakers, and butchers. Over the years, a small but sizable segment of the free black population acquired the economic resources to purchase property, including black slaves. As early as the

> 1640s, around the time that whites began to enslave blacks, there is proof of a black man, Anthony Johnson, owning a slave of his own race. The Virginia courts upheld the right of blacks to own other blacks as early as 1654; other states followed this precedent. In 1833 the Supreme Court affirmed Negro slaveholding. With relatively few exceptions, up until the Civil War, blacks enjoyed the same legal rights as whites and Indians to hold black slaves. There was no legal right to enslave whites.[15]

Did black slave owners treat their slaves with more kindness than their white counterparts? Apparently not. William Ellison, a descendent of slaves, owned more than a hundred slaves and used them to work his plantation and produce cotton gins. He had the reputation of being especially brutal with his human property. The two scholars who document Ellison's story state: "Despite his history, Ellison did not view his shop and plantation as halfway houses to freedom. He never permitted a single slave to duplicate his own experience. Nothing suggests that he wrestled with a moral dilemma. Everything suggests that Ellison held his slaves to exploit them, to profit from them, just as white slaveholders did."[16] Ira Berlin sums up the attitude black slave owners had toward their black property: "They showed little sympathy for the slave and had few qualms about the morality of slavery."[17]

When the Civil War began in 1861, the Ellison family, along with many other black slave owners, sided with the Confederacy. Blacks fought with Southerners and contributed money and other resources to the Rebel cause. Just as Yankee whites warred against Rebel whites, so Yankee blacks fought against Rebel blacks. When the North won, black slave owners, as well as their white counterparts, suffered heavy financial losses.[18]

When Morality Liberates

Slavery abounded mostly for economic reasons. There was ground to clear, land to cultivate and plant, lumber to cut, cotton to pick, tobacco to cure, errands to run, machinery to build and repair, children who needed nannies, and houses that needed cleaning. Work was plentiful and workers were not. Blacks provided cheap labor. Besides, the slave trade in black cargo was already well established. Why not tap into it? Thus early Americans joined the rest of the world in practicing slavery.[19]

Throughout the process of revolution against England and establishing an independent nation, Americans were seriously debating the institution of slavery. In keeping with their religious convictions, they had declared that "all men are created equal" and that the "Creator" had endowed all human beings with "inalienable rights," which included "life, liberty, and the pursuit of happiness." Were not the black slaves God's creatures just as whites were? Did not the inalienable rights belong to them as much as to anyone? Many Americans answered yes to both questions. For instance, in 1780 the citizens of Hardwick, Massachusetts, "demanded that the line in the state constitution that read 'all men are born free and equal' be changed to read 'all men, whites and blacks, are born free and equal.' Their fear was that the passage might otherwise 'be misconstrued hereafter, in such a manner as to exclude blacks.' "[20]

Conscientious Christians were not the only ones challenging slavery.[21] Even though he was a slave owner himself, Thomas Jefferson tried to solicit support for its abolition. He drafted a plan called the "Report of Government for the Western Territory" (1784), which called for the abolition of slavery in all the states after the year 1800. His legislation, however, was defeated by a single vote. Two years later he wrote of the defeat: "The voice of a single individual . . . would have prevented this abominable crime from spreading itself over the country. Thus we see the fate of millions unborn hanging on the tongue of one man, and heaven was silent in that awful moment! But it is to be hoped it will not always be silent, and that the friends of the rights of human nature will in the end prevail."[22]

During the hammering out of the U.S. Constitution, delegates from the northern states, some of whom were slaveholders themselves, denounced slavery with appeals to the Declaration of Independence, natural law, and the Bible. They wanted the Constitution to eliminate slavery once and for all. However, because their economic well-being depended on slave labor, the southern delegates staunchly defended the right to hold slaves. Charles Pickney of South Carolina let it be known that the southern states were prepared to abandon the Constitution or break away from the new Republic if any limitations were imposed on their "peculiar institution." As historian Page Smith explains:

> "If slavery be wrong," Pickney declared, "it is justified by the example of all the world." He cited the case of "Greece, Rome and other ancient States; the sanction given by France, England, Holland and other modern States." In all ages "one-half of mankind have been slaves." So there you have it. No compromise on the slavery issue, [or] no Constitution. It was a bitter pill for the northern delegates to swallow. Governor Morris, who had described the slav-

ery dilemma as that of doing "injustice to the southern States or to human nature," and had sworn never to put his name to a document that accepted slavery, capitulated. To him the question boiled down to "shall there be a national government or not. . . ." The alternative was "general anarchy."[23]

So the United States was born with slavery left intact. The slave population continued to grow, and the opposition to it continued to mount.

Slavery's Defeat

Ironically, Great Britain, America's former foe, became the inspiration for American abolitionists to turn up the heat. A small group of evangelical Christians within the Church of England relentlessly crusaded against England's slave trade. Led by William Wilberforce, they marshaled public opinion and set bill after bill before Parliament calling for the end of slavery. For twenty years their efforts were resoundingly defeated until on February 27, 1807, the House of Commons passed a bill abolishing slavery by a vote of 283 to 16. "In an age before mass communication, mass transit, or mass movements," writes scholar Thomas Sowell, "people were astonished to see petitions arrive in Parliament with tens of thousands of signatures, demanding an end to the slave trade. At one point, Parliament received more than 800 petitions within a month, containing a total of 700,000 signatures." The efforts of these Christians and the public support behind them were "so strong, so tenacious, so enduring, and ultimately so irresistible, that the anti-slavery crusade was swept along beyond its original goals of stopping the international trade in human beings to abolishing slavery itself throughout the British Empire, and eventually throughout the world."[24]

As the British were shutting down the slave merchants in their vast empire and persuading other countries to follow suit, the American abolitionist movement gathered momentum and intensity. "The vast majority of abolitionists were radical Protestants," states Page Smith.[25] They were the social conscience for a country that had compromised its moral will on the slavery issue. They found welcome support in the biographies and testimonies of escaped slaves. The novel *Uncle Tom's Cabin* was so powerful in fueling public opinion and moral outrage that it led Abraham Lincoln to refer to its author, Harriet Beecher Stowe, as "the little lady who started the Civil War."[26] The abolitionists preached, demonstrated, circulated periodicals and tracts, poured out books, wrote poems and songs, petitioned legislatures—all to abolish the evil that plagued their land.

> Arrested, beaten, stoned, their meeting places burned down around them, abused and reviled (one abolitionist, John Rankin, estimated he had been "mobbed" more than a hundred times), the abolitionists persevered. From a despised handful, they became a mighty army of the Lord and finally touched the conscience of a nation that called itself Christian.
>
> And so it came about that the city of God indeed triumphed over the city of man: Slavery was abolished. As sure as we can say anything about our past, we can say radical Protestants freed the slaves. The religion of the city of man could never have brought about the emancipation of the slaves. The fact was that all the "objective" evidence, the evidence of the senses, the empirical evidence, was that slaves were "inferior" to whites. Soon Darwinism would appear to confirm what the senses testified to—Africans were, according to this new school, a simpler, earlier form of human being on the evolutionary scale. Not inferior, necessarily, but "lower," more rudimentary. Since the religion of the city of man had accepted the Christian doctrines of equality and freedom, it deplored slavery, but deplored it more in the abstract and showed no inclination to man the barricades in opposition to it, or to join forces with the abolitionists in their crusade. Against the heavily prevailing social sentiment, the abolitionists had only the scriptural assurance that God made "of one blood all the nations of the earth," that he loved all creatures equally; no, that he loved the poor, the suffering, and the oppressed *more* than the rich and powerful. The black slave was the living symbol of Christ, the "suffering servant." The equality of the black slave, indeed, in certain essential ways, the *superiority* of the black slave, was quite literally an article of faith for many abolitionists. Had not Christ said that the last should be first?[27]

The largely white Christian abolitionists in America and Britain set in motion the dismantling of a globally entrenched institution that had lasted thousands of years. Within little more than a century, they won. Slavery was demolished. Economics had not been the deciding factor, nor had political expediency. Self-interest and opportunism finally fell at the feet of Christ's ambassadors as vanquished foe.[28]

The Segregations

If that were the end of the story, it would be a happy ending indeed. Abraham Lincoln's 1863 Emancipation Proclamation had freed slaves who were in states fighting against the Union. The North's victory in the Civil War and the ratification of the Thirteenth Amendment to the Constitution in 1865 had abolished slavery throughout America. And the combined effect of the 1866 Civil Rights Act and the ratification of the Fourteenth (1868) and Fifteenth Amendments (1870) had given former slaves the full rights of U.S. citizens, including the right to vote. Unfortunately, this new status did not guarantee that the populace would treat all blacks as equals. In many regions of the country, blacks became second-class citizens.

Southerners were supposed to submit gladly to Republican Reconstructionist policies that forced them to compete with their former slaves, and to accept the often underhanded actions of the northern carpetbaggers, who seemed bent on punishing southerners by squeezing them economically dry. In the eyes of southerners, this was a lousy exchange, and it led many of them to despise and abuse the blacks in their midst. These were the days that saw the rise of such white racist groups as the Ku Klux Klan, Red Shirts, and Knights of the White Camelia.[29]

Of course, northerners did not always receive blacks with enthusiasm, either. As many abolitionists saw their dreams for a southern utopia fail, they became disillusioned and wondered if it had been a mistake to force equality on the South. Abolitionist Republicans became upset when freedpeople "increasingly sought to reap the rewards of [political] office themselves rather than support their white Republicans [sic] allies."[30] Consequently the Republican party underwent a massive defection to the Democratic party, which proudly portrayed itself as the "white man's party."[31] Racism began gaining renewed political clout.

In such a mixed environment of opportunity and hostility, blacks worked out their new freedom. They simply wanted to be free of their former white masters. Sometimes freedpeople went so far as to leave the United States and return to African soil. There was a popular contingent of various "back to Africa" movements.[32] Most former slaves, however, stayed in the United States, but they too wanted to remove themselves as far as possible from their former owners. This often led to self-segregation—blacks pulling away from whites and all vestiges of society they linked to their slavery past.[33] Blacks built and ran black communities, complete with their own schools, businesses, restaurants, lodging houses, transportation centers, and churches. Many of these townships prospered well into the middle of the twentieth century.[34] Blacks frequently fought in courts and legislatures for separate-but-equal accommodations as well. Booker T. Washington, the undisputed black leader of the Reconstruction Era, spoke for the vast majority of blacks when he said, "It is not the separation that we complain of, but the unequality of accommodation."[35] Separate-but-equal policies eventually became enshrined in common law. In 1878 in *Hall v. Decuir* and in 1896 in *Plessy v. Ferguson*, the U.S. Supreme Court upheld "equal but separate accommodations for the white and colored races."[36] Egalitarian segregation became the recognized law of the land.

Hopes for land distribution, widespread in the immediate postwar months, faded by 1868, but the freedpeople continued to look for a "real" freedom that would enable them to maximize their independence and provide them with equal rights, if not equal conditions. The freedpeople had expected much from emancipation, but the gains they received were inevitably too little. "Beginning in the 1870s and accelerating in succeeding decades, blacks experienced a growing sense of despair as that freedom appeared ever more remote; in state after state, Reconstruction governments were replaced with [Democratic] administrations that sharply curtailed spending on education, rolled back civil and political rights, and created a new political climate in which violence against 'uppity' blacks flourished."[37]

Another factor that entered into this ever-hostile environment was the rise of Darwinism. All too often, blacks became the objects of derision because of this new science and its application to the social sphere. Earlier race-based judgments of the Europeans gained new scientific respectability. Darwinism applied to the realm of human behavior became Social Darwinism. The evolutionary mechanism of the survival of the fittest became enshrined in public policy and popular opinion. Racism was now scientifically and socially acceptable.[38]

The Darwinian worldview robbed black Americans of their equal humanity with whites. Now blacks were scientifically regarded as little better than their ape ancestors—almost as primitive, bearing only meager intelligence, and morally degenerate. Whites and blacks may have to share the same country, but they were not going to share the same water fountain. Segregate the races. Keep the inferior away from the superior. Let the primitives have the necessities of life, but don't let them contaminate the higher primates. It led to whites keeping blacks further away than even blacks wanted to go. Black self-segregation and separate-but-equal accommodations gave way to white-imposed segregation and separate-and-unequal treatment.

During the first half of the twentieth century,

> state after state passed new restrictive legislation designed to put blacks "in their place." Complex voting laws that included literacy

tests, poll taxes, and all-white primaries achieved the de facto disfranchisement of almost all black . . . voters. . . . Southern politics was a sordid if farcical game, one for whites only. Less complex laws provided for racial segregation of virtually every aspect of public life, from schools and transportation facilities to theaters, restaurants, hotels, parks, beaches, hospitals, cemeteries, waiting rooms, and drinking fountains. Facilities open to blacks usually received sharply limited funding and provided distinctly inferior services.[39]

Sex, Family, and Civil Rights

By the time the 1950s rolled around, racial tensions were at an all-time high. Blacks were regularly challenging society's racist segregationist policies, and many protectionist whites were responding with all the resources they could muster. The U.S. Supreme Court voiced its opposition to racial segregation in its 1954 and 1955 decisions in *Brown v. Board of Education of Topeka*, which struck a judicial blow, though a somewhat muddled one, to legal segregation in public schools.[40] But the greatest victories were being won by ordinary blacks on the streets of America. They were people who refused to give up their bus seats to whites, or to stay away from the all-white section in restaurants, or to wait demurely in a store until a white worker approached them to ask what they would like to purchase. These were the real heroes. They often underwent verbal abuse, jail time, beatings, even death in their opposition to spiteful, dehumanizing treatment. But they refused to falter. Their numbers grew, and with their white allies, social protest widened. In response, their opponents intensified their efforts to stop them.[41]

It looked as if Americans were on the verge of a race war. Marches, sit-ins, cross burnings, riots, beatings, lynchings, assassinations—pandemonium was becoming the natural state of affairs.

When the 1964 Civil Rights Bill passed Congress and was signed into law by President Lyndon Johnson, it appeared that major race conflict had been averted and the Civil Rights movement had accomplished its major objectives. School desegregation was finally national policy, and discrimination on the basis of race or nationality was finally outlawed. Everyone knew it would take time, but it was clear to all that the post–Civil War policies of racial segregation had come to an end. Now black Americans were free *and* equal before the law in all ways as whites—again. The major battles were over. Racism was legally dead—again. The Civil Rights movement had risen to the challenge and emerged victorious.

But beneath the public victory there was a much more complex and complicitous picture. There were signs that deeper problems lurked in the black experience, problems that judicial or legislative action alone could not solve. Byard Rustin, for example, found jobs for 120 black teenagers living in Harlem, New York, in 1964, soon after the Harlem riots had died down. Within just a few weeks, only twelve of the teenagers were still on the job. "One boy told Rustin he could make more playing pool than the $50 a week he had been earning; another could make more than his $60 salary by selling 'pot'; another turned down a four-year basketball scholarship to a major university because he preferred to be a 'pimp.' "[42] Something was gravely wrong, but what?

The Moynihan Report

Daniel Patrick Moynihan, undersecretary at the Department of Transportation under Johnson's administration, set about to address this matter. As a Catholic and a political leader, he was concerned about poverty among blacks and wondered what connection there might be between that and the family. His research began with a study of the Labor Department's statistics on the correlation between unemployment rates and marital disruption. His study clearly showed that much of the deterioration of black society was directly tied to the collapsing black family, and this, in turn, was putting greater pressure on national resources. Called "The Negro Family: The Case for National Action," his report observed: "Nearly a quarter of urban Negro marriages are dissolved; nearly one-quarter of Negro births are now illegitimate; as a consequence, almost one-fourth of Negro families are headed by females, and this breakdown of the Negro family has led to a startling increase in welfare dependency."[43] So the Moynihan Report proposed economic help for the heads of black families. This assistance was designed to promote the intactness and stability of black marriages and families, discourage adultery, and lower the birthrate of illegitimate children.[44]

Moynihan discovered that slavery, segregation, and racial discrimination were not the primary causes for the black family's current condition. While they had been contributing causes in many instances, blacks during and after slavery had shown that these obstacles were far from being insurmountable. Thomas Sowell makes this point in his book *Ethnic America:*

> The most important human relationships among the slaves centered on the family. Slave marriages and slave family relations had no legal standing, but usually lasted for decades, if not for a lifetime. This pattern existed throughout slave society—in all geographic

> regions, in both rural and urban settings, among field hands as well as house servants.... While premarital sex and premarital pregnancy existed among slaves, marriage itself was taken very seriously and was not lightly terminated....
>
> Most of the children of slaves grew up in two-parent families, with the father as head, and (secretly) bore his surname. Because of premarital relationships, some families contained children fathered by someone else, but a local study of nineteenth-century slave families indicated that, in three-fourths of the families, all the children had the same father and mother. In short, slave families were stable, insofar as slaves could keep them so.[45]

Blacks who had stable, intact families during slavery and after the Emancipation made their transition to freedom "without much disturbance to the routine of living. In these families, the authority of the father was firmly established, and the woman in the role of mother and wife fitted into the pattern of the patriarchal household."[46] Through the early 1900s, black marriages and families largely remained intact. Two-parent households were the norm, and they were typically headed by fathers. The unwed mother was rare.[47]

But there soon were unmistakable signs that the black family was sinking fast, much more quickly than were white families. For instance, among white women (ages 15–42) the number of illegitimate births rose from 3.6 per 1,000 in 1940 to 9.2 in 1962. Among black women, in the same age group, there was an astonishing jump from 35.6 per 1,000 in 1940 to 97.5 in 1962.[48] In 1950, the number of black one-parent, female head of households had risen to nearly one-fifth of all black families. This ratio was double that among whites.[49]

Moynihan noted in his report that by the mid-sixties, the statistics were even worse. More fathers were abandoning their families, especially in the black community. The reasons for this varied, but one of the keys was sexual promiscuity. Husbands were cheating on their wives in growing numbers, and premarital sex was increasing too. Rather than accepting responsibility for their actions, men were abandoning their lovers and the children they bore. This usually left families in deep financial and emotional straits. The problem had become so severe that E. Franklin Frazier, a black sociologist from Howard University, attributed the unfulfilled emotional needs, poor personality development, and lack of discipline and good habits among black children to "the failure of the father to play the role in family life required by American society." The solution to this problem, Frazier said, "must await those changes in the Negro and American society which will enable the Negro father to play the role required of him."[50] He believed the effort had to be a joint project between blacks and social policy, and that it had to center on the black family and its stability, which required supporting the father's role within it. Any social policy that failed to support family stability would be futile. Moynihan concurred.

President Johnson enthusiastically embraced Moynihan's analysis and decided to make the report the cornerstone of his new Civil Rights policy.[51] When he shared the report in early June 1965 with major Civil Rights leaders, including the NAACP,[52] he was delighted to hear them give it their full endorsement—that is, until the fall of that year. Within just months, Johnson's plan went from an enthusiastic thumbs up to a scathing thumbs down among the Civil Rights elite.[53] The change had nothing to do with the merits of Johnson's policy, yet it had everything to do with its consequences. More accurate still, the policy hit too close to home.

You see, the sexual revolution was off and running in the culture at large, including among the Civil Rights leadership and the liberal Left who were championing the black cause. No one wanted to sacrifice the sexual license they now enjoyed. That meant the president's family stability ideas had to go.

In two incisive essays, E. Michael Jones demonstrates this conclusion in all its decadent glory.[54] In example after example, he shows how the Left ignored moral and Christian blacks and held as their models black sexual libertines.[55] The Left wanted free love without condemnation, and that required undermining the Judeo-Christian ethic that Americans had embraced for so long. If the Left could show that it was the moral order that had enslaved and discriminated against blacks for centuries, then they could label the moral law racist and turn popular opinion against it. Undermining the moral order required subverting the traditional family. The two went hand in hand.

The Turn Against the Family

A prime example of a leader in conflict with the accepted moral order was Martin Luther King, Jr., the most central figure in the Civil Rights movement. While he preached about the sacredness of sex within the God-ordained institution of marriage, he was straining his marriage with illicit affairs. According to one of his biographers, "Three particular relationships had flowered to the status of something more than occasional one-night stands, and for almost the past two years King had grown closer and closer to one of those women, whom he saw almost daily. That relationship, rather than his marriage, increasingly became the emotional centerpiece of King's life, but it did not eliminate the incidental couplings that were a commonplace of King's travels."[56] His adulterous liaisons had even set him up for an FBI shakedown spurred on by the Bureau's director J. Edgar Hoover.[57]

When a friend confronted King about "his compulsive sexual athleticism," King excused his misconduct on the grounds that his affairs reduced the anxiety level he felt from being "away from home twenty-five to twenty-seven days a month."[58] One of his staff recalls that at the time of King's assassination many believed that King's marriage was on the verge of divorce due to his numerous affairs, absenteeism, and restraints he had placed on his wife, Coretta.[59]

One of the more radical black leaders was Black Panther Eldridge Cleaver. The Left praised Cleaver for his "sexual mysticism," which allegedly added "depth and tone to his social commentary."[60] That "sexual mysticism" was shocking and brutal, as even just a few comments from his writings reveal. Cleaver said that he arrived "at the conclusion that, as a matter of principle, it was of paramount importance for me to have an antagonistic, ruthless attitude toward white women."[61] In his words, "I became a rapist. To refine my technique and modus operandi, I started out by practicing on black girls in the ghetto—in the black ghetto where dark and vicious deeds appear not as aberrations or deviations from the norm, but as part of the sufficiency of the Evil of the day—and when I considered myself smooth enough, I crossed the tracks and sought out white prey." Cleaver raped, he said, because it gave him the chance to defy and trample "upon the white man's law, upon his system of values, and that I was defiling his woman . . . was the most satisfying to me."[62]

The "white man's law" and his "values" were references to the Judeo-Christian moral law the Left and many blacks in the Civil Rights movement sought to subvert. Cleaver cited with approval another black author who exhorts blacks to rise up and "Rape the white girls. Rape their fathers. Cut the mother's throats."[63] "I have lived those lines," Cleaver remarks, "and I know that if I had not been apprehended I would have slit some white throats."[64] For Black Panther Cleaver, social activism was advanced through despising white women and raping them. The next step would have been murder if he hadn't been stopped in time.

Given such sexual indiscretions and attitudes among many in the Civil Rights movement and their liberal supporters, it's no wonder that they chose to gut the Moynihan report. A coalition of sixty Civil Rights leaders demanded that President Johnson strike the issue of family stability from his social program. Clarence Mitchell of the NAACP criticized the Moynihan report because it "implied that it was necessary for the improvement of the Negro community to come from within."[65] Another leader made the same objection but stated it more bluntly: "Moynihan . . . emphasizes the negative aspects of the Negroes and then seems to say that it's the individual's fault when it's the [expletive] system that really needs changing."[66] The fault was with the system. Any shred of personal responsibility for change was abandoned. Instead, the Left and the Civil Rights leaders asked "the president for an 'Economic Development Budget for Equal Rights in America,' which would cost the country's taxpayers a mere $32 billion per year in 1965 dollars."[67] Handouts, not hand-ups, were the proposed cure. The answer to family and moral problems was somehow supposed to be money. The black family had lost.

The Price of Victory

When Martin Luther King, Jr., marched, it was to achieve a color-neutral society where people were treated according to their character and performance, not their race. He sought an integrated society where people of all colors would join hands as human equals with equal opportunities for self-advancement.[68] He also condemned black nationalism and black racism, particularly as expressed by the advocates of the Nation of Islam, which was led at that time by Malcolm X.[69] Unlike such groups, King's dream was racial unity and shared freedom with equal opportunity for all. The 1964 Civil Rights Act was enacted with King's endorsement as a critical means to fulfilling this dream.[70]

By the late 1960s, however, the Left and the Civil Rights establishment had turned a race-neutral dream and policies into race-preferential ones. They sacrificed personal responsibility and family stability for policies that brought political and economic gain mostly to upwardly mobile minorities. Under the guise of righting past wrongs, the Left and Civil Rights elite demanded and got from the U.S. government and judicial system affirmative-action programs, quota policies, increased welfare programs, redrawn voting districts, and a host of other race-centered policies. All the solutions politicized race. None of them addressed in any helpful way the family and related moral problems that the Moynihan Report had put at center stage. The result has been an utter policy failure.[71]

In many respects, blacks are worse off today than they were in the mid-sixties. Consider the statistics:

- Half of all black children live below the poverty level.
- In 1994, nearly half of all black children lived in one-parent households, and of those 47 percent lived with their mothers. About 26

percent of black kids lived in traditional nuclear families with both parents, and more than five percent lived with their grandparents.

- As of 1995, families headed by single black women finally outnumbered families headed by black married couples. Only a third of all black children lived with both parents.
- Almost seven of every ten black births are illegitimate.
- Twenty percent of black men and 32 percent of black women live in poverty, while seven percent of white men and 10 percent of white women do.
- The average unemployment rate for black males is 12 percent (for white males it's 5.4 percent), and for black females is 11 percent (for white females it's 5.2 percent).
- Fewer black male high school graduates go on to college than did in 1975. Black women outnumber black men in college by three to two and in graduate school by almost two to one.
- More black males are in prison than in college. In 1994, three out of every ten black men between the ages of twenty and twenty-nine were either in prison or jail, or on probation or parole. In contrast, less than five percent of black women, less than seven percent of white men, and less than two percent of white women were in the same situation.
- While blacks make up about 12 percent of the population, they account for about 45 percent of all violent criminal offenders.
- The vast majority of violent crimes committed against blacks were committed by other blacks. Ninety-three percent of black murder victims were killed by blacks in cases where there was a single offender and a single victim.[72]

It would be incredulous to claim that the current situation of the black population described in these statistics can be blamed on white racism. And yet, that's exactly what a professor of history at George Mason University flatly states, "Black people know there is an enormous amount of racism that results in the decimation of their communities."[73] Political scientist Ronald Walters agrees, stating, "If white racism is not to blame for black problems, you tell me what is."[74] Black studies professor Barbara Sizemore once thought there was a white conspiracy to keep blacks down. Today she thins otherwise: "I no longer think it's a conspiracy.... I call it outright war."[75] Despite such obviously fallacious conclusions, the Reverend Joseph Barndt can say in his book *Dismantling Racism: The Continuing Challenge to White America* that "in the United States, racism is a white problem, and only a white problem.... [I]t is exclusively a disorder of white people and not of people of color."[76]

Today, race colors everything. Whites are challenging programs and policies that they see as institutionalizing reverse discrimination. Minorities are fighting back, calling the reactions of whites "white backlash" and evidence of entrenched racist attitudes. While the clashes sometimes occur over the trivial and ridiculous, they too often color the outcomes of critical issues.

The Simpson Trial

In recent memory, few events have captured the nation's attention more than the trial of black multimillionaire actor, media personality, and former football star O. J. Simpson. He was charged with brutally murdering two whites—his former wife Nicole Brown Simpson and a waiter named Ronald Goldman.

When O. J. was first arrested, the nation—not just blacks—was stunned. No one wanted to believe that he could commit such an awful act. He was an American icon and was treated as such across all class and color distinctions. As the trial wore on for close to a year, Americans were glued to their television sets, newspapers, and radio programs for their daily dose of the O. J. saga.

The public was sharply divided over the evidence presented during the trial. And nearly 60 percent of America tuned in when the jury rendered its not-guilty verdict. The media caught the public's reaction: blacks dancing and singing, shouting with glee, and raising their fists high into the air as signs of victory and power; whites gasping in disbelief, sitting or standing stone-faced, feeling stunned and powerless, some expressing anger and rage.[77] Like anything else, of course, the racial divide was not as clear-cut as the pictures usually portrayed. A fair number of blacks thought the jury had erred. Similarly, a fair number of whites believed O. J. was innocent and rejoiced at the trial's outcome. In a *Newsweek* poll, 85 percent of blacks voiced their agreement with the jury's verdict, but only 66 percent believed he probably did not commit the murders. On the other hand, just 32 percent of whites agreed with the verdict, while a whopping 74 percent thought he was guilty. Eighty percent of blacks polled thought the jury was fair and impartial, but only half of all whites thought the same.[78]

While the numbers show a somewhat mixed reaction, they also demonstrate that the Simpson verdict provided yet another indication of the Grand-Canyon-like chasm between the universes of most blacks and whites. The reporters with *Newsweek* captured the essence of the division as well as anyone:

> Until the murders, most whites saw [O. J. Simpson] at best as the kind of star athlete and entertainer who "transcends race," at worst as a harmless pitchman. What changed that forever was the airing of the 911 tapes—of O. J. ranting and beating down the back door of the Gretna Green condo, of Nicole pleading with operator that "He's [expletive] going nuts ... He's going to beat the [expletive] out of me." That haunting voice, and the photos of Nicole's swollen and bruised face after beatings that evidently had gone on for years, convinced many whites, women in particular, that Simpson was perfectly capable of killing his ex-wife. From then on, the DNA findings and all the other prosecution evidence only hardened that sense of certainty.
>
> For many African-Americans, meanwhile, the trial turned into a parable about the criminal-justice system. For them, the clincher was the Mark Fuhrman tapes, with their hateful boasting that "anything out of a nigger's mouth ... is a [expletive] lie" ... and that "if you did the things that they teach you in the academy, you'd never get a [expletive] thing done." Those tapes confirmed what many African-Americans had always known or suspected—that many white cops hate black people, and see nothing wrong with violating civil rights or tampering with evidence to put away anyone they're convinced deserves it. The Fuhrman factor evoked a powerful story in the African-American experience: of the black man fighting a system that's rigged against him.[79]

The jury was composed of nine blacks, two Hispanics, and one non-Hispanic white. Simpson's black attorney Johnnie Cochran exploited this jury by playing the "race card" with blatant forcefulness. With "his skill at indicting the police," coupled with "his mastery of ethnic code words, clothing, and symbols," Cochran "managed to turn O. J. into a 'race man'—the kind of historical figure that African-Americans believe they must defend at all costs."[80]

Simpson was transformed into a symbol of white racist oppression, and the evidence mounted against him was depicted as a conspiracy to send one more innocent black to prison. This bigoted system had to be defeated. After 126 witnesses, 133 days of testimony, 253 days of trial proceedings, the ten-women, two-men jury spent less than four hours deliberating before arriving at their decision. The speed of their deliberations stunned everyone, and the ruling further polarized a nation.

After the verdict was read, Simpson mouthed "thank you" to the jury. One forty-four-year-old black male juror responded with a raised clenched fist. A former member of the Black Panther party in his younger days, his raised fist was a salute to black power.[81] Eldridge Cleaver would have been proud. White throats had been slit, and no black man had been convicted of the crimes.

Farrakhan's March

On the heels of the Simpson verdict, Louis Farrakhan, the controversial and charismatic black leader of the Nation of Islam, made the final preparations for the Million Man March set for the nation's capital on October 16, 1995. Farrakhan wanted black men to come and atone for their sins against black women and children.[82]

Farrakhan had created the Million-Man-March concept a year earlier, and had recruited former NAACP executive director Benjamin Chavis, Jr., to help him pull it off. Support from national black organizations was divided.[83] Farrakhan invited black men to attend the march but encouraged black women to stay away. He said he wanted "to give the world a vastly different picture of what black men are like." And that meant showing the world that "we are ready to accept the responsibility of freedom, the responsibility of being the heads of our households, the providers, the maintainers, and the protectors of our women and children and the builders of our community."[84] Certainly a message even many white Americans would welcome if that was all there was to it.

While it was declared that this was a spiritual and not racist event,[85] it was being led by a black racist and racial separatist who believed his deceased black Muslim mentor Elijah Muhammad was the Messiah.[86] Farrakhan was on record referring to Adolf Hitler as a "great man" and Judaism as a "gutter religion." He had claimed that AIDS was invented by Jewish doctors to infect black children, and he had accused Jews of "sucking the blood of the black community" and of being "watchdogs of the secret government . . . hell-bent on the destruction of America."[87] He had also found time to defame Arabs, Koreans, and Vietnamese as "bloodsuckers" who profited from the black community but never gave anything back.[88] During the march, Farrakhan's publication *The Final Call* was circulated. In it Jews are called "our enemies," America is designated the "number one enemy of freedom-loving peoples on the earth," and whites are labeled "devils."[89]

Despite his record, one poll showed that "60 percent to 70 percent of African-Americans consider Farrakhan 'an effective leader' who 'speaks the truth' and is 'good for the black community.' "[90] As Farrakhan told *Newsweek*, "My duty is to point out the wrong and the evil." And that involves pointing out that "white supremacy" is still the cause of "black inferiority" and "that's sick."[91]

During his two-and-a-half-hour speech closing the day's events, Farrakhan told the throngs of black males before him, "I'm not a malicious person, and I'm not filled with malice. But . . . I come in the tradition of the doctor who has to point out, with truth, what's wrong."[92] What was wrong with America, he said, was the "evil" of "white supremacy," which is "the idea that undergirds the setup of the Western world."[93] Gesturing at the White House, he exclaimed, "We must make them afraid to do evil to us and think they can get away with it. We must be prepared to help them if they're with us or to punish them if they're against us."[94]

I was pleased to find that not all blacks bought what Farrakhan was selling. Carl Rowan was most emphatic in his opposition to Farrakhan. "I would never," Rowan said, "follow the lead of anyone as homophobic, as anti-Semitic, as anti-female, as anti-white or as universally bigoted as Farrakhan. . . . I almost vomit at the thought of Farrakhan being my 'leader' or the 'savior of black men.' "[95]

A Peace Proposal

The struggle for Civil Rights and equal opportunity has cost America much. It has not fulfilled Martin Luther King's dream of a colorblind society. Color still matters more than character, and racial preferences still eclipse performance. Whites are now facing a growing movement of black nationalism and racism. The races are self-segregating again, with each group hanging out with "their own kind." We can't seem to talk to one another about what divides us without charges and countercharges of discrimination and bigotry. The old absolute ended in a four-year bloodbath almost a century and a half ago. The new absolute seems to be bringing us to the edge of a new civil war—one that may not be as bloody but still vicious and divisive.

What we need, I propose, is to rally around an absolute partially and imperfectly tried and long believed: *All human beings are created equal and should be treated with dignity and respect and provided equal opportunities to rise as high as their talents and drives will allow them.* This was King's vision in the 1960s, as well as Booker T. Washington's and Frederick Douglas's in the 1800s. It has its roots in Judaism and Christianity, though the adherents of these faiths sometimes distorted it and restricted its application. It will not bring equal outcomes, but then what can or even should? Marxism and socialism failed at that, as have numerous other utopian programs.

Racism is an equal opportunity employer and destroyer. We can work either to eradicate it or to leave it enshrined in our laws and public policies. I cast my vote for obliteration.

History in the Remaking

The *Old* Absolute	The *New* Absolute
(9) Western civilization and its heritage should be studied and valued above others.	(9a) Non-Western societies and other oppressed peoples and their heritage should be studied and valued above Western civilization.

- "A teacher of 'radical math literacy' warns against bombarding students with 'oppressive procapitalist ideology.' Among the practical applications of mathematics that she says should be avoided is totaling a grocery bill since such an exercise 'carries the nonneutral message that paying for food is natural.' "[1]

- Students of an elite American college claim the Holocaust didn't happen. It "has purchase, compared with the currency derived from other events," they say, "but it wasn't real." The Holocaust story, as one student summed up, is "a perfectly reasonable conceptual hallucination."[2]

- "Schoolteachers in Madison, Wisconsin, are taught how they can integrate lesbian history into the public school curriculum. They are told in district-sponsored conferences that being gay is as acceptable as being heterosexual; that gay students need role models; that lesbian teachers in the district can provide those role models; and that those who disagree are 'homophobic.'

  " 'Subtlety is the key,' the teachers are told. 'Blatant, radical

> change only invites the negative reactions of Christian parents.' The most effective way to incorporate homosexual ideas is through 'the subtle introduction of terms, questions, stories involving lesbian couples and other hidden messages.' "[3]

These are just a few examples of our tax dollars at work in America's current educational institutions. I could cite hundreds more with ease. Aside from their outrageousness, they all have at least one other characteristic in common: they are part of a relatively new approach to education called multiculturalism.

When I first heard the word *multiculturalism*, I thought it was a label describing the idea that we should seek to understand and appreciate the cultures of others. That was not a radical idea. I had been doing that much of my life and had certainly been enriched by the experience. In time, however, it began to dawn on me that the advocates of multiculturalism had a much different agenda than I had supposed. Under the guise of a new approach to education, they want to rid the classroom of what they call a eurocentric, ethnocentric, white-male-dominated, racist, heterosexist education. The emphasis on Western civilization—its history, religious foundations, intellectual and political movements, and achievements—must be marginalized in the curriculum and radically reinterpreted. In addition, they want to inaugurate studies that deride the West as bigoted and oppressive, as they uphold non-Western societies and other "oppressed peoples" as monuments to human fulfillment and keys to freedom. The multiculturalists want Euro-Americans to stop looking at the rest of the world through Western glasses, which they justly identify with the Greco-Roman-Judeo-Christian heritage. Instead, they want us to evaluate all non-Western cultures according to the standards of those cultures alone. In other words, multiculturalists are opposed to the old absolute: *Western civilization and its heritage should be studied and valued above others.* They want everyone to accept the new absolute they embrace: *Non-Western societies and other oppressed peoples and their heritage should be studied and valued above Western civilization.*

The Multiculturalist Program

Among observers of America's educational institutions, it is widely recognized that multiculturalists are political activists intent on imposing a leftist agenda on society. In his book *Inside American Education*, Thomas Sowell talks about the "prevailing vision of the left currently monopolizing many elite colleges and universities." Professors holding politically correct views, he says, "may turn their classrooms into indoctrination centers and staging areas for political activism." These same professors will accuse other professors of "insensitivity," "racism," or "sexism" on the basis of nothing more than a failure to use politically correct language—"Native American" rather than "American Indian"; "he or she," rather than the generic "he"—or a failure to include "issues of race, class, and gender" in their courses.[4]

Dinesh D'Souza describes a book required at Stanford University as part of their multicultural studies program. Entitled *I, Rigoberta Menchú: An Indian Woman in Guatemala*, the book tells "the story of a young woman who is said to be a representative voice of the indigenous peasantry," when she is nothing of the sort. States D'Souza:

> Rigoberta met the Venezuelan feminist to whom she narrates this story at a socialist conference in Paris, where, presumably, very few of the Third World's poor travel. Moreover, Rigoberta's political consciousness includes the adoption of such politically correct causes as feminism, homosexual rights, socialism, and Marxism. By the middle of the book she is discoursing on "bourgeois youths" and "Molotov cocktails," not the usual terminology of Indian peasants. One chapter is titled "Rigoberta Renounces Marriage and Motherhood," a norm that her tribe could not have adopted and survived.[5]

Why has this author and her book become required reading? "The answer is that Rigoberta seems to provide independent Third World corroboration for Western left-wing passions and prejudices. She is a mouthpiece for a sophisticated neo-Marxist critique of Western society, all the more powerful because it seems to issue not from some embittered American academic but from a Third World native."[6] Rigoberta is the perfect example of a "victim" for leftist multiculturalists. In the book's introduction she describes herself as a person of color who has suffered racism, as a woman who has endured sexism, as a native of South America that was victimized by North American colonialism, and as an Indian who has been victimized by Latino culture within Latin America.[7] Who could want more?

In his revealing book *Tenured Radicals*, Roger Kimball states, "With a few notable exceptions, our most prestigious liberal arts colleges and universities have installed the entire radical menu at the center of their humanities curriculum at both the undergraduate and the graduate level. Every special interest—women's studies, black studies, gay studies, and the like—and every modish interpretative gambit—deconstruction, poststructuralism, new historicism, and other varieties of what the literary critic Frederick Crews has aptly dubbed 'Left Eclecticism'—has found a welcome roost in the academy, while the traditional curriculum and modes of intellectual inquiry are excoriated as sexist, racist, or just plain reactionary."[8]

Academic Gregory Wolfe is even more explicit: "The ideologies which gained entry into the academy in the '60s claim that the fundamental intellectual principles of Western culture are illegitimate and must be overthrown. Indeed, the campus revolutionaries of the '60s are now members of the Establishment—tenured professors, heads of professional organizations, and directors of institutes. Perhaps the most significant aspect of the assault on the humanities is that it is now an on-going revolution from within."[9]

In a surprising article in *Newsweek*, Scott Turow looked around and asked where all the '60s radicals have gone.[10] He only needs to look in America's schools, where they are now teaching the nation's youth, espousing a refurbished Marxism and relativism that had inspired them decades earlier. They have moved from the streets into the halls of the academy.

Multiculturalism modernizes Karl Marx's ideas about class warfare. In Marx's world, capitalism and the bourgeois (ruling) class are the roots of evil, and the proletariat—the working class—is the good and source of hope. The bourgeois class oppresses the working class by owning the property and controlling the means of production. The workers can overcome their oppressed status by seizing power through a social revolution and reordering society according to communism. In a communist utopian regime, wages, money, social classes, and even state government are nonexistent. What's left is a free association of producers who control their own activities for the sake of the community. To arrive at this utopia, however, the proletariat must revolt against the dominate class, subdue it, and rule as a dictatorship until the social structure has been changed sufficiently.[11]

Multiculturalists have either knowingly adopted or unknowingly absorbed this Marxist vision while expanding the list of the oppressed and redefining the identity of the oppressor. The oppressor is now the class of white, heterosexual, capitalist, Judeo-Christian, Euro-American males. It doesn't matter whether they are poor or disenfranchised. Their economic status and control are not the primary issues anymore; they are just two among many. Multiculturalists simply assume that this redefined bourgeois class is the ruling, dominant class, and therefore it is the class they target.

Who should rise up and defeat the ruling class? Since the new oppressor is white, the oppressed must be all people of color. Since the oppressor is heterosexual, the oppressed must be bisexuals, homosexuals, and transsexuals. Since the oppressor is capitalistic, the oppressed must be those victimized by capitalism. Since the oppressor is Jewish or Christian, the oppressed must be non-Jews and non-Christians. Since the oppressor is Euro-American, the oppressed must be the rest of the world. And since the oppressor is male, the oppressed must be females, the transgendered, and all nonwhite males. Hence, the ideological reasons behind the new study programs for women, homosexuals, Asians, blacks, Native Americans, and a host of other so-called oppressed groups.

These study programs have been instituted not for the purpose of understanding other peoples but for raising oppressed classes from their oppressed condition and reinterpreting—even rewriting—history to fit the new understanding. These studies have political ends. They are educational only insofar as they advance a leftist political agenda. They are designed to shame, silence, and reeducate members of the dominant class so they will capitulate to the demands of the subjugated and thereby yield their power.

The critical weapons in this ideological war are cultural relativism, ethnocentrism, deconstruction, and myth-making. Let's take a look at each of these tools and see how they are used to accomplish the multiculturalist's ends.

The Measure of a Group, the Demise of the Individual

Relativism is like Baskin-Robbins ice cream—it comes in so many flavors that there's bound to be one to fit someone's taste. I'm not going to describe all the flavors here.[12] Instead I'll focus on just one: cultural relativism. This is the flavor served up in multicultural programs.

Philosopher James Rachels summarizes the five major tenets of cultural relativism:

(1) Different cultures have different moral codes;
(2) There is no objective standard that can be used to judge one societal code better than another;
(3) The moral code of our own society has no special status; it is merely one among many;
(4) There is no "universal truth" in ethics—that is, no moral truths hold for all peoples at all times; and, finally,
(5) The moral code of a society determines what is right within that society—that is, if the moral code of a society says that a certain

action is right, then that action *is* right, at least within that society.[13]

Cultural relativism has a long history. It first appears among some of the ancient Greek philosophers, such as Heraclitus and the Sophists.[14] But the acceptance it has earned in multicultural studies came largely from the work of nineteenth- and twentieth-century anthropologists and sociologists.

William Graham Sumner (1840–1910), one of the founders of modern sociology, was America's leading defender of Social Darwinism and Malthusian thought. In his classic book *Folkways*, he argues that moral codes grow out of cultural beliefs and practices—what he calls a culture's folkways. Right and wrong are not based on some transcultural standard; rather, they are culture-bound notions. Ethics flow from a culture's tradition. They have no other source, and they need no other justification. As he explains: "The 'right' way is the way which the ancestors used and which has been handed down. The tradition is its own warrant. It is not held subject to verification by experience. The notion of right is in the folkways. It is not outside of them, of independent origin, and brought to them to test them. In the folkways, whatever is, is right." He concludes, "Therefore, rights can never be 'natural' or 'God-given,' or absolute in any sense." Moreover, all knowledge comes from the folkways: "World philosophy, life policy, rights, and morality are all products of the folkways. They are reflections on, and generalizations from, the experience of pleasure and pain which is won in efforts to carry on the struggle for existence under actual life conditions. . . . They are all embodied in folklore, and all our philosophy and science have been developed out of them."[15]

In his study of various cultures, Sumner noticed that all cultures think they are better than others: "Each group nourishes its own pride and vanity, boasts itself superior, exalts its own divinities, and looks with contempt on outsiders. Each group thinks its own folkways the only right ones, and if it observes that other groups have other folkways, these excite its scorn." Sumner called this tendency to judge groups by one's own group *ethnocentrism*.[16]

American anthropologist Franz Boas had a different understanding of what constituted ethnocentrism. The main Social Darwinian stream of thought was to regard whites superior to other races due to their social advances. In his 1894 address to the Anthropological Section of the American Association for the Advancement of Science, Boas challenged this majority conclusion. He argued that the so-called cultural superiority of white Americans and Europeans had to do with historical circumstances, not any inherent racial capacities. He further claimed that the belief that whites were superior was simply the assessment of a naive and unwarranted ethnocentrism.[17] "Rather than judging another culture, or even any practice of another culture, by our own ethnocentric standards, Boas said that the practices and customs of another culture should be understood only in terms of its *own* context and its *own* standards. . . . [A]ll customs are relative to a particular cultural context; that is, they stem from that context, are meaningful only in that context, and should be understood only in terms of that context." Boas's understanding of ethnocentrism and its implications for cultural relativism "became the dominant philosophical stance of both anthropology and sociology."[18]

On the basis of cultural relativism and ethnocentrism, which is then mixed with heavy doses of revised Marxism, multiculturalists have persuaded schools to adopt study programs on alleged oppressed people groups. These programs are uncritical of the groups on which they focus. In fact, they usually give whatever these cultures believe or do standing ovations and their critics hisses and boos.

Multiculturalists will accuse critics of their programs of being racist ethnocentrists. This is one of the new unforgivable sins. As anthropologist Clifford Geertz says, "ethnocentric" is "the anthropologist's severest term of moral abuse."[19] How dare anyone judge whether one group should be studied and another ignored based on one's own culture-bound values, the multiculturalists will charge. Yet, when their oppressed-group study program is in place, the multiculturalists will uncritically use that group's judgments about others to demean and dismiss the characteristics and contributions of those people groups. They will use socialists to condemn capitalists, sexual libertines to exorcise advocates of sexual restraint, non-whites to accuse whites of racism, feminists to denounce the nuclear heterosexual family as an institution of reproductive and vocational slavery for women. On the other hand, the groups on the receiving end of these charges are not permitted to respond. They are the oppressors, the dominant class, hence their views are automatically biased and assumed wrong.

For multiculturalists, then, relativism and ethnocentrism only work one way. They apply to oppressed groups when they work to those groups' advantage. After that, they have no use at all. The bourgeois cannot use them to establish study programs that would promote their perspectives and values. If, as multiculturalists say out of one side of their mouth, cultures are all playing on the same field with no advantages, it would seem fair that if blacks can have study programs, then so should whites, that if feminists can have women's studies, then non-feminists should have their own study tracks as well. In reality, though, multiculturalists are not playing by these rules. Marxist ideology gives them the edge they need to keep all their critics at bay. And they use it to great effectiveness.

Deconstruction: Where Truth Goes to Die

In the hands of multiculturalists, deconstruction is a knife used to cut open and expose the West's many ways of oppressing and annihilating non-Western people groups, women, non-heterosexuals, and a host of other groups considered victims of Western imperialism and racism. The social construction that oppresses must be *de*-constructed—namely, its entrenched prejudices, superiority complex, aggressive posturing, often hidden techniques of marginalization and discrimination, and all the other tools it uses to hold others down knowingly or unknowingly must be exposed and excised.

Deconstruction assumes and builds upon the view of culture that came through Sumner and Boas. Deconstruction is not so much a literary theory as an attitude and practice that has been applied to all human knowledge, language, and behavior.[20] Its central figures are Jacques Derrida, a French philosopher who was "the chief theoretical architect of deconstruction,"[21] and the late Paul de Man, who "did more than anyone to institutionalize the 'demythologizing' tenets of deconstruction in the literature departments of American universities."[22] In their hands, and those of their followers, the search for meaning and truth becomes impossible, even laughable. While it's true that deconstruction has its critics, so far they have been unable to stem the tide of its influence.[23]

In the world of literature, deconstructionists maintain that authors cannot escape their ties to culture. Society influences them, shapes them, constructs them, so that what they write tells us as much about their culture as it does about them. But their writings do *not* tell us about a reality outside of human-making. Put another way, we can't get at a world untouched by human hands. Therefore, whatever we think we know is a distorted, impure invention humanly—more accurate still, socially—contrived.

Deconstructionism claims that we are cultural animals, mired forever in the folkways of our respective cultures. Objectivity, then, is a myth, and truth without error an illusion. "Objectivity" and "truth" are really nothing more than a group's story. Each group has a different story, and each group thinks their story is objectively true while conflicting stories are treated as objectively false. In point of fact, no story is objectively true or false. Each group's story creates a world that makes sense to that group, and that is good enough. We are all world-makers, not world-discoverers.

Furthermore, deconstructionists tell us that authors are so bound up by their cultural assumptions and biases that they are usually unaware of them. Authors are not the real creators or controllers in the communication process. They are part of the product produced by their culture and its language. This leads to the conclusion that authors can tell us little about what they are communicating. After all, they don't know the half of what they are really saying. Thus, readers are in the driver's seat for determining the meanings of any given text. And the tools deconstructionists put in the hands of readers are often some form of psychoanalysis, feminism, Marxism, or homosexism.

Of course, if deconstructionists are right about authors, then the same applies to readers and nonreaders. They are no better off than authors. They, too, are locked up in their socially constructed worlds, unable to see beyond their own social baggage. So the search for meaning and truth spins around in a vicious circle, with no one possessing a privileged or superior position that transcends culture and sees the real as it is in itself. All we see is the human, and the human is arbitrary, diverse, and contradictory.

This ultimately means that we cannot arrive at objective, universal truth about anything. For anything can be interpreted differently by different cultures, and since all interpretations are culture bound, no interpretation is better than another. In such a situation the best we can do is work to expose the hidden meanings and biases embedded in each other's knowledge claims, language usage, and behavior patterns.

Myth-Making: Past Imperfect History

Deconstructed history tears down. Reconstructed history builds on the ruins of deconstruction. The result is past imperfect myth-making. Let me show you what I mean with an appeal to the multicultural approach to Euro-American history.

In 1973, a Harvard University educator told attendees at a teacher's seminar how they should approach their profession: "Every child in America entering school at the age of five is mentally ill because he comes to school with certain allegiances toward our founding fathers, toward our elected officials, toward his parents, toward a belief in a supernatural Being, toward the sovereignty of this nation as a separate entity. It's up to you teachers to make all of these sick children well by creating the international children of the future."[24] For an American child to become an international child, educators must instill in them a sense of antagonism toward one's national, religious, and family heritage. The child's old allegiances must be severed and new ones forged. They must identify with a global community *at the expense of the child's native one.* This is largely accomplished in two ways: (1) by recasting America's history so the negatives stand out far and above the positives, and (2) by rewriting that history so it presents the contributions of minorities—whether real or imagined—far more than the contributions of white Euro-American men.

Consider, for example, the national history standards "created by the UCLA National Center for History in the Schools in cooperation with 33 national education organizations and more than 1,000 educators."[25] These standards provide teachers with guidelines about what America's students from fifth to twelfth grades should know about world history and their country's past.

The history standards were first released in 1994 in two volumes.[26] Both volumes generated a flurry of criticism due to their blatantly leftist multicultural perspective. For instance, in the U.S. history volume, Paul Revere's famous ride to warn the American colonists of the coming of British troops was not mentioned at all, nor was any word spoken about Robert E. Lee, the Confederacy's greatest general and master strategist. The Ku Klux Klan, however, rated seventeen mentions, and the black abolitionist Harriet Tubman, a woman who helped slaves escape through the Underground Railroad in the 1850s, got six honorable mentions. Abraham Lincoln's famous Gettysburg address is mentioned once, just in passing.[27] Only one modern congressional leader is mentioned, and that was Democrat Tip O'Neill calling Republican President Ronald Reagan "a cheerleader for selfishness."[28]

America's scientific and technological advances were also neglected. Notables such as Alexander Graham Bell, Albert Einstein, Jonas Salk, the Wright brothers, Thomas Edison, and Neil Armstrong received no attention. Some critics wondered if these men were omitted because they were all white males who failed to commit crimes against women and people of color. Scholar Lynne Cheney speculates that another reason for ignoring them may have been due to the low regard science and technology now have in certain parts of the academy:

> Both feminists and environmentalists argue that because of the high value that science places on objectivity and rationality, it is now in deep and deserved crisis—information that tends to come as

> a surprise to practicing scientists. Did the authors of the U.S. standards decide that in the case of a field so disdained by so many of their colleagues, the less said the better? Whatever the motive, to overlook American accomplishment in science and technology is to omit some of our most dazzling achievements.[29]

When it comes to America's early history up to 1620, "the standards suggest that students consider the architecture, labor systems, and agriculture of the Aztecs—but not their practice of human sacrifice."[30] The dark side of the native Indian cultures such as the Aztecs and Mayas are ignored or drastically played down.[31]

In the standards volume on world history, Cheney finds the section dealing with the United States dropping an atomic bomb on Hiroshima in 1945 as "the most irresponsible section." Fifth- and sixth-graders are "asked to read a book about a Japanese girl of their age who died a painful death as a result of radiation" fallout from the bomb. "No mention is made of death and suffering caused by the Japanese. The rape of Nanking is not discussed, nor is Pearl Harbor, or the Bataan death march. What fifth- and sixth-graders would be likely to conclude is that their country was guilty of a horrible—and completely unjustified—act of cruelty against innocents."[32] In fact, one question in the standards even suggests that America may have provoked Japan to attack Pearl Harbor.[33]

On the issue of slavery, the world history standards mentions the practice just twice, and both times it is attributed to white cultures—ancient Greece and the Euro-American side of the Atlantic slave trade. The standards are silent on the well-documented slave practices of many non-white peoples in North and South America, Africa, the Middle East, and Asia that preceded and followed the West's participation in slavery.[34]

When it comes to women, the standards world history volume has no problem accepting the fact that men and women in the ancient world usually had different roles. The volume refers to these role differences as "gender differentiation." However, these role differences become "restrictions on the rights and freedoms of women" when the discussion turns to the ancient Greek city-state of Athens. The reason? Historians commonly consider Athens the birthplace of Western democracy. If it's Western and democratic, it must be sexist. You may not be surprised to learn that the multicultural sin of ethnocentrism is also first introduced in the context of ancient Greek civilization. The standards conveniently omit the clear and abundant evidence showing the ethnocentricity of Asian, Arab, and African cultures.[35]

The authors of the standards went out of their way to write a politically correct multicultural version of American and world history. In so doing they trampled on the historical record in order to present Western civilization as sexist, racist, imperialistic, and oppressive, while portraying non-Western cultures in the best skewed light imaginable.

The U.S. Senate was not amused. In 1995 they voted 99 to 1 to repudiate both volumes of the standards.[36] Washington Senator Slade Gorton called the standards "perverse." Albert Shanker, the chairman of the American Federation of Teachers, denounced the standards, saying, "No other nation in the world teaches a national history that leaves its children feeling negative about their own country—this would be the first."[37]

In spite of such a resounding rejection, the authors returned to their work and attempted to answer their critics by making, in Gary Nash's words, "cosmetic" changes for the sake of clarification.[38] According to one reviewer, the revised version eliminated some "overtly biased language" and added "new material on science, technology, and the Cold War." Nevertheless, "the basic left-wing structure of the document . . . remains intact."[39]

Whether these standards are eventually accepted, undergo yet another revision, or never receive official federal sanction is not nearly as important as what their very existence reveals: a deep-seated, radical anti-Western bias among many of America's scholars.

Multiculturalism is really a camouflage for the new bigots. Under its banner intellectuals are set free to vent their rage toward any person or group that does not fit into their view of an oppressed people. It is ethnocentrism as seen through Marxist-tinted glasses. It is hypocrisy in capital letters.

Separating Fiction From Fact

Even apart from the national history standards volumes, multiculturalism is entrenched and growing in America's schools. From preschool to post-graduate work, multiculturalists are at work transforming lives through politically correct propaganda.[40] Are their efforts achieving the desired results? Tragically, yes. Young minds are the most impressionable, and the impressions left by the new bigots are creating a form of tribalism potentially far more destructive than the ethnocentrism they purport to disdain. (I will deal with this in more detail in the next chapter when I look at the new tools of control: political correctness and the new tolerance.)

Multicultural studies are having yet another troubling effect: they are turning America's youth against their own culture. A letter from a white male graduate of two major U.S. universities illustrates this point all too well:

> I am a male WASP who attended and succeeded at Choate preparatory school, Yale College, Yale Law School, and Princeton Graduate School. Slowly but surely, my lifelong habit of looking, listening, feeling, and thinking as honestly as possible has led me to see that white, male-dominated, Western, European culture is the most destructive phenomenon in the known history of the planet. . . . It is deeply hateful of life and committed to death; therefore, it is moving rapidly toward the destruction of itself and most other life forms on earth. And truly, it deserves to die. . . . We're going to have to bite the bullet of truth. We have to face our own individual and collective responsibility for what is happening—our greed, brutality, indifference, militarism, racism, sexism, blindness.[41]

It is true that Western civilization is far from innocent. Like all other peoples, Westerners have committed crimes against humanity, the environment, and deity. What sets the West apart—and this is what multiculturalists are predisposed against accepting—is that it has acted like a sponge, soaking up the values and visions of the peoples it came in contact with, expunging what it concluded was false or unhelpful, then incorporating the rest into the fabric of its life.[42] Judeo-Christianity has been the most influential and enduring worldview adopted by the West, and it has been the one that has frequently served the West as the great corrective.

As we saw in the last chapter, Euro-Americans acting on Judeo-Christian principles launched and fought a successful moral campaign to rid the world of slavery. No other peoples on earth had ever challenged this ancient institution and dismantled it. Westerners, however, did.

Contrary to feminist pronouncements, Western Judeo-Christians were also the first ones to follow the lead of Jesus of Nazareth and the first-century church in raising the status of women beyond any they ever had before. Historian Page Smith makes this clear. His comments are worth quoting at length.

> One of the most important accomplishments of the Medieval Church was to elevate the status of women far beyond that of any other culture. The seeds of this elevation lay in Christ's close relationship to women. The role of women in the world empires that

> preceded the rise of Christianity was almost uniformly deplorable.... [B]y refusing to accept the pagan division of women into wives/mothers on the one hand and sexual playthings on the other, the Church ennobled both women and the institution of marriage itself....
>
> [T]he Medieval Church gave women a kind of centrality, and spiritual dignity, not achieved elsewhere. The dominating symbol was the Holy Mother herself, but she was reinforced and supported by a number of women saints. The fact is that the iconography of the Medieval Church demonstrates more powerfully than words the central, if not primary, role of women in the life of the Church....
>
> The status that women enjoyed through church and convent was reflected in the civic world. In the words of the German historian Friedrich Heer, "The women of Paris are known to have been engaged in more than a hundred different occupations. They worked as weavers, embroiderers, and retailers; when their husbands died they carried on their businesses with resource and courage, proving themselves master craftsmen in their own right; they were teachers, doctors, and merchants."

Toward the end of his discussion, Smith challenges skeptics "to test the proposition that Christianity exalted women." The test is simple: "The industrious researcher has only to turn up other cultures where the status of women is as high. So far as I am aware no one has yet done so."[43]

The West has its blights, but history proves it has made great strides that clearly surpass those made by non-Western societies. If multiculturalism continues to get its way, the West's failures—real and contrived—will be all anyone will be taught to see. That is a formula for national suicide.

The Politically Correct Life

The *Old* Absolute	The *New* Absolute
(10) Different perspectives should be heard and tolerated, but only the true and right ones should prevail.	(10a) Only those viewpoints deemed politically correct should be tolerated and encouraged to prevail.

If you are in the market to buy or sell a house, you better beware of the new sales terminology. Real estate agents are being very careful of the words they use because they can be sued for using advertising language that someone might find offensive or discriminatory. Here is a list of several terms that many real estate agents and ad writers are striving to avoid:[1]

Red Flag Words	Reason to Avoid
Executive	Possibly racist, since most corporate executives are white
Sports enthusiast	Could discourage the disabled
Quiet neighborhood	Potential code word for "no children," hence discriminatory against families
Master bedroom	Suggests slavery
Walk-in closet	Prejudicial to people who can't walk
Spectacular view	Prejudicial to people who can't see

Convenient to jogging trails	Perhaps offensive to the disabled
Close to synagogue and deli	Constitutes religious steering
Desirable neighborhood	Constitutes racial steering
Near country club	Constitutes social class steering
Japanese garden	Might offend Asian-Americans
Rare find	If used in reference to a "nice home" in a black neighborhood, could be racist
Non-Christian	Religious discrimination
Christian	Also religious discrimination

Although the list seems overly cautious, and even comical, the concern is real. A real estate agent can be sued for violating the federal Fair Housing Act, which bars housing discrimination—including any notice or ad that "indicates any preference, limitation, or discrimination because of race, color, religion, sex, handicap, familial status or national origin or an intention to make any such preference."[2]

Newspaper publishers, real estate agencies, and local and state human relations groups are getting together to develop red-flag word lists in hopes of lowering complaints and lawsuits. One real estate representative said, "We decided to print our list on loose-leaf paper, so that people could put it in binders and add pages as we add new words.... Pretty soon we'll have the Encyclopedia Britannica in there."[3]

The message is clear: Watch what you say or it may cost you dearly. In 1991, for instance, a fair housing group in Oregon filed 150 complaints with the U.S. Department of Housing and Urban Development. "In Pennsylvania, the state human relations commission reports a 317 percent increase in housing discrimination complaints (not only ads)" in 1993 alone. In one case, three newspapers and several landlords were sued for more than one million dollars over charges of "discriminatory advertising."[4]

What has led to such an oppressive and ridiculous state of affairs? A climate filled with the odor of political correctness (PC).

The PC Virus

Are you politically correct? To the degree you subscribe to the new absolutes discussed in the previous chapters, you are PC certified. To the degree you don't, you are open to ridicule, rebuke, lawsuits, jail time, fines, and a host of other means to intimidate you into coming in line with the PC standard. PC is leftist fundamentalism, and the PC life is the one rightly ordered to that dogma.

The most critical PC virtue is the new tolerance. I call it new because it is not the kind of tolerance of less than thirty years ago. Back then being tolerant meant putting up with a slow salesclerk, restraining the desire to laugh at someone else's bizarre dress, or holding one's tongue when a person made a harmless but erroneous comment. Throughout American history, tolerant never meant condoning immoral behavior, letting beliefs that could harm someone go unchallenged, or permitting a person's dangerous lifestyle to influence others. In the past we may have disagreed about what is true, but few challenged the bedrock conviction that truth is the opposite of false, that truth does not tolerate untruth. We understood that some beliefs and lifestyles promoted the common good while others undermined it.

Not so today. In the world of PC, the tolerant person is someone who is broad-minded, open to other beliefs, lifestyles, claims to truth, and moral convictions. The tolerant person makes room for others to do as they wish, even if their behavior contradicts or mocks his own. The tolerant person believes in "live and let live." The new tolerance doesn't just put up with contrary beliefs or behaviors. It accepts them, makes room for them, honors them, even strives to protect them. The tolerant person may not adopt any of these beliefs or behaviors as his own, but he will go to the mat to uphold the desires of others to live them out. In short, the new tolerance is non-condemning and all-protecting *as long as the matters involved are PC compatible.*

The societal shift over the last thirty years is rather dramatic. Like a virus that subtley attacks its unsuspecting host, the PC virus has slowly wormed its seductive message throughout our society.

When it comes to us who are PC *in*compatible, the new tolerance is absolutely intolerant. Nonconformers are considered racists, sexists, homophobes, Victorian prudes, religious zealots, terrorist-like fundamentalists, anti everything that PC considers good. Non-PCers are never allowed to be pro anything. If we call ourselves pro-life, we are labeled anti-choice. If we say we are pro-family, we are told we are anti-women or anti-gay. If we present ourselves as pro-marriage, we are reported as being intolerant moralists and antagonistic toward single mothers. If we say we are for parental involvement and choice in education, then we are said to be against children's rights and quality education for all. If we uphold character and performance as the true measures for job placement and advancement, then we are looked upon as racists and suppressors of the poor and needy. If we are not PC, we are ostracized in the name of tolerance and diversity. The hypocrisy is blatant and venomous.

Some people have tried to make light of PC's influence or even deny its presence. In the December 1991 issue of *Harper's* magazine, a Harvard University graduate claimed that the "campuses are no more under siege by radicals than is the society at large. It has been clever of the Kimballs and D'Souzas to write as if it were so. It is always clever of those in ascendance to masquerade as victims."[5] This writer couldn't be more wrong. America is undergoing a radical shift to the Left on and off its college campuses. And the ones claimed to be "in ascendance" are the ones increasingly being marginalized and excluded from public discourse.

Still others have attempted to justify PC. Until the courts ruled these measures as violations of the First Amendment, administrators at many colleges and universities enacted speech and conduct codes for their students and sometimes for their faculty. The University of Michigan "adopted a six-page 'anti-bias code' that provides for punishment of students who engage in conduct that 'stigmatizes or victimizes an individual on the basis of race, ethnicity, religion, sex, sexual orientation, creed, national origin, ancestry, age, marital status, handicap, or Vietnam-era veteran status.' " Such codes were supposed to "send a message," especially to "minority students," that the school "board and its administration do care." They were intended to foster "unity and cohesion in the diversity which we seek to achieve, thereby creating an atmosphere of pluralism."[6] What such codes really did was squelch critical discussion of and opposition to PC dogmas and agendas. If you were PC, the schools cared. If you were not, you may have ended up in a sensitivity-awareness program to help you overcome your allegedly racist, sexist, or homophobic attitudes. Or you may have received your expulsion papers. Indeed, these things can still happen, for PC expectations still permeate the air in the academy.[7]

I believe PC and its new-tolerance companion are outlandish and destructive perversions of America's religious, moral, and political heritage. They actually contradict our founding documents and the principles that undergird them. In the balance of this chapter I would like to show how the PC establishment is working to mainstream its views and values so the PC life will become normative to Americans. In an effort to focus the discussion, I use examples from homosexuality and race relations to illustrate my case. These have been addressed from a different angle in previous chapters, so I could have just as easily drawn from a host of other PC views, such as feminism, proabortion, pro-euthanasia, and "safe-sex" promiscuity. But in today's charged atmosphere, race relations and homosexuality are two of the most contentious issues of social concern and confusion. These portraits will show how dominant and pervasive the PC perspective is, especially in American schools, politics, and law.

Looking to Africa

Black studies programs have made great strides in the PC environment. I certainly have no problems with the existence of black studies programs in schools. As long as the material developed and taught is based on sound scholarship and an appreciation for the contributions of others, including that of Western civilization, black studies can provide important insights and correctives to other academic endeavors. Thomas Sowell, Alan Keyes, and Henry Louis Gates, Jr., are just three thought-provoking black scholars writing today who exhibit these qualities. Unfortunately, within some black studies programs, a hostility is growing that blacks would readily label racist if it had a white face on it. An interpretation of the black experience called Afrocentrism is partly responsible.

Afrocentrism is an approach to history and race relations that is put forward as a substitute for Eurocentrism. Afrocentrists claim that East Africa—specifically, Egypt—is the mother of Western civilization. They claim that the ancient Egyptians were black, that they developed a theory of evolution that predates Darwin's by two millennia, and that they flew on gliders for travel, explorations, and recreation four millennia before the Wright brothers. Afrocentrists also teach that the black Egyptians discovered the wave/particle behavior of light and the theories behind quantum mechanics. The Egyptians were also to have accessed powers in the supernatural realm through "precognition, psychokinesis, remote viewing, and other underdeveloped human capabilities."[8] According to the Afrocentric view, the achievements attributed to Greece were really stolen from Egypt. Aristotle, for example, supposedly went to Egypt with Alexander the Great, stole books from the library in Alexandria, and put his name on them. African Egyptians also purportedly brought medicine, science, mathematics, and the arts to Europe. And they discovered America long before Christopher Columbus.[9]

Afrocentrists also claim that the demise of the great African civilization began when "Moorish invaders from the north plundered the black empires and sent West Africa into decline. European slave traders thereafter invented 'fantastic tales of savagery about Africans' so that the slave trade would appear an act of Christian charity. . . . The subsequent deterioration of Africa was caused by 'the greed and imperialistic goals of the European nations.' "[10] According to Afrocentrist Leonard Jeffries, this was done "as part of a conspiracy to prevent [blacks] from having a unified experience."[11]

Afrocentrists are apparently building on the views taught within some black communities for nearly two centuries. In her 1942 autobiography *Dust Tracks on a Road*, Zora Neale Hurston tells about the "great speech" she had heard all her life, one she later learned had preceded her by several generations:

> Negroes were the bravest men on earth, facing every danger like lions, and fighting with demons. We must remember with pride that the first blood spilled for American Independence was that of the daring Crispus Attucks, a Negro who had bared his black breast to the bullets of the British tyrants at Boston. . . . It was a Negro named Simon who had been the only one with enough pity and compassion in his heart to help the Savior bear His cross upon Calvary. It was the Negro troops under Teddy Roosevelt who won the battle of San Juan Hill. . . . It was the genius of the Negro which had invented the steam engine, the cotton gin, the air brake, and numerous other things—but conniving white men had seen the Negro's inventions and run off and put them into practice before the Negro had a chance to do anything about it. Thus the white man got credit for what the genius of the Negro brain had produced. Were it not for the envy and greed of the white man, the Negro would hold his rightful place—the noblest and greatest man on earth.[12]

Aside from the fact that the Afrocentric version of history has been demonstrated to be based on slender evidential threads at best and outright fabrications at worst,[13] the entire historical narrative is clearly designed to do to whites what the Afrocentrists claim whites did to blacks—dehumanize them and steal their ideas and inventions and call them their own. Like the white racists before him, Leonard Jeffries has even proposed a biological explanation for whites oppressing blacks. He argues that whites suffer from an inadequate supply of melanin, which is responsible for all skin coloration and supposedly regulates intellect and health as well. The Ice Ages caused this genetic deformity in whites, thereby making the white "ice people" and their descendants selfish, materialistic, and violent. What whites have given the world are the three D's—"domination, destruction, and death." On the other hand, because blacks lived under the warmth of the sun, their melanin remained at the proper level and their genes were enhanced by the "value system of the sun." These "sun people" and their progeny evolved biologically superior to whites. Unlike their inferior counterparts, blacks are cooperative, spiritual, and peaceful. Whites have attempted to overcome their inadequacies by committing crimes against blacks. Jeffries even contends that "rich Jews" financed the slave trade.[14]

This is not only bad science and bogus history but Social Darwinism recruited to support black racism. The disturbing part of all this is that Jeffries is a member of the academic establishment. He is the chairman of the Afro-American Studies department at City College of New York, and he is the coauthor of a multicultural curriculum used in all the public schools in New York State. According to a student who took one of his classes, he once called Diana Ross an "international whore" for her involvement with white men. And he applauded the destruction of the Challenger space shuttle because it would deter white people from "spreading their filth throughout the universe."[15]

Asa Hilliard, an educational psychologist who shares Jeffries' views, created a series called "African-American Baseline Essays." Containing multiple contributors, all Afrocentrists, the essays have been introduced into the Portland, Oregon, school system, and they have inspired "Afrocentric curricula in Milwaukee, Indianapolis, Pittsburgh, Washington, D.C., Richmond, Atlanta, Philadelphia, Detroit, Baltimore, Camden, and other cities" where "school boards and administrators [are] anxious to do the right thing."[16]

In Afrocentric studies, students are also encouraged to take African names, wear African dress, and learn and practice African rituals. They are taught to distrust and hate whites. Educators are told that the black mind works in a genetically different way. Blacks allegedly process information differently, they are more emotional, and two of their greatest kinds of intelligence are dancing and singing. They should not be taught standard English but black English. According to one black psychologist, the black way of communicating includes a lot of body language, eye movement, and positioning, "words that depend upon context for meaning and that have little meaning in themselves," and "a wide use of many coined interjections (sometimes profanity)."[17] Therefore, black children should receive a different education than whites so they don't develop feelings of inferiority when they are really superior.

In the world of PC, Afrocentrism and its racist views are acceptable. For only groups with the dominant power can be racist, and since blacks don't possess this power, they cannot be racist. Moreover, as one critic of Afrocentrism explains, with PC "since everything is political, there has never been disinterested scholarship, only power plays by various groups to justify their own claims. And even if there are some holes in Afrocentrism, the approach is useful because it raises the 'self-esteem' of black students."[18]

Education is transformed into one huge therapy session based on misinformation intended to uplift fragile egos. If I were black, I would be offended by such a condescending philosophy of education.

What will happen to the esteem of blacks taught Afrocentrism when they discover the innumerable errors of this perspective? How will they feel about their different education when they are unable to compete against other people who have received the tools they need to become successful members of society? Arthur Schlesinger makes a telling observation:

> It is hard to imagine any form of education more likely than Afrocentrism to have a "terribly damaging effect on the psyche." The best way to keep a people down is to deny them the means of improvement and achievement and cut them off from the opportunities of the national life. If some Kleagle of the Ku Klux Klan wanted to devise an educational curriculum for the specific purpose of handicapping and disabling black Americans, he would not be likely to come up with anything more diabolically effective than Afrocentrism.[19]

The Burning Issue

Yet another side of political correctness at work in race relations issues is displayed in the attention recently paid to church fires occurring in the South. *USA Today* captured the mood of many people when it exclaimed in an editorial that "racial hostility pervades the ruins [of burned churches] like the stench of smoke.... Apart from old-time lynchings, there is no more calculated act of racial hatred than burning a church."[20]

Are the burnings racially motivated hate crimes? Or is the picture more complicated than that? When we take an objective look at the facts, we find that racism is not the sole or even primary motivating factor behind the vast majority of these fires. Consider.

There are well over three hundred thousand churches across the country. Approximately six hundred churches, synagogues, and other places of worship burn each year. Most of the fires are accidental. Of those that are the work of arson, about half involve black or predominantly black churches, and nearly an equal number involve white or predominantly white churches. Arson strikes black, white, and interracial churches alike with apparent equanimity.[21]

The profile of the church-burning arsonist is revealing. It is true that some church fires are the work of racists, but even their motives are often mixed. Most race-based fires are simply not the result of pure bigotry, or even long-held, deeply entrenched racist views. Some arsonists are religious bigots, not racial ones. Many church arsonists are teenage vandals,[22] burglars, drunks, and drug addicts. In other cases they are mentally handicapped.[23]

Others are the work of pyromaniacs—people who just love to see things burn. Even fire fighters have been known to set fires.[24] Numerous churches are burned so someone can collect the insurance or carry out other fraudulent schemes. In fact, according to the Bureau of Alcohol, Tobacco, and Fire Arms (ATF), "About half of all arsons are inside jobs."[25]

Among those who have been arrested and/or convicted, one-third are black, the rest white. As far as I have been able to determine, the investigation thus far has found that black arsonists torched only black churches, while whites set fire to white and black churches and several synagogues. One anti-Protestant white man burned thirty-two white Protestant churches. That's almost a third of all the white churches torched. An angry Jewish man set ablaze a dozen synagogues. Neither man had racist motives.[26]

Some fires were clearly racially motivated. In Mississippi, three white teenagers set fire to two black churches to celebrate the anniversary of Martin Luther King, Jr.'s assassination. They were heard shouting racial epithets. They were also drunk and high on marijuana. In open court, two of the arsonists turned and faced church members and apologized for their crimes.[27]

In Tennessee, two young white men, both of whom founded a white supremacy group called Aryan Faction, set fire to a lodge house that black Baptists often used for their worship services. "They spray painted 'AF strikes again' and 'Niggers, leave or die' on the walls before dousing the place with kerosene. After torching it, they ran away, whooping and hollering." They were caught just days later by local authorities. One of the arsonists apologized in court for his wrongdoing. "I can't express the guilt that I feel," he said. "I really do feel like slime." This same person admitted that racism motivated him, but he also said that he loved "to see things burn" even as a child. He used to burn his toys and watch plastic melt. He even burned down his parents' garage once. "In religious practices," he said, "fire is purifying. And I always figure if something burns away and goes to ashes, then it exists too."[28] Race was certainly a factor, but not the only reason for this man's crime.

The federal government became involved in the arson investigations of burned churches already being conducted by local and state authorities in January 1996, when the "Justice Department launched a civil rights probe . . . into eight church fires to determine if the crimes were racially motivated." The probe was then expanded in early February to include other church fires. One FBI agent predicted in June 1996, after six months of investigative work, "We're going to find out that some of these cases will involve no racial animus, a few will be inside jobs and some will be done by extremists."[29] As it turns out, his prediction was an understatement. While the probe disproved the racial conspirator theory, it also uncovered some other fascinating facts.

Consider first the number of churches involved and their racial composition. Over the last five years, 123 church fires have been catalogued as arson or suspected as arson. The ATF says that eighty-five of these churches were white or predominantly white, while just thirty-eight were black or predominately black.[30] White churches are the targets of arson more than twice as much as black churches—a fact usually buried deep in media stories, if it is mentioned at all.

Of course, the media has had plenty of help promoting this error-ridden message. One southern black minister whose church had been destroyed referred to the burnings as a racist "conspiracy" and blamed "individuals sending out hate messages on radio and TV" for encouraging the lower classes "to do evil." As it turns out, the white man who set fire to the reverend's church was not a racist. He was "retarded and emotionally troubled," he had been "taking *Prozac*," and he had been "hospitalized repeatedly for attempted suicide," most recently days before the church burning. Hardly the profile of a hate crime.[31]

Sometimes the race message was more subtle but still quite clear. For instance, the Center for Democratic Renewal, a group that monitors racial violence, set up a fund to take contributions to help churches that had suffered loss in the fires. The fund was called the Black Church Bombing Rebuilding Fund.[32] Apparently, the CDR had no interest in helping white churches or Jewish synagogues that had been torched. They also seemingly believed that racism against blacks was the only motivating factor behind the fires. Otherwise, why would a group monitoring racial violence establish a fund for just black churches? If the act was done out of the goodness of their hearts, why restrict their goodwill to only African-American places of worship?

President Bill Clinton and Attorney General Janet Reno joined the chorus and said they thought racism was the primary motivation behind the fires, despite the fact that local and state authorities, along with FBI agents, were cautioning against conspiracy theories and downplaying the racial element. Even as late into the investigations as June 8, 1996, Clinton reasserted in his weekly radio address, "It is clear that racial hostility is the driving force behind a number of these incidents."[33] Reno later echoed this claim.[34] While their comments are true, they are only partial representations of the known facts. Like Johnnie Cochran in his defense of O. J. Simpson, Clinton and Reno played the race card, even when their own investigators have shown that race was just one factor among many and was not even the reason behind the great majority of church fires.

Like the media,[35] Clinton attempted to build a bridge between the '60s and '90s with himself postured in both eras. On one of these occasions, he told his radio audience, "I have vivid and painful memories of black churches being burned in my own state when I was a child." If that's the case, no one else can recall the incidents. Arkansas's state historian, the president of the Arkansas chapter of the NAACP, and the former president of the Regular Arkansas Baptist Convention all disputed Clinton's vivid recollections. They said they "couldn't recall any church burnings in Arkansas during the Civil Rights era."[36]

One of the biggest ironies in this whole saga has been the incredible outpouring of support from the American people for the members of these destroyed houses of worship. Organizations such as Promise Keepers, the National Council of Churches, Habitat for Humanity, the Southern Baptist Convention, the Anti-Defamation League, and corporations such as AT&T have raised money and pledged other kinds of support to help rebuild and refurbish the wrecked churches and synagogues. Many local churches have reached out with resources as well. Local whites restored two black churches in Tennessee so quickly that neither church missed a worship service.[37] One black pastor of a burned-out church said, "People have been kind and very supportive and a great majority of them have been from white congregations."[38] A middle-aged white woman in this pastor's community told one reporter, "Racism isn't right. Just because it was a colored church [that burned] makes no difference.... There's some things that decent folks just don't accept."[39]

This is not PC-compatible behavior. According to the PC theory of race relations, only whites can be racist since they are the most powerful class, and blacks in American society are routinely discriminated against because whites hold the reins of power. Jesse Jackson made this crystal clear when he made these remarks in June 1996 about the church burnings: "It seems to me that the blue suits are engaging in anti-civil rights propaganda and legislation in Congress and the black robes are handing out restrictive rulings in the courts, and the white sheets are doing the burning. There is a kinship among these things."[40] There is a kinship, all right, but not between these groups and the arsonists. The conspiratorial kinship is in the fertile imaginations of those people who, like Jackson, practice reverse racism while calling it "telling it like it is." That's one of those things decent folks just don't accept.

It is an example of tragic destruction being used by the PC community to give credence to their racial conspiracy theories. Yes, church burnings have occurred. Yes, they are usually the acts of sick people. But are they a result of a deeply seated racial hatred toward our fellow black Americans? I think not.

The truth is, children of any race are not born bigots. Bigots are bred. And they are usually bred by members of their own race—white or black, brown or yellow, it doesn't matter. Until we all face up to reality, our fantasies will keep perpetuating divisions in the name of racial healing.

The Homosexualization of America

For three years, in the early '70s, homosexual activists physically and psychologically bullied their way into the American Psychiatric Association's professional meetings and demanded that the APA alter its position on homosexuality. Even a highly sympathetic account of the activists' behavior described their efforts as "[g]uerilla theater tactics" and "shouting matches" that shocked, intimidated, and distressed conferees. To cite a typical example, one psychiatrist, while he was discussing the use of "aversive conditioning techniques" in the treatment of sexual deviation, was verbally assaulted by activists. "Shouts of 'vicious,' 'torture,' and 'Where did you take your residency, Auschwitz?' " rang out throughout the crowded room.[41] The barrage on the APA establishment and its members was so effective that the APA finally caved in and gave the activists what they wanted. After most of a century of regarding homosexuality as a curable mental illness, the APA granted homosexuality normalcy status in 1973. The politics of intimidation had won the day.

Homosexual activists are still bullying their way into the American mainstream. At times their tactics are more subtle than they were with the APA, but they still manage to convince people that homosexuals are victims of hatred and bigotry and therefore deserve society's protection. Consider the victories they won at one of America's most prestigious universities—Stanford.

The Stanford Case

At Stanford University, homosexual activists were having a hard time getting the school's administration to sympathize with their agenda. It seems no homosexuals were being victimized. Attacks on homosexuals were virtually nonexistent, and expressions of disapproval of the homosexual lifestyle were almost as rare. What to do?

A computer science lecturer named Stuart Reges came up with the winning suggestion: when you lack evidence, create it yourself. He suggested that homosexuals put out fliers at fraternities advertising a gay dance with the hope that fraternity members would become angry and tell them to leave. He also thought it would be a good idea for homosexual couples to attend fraternity parties and flaunt their sexuality to see if their actions might solicit a hostile response. Yet another provocative idea was for homosexuals to stage "a kiss-in outside the gym some afternoon" just long enough to "force the football team" to walk past them "at the end of practice." If homosexuals could "collect a lot of powerful anecdotes" of homophobic hatred, then they could achieve victim status and thereby win the sympathetic ear of the university.[42]

When the staged provocations failed to bring about the desired results, the homosexual activists grasped at an even more desperate straw. "When the *Stanford Review* reprinted Reges' advice in a news story, he declared that the article itself provided the much-needed evidence of a pervasive 'anti-gay' bias; the very existence of such students who wrote for the *Review*, according to Reges, suggested that things had gotten 'even worse' for campus homosexuals." Amazingly enough, this tactic—along with similarly silly claims of rampant homophobia on campus—worked.

> In the fall of 1988, the university began funding the Lesbian, Gay, and Bisexual Community Center . . . in order for the group to pay for "coming out" days, Gay and Lesbian Awareness Week, and other events to combat homophobia. In 1991, married-student housing was made available to homosexual partners who wished to live together (the fact that the children of married couples would gain exposure to homosexual relationships was seen as an additional plus). And in 1991, Stanford Law School hired its first openly homosexual faculty member under a new affirmative action policy that gave preferences to openly homosexual applicants. The law school's hiring committee argued that those who had proclaimed their homosexuality would provide positive role models for students to emulate. The professor's arrival itself became the occasion for more awareness, as the entire law school was decorated with a display of lavender balloons to mark the festive day. . . .

> In early 1993 . . . Stanford extended employee housing and health benefits to the "domestic partners" of homosexual faculty and staff. The university's explanation hardly drew notice when it declared, "We think that redefining 'family' for purposes of the benefits program to include long-term, committed domestic partnerships, appropriately reflects the changing social reality and values of the Stanford community." With this rhetoric, the university carried the irrational fear of homophobia to a logical conclusion.[43]

This isn't all the university did to help the homosexual community overcome its fabricated victimhood. Stanford's Office of Residential Education now actively recruits homosexuals to accept positions in which they will "promote openness to issues of sexuality and sexual preference" to the dormitory student residents. Stanford has also erected a "Gay Liberation" statue near the campus's central Quad. The statue depicts homosexual men and women caressing each other.[44]

Perhaps the most outrageous allowance the school has made is to permit the holes drilled between the walls of toilet stalls in the men's bathrooms to remain. Homosexuals created the "glory holes" so they could engage in anonymous bathroom sex. An interested party goes into a stall and waits for someone to enter the adjoining stall. When a person does, the sex-seeker taps his foot. If the newcomer taps his foot in response, the match is made and consummated in the bathroom.[45]

The Politics of Desire

Homosexuals want far more than "glory holes" and statues. They want their disordered sexual appetite recognized as a civil right. And while many people are opposing their desire, many others who are not homosexual have agreed with them and have chosen to fight alongside them on this issue.

Homosexuals could not be more pleased. They see this shift in perception as a victory for the homosexual movement. Homosexual author Dennis Altman makes this observation in his book *The Homosexualization of America:*

> The greatest single victory of the gay movement over the past decade has been to shift the debate from behavior to identity, thus forcing opponents into a position where they can be seen as attacking the civil rights of homosexual citizens rather than attacking specific and (as they see it) antisocial behavior.
>
> . . . Once the homosexual is perceived as part of a people with his or her particular lifestyle, she/he will likely be treated as are other

members of recognized minorities and accorded a particular identity that is a far cry from the stigmatized one implied in earlier definitions. Moreover, the impact on homosexuals themselves is enormous; the sense of being isolated, exceptional, doomed to a lonely and miserable life, which was the experience of so many gay women and men in the past, is far less likely in a society that acknowledges the existence of a homosexual minority and culture.[46]

In an attempt to achieve Civil Rights status, homosexuals also want the very words *family* and *marriage* redefined. As one lesbian author said, "Cleaving [which is what occurs in a traditional marriage] is an activity which should be left to snails for cleaning ponds and aquariums. Multiplicity of relationships does not create the number of conflicts the morality tales of our culture would have us believe, if the basis of each relationship is the autonomy of the self and the freedom of the other."[47]

Homosexuals have tried to turn the traditional understanding of marriage and family into a hideous monster better slain than served. "We should put an end to our embarrassment about transcending monogamy, for by moving beyond it we have also transcended the possessiveness and jealousy adopted from traditional heterosexual relationships in which males 'own' women, who are in turn dependent. By openly and honestly incorporating recreational sex into our relationships we have tapped a rich quarry of 'resistance,' that essential quality needed for rewarding, ongoing sexuality in a relationship."[48]

Unfortunately, homosexuals have found many influential allies in the media, literature, education, politics, psychology, and law. As a consequence, the homosexual movement has been demanding, and in many states getting, parts of its social agenda fulfilled by legislative fiat.[49]

The most recent and far-reaching instance of this came in May 1996 at the level of the U.S. Supreme Court. Four years previous, 53 percent of the citizens of the State of Colorado voted in favor of Amendment 2, thereby officially amending their state constitution. Amendment 2 expressly forbade the enactment of laws in Colorado that would give homosexuals, lesbians, or bisexuals special treatment on the basis of their "orientation, conduct, practices or relationships." It specifically prohibited laws that would grant these groups entitlement claims due to "minority status, quota preferences, protected status or claim of discrimination."[50] In other words, Amendment 2 banned special rights to homosexuals. They had all the other legal rights everyone else did, but they could not claim the additional rights reserved for minorities. Affirmative action programs would be out of their reach.

In a six-to-three decision, the U.S. Supreme Court struck down

Amendment 2, arguing that it was "born of animosity toward the class that it affects." The majority opinion falsely claimed that the "amendment imposes a special disability upon [homosexuals and bisexuals] alone" and makes them "unequal to everyone else."[51] With the stroke of a pen, the Court granted homosexuals the equivalence of minority status based on their sexual behavior. And they did so by labeling the people of Colorado as homophobic hatemongers. The Justices in their majority opinion never even mentioned the Court's 1986 decision in *Bowers v. Hardwick*, which upheld the rights of states to enact criminal statutes against homosexuality and bestiality. So the Court left the law in utter confusion. States can criminalize homosexual conduct, but they cannot deny homosexuals special rights.

This display of irrationality is stupefying. And yet, it is also to be expected. Remember, in the world of PC, objectivity is deemed impossible, truth is created by groups, public policy is set by opinion polls, and judges can rule according to their whims. Writing the opinion for the dissent, Justice Scalia penned words of sanity and objective truth:

> Today's opinion has no foundation in American constitutional law, and barely pretends to. The people of Colorado have adopted an entirely reasonable provision which does not even disfavor homosexuals in any substantive sense, but merely denies them preferential treatment. Amendment 2 is designed to prevent piecemeal deterioration of the sexual morality favored by a majority of Coloradans, and is not only an appropriate means to that legitimate end, but a means that Americans have employed before. Striking it down is an act, not of judicial judgment, but of political will.[52]

This exercise in raw judicial power is but another step in America's march to sanctioning deviancy in all its forms.

How Long?

How long will Americans let the forces of PC lead the way to darker ignorance and more degrading forms of deviancy? How long will Americans be intimidated into silence and submission by the dictates of the new tolerance? Can the tide be turned? If so, how? This book's last two chapters are dedicated to addressing these questions. I believe the PC perspective can be defeated, but it will take a new cultural revolution to do it. That transformation work has already begun, but it needs the constant infusion of intelligent, persistent activism if it's going to succeed.

PART THREE

Absolutely for the Common Good

Chapter 14

When Worlds Collide

"How do you know there is a real, tangible world outside our minds?" the television interviewer asked.

The camera turned its attention to Mortimer Adler in expectation of an answer.

I sat forward in my chair anxious for his reply. I had read several of Adler's books and found them level-headed and insightful. He certainly lived up to his reputation as the layman's philosopher. A lifelong educator, editor of the impressive *Great Books of the Western World* series, and author of nearly sixty books himself, this was a man who knew the issues inside and out.

Adler slowly turned his head toward the interviewer and, without cracking a smile, said, "It's no great mystery. The world outside of my mind never lets me forget it is there. When I run into a wall, reality abruptly stops me. When I throw cold water on my face, reality wakes me up. If I stub my toe or burn myself, reality brings me a taste of pain. If I ever think the external world is not there, reality finds a way to slap some sense into me. The external world is there. I have the bruises to prove it."

I have met some who think Adler is wrong. The world, they have said, is nothing more than our interpretation of it. We create reality; we make it what it is. One university professor said that the world was really an illusion. Even she didn't exist, nor did I. I found the idea so absurd that I decided to challenge her.

"Tell me," I began. "If everything is an illusion, why do you look both ways before you cross a busy street? I know you do that because I've seen you do it."

"I don't understand," she said. "What's your point?"

"My point is simple: If you are right—that you don't exist and neither does anything else—then streets aren't really there, the cars on those streets aren't there, and the big truck rigs barreling down on you aren't there either. So, why look both ways before stepping out onto a street that isn't there and into traffic that isn't there either? You can't get hurt. After all, you don't exist either."

She just glared at me and wouldn't answer. What could she say? Reality had slapped her in the face, and she didn't like the sting. At the same time, she didn't want to give up belief in her ability to create a world of her choosing. She sat defiantly resisting the hard evidence impinging on her self-imposed delusion.

Still somewhat perturbed, she got out of her nonexistent chair, walked out of the nonexistent room, through the nonexistent door, and into the nonexistent hallway. I watched this nonexistent woman leave. It was a lot to assimilate.

Believers in the ten new absolutes are in no better shape than this university professor. They, too, have placed their faith in "truths" that are not true. They have accepted a reality that isn't real, that doesn't square with either the physical or the moral order that is really there. They keep trying to live in the worlds of their own creation, but they keep running up against the real world, and they become bruised and broken in the collision. Rather than succumb to common sense, many dig in their heels and keep rationalizing away their injuries. It's within this group that the most avid activists are born. They become the teachers, the authors, the speakers, the lawyers, the judges, the legislators . . . who fight for the right to live a lie and recruit others to share in their happy lifestyle and their righteous crusade.

The people who are the new absolutists make poor gods. They try hard to create an alternative world to the real one and pursue their desires within their own creation. But they are bucking reality and getting beat up in the process.

Contrary to the new absolutists, the rest of us try to come to terms with what is. We often misjudge and occasionally take off into flights of fancy. But we know the world beyond us is real and that it makes demands and grants rewards. Thus we are the ones who marry till death do us part and see love as work, not a fleeting emotion. We are the ones who value children for their own sake, which is why we conceive and adopt children, and raise them the best we can. We teach them to live responsibly, honorably, and honestly. We proclaim that they can succeed if they work hard for their dreams and never give up. We share our lives and instruct them in our faith and values. We also strive to ingrain in them a sense of discipline, and expect them to respect us as we respect them. We are also the ones concerned over what the new absolutes are doing to our marriages, families, communities, and country. We want to fight back, but we are overwhelmed by the sheer force of the assault. So most of us stay huddled in our hamlets, restricting our social involvement to spouse, kids, work, and worship.

Fallen Fantasies

I must admit that at times I have wanted to pull the covers over my head, too. But over the years of watching the new absolutists live, I realize how fragile their efforts really are. Their self-created worlds are crashing into the world of reality. The explosions you hear are from worlds colliding. The new absolutists are flailing away at reality, striking out at it blindly. These are not the actions of all-powerful creative gods, but stubborn, rebellious mortals. Let me illustrate what I mean.

Intolerant Tolerance

While homosexuals promote the message that they are victims of an oppressive, heterosexist, homophobic society, nearly a hundred of them terrorized Christians on a Sunday evening while they were attending church services. Homosexual activists "vandalized church property, replaced the church's Christian flag with a homosexual flag, harassed and scared children, pounded on doors during the service, and hurled eggs and rocks at churchgoers." Activist couples were arrayed in "bondage attire," and many men and women displayed their "bare breasts, bare genitals and buttocks." Some male couples were "totally naked" and publicly "engaged in acts of mutual masturbation and oral sex."[1] At another church they shouted "Bring back the lions. Bring back the lions," as they disrupted the guest speaker's talk.[2]

One has to wonder who the real victims are.

Lonely by Choice

Look too at the many women who fell for the feminist line that pregnancy was a disease and motherhood a slavery condition and environmental burden. They have been having second thoughts, even while they hug ever closer the myths they've tried to live out. Listen to the voice of Michele Patenaude:

> In a world that can no longer provide for those already born, the last thing needed is another child to add to the already-born five billion. What Mother Earth needs, I tell myself, is more women like me

> who do not want to be mothers.... I self-righteously comfort myself with the idea that childlessness is environmentally altruistic....
>
> Still, I'm ambivalent. I wonder if when I'm seventy, I'll look back to regret my choice. Secretly, I sometimes worry that I will spend my old age alone....
>
> We stake our claim to immortality through our children. We aim a collection of our genes at eternity. Through them we hope to be kept alive in memory.
>
> I will have no descendants to keep me alive, in memory or genetics. On my family tree I am a terminal bud. A biological *cul-de-sac.* A genetic dead end.
>
> By choice.[3]

Or consider Jyl Felman:

> The heart of the matter is that I have made a commitment to myself, to my creative powers until the day I die. This commitment is based on a relationship with myself that is not distracted by the dependence of another vulnerable human being. It means that the "I" of me can have no rival for my attention. For a woman, a Jew, and a lesbian, saying this is close to speaking heresy.
>
> ... I do wake up at night terrified that my life has no meaning. I do imagine that I am all alone despite my life partner and my friends. I despair that my writing is meaningless; that I have made a huge mistake. But in my terror I do not long for a child, although I know that my despair would have an immediate answer if I did. Someone would need me. ME. Someone else's life would depend on me and the quality of loving attention that I could offer. If I am not careful, at this point in my ruminations all my self-loathing sets in.[4]

Ambivalence. Loneliness. Self-loathing. Unmet needs. A sense of meaninglessness. Emptiness. Terror. The bitter fruit from the tree of childless-by-choice.

Exposing Pro-choice Subterfuge

The "pro-choice" mantra "The fetus is not a baby" leads to a callous flippancy toward life and rationalizations that distort the truth. Some proabortionists are beginning to face this, even while they refuse to let go of abortion on demand. Bestselling proabortion feminist Naomi Wolf recently admitted, "The pro-life slogan 'Abortion stops a beating heart' is incontrovertibly true.... While images of violent fetal death work magnificently for pro-lifers as political polemic, the pictures are not polemical in themselves: they are biological facts. We know this.... How can we charge that it is vile and repulsive for pro-lifers to brandish vile and repulsive images if the images are real? To insist that the truth is in bad taste is the height of hypocrisy."

Wolf also challenges the proabortion assertion that all women who choose to abort their children are acting on high moral ground. "Of the abortions I know of," she states, "these were some of the reasons: to find out if the woman could get pregnant; to force a boy or man to take a relationship more seriously; and again and again, to enact a rite of passage for affluent teenage girls." After adding that 57 percent of unwanted pregnancies are the consequence of failures to use contraception, Wolf draws this remarkably frank conclusion: "With the pro-choice rhetoric we use now, we incur three destructive consequences . . . hardness of heart, lying, and political failure."

What brought about this turnaround in Wolf's thinking? Pregnancy. "When I was four months pregnant, sick as a dog and in the middle of an argument," she confesses, "I realized that I could no longer tolerate the fetus-is-nothing paradigm of the pro-choice movement."

Well, then, if the fetus is really a baby, should we stop the killing? Wolf isn't ready to take that logical step—not yet, anyway. Instead, she calls on proabortionists to use more honest moral rhetoric and work toward a better moral policy. According to columnist Mona Charen, Wolf also wants "pro-choice feminists to mourn the deaths of the fetuses who die in abortions, she wants the women themselves to rediscover a sense of sin, and she hopes all will turn to God for redemption."[5] Incredible concessions to reality, indeed. Yet still some distance to go.

Post-Roe Conversion

On the abortion front, one of the most startling conversions has been that of Norma McCorvey. She was the *Roe* side of the equation in the U.S. Supreme Court decision on *Roe v. Wade*, the case that effectively legalized abortion on demand in 1973. She had been given the name Jane Roe to protect her privacy during the court battles. In her lawsuit she had claimed that she had become pregnant by a rapist, which was why she wanted to abort the child. Years later she admitted she lied about the rape. By the time her case reached the Supreme Court, she had already given birth and put the baby up for adoption. In a 1994 interview she gave for the *New York Times*, the reporter described this lesbian mother of three grown children as a troubled, adolescent-like woman. "It seems as if some aspects of her grew up and some didn't," the reporter says, "some grew wrong, while others grew right. Her personality is fractured, and like a prism, different moods glint through, some lasting seconds, others staying longer.

Through it all, the constant is how hard she tries to be liked."[6]

In 1995, Norma McCorvey, alias Jane Roe, had a conversion. She became a Christian. She also resigned her marketing director's position at a north Dallas, Texas, women's abortion clinic and began work for the pro-life organization Operation Rescue. When she came forward about her change of heart, she announced, "I'm pro-life. I think I've always been pro-life. I just didn't know it." On ABC's *World News Tonight* program, she stated, "I think abortion's wrong. I think what I did with *Roe v. Wade* was wrong. I just have to be pro-life."[7] She also told reporters that she believed *Roe v. Wade* "literally" handed women "the right to slaughter their own children."[8]

McCorvey had been struggling for a long time. Her work at an abortion clinic added to her internal strain. Day in and day out, she saw women who looked sad and resigned coming to the clinic to have the life they carried extinguished. She was particularly disturbed when she came upon a freezer packed with the bodies of the aborted. She drank herself to sleep each night, trying to drown the guilt and anguish within and cope with the visions of death that haunted her dreams. Finally, McCorvey's troubled conscience couldn't live with itself anymore. Her moral turmoil came to a head when she was sitting in a park one day looking at the empty swings. "Oh my God," she thought, "the playgrounds are empty because there're no children, because they've all been aborted." She had been befriended by pro-lifers, including the Reverend Flip Bentham, the leader of Operation Rescue in Dallas. From them she found acceptance and love. From them she heard a message of hope that would lead to reconciliation with herself and the God of all life. She had not had such experiences with the proabortion community. "I wasn't good enough for them," she stated. "I can't really remember a pro-choice person here in Texas ever calling me and saying, 'Good morning, Norma, are you having any trouble in your life?' "[9] She said she felt the proabortion movement had used her, and she was determined to not let that happen ever again. "I've already been exploited enough to last a lifetime," she told NBC's *Nightline*.[10]

While McCorvey reconciled herself with reality, the proabortion establishment would not. Sarah Weddington, McCorvey's attorney in the *Roe* case, voiced her conviction that the "opposition" would use her former client's change of mind as "PR" for their anti-abortion movement.[11] What Weddington didn't say is that she had had an abortion herself, even before she represented McCorvey in the *Roe* case, and that she had used McCorvey to strengthen her legal case against restrictions on abortion.[12]

Weddington also failed to mention that McCorvey had accused her of lying about the availability of abortion. Apparently Weddington didn't want to share that information because she thought it would have hampered her legal case.[13]

Kids Know Best

Children pay some of the highest cost of our new absolutist society. Take the kids from broken families, the kids raised under the new absolute that made divorce as easy and frequent as marriage. How has reality struck them? Some teenagers from an American high school give us a few clues.

"I just assume anybody I meet, their parents are divorced," says Rachel, a dark-haired girl whose parents divorced when she was in third grade. "A couple of weeks ago I asked a new friend of mine if he lived with his mom or his dad. And he kind of went, 'What?' I was embarrassed. To me it was just a given that he lived with one of them, and he said, 'I live with both my parents.' And it was like, '*Oh*, oh, I forgot.' People can still be *married*, you know. It never even crosses my mind that somebody's parents might still be married."

Rachel grows angry. She turns to the adult in the classroom moderating the discussion about families and, with bitterness in her voice, says, "Your generation didn't want to be stable, did you? . . . Well, to me, stability is just a dream," she laments. "I think it's just gonna get worse and worse. I think family is just gonna be gone. I don't have the slightest idea how a family works. How can I know what to do if I've never experienced it?"

The moderator turns to the rest of the class and asks them what might replace the nuclear family. One teenage boy responds: "I think the family'll still exist as more of an—outline. There might be two people and they might be married or living together and they'll have a child and maybe they'll get divorced and people will come and go and the unit will look about the same, but the people themselves will behave more as separate entities, especially the children." Then he adds that the future family "seems more empty, more—people out for themselves, mostly." Trying to find something to salvage from this futuristic scenario, he asserts, "I think it would be good for the children. . . . I personally prefer to be independent. Mostly adults will be oblivious to it. They'll either ignore it deliberately or they won't notice that people are just drifting away emotionally. That's basically the way it is now, anyway, among my friends."[14]

And yet, the new absolutists insist that the nuclear family must go for the benefit of all. Who's ignoring reality?

Multicultural Hypocrisy

The multiculturalists are the most hypocritical of the gods. As they claim that all cultures have equal value and should be of equal importance to us, they look with disdain on the West and teach others to denigrate it.

In 1990, the president of Yale University approached Lee Bass, one of the school's wealthy contributors, to give money to help the university establish a Western civilization program. Bass came through with twenty million dollars. Multiculturalists at the university were outraged. "Western civilization?" asked one professor. "Why not a chair for colonialism, slavery, empire, and poverty?" Historian Geoffrey Parker, who teaches some of the school's courses in Western civilization, commented that the "major export of Western civilization is violence." Opposition to the program mounted, complete with political power plays to squelch efforts to hire four new faculty members for the proposed program. After four years of heated wrangling, the program was effectively rebuffed. Yale had to return the money—with interest—to Bass.[15]

As it turns out, the Western civilization program was not just killed for ideological reasons. A campus magazine reported that "a number of faculty have even tried to have the funds redirected to their own projects or departments after succeeding in killing the original proposal."[16] Haggling over money, greed, and good old-fashioned capitalism brought the death knell. When it came down to it, the school's multiculturalists revealed not simply their bigotry toward the West, but their love of money to meet their own self-centered ends.

The ultimate irony is that multiculturalism could only have arisen in the West. One astute observer makes this clear:

> No doubt multiculturalists won much approval by employing the Western notion that it is desirable to know something about nations and other peoples. They have gained even more approval by appealing to the need for empathy, by insisting that it is not enough to know about other people, we should also know what those people think about themselves. In short, we should seek knowledge with the least possible amount of prejudice.
>
> No place but the West, with its legacy of scientific knowledge and cultural toleration, could have spawned anything like multiculturalism. What is disturbing, of course, is that the multiculturalists have enlisted Western values to promote the denunciation of the West.[17]

Multiculturalists steal Western values, attitudes, and theories, then use them for their own ends. Then they turn around and have the audacity to slam their source as racist, heterosexist, homophobic, and imperialistic.

Who is ripping off whom in this ideological tug-of-war? It is the ungrateful squatters. The real imperialists and racists are the multiculturalists—tenured thieves who rape the West then blame the victim for the crime.

The Wisdom of Religion

Despite efforts of groups such as the federal government, ACLU, People for the American Way, and Americans United for Separation of Church and State to purge the public square of religion's influence, studies show the powerfully positive role that religion plays in the well-being of individuals, marriages, families, and communities. In a special report by the Cultural Policy Studies Project of the Heritage Foundation, Patrick Fagan summarizes the findings of these studies. There is "ample evidence," he states, that:

- The strength of the family unit is intertwined with the practice of religion. Churchgoers are more likely to be married, less likely to be divorced or single, and more likely to manifest high levels of satisfaction in marriage.
- Church attendance is the most important predictor of marital stability and happiness.
- The regular practice of religion helps poor persons move out of poverty. Regular church attendance, for example, is particularly instrumental in helping young people to escape the poverty of inner-city life.
- Religious belief and practice contribute substantially to the formation of personal moral criteria and sound moral judgment.
- Regular religious practice generally inoculates individuals against a host of social problems, including suicide, drug abuse, out-of-wedlock births, crime, and divorce.
- The regular practice of religion also encourages such beneficial effects on mental health as less depression (a modern epidemic), more self-esteem, and greater family and marital happiness.
- In repairing damage caused by alcoholism, drug addiction, and marital breakdown, religious belief and practice are a major source of strength and recovery.
- Regular practice of religion is good for personal physical health: It increases longevity, improves one's chances of recovery from illness, and lessens the incidence of many killer diseases.

Some 81 percent of the studies showed the positive benefit of religious practice, 15 percent showed neutral effects, and only four percent showed harm. Each of these systematic reviews indicated more than 80 percent benefit, and none indicated more than 10 per-

> cent harm. Even this 10 percent may be explained by more recent social science insights into "healthy religious practice" and "unhealthy religious practice."... Unfortunately, the effects of unhealthy religious practice are used to downplay the generally positive influence of religion. This both distorts the true nature of religious belief and practice and causes many policymakers to ignore its positive social consequences.[18]

It's really amazing. The same forces trying to mitigate religion's influence in American life struggle to come to grips with America's cultural decline, but they show no real understanding of why it is happening. Consider Barry Lynn, the executive director of Americans United for Separation of Church and State. While he urges the erection of an "impenetrable barrier" between church and state, he says we should not "worry about defining what or who constitutes a family." Instead "we should promote the values of stability and commitment in all relationships."[19] He just doesn't understand that it's in the family unit that we learn what stablility and commitment are all about. The teenagers from Franklin High School figured this one out.

Lynn has also said that "when we restrict the right of women to make reproductive choices we do make it less possible for those women to play a full and open role in the marketplace."[20] He doesn't seem to understand that the exercise of "reproductive choice" makes it impossible for the preborn to play any role in society since it kills them. He doesn't seem to realize the post-abortion agony most women suffer when they choose the death option. He doesn't deal with how the guilt and shame affect the relationships, job performance, and self-perception of women who abort. He just doesn't grasp the fact that abortion destroys something in all the lives it touches.

He just doesn't get it. Reality is still elusive.

Back to Reality

Reality's classroom can be tough, but it's much better to be inside the classroom receiving the instruction than outside ignoring the lessons. The new absolutists are on the outside casting stones at those of us on the inside while they shout, "We're the tolerant ones, we're in the know." Americans have listened and lived out their message far too long. The new absolutes are an abysmal failure. Even those who accept the new absolutes cannot live with them. Among them lay scattered and broken marriages, confused and angry kids, racial distrust and animosity, millions of aborted babies, and a host of other problems.

We must stop the insanity.

A Plea for Intolerance

In 1948 Richard Weaver wrote in his book *Ideas Have Consequences*, "There is ground for declaring that modern man has become a moral idiot."[1] An ominous declaration when you consider that there is more evidence to support that claim today than when he wrote it. We have turned our backs on the institutions and safeguards that have prospered and protected us for centuries. We are paying dearly for this choice. The West is unraveling before our very eyes.

But despite the insurmountable evidence, some do not think the West is in trouble. They look around and conclude that Western civilization is just going through some growing pains. Families are taking different shapes, and that's okay. New sexual freedom is being explored, and that's good. Past prejudices toward women, the poor, and people of color are being overcome, and that's needed too. Through speech and behavior codes, people are trying to be more sensitive toward individuals and groups that were once demeaned. Occasionally, we may be a bit overzealous, but that is simply part of feeling our way through this new and exciting territory. We are progressing, not regressing; we can take comfort in that.

While this is a nice-sounding explanation, it is just not true. Some mid-course corrections have been definitely needed, some of which I've mentioned in earlier chapters. The old absolutes were not all true, and they certainly were not always applied well. But for the most part, the old absolutes did guide us forward, while the new ones have done nothing of the kind. If anything, the new absolutes have brought us misery—individually and collectively. America is a nation in moral and social decline. She is coming undone. The signs are there for all who have eyes to see.

Family—the Decisive Institution

In his book *Family and Civilization*, published in 1947, Harvard University sociologist Carle Zimmerman traces the history of the family from its prehistoric days to its contemporary setting. He argues that the heart of society is the nuclear family—mother, father, and the children they raise. He also makes the case that as the family goes, so goes society. He demonstrates that the link between the family and society is so strong that one can tell when a society is in decline by looking through the prism of the family. What he reveals is disturbing but true.

He lists some "forms of behavior" that "gain great prominence" when the individual becomes more important in the fabric of society than the "domestic family."[2] I couldn't help but notice the parallels between Zimmerman's list and the new absolutes:

1. Quick, easy, no-fault divorces and increasing divorce rates. (See *The New Absolutes*, chapter 6.)
2. "Decreased number of children, population decay, and increased public disrespect for parents and parenthood." (See *The New Absolutes*, chapters 5, 7, 8, and 10.)
3. "Elimination of the real meaning of the marriage ceremony." People get married for the wrong reasons and with a faulty view of what marriage is all about. So when times get tough in the relationship or expectations, no matter how trivial, don't get met, spouses seek to end the relationship. (See *The New Absolutes*, chapters 6 and 10.)
4. "Popularity of pessimistic doctrines about the early heroes." Multiculturalism's rewriting of Euro-American history to play down and even ignore the good while holding up the bad and blowing it out of proportion is just one example of how we are indoctrinating our youth to despise our early heroes. (See *The New Absolutes*, chapter 12.)[3]
5. A rise in theories that promote cohabitation over marriage and a "looser" understanding of family as a solution to social problems. (See *The New Absolutes*, chapters 6 and 7.)
6. People from domestic families refuse to "maintain" the "traditions" of their family and society after they marry, "while other people escape these obligations" altogether. Zimmerman cites examples from ancient Greece and Rome in which "mothers refused to stay home and bear children," even though these activities had been the social norm for centuries. (See *The New Absolutes*, chapters 5–13.)
7. The spread of anti-family attitudes and practices to the farthest

reaches of civilization. America is leading the West in its advocacy of anti-family views on contraception, abortion, marriage, and children's rights. (See *The New Absolutes*, chapters 3 and 10.)[4]

8. "Breaking down of most inhibitions against adultery." (See *The New Absolutes*, chapters 6, 7, 8, and 10.)
9. "Revolts of youth against parents so that parenthood [becomes] more and more difficult for those who [do] try to raise children." I don't address this particular point in this book, but it hardly needs substantiation. Raising kids forty years ago was much easier than trying to raise them in today's environment where the culture works against the best efforts of parents by telling youth that self-expression, self-fulfillment, and self-gratification should be their primary guiding lights. One revealing indication of this situation is cited by former U.S. Secretary of Education William Bennett: "Over the years teachers have been asked to identify the top problems in America's public schools. In 1940, teachers identified talking out of turn; chewing gum; making noise; running in the halls; cutting in line; dress code infractions; and littering. When asked the same questions in 1990, teachers identified drug abuse; alcohol abuse; pregnancy; suicide; rape; robbery; and assault."[5]
10. "Common acceptance of all forms of sex perversions." Except for approving the practice of adults having sex with children, America has already fulfilled this step. (See *The New Absolutes*, chapters 8 and 9.)

Zimmerman notes that these behaviors signaled and contributed to the eventual demise of ancient Greek and Roman civilizations. He is quick to point out, though, that these actions are results, not initial causes, of family breakdown. They are "symptoms of the final decay of the basic postulates upon which the 'human' part of society is built."[6] The human part is summed up in "two fundamental attributes of human life" that Zimmerman labels *fides* and *sacramentum*. These are Latin words that come from "the Christian doctrine on the nature of the family." Zimmerman explains what these terms mean and how critical they are to a society's foundations:

> Essentially fides means *loyalty in human relationships*. Sacramentum means that basic human relations are considered as *products of a system of values coming from the infinite world*; it means that loyalty between peoples in their basic relationships is a *way* of life without which there cannot be long-continued order in the social universe.

> Both separately and together, fides and sacramentum mean that *other persons* are considered human beings like us. Unless there are strong reasons to the contrary, they are to be treated as a special class, very different from the physical, botanical, and animal forces in the universe. All social life is built upon these basic assumptions. Self-sacrifice for group interests, the recognition of contracts, legal and moral norms, and the inviolability of standards of international law depend upon the acceptance and preservation of this conception of humanity. *The belief that human beings and human relations are sacred is the cornerstone upon which the total social structure is built.*[7]

Zimmerman found that historically and sociologically these core religious beliefs about human beings are bound up in the domestic family. The family cannot sustain itself without them. No other beliefs would lead individuals to consider others as more important than themselves and therefore worthy objects of self-sacrificial acts. "Mothers will not bear the pains of childbirth nor fathers the worries of parenthood for economic rewards alone. Fundamentally, people are familistic because they think it right and for no other reason."[8] They tough out difficult times during marriage and childhood rebellion because they believe in the dignity of the human person and the value of reaching out even at one's own expense.

In the West, these religious values about human life came out of the Judeo-Christian worldview. This view holds that God established these values, and they are critical for the right ordering of society. With them firmly in place, the common good flourishes. Without them, the common good suffers and collapses. For there can be no common good unless all human beings and their relationships have a shared worth, and all of this is grounded in a God in which the family and much of the larger community have placed their faith.

If this is true, then it stands to reason that familial and social decay occur during periods of disbelief in that one God. This is exactly what Zimmerman discovered.[9] Monotheistic religion and the domestic family need each other. Religion presents the ultimate unity and intrinsic dignity of all humankind, and the family incorporates this view and works out its implications within the family's sphere of influence. When the family's children strike out on their own, if they keep living by the values of this religious view, then they live beyond themselves, making sacrifices for the benefit of others, including the society at large. Everyone reaps the advantages of this arrangement.

On the other hand, when this critical balance is tilted away from upholding the nuclear family unit and the religious viewpoint that undergirds it, everything and everyone suffers. The family, society, even individuals lose. No person or group can long survive with the individual exalted over the family, selfishness granted sway over self-sacrifice, and disbelief in the infinite God and the values he established gaining ground over belief in that God and those religious values. And yet, this is exactly what is happening in the United States and the rest of the Western world. What was once fertile ground for Judeo-Christianity and the family has become hard and drained of its nutrients. Weeds mostly grow where flowers once bloomed and the field has become an eyesore.

Zimmerman observes that familial and social corruption can be stopped and even reversed, but it takes forces outside of the family unit to do it. When the family collapses and selfism rules the day, people "do not seem to turn back willingly toward the familism necessary to preserve the social system." Why should they? That would require self-sacrifice, a value antithetical to the individualistic mind-set.

Zimmerman points out that after the Roman Empire fell, the outside force that restored social and family order was the Christian church. With its firm belief in fides, sacramentum, and the God who establishes them, the church rebuilt the foundation needed for social relationships, harmony, and growth. And central to that process was a focus on the family, especially "the childbearing function of the family."[10]

I believe Zimmerman is right. The new absolutes and the behaviors they are supposed to justify are symptoms of a deeper disbelief in the one God of the Judeo-Christian faith and the moral code he gave us. Religion, particularly the Judeo-Christian view, is regarded as a social hindrance to be contained to the private sphere. Human life is no longer sacred but expendable for the flimsiest of reasons. Human relationships have only utilitarian value: as long as they serve me and my interests. Childbearing has been devalued: pregnancy is increasingly treated as a curable disease, and motherhood as a state of oppression. The value of children is defined in terms of the contribution they might make to the perceived well-being of the mother or father or to the community's job market or tax base. When children are seen as a burden, especially if they are still residents in the mother's womb, their lives may be at risk.

The West has become a hostile place for families and people of faith. But for people who care little for God, morality, or family, the West is a safe haven. The new absolutists are seeing to that.

- If people want to indulge their sexual lusts, what better "truths" could they embrace than the new absolutes that open virtually all the doorways promising sensual pleasures galore?

- If people find it easier to shift the responsibility for their unhappy condition and poor choices on to others, what better justification could they find than the one provided by the new absolutes?
- For those individuals who want everything in life without worrying about children getting in the way, where could they find more plentiful and accommodating escape hatches than in the new absolutes?
- The new absolutes promise sex without consequence and love without commitment. They say they can deliver politics without religious conscience and family without bonds. They make history so malleable that it can be made to fit any personal or social cause or grievance. They give people benefits they don't have to earn and honors undeserved. They disarm and discredit objectors with charges of hateful discrimination and irrational fears.

In short, the new absolutes are the perfect cover for indulging in a host of self-serving behaviors Americans did not tolerate in the past. Will we keep putting up with them, or will we put a stop to them? Our choice will determine our future and the futures of those who must live with our choice.

The End of Tolerance

If we hope to stop the social disintegration, I believe we must begin by becoming antagonistic rather than accommodating to the new absolutes. We must violate the new tolerance and become people marked by intolerance. Not an intolerance that unleashes hate upon people, but an intolerance that's unwilling to allow error to masquerade as truth. An intolerance that calls evil *evil* and good *good.* An intolerance that keeps fantasy where it belongs—in the realm of fiction, not in the realm of reality. An intolerance that refuses to allow any race to get away with racism and hate crimes. An intolerance that will not put up with the contemporary assaults on heterosexual, lifelong marriage, and the nuclear family. An intolerance that defends the preborn, newborn, disabled, ill, and elderly from attacks on their persons and inherent dignity. An intolerance that will not permit the politicization of history for any purpose. An intolerance that will not let educators confuse and abuse our youth with impunity. An intolerance unwilling to bow to intimidation tactics carried out by those caught up in moral stupidity and intellectual nonsense. An intolerance that permits disbelief in religious faith without allowing it to set public policies that undermine the exercise of religious faith in any social sphere.

Let's face it. The new absolutists are anything but tolerant. The most intolerant people I have ever met are those who believe in the new absolutes. When they enjoin others to be tolerant, what they want is the assurance that they will have free reign to do what they wish. They are not interested in anything as virtuous or abstract as respect for all peoples. If they really respected others, they would not indulge in the kind of practices that wreck lives. No, what they want is uninhibited freedom for themselves. As I've shown, their behavior betrays their real intent.

With some rare though important exceptions, I have argued that the old truths are better for the common good, while the new absolutes represent cultural regression—old lies dressed in contemporary garb, unsuitable for any human being to embrace regardless of his or her culture. If I am right, then we cannot bring about needed social changes with any aspect of the new tolerance at our side. In fact, the new absolutists would also be unable to change society with the new tolerance as their operative guide. History teaches us that cultural change for the common good is never wrought by the tolerant. Those who have been intolerant of racial injustice have brought about racial change. Those who have rejected religious hypocrisy have instituted religious revivals and reforms. Those who have valued all human life have even sacrificed their own lives for the good of others. Those who have stood against hatred and violence have brought about reconciliations and peace settlements. Those who have fought against ignorance have advanced education and the pursuit of knowledge. Advocates of the new tolerance could not have brought about social change on these issues. A live-and-let-live stance is simply not conducive to social progress.

So, in the spirit of intolerance, I put forward these suggested steps as ways to begin to purge America's social system.

The West Is *the Best*

We must get over the historically fallacious notion that Western civilization has been a blight of oppression in human history. This is simply untrue. If anything, the Western tradition has done more to improve the human condition than anything it has done to harm it. The bedrock institutions of marriage and family found their most conducive safe haven in the West. A deep, abiding belief in the worth of all human beings found its most profound expression in the West. And even though the West participated in slavery, it was the West that brought an end to the practice because of its respect for all human life.

An openness to learning from other cultures and a conviction that the world was rational and knowable turned the West into a sanctuary of higher education, scientific progress, and agricultural and industrial advancement. The West far surpassed the rest of the world in these kinds of achievements.

The West is also the founder of democracy, which has proven so far to be the best humanly devised political framework for exercising maximal freedom while imposing responsible restraints.

Western civilization has been far from perfect. It has countenanced its share of evils. But it's one thing to point out the West's flaws amidst its beauty, and quite another to see in the West only ugliness. The former is the way of critical appreciation; the latter the way of destructive obsession. We need an objective, even-handed view of the West and its contributions to the American experience. We don't need multicultural propaganda that denigrates the West's contributions while blowing out of all proportions its mistakes. I agree with the proposal of Jonathan Chaves, a professor of Chinese language and literature at George Washington University. When his school seriously debated whether multicultural studies would become part of the curriculum, professor Chaves made the following plea:

> Let us require the students to receive a solid grounding in the great classics of the West and in the entire Western heritage. Our own university and the whole system of higher education of which it forms a part is a product of the West. The academic freedom which allows us to explore the complete range of knowledge is a product of the West. The very enterprise of systematically and dispassionately studying another civilization, while empathetically entering into its aesthetic sensibility, historically has emerged only in the West. If we repudiate a grounding in the West under the influence of a radical egalitarian ideology which holds all cultures to be of equal value and importance, and of equal interest to us, we will undermine the very ground we stand on.
>
> ... [L]et the "multiculturalists" take note: the sins we commit against our ancestors will be atoned by our children.[11]

All Life Is Precious

We must also challenge the notion that the stronger can make decisions about the weaker, even if that means death for the vulnerable.

There's a bumper sticker that reads: "Every child a wanted child." To a pro-life advocate, that slogan could mean that no child, born or unborn, should be or truly is unwanted. Someone, somewhere, wants that person to have life and be loved and love in return. To a proabortion advocate, on the other hand, those same words have a very different meaning: Only those children wanted by their mother should be allowed to live. In other words, the desires of the stronger take precedence over the lives of the weaker. Want makes right, even if it leads to the death of the unwanted.

This draconian approach to moral decision-making has moved beyond the world of the unborn and entered the worlds of the newborn, differently-abled, infirm, and elderly. This slippery slope will soon put all of our lives at risk. We must stop the killing, and that must include ridding our public policies and laws of this immoral "moral" view.

Think about it. Would we consider a person to be a fit, loving parent if she lined up her children against a wall and chose some to live and others to be executed on the basis of her desires? Absolutely not. We would view this as a cold-hearted, profoundly selfish act worthy of condemnation, not emulation. And yet, isn't this what abortion on demand sanctions?

Of course, the proponents of the culture of death don't want us to see the criterion of wantedness in such a stark, unattractive light. They want us to consider how miserable it would be to be born into a family who didn't want us, who might be too poor or too emotionally unstable to meet our needs. They want us to consider the possibility that being born into such circumstances could lead us to become victims of abuse. Therefore, they argue, wouldn't it be better that we never saw life outside the womb? Or, if already born, that our misery be mercifully ended with our deaths?

This reasoning is frightening. The intentional killing of an innocent party is being heralded as the solution to family economic and psychological problems. Imagine a family killing one of its members to save money or relieve stress. Would we accept that as moral justification for the commitment of murder? This should be an outrage. But as a society, we have given legal sanction to this morally reprehensible "solution."

It's tragically ironic that in a culture obsessed with helping the adult victims of childhood sexual, emotional, and physical abuse that we would wage war against our weaker members by sanctioning the greatest abuse of all—their physical termination. If love is a choice and a cherished treasure in the world of the abused adult, how much more so is it in the world of the abused child. Rather than kill the weaker among us, we should reach out to them as Mother Teresa has. Let her appeal linger long in our ears: "The child is God's gift to the family. Each child is created in the special image and likeness of God for greater things—to love and to be loved. . . . [W]e must bring the child back to the center of our care and concern. This is the only way that our world can survive because our children are the only hope for the future."[12]

How much we miss when we destroy a human life.

We must re-embrace the truth that all human beings have intrinsic worth and dignity, that none should be treated as objects, as property to be handled as the stronger see fit. Want does not make right. It didn't during the days of slavery, and it doesn't now, no matter what the Supreme Court or Congress decrees.

Relativism Is False

The new absolutists do not believe in relativism, not really. Many may use the rhetoric of relativism to deflect objections or to help gain a tolerant and accepting stance toward their views. Nonetheless, their behavior belies the fact that they believe their perspective should be dominant and universal. They are absolutists, not relativists.

I realize, though, that many people do not accept the idea that relativism is false. Some have developed and defended sophisticated ideas about relativism, while others have embraced and pushed more popular notions. It would take an entire book to venture into the ins and outs of the varieties of relativism and their strengths and weaknesses.[13] If my argument is sound, relativism is really not an issue of great concern anyway. The central issues are over which rival absolutes we should accept. However, since new absolutists sometimes appeal to relativism, I will give some arguments against it to show how shaky the relativist view really is.

Recall that by the term *absolute* I mean that which is true or right for all people at all times and in all places. The statement "George Bush was president of the United States between 1988 and 1992" is true, not just for Americans, but also for Europeans, Asians, and South Americans. It will always be true for everyone regardless of where they live or when that "George Bush was president of the United States between 1988 and 1992." In contrast, I use the word *relative* to mean that which is true or right for some people at some times and in some places. In other words, truth and morality vary. My truth may not be your truth. My code of behavior may not square with yours.

One of the most critical consequences of relativism is that there is no objective, unchanging standard by which we can discover what is really true and right. Your understanding of reality is just as good as mine. No one has an edge on anyone else. We are on equal footing, which is no good footing at all. So when we disagree, we are only left with each other's opinion.

Assuming this view is true, then no one could ever be wrong. If you believed the earth was flat or that human beings have wings, you would be right if relativism is true. No matter how fantastic or incredulous your beliefs, you could not be judged mistaken. Nor could you correct anyone else even if they held beliefs that contradicted yours. Just as you are right, so they must be too. This puts relativists in a fascinating dilemma. If they run across an absolutist, they must not try to correct or challenge his views. After all, he is just as right as they are! The absolutist, on the other hand, can criticize relativists, since he believes that people can be mistaken about what they believe. So relativists, to be consistent, should not try to convince others of their view. Absolutists, however, can spread their views far and wide and challenge the views of relativism as much as they want.

Another problem with relativism is that it leads to the conclusion that reality actually contains contradictory conditions and truths. The earth would be flat and round. Tooth fairies would be fictional and real-life creatures. The claims of gender feminism would be true and false. The Holocaust really happened and it was just a figment of someone's imagination. These are just a handful of the absurdities relativism would force us to accept. For the relativist, this is an uncomfortable situation. For the absolutist can say, "In my version of reality, relativism is false and relativists do not exist. Therefore, I refuse to listen to your babbling about a false theory. In fact, I deny you are even present to listen to." What could the relativist say? No one can be wrong.

Now, if you could never be wrong, then you could not learn either. Learning involves gaining new knowledge and correcting false beliefs. If nothing could be corrected, then we could never grow in our understanding of anything. Schools would become unnecessary, as would discipline to correct immoral or dangerous behavior. We would have to abandon attempts to educate our children, to guide their decisions and choices, to keep them from walking in front of moving vehicles. Remember, they can't make mistakes. If more relativists really lived out this view, the population of relativists would decrease quite quickly, and they would be easy to spot. They would be the uneducated with tire marks covering their lifeless bodies.

One more problem with relativism is that it is self-refuting. It cuts its own intellectual legs out from under itself. With regard to the truth issue, relativism says, "All truth is relative." The word *all* means there are no exceptions. "All truth is relative" must be true universally—for all people, at all times, in all places. The word *relative*, however, means that nothing is true for all people at all times in all places. In other words, the claim "All truth is relative" means that no truth is absolute.

But if no truth is absolute, then the claim that "All truth is relative" cannot be true, because it claims to be absolutely—that is, universally—true. So if the claim is true, it must be false. Its very criteria for truthfulness, when applied to itself, contradicts itself.

The relativist can avoid this conclusion by saying that "All truth is relative" is itself relative. That is, "All truth is relative" is true for some people at some times and in some places but not for all people at all times and in all places. So in Lubbock, Texas, let's say, "All truth is relative" is true, but in Boise, Idaho, it is false. If we accept this avoidance strategy, it doesn't help the case for relativism. It leaves ample room for the reality of absolute truths among some groups in some locales. In short, this move reduces "All truth is relative" to "Some truths are relative." Now if only some truths are relative, then some truths must be absolute. Therefore relativism is not universally true. In fact, one absolute truth might be that *no* truths are relative. This would certainly put the relativist in a precarious position.

The same problems surface when someone tries to argue that "All *morals* are relative." If *all* really means "all," then the position must be false because it says that for all persons in all places at all times that nothing is moral for all persons in all places at all times. This is self-refuting. On the other hand, if the relativist says that "All morals are relative" really means that "Some morals are relative," then this allows for at least some absolute moral laws. One of these moral laws might very well be that there are no relative morals, once again bringing the relativist to a difficult spot.[14]

Therefore, we need not bow at the altar of relativism or be driven to silence by those who condemn us for believing in universal truths and universal moral standards. Truth and morals are not relative but absolute. Exactly what is true and which morals we should accept—that is what the culture war is really about. Relativism is usually a subterfuge used to smuggle in new absolutes and squelch opposition to them. We do not need to fall prey to this maneuver any longer.

The Moral Law Is Real

Two millennia ago Paul, the Christian-Jewish missionary, claimed that even people who have not read God's moral law in the Bible still show that they know it. The "requirements of the law are written on their hearts, their consciences also bearing witness, and their thoughts now accusing, now even defending them," Paul wrote.[15] How can this be? The law says people should not commit adultery, yet many do. The law tells people not to lie or cheat, yet they often do. How can Paul say that they show the law of God is written on their hearts when they frequently break that law? There are many ways to answer this question, but the three I want to focus on here are reaction, excuse-making, and blame-shifting.

People do lie and cheat, usually to get something they want or to cover up something they did. They will use all kinds of rationalizations in an attempt to justify their actions and thereby keep the pangs of guilt and blame at bay. But watch them when someone lies to them or cheats them. They rise up in indignation. They just can't believe that someone would rip them off. How dare she deceive me! Their reaction shows the moral law resident within them. They really know that lying is wrong and truth-telling is right, that cheating is immoral, and honesty and faithfulness are moral. That's why they react as they do. Their behavior in regard to injustices perpetrated against them shows how deeply a sense of justice is rooted in them.

Moreover, the very fact that people try to justify their wrongdoing or blame others for it indicates the moral law at work in their being. We don't try to excuse our good behavior. We sense it is right; no excuses are needed for right actions. And we don't blame others for our good behavior; we credit ourselves with the good while shifting the responsibility for the bad to someone or something else.

These aspects of human behavior are universal. They are found in every culture. Despite the great diversity of religious systems, all religions try to account for human guilt and prescribe remedies for it. Also consider that all societies have laws to protect themselves from wrongdoers. Granted, some societies encourage violations to the moral order affirmed in the Judeo-Christian worldview. For instance, a society may urge its members to steal from its neighbors. But those societies will condemn their members for stealing each other's goods.

These are just a few of the signs that show the existence of a universal moral law. We all know there are real rights and real wrongs, objective rules of morality we should obey and often don't. We may differ on some of the particulars of what these rules are, but, in more instances than we usually care to admit, we know when we are violating them, and we always know when someone has violated them against us. Our reactions, the excuses we generate for ourselves, and the blame we cast on others when it really belongs on us all show God's moral law written on our hearts.[16]

There is a moral law, then, embedded in the nature of things. It is not culture bound but instead transcends culture. It is not in the folkways but in nature's ways. When we obey it, we benefit ourselves and our communities. When we disobey it, we hurt ourselves and frequently others as well. Right now, the West, particularly America, is violating this natural moral law. The violations are destroying lives and relationships in unprecedented numbers. The wrongdoings have terrible, long-lasting consequences that will likely take several generations to overcome. We can repair much of the damage, but we will have to begin by rejecting the new absolutes.

Religion Is Essential

The moral law inscribed in our being comes from the Law-Giver most fully revealed in the Judeo-Christian religion. America's founders understood this, which is why they built the Republic on "the laws of nature and [on] nature's God." The "Creator" is the one who creates all human beings as equals. He is also the one who endows human beings "with certain unalienable rights," among which are "life, liberty, and the pursuit of happiness." This is what the Declaration of Independence affirms, and this is the foundation undergirding the U.S. Constitution, the Bill of Rights, our jurisprudence, and our educational system.

Without these religious and moral convictions, our government will not last. In 1798, President John Adams said as much: "We have no government armed with power capable of contending with human passions unbridled by morality and religion. Avarice, ambition, revenge, or gallantry, would break the strongest cords of our Constitution as a whale goes through a net. Our Constitution was made only for a moral and religious people. It is wholly inadequate to the government of any other."[17] James Madison, the architect of the U.S. Constitution, concurred with Adams' assessment. Madison wrote: "We have staked the whole future of American civilization, not upon the power of government, far from it. We have staked the future of all of our political institutions upon the capacity of mankind for self-government; upon the capacity of each and all of us to government ourselves, to control ourselves, to sustain ourselves *according to the Ten Commandments of God.*"[18]

In the last half of the twentieth century, we have lost control of ourselves because we have walked away from our Creator and his moral prescriptions. We have put ourselves in his place. We are legislating our own morality—a morality that violates his. We are replacing his ten commandments with the ten new absolutes. The trade has already shown what poor gods we make. We are reaping the whirlwind of our own creation. The signs of devastation are everywhere for those who choose to see. To stop the destruction, we must return to the Creator and seek to order our lives and culture according to his ways, not ours.

I am not suggesting that the Bible become the law of the land or that we force people to accept the Judeo-Christian faith. My position is in line with that of Madison's, who said: "Religion, or the duty we owe to our Creator, and manner of discharging it, can be directed only by reason and conviction, not by force or violence; and, therefore, that all men should enjoy the fullest toleration in the exercise of religion according to the dictates of conscience, unpunished and unrestrained by the magistrate, unless under color of religion any man disturb the peace, the happiness, or safety of society, and that it is the mutual duty of all to practice Christian forbearance, love, and charity toward each other."[19] Liberty in religious belief should always be guaranteed. Liberty in behavior, on the other hand, should be regulated so it does not threaten society's well-being. The early Americans sought to achieve this balance. Though they sometimes failed, the goal was right, and it was based on their Judeo-Christian convictions. True liberty is found in the Judeo-Christian religion—nowhere else.

A New Beginning

What these few steps suggest is that we must not permit the new absolutists to define the terms of the debate any longer. We have a great religious and social heritage that gives us all the resources we need to push back the night. That is what we must draw on. We stand on the shoulders of giants—the men and women who have gone before us and sacrificed so much so that we may have so much more. The new absolutes are taking this heritage from us. They are leading us to commit cultural suicide.

We must stand up and contend for our convictions, bringing to their support whatever evidence we believe justifies them. If our convictions are truly justifiable and apply to the culture at large, then we should fight for them through the legal and peaceful means available to us until they become part of our cultural belief system and civil law. If, on the other hand, they prove to be false or in need of revision, then we should be grateful for the exposure and alter our beliefs and behavior accordingly.

This is the way of *authentic* absolutism.

This is the way of rational discourse and sound public policy-making.

This is the way to civil order, especially in a democratic society.

This is the way toward moral progress and away from moral idiocy.

This is the path we need to travel . . . can travel . . . must travel for the good of us all.

Endnotes

Chapter 1: "God" in Fresno

1. Allan Bloom, *The Closing of the American Mind* (New York: Simon & Schuster, 1987), p. 25.
2. Richard M. Weaver, *Ideas Have Consequences* (Chicago: University of Chicago Press, 1948), p. 1.
3. Weaver, p. 2.
4. Weaver, p. 2.

Chapter 2: The Rule of Relativism

1. James Davison Hunter, *Culture Wars: The Struggle to Define America* (New York: HarperCollins, 1991), p. 246.
2. Clifford Geertz, *Local Knowledge: Further Essays in Interpretive Anthropology* (New York: Basic Books, 1983), p. 44.
3. George Barna, *Virtual America* (Ventura, Calif.: Regal Books, 1994), pp. 155–156.
4. Barna, pp. 81–83.
5. Barna, pp. 83, 86.
6. Barna, p. 18.
7. Barna, p. 83.
8. Barna, pp. 17–18.
9. Barna, pp. 83–84.
10. Barna, p. 85.
11. Barna, p. 84.
12. James Patterson and Peter Kim, *The Day America Told the Truth* (New York: Plume, 1992), p. 6.
13. Patterson and Kim, p. 27.
14. Patterson and Kim, p. 27.

15. Patterson and Kim, p. 31.
16. Patterson and Kim, p. 32.
17. As quoted by Hunter, *Culture Wars*, p. 113.
18. Paul C. Vitz, "An American Disaster: Moral Relativism," in *In Search of a National Morality: A Manifesto for Evangelicals and Catholics*, ed. William Bentley Ball (Grand Rapids, Mich.: Baker Book House; San Francisco, Calif.: Ignatius Press, 1992), p. 43.
19. S. D. Gaede, *When Tolerance Is No Virtue: Political Correctness, Multiculturalism, and the Future of Truth and Justice* (Downers Grove, Ill.: InterVarsity Press, 1993), p. 44.
20. Jon D. Hull, "The State of the Union," *Time* (January 30, 1995), p. 54.
21. Hull, p. 54.
22. Hull, p. 53.
23. Hull, p. 54.
24. Richard N. Ostling, "In So Many Gods We Trust," *Time* (January 30, 1995), p. 72.
25. Harold O. J. Brown, "The Decline of Morality," in *In Search of a National Morality*, p. 65.
26. William J. Bennett, *The De-Valuing of America: The Fight for Our Culture and Our Children* (New York: Summit Books, 1992), p. 33.
27. Gaede, p. 45.
28. Jim Nelson Black, *When Nations Die: Ten Warning Signs of a Culture in Crisis* (Nashville, Tenn.: Thomas Nelson, 1994), p. 177.
29. Charles Colson with Ellen Santilli Vaughn, *Kingdoms in Conflict* (New York: William Morrow; Grand Rapids, Mich.: Zondervan, 1987), pp. 225–226.

Chapter 3: The Betrayal of Behavior

1. For several excellent examples of this phenomenon, see James Davison Hunter, *Culture Wars: The Struggle to Define America* (New York: Basic Books, 1991), chap. 5.
2. *Contract with America*, Ed Gillespie and Bob Schellhas, eds. (New York: Times Books, 1994), p. 144.
3. Mary Ann Glendon, *A Nation Under Lawyers: How the Crisis in the Legal Profession Is Transforming American Society* (New York: Farrar, Straus and Giroux, 1994), p. 3.
4. Maurice Cranston, "What Are Human Rights?" in *The Human Rights Reader*, rev. ed., Walter Laqueur and Barry Rubin, eds. (New York: New American Library, 1989), pp. 21–23.
5. See Steven Lukes, "Five Fables about Human Rights," in *On Human Rights: The Oxford Amnesty Lectures, 1993*, Stephen Shute and Susan Hurley, eds. (New York: Basic Books, 1993), pp. 19–40. In this essay Lukes identifies some intellectuals and philosophies that reject human rights. Among the individuals he names are Jeremy Bentham, Edmund Burke, Alasdair MacIntyre, Karl Marx, and Lenin. Three philosophical views he identifies are utilitarianism, communism, and communitarianism.

6. See E. Michael Jones, "Bela Does Cairo: The Great Satan Swings and Misses at the Cairo Conference on Population and Development," *Liberty, Life and Family* 2:1 (1995): 1–37; Jacqueline R. Kasun, "Cairo: A Second Opinion," *Culture Wars* (May 1995), pp. 23–27, 39–41; George Weigel, "What Really Happened at Cairo," *First Things* (February 1995): 24–31.
7. Kasun, p. 41.
8. Norman L. Geisler, "The Hermeneutics of Natural Law," pp. 10–11, unpublished paper delivered at the Evangelical Theological Society annual meeting in Lisle, Chicago, on November 19, 1994.

Chapter 4: Freedom From Religion

1. Johnny Hart, "B.C.," *The Tennessean* (July 17, 1994).
2. William A. Donohue, *The Politics of the American Civil Liberties Union* (New Brunswick, N.J.: Transaction, 1985), p. 308.
3. Donohue, pp. 308–310.
4. Donohue, p. 310.
5. Ira Glasser, *Visions of Liberty: The Bill of Rights for All Americans* (New York: Arcade, 1991), pp. 77, 74.
6. Gerald Parshall, "Hanging Offenses," *U.S. News and World Report* (March 6, 1995), p. 15.
7. Cathy Lynn Grossman, "Season Fuels Debate Over Church, State," *USA Today* (December 15, 1993), pp. 1A, 2A.
8. "Ongoing Legal Activities," *Law & Justice* 3:1 (1994): 9.
9. Tony Mauro, "Court Rules against Jewish School District," *USA Today* (June 28, 1994), p. 3A.
10. Jay Alan Sekulow, "We Still Have a Prayer," *Law & Justice* 4:3 (1995): 1.
11. "Docket List," *Law & Justice* 1:4 (Summer 1992): 6.
12. *National Review* (May 6, 1996), pp. 14, 16.
13. Thomas P. Monaghan, "Misusing the Constitution," *Law & Justice* 2:3 (May/June 1993): 10.
14. Associated Press, "Quoting Bible Wins New Trial," *The Tennessean* (October 17, 1993).
15. "Docket List," *Law & Justice* 1:4 (Summer 1992): 6.
16. Jay Alan Sekulow, "Second Grader Formally Disciplined for Typing 'Jesus' on School Computer," *CaseNote* 2:5 (1995): 1–3.
17. "Case Briefs," a pamphlet published by the Alliance Defense Fund, Scottsdale, Arizona, n.d.
18. Jay Alan Sekulow, "A Reason for Hope," *CaseNote* (February 1994): 1–3.
19. "She Won a License to Pray," *Woman's World* (May 31, 1994).
20. Patrick K. Lackey, "DMV OKs 'God' on License Plates," *Virginia Pilot* (January 14, 1994), p. B4.
21. "Recent Victories and Other Legal Activities," *Law & Justice* 2:3 (May/June 1993): 8.
22. Jay Sekulow, "The Abortion Distortion," *Law & Justice* 2:1 (Fall 1992): 3.
23. "Docket List," *Law & Justice* 1:3 (Winter 1993): 6.

24. Tony Mauro, "Court Mulls Aid For Christian Magazine," *USA Today* (November 1, 1994), p. 5A.
25. James P. Gannon, "Christian Speech Only One to Face Discrimination Ax," *The Tennessean* (November 6, 1994), p. 5D.
26. Keith A. Fournier, "In Defense of Liberty," *Law & Justice* 2:2 (Spring 1993): 6.
27. "Two Major Court Decisions and Other Recent Victories and Activities," *Law & Justice* 2:2 (Spring 1993): 8.
28. "Docket List," *Law & Justice* 1:3 (Winter 1993): 6.
29. Jay Alan Sekulow, "Quick Action Provides Avenue for Gospel!" *CaseNote* (September 1994): 1–4.
30. Jay Alan Sekulow, "Religious Speech and the First Amendment," *Law & Justice* 2:3 (May/June 1993), p. 3, 7.
31. See Thomas Bokenkotter, *A Concise History of the Catholic Church*, rev. ed. (New York: Image Books, 1990), pp. 328–29; Mark A. Noll, *A History of Christianity in the United States and Canada* (Grand Rapids, Mich.: William B. Eerdmans, 1992), chap. 1.
32. Noll, *A History of Christianity in the United States and Canada*, chaps. 2–3; William W. Sweet, *The Story of Religion in America* (Grand Rapids, Mich.: Baker Book House, 1973), chaps. 3–7. In fact, English Catholics had founded Maryland, but Anglicans considerably reduced their influence by the mid 1700s. See Edwin S. Gaustad, *Faith of Our Fathers: Religion and the New Nation* (San Francisco, Calif.: Harper & Row, 1987), pp. 15–16.
33. Noll, *A History of Christianity in the United States and Canada*, pp. 32–35, 40–48.
34. For some excellent documentation of my comments about the Declaration of Independence, see Gary T. Amos, *Defending the Declaration: How the Bible and Christianity Influenced the Writing of the Declaration of Independence* (Brentwood, Tenn.: Wolgemuth & Hyatt, 1989).
35. While the vast majority of the Declaration's drafters and signers were Christians, its key author was Thomas Jefferson, a deist. Jefferson rejected many cardinal doctrines of orthodox Christianity, including the Trinity, original sin, the infallibility of the Bible, and the deity, virgin birth, substitutionary death, resurrection, and ascension of Jesus Christ. Like Christians, he believed God created, sustains, and manages the world, but he rejected the Christian teaching that God performed miracles or revealed his will in the Bible. He thought such ideas were the result of human fabrications, superstition, or fanaticism. A case in point is the Christian view of Jesus' virgin birth. According to Jefferson, "The day will come when the account of the birth of Christ as accepted in the Trinitarian churches will be classed with the fable of Minerva springing from the brain of Jupiter." (Henry Wilder Foote, *Thomas Jefferson: Champion of Religious Freedom, Advocate of Christian Morals* (Boston, Mass.: Beacon, 1947), p. 49. Jefferson regarded himself a Christian in morals, not in metaphysics. In his words, "I am a Christian in the only sense in which I believe Jesus wished anyone to be, sincerely attached to his doctrines [i.e., moral teachings] in preference to all others; ascribing to himself every human excellence, and believing that he never claimed any other." (Foote, p. 4.) For a succinct summary of Jefferson's

deistic views, see Norman L. Geisler and William D. Watkins, *Worlds Apart: A Handbook on World Views* (Grand Rapids, Mich.: Baker Book House, 1989), pp. 155–62. Fuller discussions can be found in Foote's *Thomas Jefferson*; Saul K. Padover, *Thomas Jefferson and the Foundations of American Freedom* (New York: Van Nostrand Reinhold, 1965); and Francis I. Fesperman, "Jefferson's Bible," *Ohio Journal of Religious Studies* 4:2 (October 1976): 78–88. An excellent selection of Jefferson's writings is available in *The Portable Thomas Jefferson*, Merrill D. Peterson, ed. (New York: Penguin Books, 1975).

36. Thomas Jefferson, *Notes on Virginia*, in *The Writings of Thomas Jefferson*, Albert E. Bergh, ed. (Washington, D.C.: Thomas Jefferson Memorial Association, 1905), vol. 1, p. 227.
37. Patricia U. Bonomi, *Under the Cope of Heaven: Religion, Society, and Politics in Colonial America* (New York: Oxford University Press, 1986), p. 3.
38. Barry Alan Shain, *The Myth of American Individualism: The Protestant Origins of American Political Thought* (Princeton, N.J.: Princeton University Press, 1994), p. 195, n. 6.
39. Joyce Appleby, "The American Heritage—the Heirs and the Disinherited," in *Liberalism and Republicanism in the Historical Imagination*, Joyce Appleby, ed. (Cambridge: Harvard University Press, 1992), p. 225.
40. Donald J. D'Elia, "We Hold These Truths and More: Further Catholic Reflections on the American Proposition," in *We Hold These Truths and More: Further Catholic Reflections on the American Proposition*, Donald J. D'Elia and Stephen M. Krason, eds. (Steubenville, Ohio: Franciscan University Press, 1993), p. 65.
41. *Licentiousness Unmask'd* (1776), p. 9, as cited in Shain, p. 221.
42. Thomas Paine, *Rights of Man, Part Second* (1792), p. 390, as cited in Shain, p. 297. See also the Declaration of Independence.
43. James Madison, *Annals of the Congress*, vol. I, p. 434, as cited in Robert L. Cord, *Separation of Church and State: Historical Fact and Current Fiction* (New York: Lambeth, 1982), p. 7. The italics in the quote were added by Cord.
44. Cord, pp. 6–7.
45. Cord, p. 7.
46. *Annals of Congress*, vol. I, p. 730, as cited in Cord, p. 10.
47. Gaustad, p. 114.
48. Gaustad, pp. 114–115. See also his Appendix B.
49. *Article III* of *An Ordinance for the Government of the Territory of the United States, North-West of the River Ohio*, as cited in *America's God and Country: Encyclopedia of Quotations*, compiled by William J. Federer (Coppell, Tex.: Fame, 1994), p. 165.
50. *Wallace v. Jaffree*, 472 U.S. 38 (1985), Justice William H. Rehnquist, dissenting, in *Religious Liberty in the Supreme Court: The Cases That Define the Debate over Church and State*, Terry Eastland, ed. (Grand Rapids, Mich.: William B. Eerdmans, 1993), p. 359.
51. Cord, p. 15.
52. John Quincy Adams, as quoted in Benjamin Hart, *Faith and Freedom: The Chris-*

tian Roots of American Liberty (San Bernardino, Calif.: Here's Life Publishers, 1988), p. 16.

53. John Adams, "Letter to Officers of the First Brigade of the Third Division of the Militia of Massachusetts, October 11, 1798," in *The Works of John Adams, Second President of the United States,* Charles Francis Adams, ed. (Freeport, N.Y.: Books for Libraries Press, 1969), vol. 9, p. 229.
54. Stephen L. Carter, *The Culture of Disbelief: How American Law and Politics Trivialize Religious Devotion* (HarperCollins, 1993), p. 21.
55. Carter, pp. 21–22.
56. Keith A. Fournier with William D. Watkins, *A House United? Evangelicals and Catholics Together—A Winning Alliance for the Twenty-first Century* (Colorado Springs, Colo.: NavPress, 1994), p. 152. Also see Fournier's *Religious Cleansing in the American Republic* (Virginia Beach, Va.: Liberty, Life and Family, 1993).

Chapter 5: Death, What a Beautiful Choice

1. Randy Frame, "Ad Campaign Filled with Life," *Christianity Today* (April 27, 1992), p. 43.
2. Frame, p. 43.
3. See Philip G. Ney, "Is Elective Abortion a Cause of Child Abuse?" *Sexual Medicine Today* 40:6 (June 1980): 31; Francis J. Beckwith, *Politically Correct Death: Answering Arguments for Abortion Rights* (Grand Rapids, Mich.: Baker Book House, 1993), pp. 63–65; Randy Alcorn, *Pro-Life Answers to Pro-Choice Arguments* (Sisters, Ore.: Multnomah, 1992), pp. 111–13; Francis J. Beckwith and Norman L. Geisler, *Matters of Life and Death* (Grand Rapids, Mich.: Baker Book House, 1991), pp. 101–102.
4. "Ads Rankle Planned Parenthood," *Christianity Today* (March 7, 1994), p. 45.
5. Genesis 1:27, NIV.
6. Genesis 5:1–3.
7. Genesis 9:6, NIV.
8. James 3:9; 2 Corinthians 4:4; Colossians 1:15; Hebrews 1:3.
9. Genesis 2:22–24; Matthew 19:4–6.
10. See "Image, Idol, Imprint, Example," *The New International Dictionary of New Testament Theology,* Colin Brown, ed. (Grand Rapids, Mich.: Zondervan, 1976), vol. 2, pp. 284–93; Bruce K. Waltke, "Reflections from the Old Testament on Abortion," *Journal of the Evangelical Theological Society* 19:1 (Winter 1976): 3–13; Claus Westermann, *Genesis 1–11: A Commentary,* John J. Scullion, trans. (Minneapolis, Minn.: Augsburg, 1984), pp. 148–58; J. Barton Payne, *The Theology of the Older Testament* (Grand Rapids, Mich.: Zondervan, 1962), pp. 226–228; Henri Blocher, *In the Beginning: The Opening Chapters of Genesis* (Downers Grove, Ill.: InterVarsity, 1984), chap. 4; Robert L. Saucy, "Theology of Human Nature," in *Christian Perspectives on Being Human: A Multidisciplinary Approach to Integration,* J. P. Moreland and David M. Ciocchi, eds. (Grand Rapids, Mich.: Baker Book House, 1993), pp. 21–29; H. D. McDonald, *The Christian View of Man* (Westchester, Ill.: Crossway, 1981), chap. 3; Ronald B. Allen, *The Majesty of Man: The Dignity of Being Human* (Portland, Ore.: Multnomah, 1984), chap.

6; G. C. Berkouwer, *Man: The Image of God*, Studies in Dogmatics (Grand Rapids, Mich.: William B. Eerdmans, 1981).

11. Sherwood Eliot Wirt, *The Social Conscience of the Evangelical* (New York: Harper and Row, 1968), p. 31.
12. Leslie D. Weatherhead, *It Happened in Palestine* (London: Hodder and Stoughton, 1936), pp. 267–269.
13. Nigel M. de S. Cameron, *The New Medicine: Life and Death after Hippocrates* (Wheaton, Ill.: Crossway, 1991), chap. 1.
14. Joseph P. Witherspoon, professor at the University of Texas Law School, in testimony before the House Subcommittee on Civil and Constitutional Rights of the House Committee on the Judiciary, 94th Congress, 2nd Session 17 (1976), as cited in Thomas Patrick Monaghan, "The Abiding Unconstitutionality and Illegitimacy of *Roe v. Wade*," *Liberty, Life and Family* 1 (1994): 123–124.
15. See Monaghan, pp. 121–43; Robert R. Reilly, "The Truths They Held: The Christian and Natural Law Background to the American Constitution," in *We Hold These Truths and More: Further Catholic Reflections on the American Proposition*, Donald J. D'Elia and Stephen M. Krason, eds. (Steubenville, Ohio: Franciscan University Press, 1993), chap. 6; D. James Kennedy and Jerry Newcombe, *What If Jesus Had Never Been Born?* (Nashville, Tenn.: Thomas Nelson, 1994); *Abortion and the Constitution: Reversing Roe v. Wade Through the Courts*, Dennis J. Horan, Edward R. Grant, and Paige C. Cunningham, eds. (Washington, D.C.: Georgetown University Press, 1987), especially these essays: Dennis J. Horan and Thomas J. Balch, "*Roe v. Wade*: No Justification in History, Law, or Logic," pp. 57–88; John R. Connery, "The Ancients and the Medievals on Abortion: The Consensus the Court Ignored," pp. 123–135; Joseph W. Dellapenna, "Abortion and the Law: Blackmun's Distortion of the Historical Record," pp. 137–158; and Martin Arbagi, "*Roe* and the Hippocratic Oath," pp. 159–181.
16. He penned two major editions of this work. The first was published in 1798 and the second in 1803. There are significant differences between these versions, but we won't go into them here. Historian Gertrude Himmelfarb does a fine job pointing out the differences and their significance in her book *Victorian Minds* (Gertrude Himmelfarb, *Victorian Minds: A Study of Intellectuals in Crisis and Ideologies in Transition* (Chicago, Ill.: Elephant, 1968), pp. 108–109. She quotes Walter Bagehot, who she says "went to the heart of the matter" regarding the changes Malthus made in the two editions. According to Bagehot, "In its first form the *Essay on Population* was conclusive as an argument, only it was based on untrue facts; in its second form it was based on true facts, but it was inconclusive as an argument." Bagehot was right. Neither version of Malthus's essay has proved true, but that has not damaged the essay's credibility or influence in the minds of its true believers.
17. E. Michael Jones, "Bela Does Cairo: The Great Satan Swings and Misses at the Cairo Conference on Population and Development," *Liberty, Life, and Family* 2:1 (1995): 15.
18. Himmelfarb, pp. 90–91.
19. T. R. Malthus, *A Summary View of the Principle of Population*, reprinted in

Thomas Robert Malthus, *An Essay on the Principle of Population* and *A Summary View of the Principle of Population*, Antony Flew, ed. (New York: Penguin, 1970), pp. 271–272.

20. See Paul Johnson, *The Birth of the Modern: World Society 1815–1830* (New York: HarperCollins, 1991), p. 207.
21. Himmelfarb, chap. 3.
22. Paul Ehrlich, *The Population Bomb* (New York: Ballantine, 1968), as cited in Walter Williams, "Why Do We Listen to Fools?" *Conservative Chronicle* (March 1, 1995), p. 29.
23. Boyce Rensberger, "Damping the World's Population," *Washington Post National Weekly Edition* (September 12–18, 1994), p. 10.
24. Tim Stafford, "Are People the Problem?" *Christianity Today* (October 3, 1994), p. 49.
25. Stephen Budiansky, "Population Wars," *U.S. News and World Report* (September 12, 1994), p. 60.
26. For a pro-population-control perspective, see Paul R. Ehrlich and Anne H. Ehrlich, *The Population Explosion* (New York: Simon and Schuster, 1990). For a contrary view, see Michael Cromartie, ed., *The Nine Lives of Population Control* (Grand Rapids, Mich.: William B. Eerdmans, 1995).
27. Robert Jastrow, "The Background to Darwin's Theory," in *The Essential Darwin*, Masters of Modern Science Series, Robert Jastrow, gen. ed., commentary and selections by Kenneth Korey (Boston, Mass.: Little, Brown and Co., 1984), p. xiii.
28. Charles Darwin, *On the Origin of Species*, in *The Essential Darwin*, p. 80–81.
29. See Antony Flew, "Introduction," in Malthus, *An Essay on the Principle of Population*, pp. 49–50.
30. Adrian Desmond and James Moore, *Darwin: The Life of a Tormented Evolutionist* (New York: Warner, 1991), p. 265.
31. Desmond and Moore, p. 449.
32. Desmond and Moore, p. 573.
33. Bertrand Russell, *Why I Am Not a Christian* (New York: Simon and Schuster, 1957), p. 54.
34. Sherwin B. Nuland, *How We Die: Reflections on Life's Final Chapter* (New York: Alfred A. Knopf, 1993), page xv.
35. Robert E. D. Clark, *Darwin: Before and After* (Grand Rapids, Mich.: Grand Rapids International, 1958), p. 106.
36. Gil Elliot, *Twentieth-Century Book of the Dead* (New York: Charles Scribner, 1972), p. 1.
37. Phillip E. Johnson, *Reason in the Balance: The Case Against Naturalism in Science, Law and Education* (Downers Grove, Ill.: InterVarsity Press, 1995), pp. 33, 38.
38. Desmond and Moore, pp. 572, 609.
39. Daniel J. Kevles, *In the Name of Eugenics: Genetics and the Uses of Human Heredity* (Cambridge, Mass.: Harvard University Press, 1995), pp. 3–4.
40. Kevles, p. 94.
41. For just one of many examples showing the influence of Malthus, Darwin, and

eugenics on Margaret Sanger, see her article "Birth Control—Past, Present and Future," *The Birth Control Review* (June 1921): 5–6, 11–13. See also Ellen Chesler, *Woman of Valor: Margaret Sanger and the Birth Control Movement* (New York: Doubleday, 1992), pp. 86–87, 122–125, 180, 235–236. Chesler's book is strongly pro Sanger and birth control.

42. Margaret Sanger, "Birth Control or Abortion?" *The Birth Control Review* (December 1918): 3.
43. Sanger, "Birth Control or Abortion?" pp. 3–4; "Why Not Birth Control in America?" *The Birth Control Review* (May 1919): 10; "The Case for Birth Control," *The Woman Citizen* (February 23, 1924): 17.
44. Margaret Sanger, "Birth Control—Past, Present and Future," *The Birth Control Review* (August 1921): 19.
45. Margaret Sanger, "The Pope's Position on Birth Control," *The Nation* (January 27, 1932), p. 103.
46. Sanger, "The Pope's Position on Birth Control," p. 103. Also see her article "Birth Control," *State Government/American Legislator* (September 7, 1934): 187.
47. Sanger, "Birth Control or Abortion?" p. 4.
48. Margaret Sanger, "Preparing for the World Crisis," *The Birth Control Review* (April 1920): 8.
49. Sanger, "Birth Control—Past, Present and Future" (August 1921), p. 19. See also the preceding part of this article that appears under the same title in the July 1921 issue of *The Birth Control Review*, pp. 5–6, 15.
50. Sanger, "Birth Control—Past, Present and Future" (August 1921), p. 5.
51. Margaret Sanger, "A Parents' Problem or Woman's?" *The Birth Control Review* (March 1919): 6; "Morality and Birth Control," p. 11.
52. Sanger, "A Parents' Problem or Woman's?" p. 6.
53. Sanger, "A Parents' Problem or Woman's?" p. 6.
54. Sanger, "A Parents' Problem or Woman's?" p. 7.
55. Margaret Sanger, "Birth Control and Racial Betterment," *The Birth Control Review* (February 1919): 11–12.
56. Margaret Sanger, "The Eugenic Value of Birth Control Propaganda," *The Birth Control Review* (October 1921): 5.
57. Sanger, "Birth Control and Racial Betterment," p. 12. See also her article "Wasting Our Human Resources," *The Birth Control Review* (March 1920): 9–11.
58. Margaret Sanger, "When Should a Woman Avoid Having Children?" *The Birth Control Review* (November 1918): 6.
59. Margaret Sanger, "Women and Birth Control," *The North American Review* (May 1929): 534.
60. Sanger, "When Should a Woman Avoid Having Children?" p. 6.
61. Sanger, "Birth Control and Racial Betterment," p. 11.
62. Margaret Sanger, "The Function of Sterilization," *The Birth Control Review* (October 1926): 299.
63. Margaret Sanger, "The Need for Birth Control," *The Birth Control Review* (August 1928): 228.

64. Margaret Sanger, "War and Population," *The Birth Control Review* (June 1922): 106.
65. Margaret Sanger, *Woman and the New Race* (New York: Brentano's, 1920), p. 67.
66. Margaret Sanger, "No Healthy Race without Birth Control," *Physical Culture* (March 1921): 125–126.
67. Sanger, "No Healthy Race without Birth Control," pp. 123–124.
68. Margaret Sanger, "The Tragedy of the Accidental Child," *The Birth Control Review* (April 1919): 5.
69. Sanger, "The Case for Birth Control," p. 17.
70. Sanger, "Birth Control—Past, Present and Future" (August 1921), p. 19.
71. Margaret Sanger, "Morality and Birth Control," *The Birth Control Review* (March 1919): 14.
72. Sanger, "Birth Control—Past, Present and Future" (August 1921): 19.
73. Margaret Sanger, "Birth Control—Past, Present and Future," *The Birth Control Review* (June 1921): 5–6, 11–13.
74. Sanger, "Birth Control—Past, Present and Future" (August 1921): 20.
75. Robert G. Marshall and Charles A. Donovan, *Blessed Are the Barren: The Social Policy of Planned Parenthood* (San Francisco: Ignatius, 1991), pp. 6–7.
76. Jones, p. 28.
77. Chesler, p. 136.
78. Jones, p. 28.
79. See Roselle K. Chartock and Spencer, eds., *Can It Happen Again? Chronicles of the Holocaust* (New York: Black Dog and Leventhal, 1995), pp. xix, 65.
80. Keith A. Fournier and William D. Watkins, *In Defense of Life* (Colorado Springs, Colo.: NavPress, 1996), pp. 16, 23.
81. James Patterson and Peter Kim, *The Second American Revolution* (New York: William Morrow and Co., 1994), p. 250.
82. Lawrence F. Roberge, *The Cost of Abortion: An Analysis of the Social, Economic, and Demographic Effects of Abortion on the United States* (LaGrange, Ga.: Four Winds, 1995).
83. "Witness Abortion, Senators Urged," *The Tennessean* (November 18, 1995), p. 15A.
84. Keith Fournier, "Not Just Speaking for Catholics," *Washington Times* (May 5, 1996).
85. See "Witness Abortion, Senators Urged," p. 15A; "Attack on Rare Abortion Procedure Invites Misery," *USA Today* (November 3, 1995), p. 10A.
86. Mimi Hall, "Partial Birth Abortions Face House Vote," *USA Today* (November 1, 1995), p. 6A.
87. See Mimi Hall, "House Approves Ban on Partial Birth Abortions," *USA Today* (November 2, 1995), p. 7A; Kate O'Beirne, "Bread & Circuses," *National Review* (May 6, 1996), p. 24; Carter Brothers, "No Right Exists for Late-Term Abortion," *The Tennessean* (November 28, 1995), p. 10A; Susan Page, "Late-Term Abortion Bill Vetoed," *USA Today* (April 11, 1996), p. 1A.
88. For evidence that the fetus is a human person with potential, not a potential human person, see Jerome Lejeune, *The Concentration Can: When Does Human*

Life Begin? An Eminent Geneticist Testifies (San Francisco, Calif.: Ignatius, 1992); Landrum Shettles and David Rorvik, *Rites of Life: The Scientific Evidence for Life Before Birth* (Grand Rapids, Mich.: Zondervan, 1983); Fournier and Watkins, chap. 2.

89. Peter Singer and Helga Kuhse, "On Letting Handicapped Babies Die," in *The Right Thing to Do: Basic Readings in Moral Philosophy,* 1st ed., James Rachels, ed. (New York: Random House, 1989), p. 146.
90. Joseph Fletcher, as cited in Melinda Delahoyde, *Fighting for Life: Defending the Newborn's Right to Live* (Ann Arbor, Mich.: Servant, 1984), p. 11.
91. James Manney and John C. Blattner, *Death in the Nursery: The Secret Crime of Infanticide* (Ann Arbor, Mich.: Servant, 1984), pp. 22–23. See also Fournier and Watkins, chap. 3.
92. J. P. Moreland, "James Rachels and the Active Euthanasia Debate," *Journal of the Evangelical Theological Society* 31:1 (March 1988), p. 81.
93. Fournier and Watkins, chap. 4.
94. Paul Leavitt, " 'Dr. Death' Case," *USA Today* (July 11, 1996), p. 3A.
95. Fournier and Watkins, pp. 53–54.
96. Fournier and Watkins, chap. 4.

Chapter 6: I Do, for Now

1. Genesis 2:24–25, NIV.
2. For some helpful background on the Judeo-Christian tradition on marriage and divorce European Christians brought to America, see William A. Heth and Gordon J. Wenham, *Jesus and Divorce: The Problem With the Evangelical Consensus* (Nashville, Tenn.: Thomas Nelson, 1984), chap. 3.
3. Ferdinand Mount, *The Subversive Family: An Alternative History of Love and Marriage* (New York: The Free Press, 1992), p. 200.
4. Mount, p. 202.
5. Barry Alan Shain, *The Myth of American Individualism: The Protestant Origins of American Political Thought* (Princeton, N.J.: Princeton University Press, 1994), p. 97.
6. Jonas Clark, *Massachusetts Election Sermon* (1781), p. 37, as cited in Shain, p. 199.
7. Shain, p. 201.
8. Shain, p. 209.
9. Shain, p. 98.
10. Bryce J. Christensen, *Utopia Against the Family: The Problems and Politics of the American Family* (San Francisco, Calif.: Ignatius Press, 1990), p. 20.
11. William J. Bennett, *The Index of Leading Cultural Indicators: Facts and Figures on the State of American Society* (New York, N.Y.: Simon and Schuster, 1994), p. 59.
12. Elizabeth Gleick, "Should This Marriage Be Saved?" *Time* (February 27, 1995), p. 50; Kim A. Lawton, "No Fault Divorce Under Assault," *Christianity Today* (April 8, 1996), p. 85.
13. Michael J. McManus, *Marriage Savers: Helping Your Friends and Family Stay Married* (Grand Rapids, Mich.: Zondervan, 1993), p. 28.
14. McManus, p. 28.

15. James Patterson and Peter Kim, *The Day America Told the Truth: What People Really Believe About Everything That Really Matters* (New York: Plume, 1991), p. 93.
16. McManus, p. 36.
17. Karen S. Peterson, "Cohabiting First Doesn't Secure Knot," *USA Today* (May 10, 1995), p. 2D.
18. McManus, p. 37.
19. Peterson, p. 2D.
20. McManus, p. 37.
21. Patterson and Kim, p. 88.
22. Patterson and Kim, p. 88.
23. Patterson and Kim, p. 88.
24. Herbert Muschamp, "A Sanctuary, Yes, But This Is Not a Place to Hide," *New York Times* (November 28, 1994), p. H37; Carrie Ferguson, "A Union of Fidelity, Honor, Respect," *The Tennessean* (February 21, 1994), p. D2.
25. " 'Defense of Marriage Act' Sprints Toward Promised Presidential Nod," *Family Issues Alert* (May 29, 1996), p. 1.
26. Elizabeth Fox-Genovese, "Better or Worse, Mostly Worse," *National Review* (May 6, 1996), p. 51.
27. Jeffrey L. Sheler, "Spiritual America," *U.S. News & World Report* (April 4, 1994), p. 48.
28. See Laura Garcia, "Can Marriage Be Saved?" *Catholic Dossier* 1:4 (November-December 1995): 7–8.
29. Deuteronomy 6:5, NIV. See also Matthew 22:37.
30. Barbara Dafoe Whitehead, "The Moral State of Marriage," *The Atlantic Monthly* (September 1995), p. 118.
31. Whitehead, p. 118.
32. Whitehead, p. 119.
33. 1 Corinthians 13:4–8, NIV.
34. Mike Mason, *The Mystery of Marriage* (Portland, Ore.: Multnomah Press, 1985), pp. 34–35, 45.

Chapter 7: Family Is Who You Come Home To

1. Tony Bizjak, "Family Images: Focusing in on New Definitions," *Sacramento Bee* (June 28, 1992), p. F3.
2. Margaret L. Usdansky, " 'Blended,' 'Extended' Now All in the Family," *USA Today* (August 30, 1994), p. 3A.
3. Associated Press, "Census Counts More Two-Parent Families," *The Tennessean* (October 16, 1995), p. 9A.
4. Associated Press, p. 9A.
5. Gannett News Service, "Nontraditional Families Gaining," *The Tennessean* (July 30, 1994), p. 7A.
6. Gannett News Service, p. 7A.
7. American Home Economics Association, *A Force for Families* (Washington, D.C.: AHEA, n.d. [c. 1976]), p. 4.

8. Ellen Willis, "Abortion: Is a Woman a Person?" in *Feminist Philosophies: Problems, Theories, and Applications*, Janet A. Kourany et al., eds. (Englewood Cliffs, N.J.: Prentice-Hall, 1992), pp. 84–85.
9. Willis, p. 86.
10. Margaret Sanger, "The Case for Birth Control," *The Crisis* 4:6 (1934): 177.
11. Margaret Sanger, "The War Against Birth Control," *The American Mercury* 2:6 (July 1924), p. 231.
12. Ellen Chesler, *Woman of Valor: Margaret Sanger and the Birth Control Movement* (New York: Doubleday, 1992), pp. 13–14.
13. David G. Allen, "Critical Social Theory as a Model for Analyzing Ethical Issues in Family and Community Health," *Family and Community Health* 10 (May 1987): 63–72.
14. Letty Cottin Pogrebin, *Family Politics: Love and Power on an Intimate Frontier* (New York: McGraw-Hill, 1983), pp. 3–5.
15. George Barna, *The Future of the American Family* (Chicago: Moody Press, 1993), p. 31.
16. Robin Lane Fox, *Pagans and Christians* (San Francisco: HarperSanFrancisco, 1986), p. 343.
17. W. G. Hardy, *The Greek and Roman World*, rev. ed. (Cambridge, Mass.: Schenkman, 1970), p. 92.
18. Beryl Rawson, "Family Life Among the Lower Classes at Rome in the First Two Centuries of the Empire," *Classical Philology* 61:2 (April 1966): 71–83.
19. Hardy, p. 92; Fox, p. 343; Robert W. Shaffern, "Christianity and the Rise of the Nuclear Family," *America* (May 7, 1994), p. 14; David Herlihy, "The Making of the Medieval Family: Symmetry, Structure, and Sentiment," *Journal of Family History* (Summer 1983): 118.
20. E. L. Hebden Taylor, *The Reformational Understanding of Family and Marriage* (Nutley, N.J.: Craig Press, 1975), p. 5.
21. Ulpian, *Digest*, 50. 16. 195.
22. Hardy, pp. 92–93.
23. Carle C. Zimmerman, *Family and Civilization* (New York: Harper and Brothers, 1947), p. 758.
24. Fox, pp. 343–351.
25. Fox, p. 343.
26. Will Durant, *Caesar and Christ: A History of Roman Civilization and of Christianity from Their Beginnings to* A.D. *325* (New York: Simon & Schuster, 1972), pp. 134, 369.
27. 1 Corinthians 6:12–20; D. H. Madvig, "Corinth," in *The International Standard Bible Encyclopedia*, rev. ed. (Grand Rapids, Mich.: William B. Eerdmans, 1979), vol. 1, p. 773; Jerome Murphy-O-Connor, "Corinthian Slogans in 1 Corinthians 6:12–20," *The Catholic Biblical Quarterly* 40:3 (July 1978): 391–96; Kenneth E. Bailey, "Paul's Theological Foundation for Human Sexuality," *Theological Review* 3:1 (1980): 27–41.
28. Fox, pp. 344–45; Herlihy, p. 121.
29. Shaffern, p. 13.

30. Zimmerman, pp. 769–72; Shaffern, pp. 13–15; Herlihy, pp. 116–130.
31. Shaffern, p. 13.
32. Shaffern, p. 14.
33. Shaffern, p. 14.
34. Herlihy, pp. 122–123.
35. Herlihy, p. 123.
36. Herlihy, p. 127.
37. Shaffern, p. 15.
38. Zimmerman, pp. 771–772.
39. Shaffern, p. 14.
40. Shaffern, p. 15.
41. *Editorial Research Reports on the Changing American Family* (Washington, D.C.: Congressional Quarterly, 1979), p. 12.
42. Allan C. Carlson, *From Cottage to Work Station: The Family's Search for Social Harmony in the Industrial Age* (San Francisco, Calif.: Ignatius, 1993), p. 10.
43. Adam Smith, *An Inquiry Into the Nature and Causes of the Wealth of Nations,* cited in Carlson, p. 14.
44. *Editorial Research Reports on the Changing American Family,* p. 13.
45. *Editorial Research Reports on the Changing American Family,* p. 13.
46. Barry Alan Shain, *The Myth of American Individualism: The Protestant Origins of American Political Thought* (Princeton, N.J.: Princeton University Press, 1994), p. 96.
47. Beth Frerking, "Americans Clinging to the Family Style of 'Ozzie & Harriet,' " *Patriot* (May 24, 1992), p. E12.
48. Margaret Sanger, *My Fight for Birth Control* (New York: Farrar and Rinehart, 1931), p. 5, as cited in Robert Marshall and Charles Donovan, *Blessed Are the Barren: The Social Policy of Planned Parenthood* (San Francisco, Calif.: Ignatius, 1991), p. 57.
49. Bryce J. Christensen, "The Definition of Family Should Remain Limited," in *The Family in America: Opposing Viewpoints,* Viqi Wagner, ed. (San Diego, Calif.: Greenhaven Press, 1992), p. 50.
50. Simone de Beauvoir, as cited in Christina Hoff Sommers, "Philosophers Against the Family," in *Person to Person,* Hugh LaFollette and George Graham, eds. (Philadelphia, Pa.: Temple University Press, 1987), p. 85.
51. Warren M. Hern, "Is Pregnancy Normal?" *Family Planning Perspectives* 3:1 (January 1971): 9.
52. Claudia Wallis, "The Nuclear Family Goes Boom!" *Time* (Fall 1992), p. 42.
53. Judith Stacey, "Good Riddance to 'The Family': A Response to David Popenoe," *Journal of Marriage and the Family* 55 (August 1993): 547, italics added.
54. Penelope Leach, *Children First: What Our Society Must Do—and Is Not Doing—For Our Children Today* (New York: Alfred A. Knopf, 1994), p. 8.
55. Elizabeth Debold, Marie Wilson, and Idelisse Malavé, *Mother/Daughter Revolution: From Betrayal to Power* (Reading, Mass.: Addison-Wesley, 1993), p. 226, italics added.

Chapter 8: Love the One You're With

1. Kim Painter, "Teens and Sex a Fact of American Life," *USA Today* (June 7, 1994), p. 6D.
2. Robert T. Michael, John H. Gagnon, Edward O. Laumann, and Gina Kolata, *Sex in America: A Definitive Survey* (Boston, Mass.: Little, Brown and Co., 1994), p. 92.
3. Michael et al., p. 95.
4. Michael et al., p. 99.
5. Painter, p. 6D.
6. William J. Bennett, *The Index of Leading Cultural Indicators: Facts and Figures on the State of American Society* (New York: Simon and Schuster, 1994), p. 72.
7. Allan C. Carlson, "By the Decades: The Troubled Course of the Family, 1945–1990 . . . and Beyond," *The Family in America* 4:5 (May 1990): 4. Estimating the number of illegal abortions has always been a tricky and speculative endeavor. While some people may dispute Carlson's 100,000 figure as too low, the claims of many abortion advocates that one to two million illegal abortions occurred yearly prior to *Roe* is manifestly absurd and has been completely discredited. See Francis J. Beckwith, *Politically Correct Death: Answering Arguments for Abortion Rights* (Grand Rapids, Mich.: Baker, 1993), pp. 55–59.
8. Beckwith, p. 58; Francis J. Beckwith and Norman L. Geisler, *Matters of Life and Death: Calm Answers to Tough Questions about Abortion and Euthanasia* (Grand Rapids, Mich.: Baker 1991), p. 43.
9. Carlson, p. 4.
10. Bryce J. Christensen, *Utopia against the Family: The Problems and Politics of the American Family* (San Francisco, Calif.: Ignatius Press, 1990), p. 20.
11. Michael et al., p. 40.
12. Michael et al., pp. 96–97.
13. Michael et al., p. 105.
14. James Patterson and Peter Kim, *The Day America Told the Truth: What People Really Believe About Everything That Really Matters* (New York: Plume, 1991), p. 94.
15. Patterson and Kim, p. 95.
16. Of course, if recent studies are accurate, a little forcefulness is not necessarily taboo either, at least in the fantasy lives of many Americans. Twenty-seven percent of men and 19 percent of women fantasize about being sexually dominate or sexually submissive, and about 13 percent of men and four percent of women would like some violence mixed with their sexual activities. (Patterson and Kim, p. 77.)
17. Patterson and Kim, p. 77. Also on the list of fantasies were incest, bestiality, and sex with defecation.
18. The material in the following chart comes from a chart with many more categories in Patterson and Kim, p. 81.
19. Barbara Ehrenreich, "The Bright Side of Overpopulation," *Time* (September 26, 1994), p. 86.
20. Ehrenreich, p. 86.

21. Ehrenreich, p. 86.
22. Ehrenreich, p. 86.
23. Genesis 2:24; Matthew 19:5; 1 Corinthians 6:16.
24. Robert Kimball Shinkoskey, "Without Law," *The Family in America* 7:1 (January 1993): 5.
25. Shinkoskey, p. 6.
26. Genesis 1:27–28; 2:23–24; 5:1–3; Psalm 113:9; 127:3–5.
27. Shinkoskey, p. 6.
28. See the entire Song of Solomon which depicts "love in all its spontaneity, beauty, power and exclusiveness—experienced in its varied moments of separation and intimacy, anguish and ecstasy, tension and contentment. . . . God intends that such love—grossly distorted and abused by both ancient and modern people—be a normal part of marital life in his good creation (see Genesis 1:26–31; 2:24)." "Introduction: Song of Songs," in *The NIV Study Bible*, Kenneth Barker, gen. ed. (Grand Rapids, Mich.: Zondervan, 1985), pp. 1003–1004.
29. DeNeen L. Brown, "The New Age of Innocence?" Washington Post National Weekly Edition (November 29–December 5, 1993), p. 33.
30. "Teens Talk About Sexuality," *USA Weekend* (September 22–24, 1995), p. 4; Gayle Jo Carter, "Tipper Gore and Teens Talk Tough," *USA Weekend* (March 4–6, 1994), p. 12.
31. Frank H. Boehm, "Never Learn?" *The Tennessean* (January 11, 1994), p. 9A.
32. Julie Stacey, "Children Bearing Children," *USA Today* (February 22, 1994), p. 2A.
33. Robert G. Marshall and Charles A. Donovan, *Blessed Are the Barren: The Social Policy of Planned Parenthood* (San Francisco: Ignatius Press, 1991), p. 63.
34. Marshall and Donovan, p. 104.
35. For some insightful and critical discussions of sex education in America, see Marshall and Donovan, chap. 4; Eric Buehrer, *The Public Orphanage: How Public Schools Are Making Parents Irrelevant* (Dallas, Tex.: Word, 1995), chaps. 7, 8, 12, 13; Barbara Dafoe Whitehead, "The Failure of Sex Education," *The Atlantic Monthly* (October 1994).
36. Buehrer, pp. 87–88.
37. Claudia Dreifus, "Joycelyn Elders," *The New York Times Magazine* (January 30, 1994), p. 18.
38. K. D. Whitehead, "Is It Time to Get Rid of the Surgeon General? Part I: The Rise and Fall of Joycelyn Elders," *Culture Wars* (July/August 1995), p. 34.
39. M. Jocelyn Elders, "Adolescent Health Issues: What Is Our Role?" *North Carolina Medical Journal* 52:5 (May 1991): 217.
40. Elders, "Adolescent Health Issues," p. 218.
41. Joycelyn Elders, as cited by Hilts, p. B7.
42. Elders, "Adolescent Health Issues," p. 219.
43. M. Joycelyn Elders, "Schools and Health: A Natural Partnership," *Journal of School Health* 63:7 (September 1993): 314.
44. Philip J. Hilts, "Blunt Style on Teen Sex and Health," *New York Times* (September 14, 1993), p. B7.

45. Joycelyn Elders, "The Future of U.S. Public Health," *Journal of the American Medical Association* 269:17 (May 1993): 2293.
46. Elders, as cited in Chris Bull, "The Condom Queen Reigns," *The Advocate* (March 22, 1994), p. 37.
47. Elders, "Adolescent Health Issues," p. 219.
48. Kay Coles James, "A Condom for Every Kid," *World* (July 31, 1993), p. 30.
49. Bull, p. 38.
50. James, p. 30; Jim Nelson Black, *When Nations Die: Ten Warning Signs of a Culture in Crisis* (Wheaton, Ill.: Tyndale House, 1994), p. 182.
51. "Condom Controversy," *World* (July 993), p. 13.
52. James, p. 30.
53. Elders, as cited in Bull, p. 37.
54. President Bill Clinton, as cited in Bull, p. 37.
55. Kerry Lobel, as cited in Bull, p. 37.
56. Elders, as cited in Dreifus, p. 19.
57. President Bill Clinton, as cited in Whitehead, p. 34.
58. Roy Maynard, "Non-Sexual Revolution," *World* (December 11, 1993), p. 11; Evangelical Press, "Elders Wants Sex Education for Two-Year-Old Children," *Dallas/Fort Worth Heritage* (January 1994), p. 14.
59. Dreifus, p. 19.
60. Elders, as cited in Bull, p. 37.
61. Joycelyn Elders, as cited in "A Lightning Rod Is Struck," *The Catholic World Report* (January 1995), p. 17.
62. Joycelyn Elders, as cited in the Associated Press, "Abortion Coverage Strategy: Use the Vote," *New York Times* (October 8, 1993), p. A14.
63. Elders, as cited in Dreifus, p. 19.
64. Elders, as cited in Dreifus, p. 19.
65. Joe S. McIlhaney, Jr., *Why Condoms Aren't Safe* (Colorado Springs, Colo.: Focus on the Family, 1993). According to Dr. McIlhaney, a gynecologist who specializes in treating infertility, "In one study *by promoters of condom use*, more than 13 percent of unmarried white teenagers became pregnant *in the first year* they used condoms for contraception. Among non-white unmarried girls, the comparable figure was 22 percent. These numbers are even more significant when you remember that a woman can get pregnant only two or three days each month" (p. 6).
66. McIlhaney, p. 6.
67. McIlhaney, pp. 6–7.
68. Elders, as cited in Bull, p. 35.
69. Joycelyn Elders, as cited in Mimi Hall, "Drumbeat Growing against Elders," *USA Today* (June 29, 1994), p. 8A.
70. Bull, p. 35.
71. Elders, as cited in Bull, p. 35.
72. Joycelyn Elders, as cited in Hilts, p. B7.
73. Joycelyn Elders, as cited in Douglas Jehl, "Surgeon General Forced to Resign by White House," *New York Times* (December 10, 1994), p. A9.

74. Whitehead, p. 35.
75. President Bill Clinton, as cited in Whitehead, p. 35.
76. Joycelyn Elders, as cited in Mimi Hall, " 'Differences' Are Surgeon General's Downfall," *USA Today* (December 12, 1994), p. 6A.
77. Clare Boothe Luce, *Is the New Morality Destroying America?* (Washington, D.C.: Ethics and Public Policy Center, 1979), p. 10.

Chapter 9: Dial Deviant for Normal

1. William Blackstone, "Introduction," *Commentaries on the Laws of England*, vol. I, sec. 2, pp. 29–31, as cited in Charles Rice, *Fifty Questions on the Natural Law: What It Is and Why We Need It* (San Francisco, Calif.: Ignatius Press, 1993), p. 33.
2. James Otis, "Rights of the British Colonies" (1764), as cited in Barry Alan Shain, *The Myth of American Individualism: The Protestant Origins of American Political Thought* (Princeton, N.J.: Princeton University Press, 1994), p. 132.
3. Alexander Hamilton, as cited in Rice, pp. 33–34. Similarly, the author of the 1776 Virginia Bill of Rights, George Mason, spoke out against a slavery statute under consideration before the General Court of Virginia in 1772. He based his case on divinely established natural law: "All acts of legislature apparently contrary to natural right and justice are, in our laws, and must be in the nature of things, considered as void. The laws of nature are the laws of God; Whose authority can be superseded by no power on earth. A legislature must not obstruct our obedience to him from whose punishments they cannot protect us. All human constitutions which contradict his laws, we are in conscience bound to disobey. Such have been the adjudications of our courts of Justice." (cited in Rice, p. 34.)
4. Blackstone, as cited in William Dannemeyer, *Shadow in the Land: Homosexuality in America* (San Francisco, Calif.: Ignatius Press, 1989), p. 57.
5. Dannemeyer, chap. 2; Richard F. Duncan and Gary L. Young, "Homosexual Rights and Citizen Initiatives: Is Constitutionalism Unconstitutional?" *Notre Dame Journal of Law, Ethics and Public Policy* 9:1 (1995): 93–94.
6. E. Michael Jones, *Degenerate Moderns: Modernity as Rationalized Sexual Misbehavior* (San Francisco, Calif.: Ignatius Press, 1993), pp. 93–94, 104–105.
7. Cornelia Christenson, *Kinsey: A Biography* (Bloomington, Ind.: Indiana University Press, 1971), p. 32.
8. Jones, p. 96.
9. Judith A. Reisman and Edward W. Eichel, *Kinsey, Sex and Fraud: The Doctrination of a People* (Lafayette, La.: Huntington House, 1990).
10. Reisman, as cited in Jones, p. 96.
11. Kinsey, as cited in Jones, p. 99.
12. Kinsey, as cited in Jones, p. 96.
13. Kinsey, as cited in Jones, pp. 96–97.
14. Alfred C. Kinsey, Wardell B. Pomeroy, and Clyde E. Martin, *Sexual Behavior in the Human Male* (Philadelphia, Pa.: W. B. Saunders, 1948); Alfred C. Kinsey, Wardell B. Pomeroy, Clyde E. Martin, and Paul H. Gebhard, *Sexual Behavior in*

the Human Female (Philadelphia, Pa.: W. B. Saunders, 1953).

15. Bruce Westfall, "The Sex Revolution's Phony Foundation," *Citizen* (September 16, 1991), p. 2.
16. Westfall, p. 2.
17. Kinsey, as cited in Christenson, p. 107.
18. Robert T. Michael, John H. Gagnon, Edward O. Laumann, and Gina Kolata, *Sex in America: A Definitive Survey* (Boston, Mass.: Little, Brown and Co., 1994), p. 20.
19. Kinsey, as cited in Michael et al., p. 20.
20. Michael et al., pp. 20, 173; Dannemeyer, p. 60.
21. Kinsey, as cited in Jones, p. 102.
22. Michael et al., p. 173.
23. Kinsey, as cited in Michael et al., p. 20.
24. Jones, p. 104.
25. Abraham Maslow and James M. Sakoda, "Volunteer Error in the Kinsey Study," *The Journal of Abnormal and Social Psychology* 42:2 (April 1952): 26.
26. Michael et al., in their book *Sex in America,* make this same criticism of Kinsey's work, but they are more sympathetic, although they arrive at the same conclusion. See pp. 18–19.
27. Jones, p. 102.
28. Jones, pp. 100–101.
29. The Reverend John Beckman, "Kinsey's Gals," *Fidelity* (October 1993), p. 7.
30. Dannemeyer, pp. 59–60.
31. Jones, p. 102.
32. Dannemeyer, p. 60.
33. Wardell B. Pomeroy, *Dr. Kinsey and the Institute for Sex Research* (New York: Harper and Row, 1972), p. 138.
34. Kinsey et al., *Sexual Behavior in the Human Male,* p. 160.
35. Kinsey et al., p. 178.
36. Kinsey et al., p. 161.
37. Jones, p. 107.
38. John Gargon, *Human Sexualities,* as cited in Jones, p. 107.
39. Paul Gebhard, as cited in Westfall, p. 2.
40. Jones, p. 104.
41. Christenson, p. 19.
42. Gebhard, as cited in Jones, p. 111.
43. Samuel A. Steward, "Remembering Dr. Kinsey: Sexual Scientist and Investigator," *The Advocate* (November 13, 1980), pp. 21–22.
44. Steward, p. 21.
45. Steward, p. 21.
46. Jones, chap. 5. Jones's observations on the Kinsey Institute's cloak of secrecy surrounding Kinsey's sex life and personal records are at once disturbing and revealing.
47. The associate was Wardell Pomeroy, who was one of Kinsey's coauthors on his two books concerning male and female sexuality. See Jones, p. 113.

48. Dannemeyer, p. 161.
49. Chris Corcoran, "A Church-Backed Sex-Ed Program Stirs Furor Among Parents, Clergy," *New York City Tribune* (July 18, 1988), p. 5.
50. Sex therapist Edward Eichel, as cited in Corcoran, p. 5.
51. Dannemeyer, p. 162.
52. Dannemeyer, pp. 162–164.
53. Deryck Calderwood, *About Your Sexuality*, as cited in Dannemeyer, p. 164.
54. Calderwood, as cited in Dannemeyer, p. 164.
55. Westfall, p. 3.
56. Mary Calderone, as cited in Christine Richert, "Sex Education Encourages Promiscuity," in *Sexual Values: Opposing Viewpoints*, Bruno Leone and M. Teresa O'Neill, eds. (St. Paul, Minn.: Greenhaven Press, 1983), p. 55.
57. "Gay Students Have a Safe Haven in Oregon," *USA Today* (July 10, 1996), p. 6D.
58. Patricia Smith, "School Programs Should Not Stress Acceptance of Homosexuality," in *Homosexuality*, p. 114; Rosie Mestel, "Sex by the Numbers," *Discover* (January 1994), p. 70; Kim Painter, "More Figures on Homosexuality," *USA Today* (October 7, 1994), p. 4D; Michael et al., pp. 174–77; David W. Dunlap, "Gay Survey Raises a New Question," *New York Times* (October 18, 1994), p. A10; Thomas E. Schmidt, *Straight and Narrow? Compassion and Clarity in the Homosexuality Debate* (Downers Grove, Ill.: InterVarsity Press, 1995), pp. 102–105.
59. Smith, p. 116. Along with student proselytizing, Uribe is not beyond giving her support to teachers who have kept quiet about their nontraditional lifestyles. In a *New York Times* report, Uribe is attributed with encouraging a lesbian high school teacher to let her school in on her secret. After a professional workshop for educators, Uribe told the conflicted teacher, "Honey, it's your civil right" to come out of the closet. Uribe then supplied her with information about "the protections offered by union contracts and civil rights law" against sexual discrimination. This was the counsel that finally pushed the teacher into declaring her homosexuality before her students and school administrators, a coming out that was greeted with little resistance and a lot of support from her peers and students. (Jane Gross, "In School," *New York Times* (July 27, 1994), p. B8.
60. Eric Buehrer, *The Public Orphanage: How Public Schools Are Making Parents Irrelevant* (Dallas, Tex.: Word, 1995), p. 136.
61. Buehrer, p. 136.
62. Warren Duzak, "Commission Cites Bible in Gay Vote," *The Tennessean* (November 21, 1995), p. 1B.
63. Dale Buss, "Homosexual Rights Go to School," *Christianity Today* (May 17, 1993), p. 70; see also p. 71.
64. Buss, p. 70; Joseph P. Gudel, "That Which Is Unnatural: Homosexuality in Society, the Church, and Scripture," *Christian Research Journal* 15:3 (Winter 1993): 10–11.
65. Buss, p. 70.

66. Leslea Newman and Diana Souza, *Heather Has Two Mommies* (Boston, Mass.: Alyson Publications, 1989).
67. Michael Willhoite, *Daddy's Roommate* (Boston, Mass.: Alyson Wonderland, 1990). A new book will soon be released called *Daddy's Wedding*, where the father marries his male roommate.
68. David Gelman with Debra Rosenberg, Vicki Quade, Elizabeth Roberts, and Danzy Senna, "Tune In, Come Out," *Newsweek* (November 8, 1993), pp. 70–71.
69. Bruce Mirken, "School Programs Should Stress Acceptance of Homosexuality," in *Homosexuality: Opposing Views*, William Dudley, ed. (San Diego, Calif.: Greenhaven Press, 1993), pp. 110, 111.
70. Dannemeyer, pp. 58–59.
71. Dannemeyer, pp. 60–61.
72. *Bowers v. Hardwick*, 478 U.S. 186 (1986).
73. Justice Byron R. White, *Bowers v. Hardwick*, as cited in *May It Please the Court: The Most Significant Oral Arguments Before the Supreme Court Since 1955*, Peter Irons and Stephanie Guitton, eds. (New York: New Press, 1993), pp. 370, 371.
74. Justice White, p. 372.
75. Chief Justice Warren E. Burger, *Bowers v. Hardwick*, as cited in Richard F. Duncan, "Who Wants to Stop the Church: Homosexual Rights Legislation, Public Policy, and Religious Freedom," *Notre Dame Law Review* 69:3 (1994): 404, n. 40.
76. Wardell Pomeroy, as cited in John Leo, "Cradle-to-Grave Intimacy," *Time* (September 7, 1981), p. 69.
77. Pomeroy, as cited in Michael Ebert, "Pedophilia Steps into the Daylight," *Citizen* (November 16, 1992), p. 6.
78. Larry Constantine, as cited in Francis J. Beckwith, *Politically Correct Death: Answering Arguments for Abortion Rights* (Grand Rapids, Mich.: Baker Book House, 1993), p. 176.
79. John Money, as cited in Joseph Geraci and Donald Mader, "Interview: John Money," *Paidika* (Spring 1991), p. 5.
80. Geraci and Mader, p. 5.
81. Money, as cited in Geraci and Mader, p. 9. Although *Paidika* is published in the Netherlands, its editorial board includes a number of Americans, including "Dr. Vern Bullough, dean of faculty of natural and social science at State University College at Buffalo, New York; Dr. Wayne Dynes of Hunter College; Dr. John DeCecco from the department of psychology at San Francisco State University; and Dr. Hurbert Kennedy, a research associate at the Center for Research and Education in Sexuality at San Francisco State University." (Buehrer, p. 144.)
82. Editors, "Statement of Purpose," *Paidika* (Summer 1987).

Chapter 10: I Am Woman, Hear Me Roar

1. 1 Peter 3:7.
2. Robert Kimball Shinkoskey, "Without Law," *The Family in America* 7:1 (January 1993): 3.
3. Shinkoskey, p. 3.

4. Shinkoskey, p. 3. I am not referring to child labor abuses that occurred in the factories, nor am I implying that child labor should be brought back. I am dealing with families running businesses out of their homes.
5. *Editorial Research Reports on the Changing American Family,* Hoyt Gimlin, ed. (Washington, D.C.: Congressional Quarterly, 1979), p. 13.
6. Sally Quinn, "The Feminist Betrayal," *Reader's Digest* (June 1992), p. 86.
7. Christina Sommers, *Who Stole Feminism: How Women Have Betrayed Women* (New York: Simon and Schuster, 1994), p. 22. For some helpful discussions on the history of feminism and its contemporary divisions, see Sommers; Elizabeth Fox-Genovese, *Feminism without Illusions: A Critique of Individualism* (Chapel Hill, N.C.: University of North Carolina Press, 1991); Dinesh D'Souza, "The New Feminist Revolt: This Time It's against Feminism," *Policy Review* (Winter 1986): 46–52; Wendy Kaminer, "Feminism's Identity Crisis," *The Atlantic Monthly* (October 1993), pp. 51–68; Rene Denfeld, *The New Victorians: A Young Woman's Challenge to the Old Feminist Order* (New York: Warner Books, 1995); Eloise Salholz, with Pamela Abramson, Shawn Doherty, Renee Michael, and Diane Weathers, "Feminism's Identity Crisis," *Newsweek* (March 31, 1986), pp. 58–59; Karen Offen, "Defining Feminism: A Comparative Historical Approach," *Signs: Journal of Women in Culture and Society* 14:1 (1988): 119–57; Katherine Kersten, "What Do Women Want? A Conservative Manifesto," *Policy Review* (Spring 1991): 4–15.
8. Frederica Mathewes-Green, *Real Choices: Offering Practical, Life-Affirming Alternatives to Abortion* (Sisters, Ore.: Multnomah, 1994), pp. 249–250. In another study conducted between May 1993 and April 1994, among groups made up of women who had undergone abortions, the top five reasons they gave for choosing abortion were: (1) They felt pressured by their husband or boyfriend (38.2 percent); (2) they felt pressure from their parents, especially their mother (20.5 percent); (3) they wanted to protect their parents (11.7 percent); (4) their husband or boyfriend was weak and unsupportive (8.8 percent); (5) they feared their parents' disapproval (8.8 percent) (Mathewes-Green, p. 247–248). In this study no one cited health concerns, rape, incest, population control, liberation, or womb-control as motivating factors.
9. Mathewes-Green, p. 243.
10. Mathewes-Green, p. 242.
11. Mathewes-Green, pp. 234–235.
12. James T. Burtchaell, *Rachel Weeping: The Case against Abortion* (San Francisco, Calif.: Harper and Row, 1982), pp. 18–19.
13. Burtchaell, p. 20.
14. Polly Bergen, as cited in *The Choices We Made: Twenty-Five Women and Men Speak Out about Abortion,* Angela Bonavoglia, ed. (New York: Random House, 1991), p. 27.
15. Mathewes-Green, pp. 40, 42.
16. Mathewes-Green, p. 66.
17. Pam Koerbel, *Does Anyone Else Feel Like I Do?: And Other Questions Women Ask Following An Abortion* (New York: Doubleday, 1990), p. 15.

18. Mathewes-Green, p. 152.
19. Koerbel, p. 17.
20. Mathewes-Green, p. 39.
21. Koerbel, p. 80.
22. Mathewes-Green, p. 117.
23. Mathewes-Green, p. 156.
24. Linda Bird Francke, *The Ambivalence of Abortion* (New York: Random House, 1978), p. 32.
25. In her book *Passage Through Abortion,* Mary Zimmerman reports that half of all abortion cases led "quickly" to the "disruption and termination of the relationship with the man involved" (as cited in Mathewes-Green, p. 71). The Open Arms Abortion Information Survey Project found that 52 percent of women questioned said that the father of the child left "soon after the abortion" (Mathewes-Green, p. 243). In another study with four hundred couples, researcher Emily Milling found that 70 percent of the relationships "failed within one month after the abortion" (Koerbel, p. 66).
26. Burtchaell, p. 16.
27. Burtchaell, p. 17.
28. Koerbel, p. 80, italics added.
29. Gloria Steinem, "Foreword," in *The Choices We Made,* pp. x, xii.
30. Carolyn G. Heilbrun, *The Education of a Woman: The Life of Gloria Steinem* (New York: Dial Press, 1995).
31. John J. Reilly, "The Fish Rots First at the Head," *Culture Wars* (March 1996), p. 19.
32. Steinem, "Foreword," in *The Choices We Made,* pp. xii-xiii.
33. Andrea Dworkin, as cited in Richard John Neuhaus, "The Feminist Revelation," *First Things* (December 1991), p. 56. On the dedication page of her book *Outrageous Acts and Everyday Rebellions,* 2d ed. (New York: Henry Holt and Co., 1995), Steinem says of Dworkin, "This book is gratefully dedicated . . . to Andrea Dworkin for an anger so righteous that it keeps others from confronting injustice without it" (italics deleted). Whether it's a righteous anger, I don't think so. But that it's anger is unequivocally true. A better description would be irrational rage.
34. Steinem, pp. 161–175.
35. Steinem, p. 169.
36. Steinem, pp. 164, 165, 334, 335, 340.
37. Steinem, pp. 168–169.
38. Steinem, p. 164.
39. Steinem, p. 335.
40. Jerome LeJeune, as cited in *The Human Life Bill—S. 158, Report Together with Additional and Minority Views to the Committee on the Judiciary, United States Senate, Made by Its Subcommittee on Separation of Powers,* 97th Congress, 1st session, 1981, p. 9.
41. Steinem, p. 165
42. Steinem, "Foreword," in *The Choices We Made,* pp. xi-xii.

43. Reilly.
44. D'Souza, pp. 50–51.
45. Jo McGowan, "In India, They Abort Females," *Newsweek* (January 30, 1989), p. 12.
46. Francis J. Beckwith, *Politically Correct Death: Answering the Arguments for Abortion Rights* (Grand Rapids, Mich.: Baker Book House, 1993), p. 31.
47. Francis J. Beckwith and Norman L. Geisler, *Matters of Life and Death: Calm Answers to Tough Questions about Abortion and Euthanasia* (Grand Rapids, Mich.: Baker Book House, 1991), pp. 118–19. They conclude that about 15,000 sex-selection abortions per year are performed in the United States, but they base their calculations on a total annual abortion rate of 1.5 million. My sex-selection abortion figure is higher because I am working with a 1.6 million annual abortion rate.
48. Marilyn French, *The War against Women* (New York: Ballantine, 1992), pp. 115–116.
49. Steinem, *Outrageous Acts and Everyday Rebellions*, p. 340.
50. Reilly, p. 18.
51. Gloria Steinem, as cited in John Leo, "The Trouble with Feminism," *U.S. News and World Report* (February 10, 1992), p. 19.
52. Catharine MacKinnon, as cited in Christina Sommers, "Hard-Line Feminists Guilty of Ms.-Representation," *Wall Street Journal* (November 7, 1991), p. A14.
53. Steinem, *Outrageous Acts and Everyday Rebellions*, p 166.
54. Steinem, *Outrageous Acts and Everyday Rebellions*, p. 183.
55. Steinem, p. 232.
56. Betty Friedan, as cited in Carol Iannone, "What Moderate Feminists?" *Commentary* (June 1995), p. 47.
57. Simone de Beauvoir, as cited in Nicholas Davidson, *The Failure of Feminism* (Buffalo, N.Y.: Prometheus, 1988), p. 17.
58. Bonnie Gangelhoff, "Gloria Steinem Fights a Women's Revolution Within," *Houston Post* (December 6, 1992), p. C14.
59. Reilly, p. 19.
60. Quinn, p. 84
61. Steinem, as cited in Gangelhoff, p. C14. See also Karen Lehrman, "The Feminist Mystique," *The New Republic* (March 16, 1992), pp. 32–33.
62. Steinem, *Outrageous Acts and Everyday Rebellions*, pp. 173–174.
63. Betty Friedan, as cited in Reilly, p. 19. See also Rita Mae Brown, "Reflections of a Lavender Menace," *Ms.* (July/August 1995), pp. 40–47.
64. Steinem, p. 26.
65. Steinem, p. 165.
66. Laura Garcia, "Can Marriage Be Saved?" *Catholic Dossier* 1:4 (November-December 1995): 8.
67. Betty Friedan, *The Feminine Mystique*, as cited in Iannone, p. 48.

Chapter 11: Race Colors Everything

1. The panelists were Jay Sekulow (chief counsel of the American Center for Law and Justice); Robert Peck (legislative counsel in the Washington, D.C., national

office of the American Civil Liberties Union); Don Feder (nationally syndicated columnist with the *Boston Herald*); Clarence Page (Pulitzer Prize-winning journalist and columnist for the *Chicago Tribune*); Mona Charen (nationally syndicated columnist, and political analyst on CNN's *The Capital Gang*); Elliot Mincberg (legal director of People for the American Way); Barry Lynn (executive director of Americans United for Separation of Church and State); and Alan Keyes (see the text for his credits).

2. Alan Keyes, "Defining American Culture: A Panel Discussion," *Liberty, Life and Family* 2:1 (1995): 180.
3. Dinesh D'Souza, *The End of Racism: Principles for a Multiracial Society* (New York: The Free Press, 1995), p. 59.
4. D'Souza, chap. 2. See also Thomas Sowell, *Race and Culture: A Worldview* (New York: Basic Books, 1994), passim.
5. D'Souza, pp. 51–52.
6. For a classic statement of this position, see the nineteenth-century work by French scholar and diplomat Arthur de Gobineau entitled *The Inequality of Human Races*, Adrian Collins, trans. (New York: Howard Fertig, 1967).
7. Sowell, chap. 7; D'Souza, chaps. 2–3; Michael Grant, *The World of Rome* (New York: Meridian, 1960), chap. 4; "Slave, Slavery," in *New Bible Dictionary*, J. D. Douglas, ed. (Downers Grove, Ill.: InterVarsity Press, 1982), pp. 1121–25; Francis Lyall, *Slaves, Citizens, Sons: Legal Metaphors in the Epistles* (Grand Rapids, Mich.: Zondervan, 1984), chap. 2; Derek Tidball, *The Social Context of the New Testament: A Sociological Analysis* (Grand Rapids, Mich.: Zondervan, 1984), pp. 114–16; Norman F. Cantor, *The Civilization of the Middle Ages*, rev. ed. (New York: HarperCollins, 1993), pp. 38, 43; Owen Chadwick, *A History of Christianity* (New York: St. Martin's Press, 1995), pp. 189–190; Paul Johnson, *A History of Christianity* (New York: Atheneum, 1976), pp. 149, 176; Thomas Sowell, *The Economics and Politics of Race: An International Perspective* (New York: Quill, 1983), chap. 4.
8. Sowell, *Race and Culture*, pp. 194–195. "Neither a national policy nor a racial ideology was necessary for enslavement to take place. All that was necessary was the existence of vulnerable people, whoever and wherever they might be—and regardless of whether they were racially similar or different from those who victimized them. . . . Enslavement was based on self-interest and opportunity, not ideology" (Sowell, *Race and Culture*, p. 195).
9. Audrey Smedley, *Race in North America* (Boulder, Colo.: Westview Press, 1993), p. 95; Winthrop Jordan, *The White Man's Burden* (New York: Oxford University Press, 1974), p. 40.
10. John Hope Franklin, *Race and History* (Baton Rouge, La.: Louisiana State University Press, 1989), p. 334; Smedley, pp. 95–96. For more on the legal status of slaves in colonial America, see A. Leon Higginbotham, Jr., *In the Matter of Color: Race and the American Legal Process: The Colonial Period* (New York: Oxford University Press, 1978).
11. U.S. Bureau of the Census, *Negro Population of the United States: 1790–1915* (Washington, D.C.), p. 56.

12. D'Souza, p. 75.
13. D'Souza, pp. 75–76.
14. Abram Harris, *The Negro As Capitalist* (New York: Arno Press, 1936), p. 4; Kenneth Stampp, *The Peculiar Institution: Slavery in the Antebellum South* (New York: Vintage, 1956), p. 194.
15. D'Souza, p. 76.
16. Michael P. Johnson and James L. Roark, *Black Masters: A Free Family of Color in the Old South*, as cited in D'Souza, p. 78.
17. Ira Berlin, *Slaves Without Masters: The Free Negro in the Antebellum South* (New York: Pantheon, 1974), p. 275.
18. Gary B. Mills, *The Forgotten People: Cane River's Creoles of Color* (Baton Rouge, La.: Louisiana State University Press, 1977), p. xxix; Thomas Holt, *Black Over White: Negro Political Leadership in South Carolina During Reconstruction* (Urbana, Ill.: University of Illinois Press, 1977), pp. 63, 230.
19. D'Souza, chap. 3; Sowell, *Race and Culture*, chap. 7; Barry Alan Shain, *The Myth of American Individualism: The Protestant Origins of American Political Thought* (Princeton, N.J.: Princeton University Press, 1994), chap. 8.
20. Shain, p. 293.
21. The earliest voices raised against slavery were the Quakers, who were followed by Baptists, Congregationalists, Methodists, and varied sorts of millennialists. They had spoken out at least since the turn of the eighteenth century. See Shain, p. 293.
22. Thomas Jefferson, as cited in Henry Wilder Foote, *Thomas Jefferson: Champion of Religious Freedom, Advocate of Christian Morals* (Boston, Mass.: Beacon Press, 1947), p. 18.
23. Page Smith, *Rediscovering Christianity: A History of Modern Democracy and the Christian Ethic* (New York: St. Martin's Press, 1994), pp. 123–124. See also Higginbotham, chap. 11; Peter Kolchin, *American Slavery, 1619–1877* (New York: Hill and Wang, 1993), chap. 3; William Lee Miller, *Arguing About Slavery: The Great Battle in the United States Congress* (New York: Alfred A. Knopf, 1996), chap. 2; Jack N. Rakove, *Original Meanings: Politics and Ideas in the Making of the Constitution* (New York: Alfred A. Knopf, 1996), chap. 4.
24. Sowell, *Race and Culture*, p. 211. See also John C. Pollock, "William Wilberforce and the Abolition of Slavery," in *Great Leaders of the Christian Church*, John D. Woodbridge, ed. (Chicago, Ill.: Moody Press, 1988), pp. 301–305.
25. Smith, p. 143.
26. Abraham Lincoln, as cited in Sowell, *Race and Culture*, p. 209.
27. Smith, pp. 147–148.
28. Sowell, *Race and Culture*, pp. 210–214; Johnson, pp. 370–371, 444–445; Chadwick, pp. 242, 274. Chadwick states that slavery has made a modern-day comeback: "There has been some evidence in the 1990s of a revival of slavery, perhaps in Brazil and elsewhere in Latin America, perhaps in North Africa, perhaps in the Middle East"(p. 243).

    In relationship to Africa, Joseph R. Gregory confirms this awful fact in his article "African Slavery 1996," *First Things* 63 (May 1996): 37–39. As Gregory reports: "In the West African nation of Mauritania, between eighty and ninety thousand human beings are owned outright by other people, according to the American Anti-Slavery Group, Human Rights Watch/Africa, and the U.S. State Department. Most are black tribesmen owned by the dark-skinned Berbers known as the Moors. Across the continent, in the war-ravaged Sudan, chattel slaves number in the tens of thousands, according to Christian Solidarity International. Most are the children of black Christian and animist villagers, taken in raids by their traditional Arab enemies, now formed into militia by the Muslim government in Khartoum in its war to subdue the south" (p. 37).

29. Kolchin, pp. 233–235.
30. Kolchin, p. 231.
31. Kolchin, pp. 230–235.
32. William J. Watkins, Jr., "*Plessy* v. *Ferguson*—One Hundred Years Later," *Chronicles* (August 1996), p. 45.
33. Kolchin, pp. 216–229.
34. See "Black Southerners Versus the North: A Different Kind of Solidarity," *Issues and Views: An Open Forum on Issues Affecting the Black Community* (Fall/Winter 1996), pp. 1–2, 6.
35. Watkins, p. 45.
36. Watkins, p. 45.
37. Kolchin, pp. 231–232.
38. Richard Hofstadter, *Social Darwinism in American Thought* (Boston, Mass.: Beacon Press, 1983), especially chap. 9; Daniel J. Kevles, *In the Name of Eugenics: Genetics and the Uses of Human Heredity* (Cambridge, Mass.: Harvard University Press, 1995); Pat Shipman, *The Evolution of Racism: Human Differences and the Use and Abuse of Science* (New York: Simon and Schuster, 1994); Robert E. D. Clark, *Darwin: Before and After—An Examination and Assessment* (Grand Rapids, Mich.: Grand Rapids International, 1958), chap. 6; Bolton Davidheiser, *Evolution and Christian Faith* (Grand Rapids, Mich.: Baker Book House, 1969), chap. 9; Peter J. Bowler, *The Non-Darwinian Revolution: Reinterpreting a Historical Myth* (Baltimore, Md.: Johns Hopkins University Press, 1988), chap. 7.

    Many scientists, historians, and sociologists have claimed that Social Darwinism was a perversion of Darwin's thought. He was a scientist, not a sociologist or social engineer. He never intended his ideas to be applied to society at large. In their monumental biography on this ground-breaking scientist, Adrian Desmond and James Moore show unequivocally that these defenders of Darwin are wrong. Darwin, they write, "thought blacks inferior but was sickened by slavery; he subordinated women but was totally dependent on his redoubtable wife. . . . Social Darwinism is often taken to be something extraneous, an ugly concretion added to the pure Darwinian corpus after the event, tarnishing Darwin's image. But his notebooks make plain that competition, free trade, imperialism, racial extermination, and sexual inequality were written into the equation from the start—Darwinism was always intended to explain human society." (Adrian Desmond and James Moore, *Darwin: The Life of a Tormented Evolutionist* [New York: Warner Books, 1991], p. xxi.)

39. Kolchin, pp. 235–236.
40. Dennis J. Hutchinson, "Brown v. Board of Education," in *The Oxford Companion to the Supreme Court of the United States*, Kermit L. Hall, ed. (New York: Oxford University Press, 1992), pp. 93–96.
41. See David J. Garrow, *Bearing the Cross: Martin Luther King, Jr., and the Southern Christian Leadership Conference* (New York: William Morrow and Co., 1986), chaps. 1–2; Sara Rimer, "Trip to History for Boston Teenagers: To the South of the Civil Rights Fight," *New York Times* (July 29, 1994), p. A6; Jeannye Thornton, " 'I'm Not Going to Ride the Bus,' " *U.S. News and World Report* (December 11, 1995), pp. 52, 54.
42. E. Michael Jones, "The Beloved Community Gets Down: How the Civil Rights Movement Destroyed the Black Family," *Culture Wars* (October 1995), p. 20.
43. The Moynihan Report, as cited in *Editorial Research Reports on The Changing American Family* (Washington, D.C.: Congressional Quarterly, 1979), p. 71.
44. Jones, p. 22.
45. Thomas Sowell, *Ethnic America: A History* (New York: Basic Books, 1981), pp. 188–189. Slave owners occasionally broke up slave families by selling spouses and children. The anguish this caused was great, but it did not lead to blacks giving up on their marriages or families. In fact, in the post-Civil War period, it was common to see freed black spouses searching for their mates. Parents looked for their children and vice versa. As Sowell notes, "The search for lost family members continued through newspaper advertisements that filled the newly established black newspapers on into the 1880s." (Sowell, *Ethnic America*, p. 198.)
46. E. Franklin Frazier, *The Negro Family in the United States*, as cited in Jones, pp. 24–25.
47. Sowell, *Ethnic America*, p. 213.
48. Allan C. Carlson, "By the Decades: The Troubled Course of the Family, 1945–1990 . . . and Beyond," *The Family in America* 4:5 (1990): 3.
49. Sowell, *Ethnic America*, p. 222.
50. Frazier, as cited in Jones, p. 25.
51. Jones, p. 22.
52. The National Association for the Advancement of Colored People.
53. Jones, p. 22.
54. Jones, pp. 18–35; E. Michael Jones, "Dionysos Goes Free Again: The Cultural Scenario That Let O. J. Walk," *Culture Wars* (November 1995), pp. 10–13.
55. Norman Mailer, himself an avid advocate of liberal causes, claimed that the black gave himself over to the "pleasures of the body," and his music "gave voice to the character and quality of his existence, to his rage and the infinite variations of joy, lust, languor, growl, cramp, pinch, scream, and despair of his orgasm." Norman Mailer, "The White Negro," in his book *Advertisements for Myself*, as cited in Jones, "Dionysos Goes Free Again," p. 11.
56. Garrow, p. 375.
57. David J. Garrow, *The FBI and Martin Luther King, Jr.: From "Solo" to Memphis* (New York: W. W. Norton and Co., 1981), especially chap. 4.

58. Martin Luther King, Jr., as cited in Garrow, *Bearing the Cross*, p. 375.
59. Garrow, *Bearing the Cross*, p. 617.
60. Maxwell Geismar, *Soul on Ice*, as cited in Jones, "Dionysos Goes Free Again," p. 10.
61. Eldridge Cleaver, as cited in Jones, "Dionysos Goes Free Again," p. 11.
62. Cleaver, as cited in Jones, p. 12.
63. LeRoi Jones, as cited in Jones, p. 12.
64. Cleaver, as cited in Jones, p. 12.
65. Clarence Mitchell, as cited in Jones, "The Beloved Community Gets Down," p. 30.
66. Floyd McKissick, as cited in Jones, "The Beloved Community Gets Down," p. 30.
67. Jones, p. 30.
68. See, for example, Martin Luther King, Jr., "I Have a Dream," in *A Testament of Hope: The Essential Writings of Martin Luther King, Jr.*, James Melvin Washington, ed. (San Francisco, Calif.: Harper and Row, 1986), chap. 36.
69. Martin Luther King, Jr., "I Have a Dream," pp. 296–297; "Kenneth B. Clark Interview," pp. 335–336; "*Playboy* Interview: Martin Luther King, Jr.," pp. 364–365.
70. Garrow, *Bearing the Cross*, chap. 6.
71. See D'Souza, chap. 8; these two titles by Thomas Sowell: *Civil Rights: Rhetoric or Reality?* (New York: William Morrow, 1984), and *Preferential Policies: An International Perspective* (New York: William Morrow, 1990); and consider the collection of articles in *Debating Affirmative Action: Race, Gender, Ethnicity, and the Politics of Inclusion*, Nicolaus Mills, ed. (New York: Dell, 1994).
72. D'Souza, pp. 6–7; Carlson, pp. 3–4, 6; David Popenoe, "American Family Decline, 1960–1990: A Review and Appraisal," *Journal of Marriage and the Family* 55 (August 1993): 527–555; William J. Bennett, *The Index of Leading Cultural Indicators: Facts and Figures on the State of American Society* (New York: Simon and Schuster, 1994), pp. 26–27, 64–65; Associated Press, "Look at the Stats," *The Tennessean* (October 12, 1995), p. 17A; Julie Stacey, "Children Bearing Children," *USA Today* (February 22, 1994), p. 2A; Kim Painter, "Teens and Sex a Fact of American Life," *USA Today* (June 7, 1994), p. 6D; Marilyn Elias, "One in Four Kids Suffers Some Form of Abuse," *USA Today* (October 3, 1994), p. D1; Gannett News Service, "Nontraditional Families Gaining," *The Tennessean* (July 30, 1994), p. 7A; "Census Report on Children Paints a Diverse Picture of Family Life," *New York Times* (August 30, 1994), p. A9; Margaret L. Usdansky, " 'Blended,' 'Extended' Now All in the Family," *USA Today* (August 30, 1994), p. 3A; Connie Cass, "The Black Male Takes His Plight to the Streets of Washington," *The Tennessean* (October 15, 1995), p. 1D; Linda Kanamine, "Number of Two-Parent Families Up," *USA Today* (October 16, 1995), p. 1A; "Message of Today's March Is Self-Help, Not Racism," *USA Today* (October 16, 1995), p. 12A; Bob Herbert, "The Crowd Was There, But Where the Leader?" *The Tennessean* (October 23, 1995), p. 11A.
73. Roger Wilkins, as cited in Jared Taylor, *Paved With Good Intentions: The Failure*

of Race Relations in Contemporary America (New York: Carroll and Graf, 1992), p. 102.

74. Ronald Walters, as cited in D'Souza, p. 9.
75. Barbara Sizemore, as cited in Taylor, p. 102. A black student at Penn State, after citing "proof" that AIDS is a devilish plot hatched by whites to "exterminate black people," wrote: "After looking at all of the evidence there is only one conclusion: white people are devils. . . . I believe that we must secure our freedom and independence from these devils by any means necessary, including violence. . . . To protect ourselves we should bear arms (three handguns and two rifles, maybe an M–16) immediately and form a militia. . . . So black people, let us unite, organize, and execute." (Taylor, p. 104.)
76. Joseph Barndt, *Dismantling Racism: The Continuing Challenge to White America* (Minneapolis, Minn.: Augsburg, 1991), pp. 34, 35.
77. Roger Rosenblatt, "A Nation of Pained Hearts," *Time* (October 16, 1995), pp. 40–45; John McCormick, Mark Starr, Vern E. Smith, and Howard Fineman, "Whites v. Blacks," *Newsweek* (October 16, 1995), pp. 28–35; "One Verdict, Clashing Voices," *Newsweek* (October 16, 1995), pp. 46, 51; Michael Isikoff, "The Silly Season," *Newsweek* (October 16, 1995), pp. 63–65; Jonathan Alter, "White and Blue," *Newsweek* (October 16, 1995), pp. 66–67; Barbara Reynolds, "Guilty Get Away, Innocents Die When Justice Fails," *USA Today* (October 6, 1995), p. 12A; Kurt Mack, "O. J. Is Not a Black Hero," *Newsweek* (October 30, 1995), p. 20; Richard Price, "For the Public, Deliberations Go On," *USA Today* (October 6, 1995), p. 4A; Debbie Howlett, "Clark Says Verdict Was Based on Race," *USA Today* (October 6, 1995), p. 4A; K. Sheffield, "Wrong to Categorize All 'Blacks' As One," *The Tennessean* (October 15, 1995), p. 4D; Fred Bayles, "Simpson—Racial Split," Associated Press (October 4, 1995); Anne Thompson, "Simpson—Money or Race?" Associated Press (October 4, 1995); Christopher Sullivan, "Simpson—Blacks Reflect," Associated Press (October 3, 1995); Marianne Means, "What Planet Were Those Women On?" *The Tennessean* (October 14, 1995), p. 9; "Still Fuming Over the O. J. Verdict," *Newsweek* (October 30, 1995), pp. 16, 18; Bill Compton, "Trial Shows Juries Not Totally Objective," *The Tennessean* (October 13, 1995), p. 12A; James Nuechterlein, "O. J. Simpson and the American Dilemma," *First Things* 58 (December 1995): 10–11.
78. "Decision . . . Division," *Newsweek* (October 16, 1995), pp. 30, 34, 39.
79. McCormick et al., pp. 33–34.
80. McCormick et al., p. 34.
81. Jones, "Dionysos Goes Free Again," p. 10.
82. Dwight Lewis, "Hopefully, a Million Men Will Walk for Responsibility," *The Tennessean* (September 17, 1995), p. 5D.
83. Supporters of the march included the SCLC, the Congressional Black Caucus, the National Black Women's Political Congress, and the National Council of Negro Women. (Desda Moss, "Islam March Is Tapping Into Mainstream," *USA Today* (September 25, 1995), p. 3A; Desda Moss and Gary Fields, "Mobilizing One Million," *USA Today* (October 13–15, 1995), p. 2A.) Among those who declined to support the event were the NAACP, the Black Urban League,

and the country's two largest black religious groups—"the 8.2 million-member National Baptist Convention and the two million-member Progressive National Baptist Convention." (Moss and Fields, "Mobilizing One Million," p. 2A. See also Desda Moss and Gary Fields, "Jackson Finds He's in Tight Spot," *USA Today* (October 16, 1995), p. 3A.)

84. Louis Farrakhan, as cited in Larisha Butler, "Thousands Reported Heeding Farrakhan's Call," *The Tennessean* (October 13, 1995), p. 9A.
85. Colin Powell who, while deciding not to show up at the march for apparent political reasons, said that the "march is not about racism, or the O. J. Simpson trial or Rodney King, but about a spiritual revolution." As cited in Karen S. Peterson, "A Million Men, a Single Message," *USA Today* (October 13, 1995), p. 5D.
86. Howard Fineman and Vern E. Smith, "An Angry 'Charmer,'" *Newsweek* (October 30, 1995), p. 38.
87. Louis Farrakhan, as cited in Abraham Cooper and Harold Brackman, "Given Track Record, Why Back Farrakhan?" *USA Today* (October 13, 1995), p. 13A.
88. Desda Moss and Gary Fields, "Men Ready for Rally Today," *USA Today* (October 16, 1995), p. 1A.
89. "Farrakhan's Critics Look at Million Man March," *Family Issues Alert* (October 25, 1995), p. 2.
90. Cooper and Brackman, p. 13A. Another poll showed smaller but still substantial numbers, indicating that 41 percent of blacks viewed Farrakhan favorably and an equal percentage had an unfavorable view of him. (Fineman and Smith, p. 33.)
91. Farrakhan, as cited in "'My Duty Is to Point Out the Wrong and the Evil,'" *Newsweek* (October 30, 1995), p. 36.
92. Farrakhan, as cited in Susan Page, "Clinton Urges Both Races to 'Clean House,'" *USA Today* (October 17, 1995), p. 1A.
93. Farrakhan, as cited in Hoversten, "Attendance in Dispute," p. 3A.
94. Farrakhan, as cited in Judy Keen, "March Affirms Farrakhan's Clout," *USA Today* (October 17, 1995), p. 3A.
95. His thoughts about Chavis were just as condemning: "I would never walk two seconds behind Chavis, a notorious womanizer whose pursuit of women other than his wife almost wrecked the NAACP. I would never pay a march fee to hear Chavis tell me how to be a responsible black husband and father, no matter how great the pressures for 'black solidarity.'" Carl Rowan, "Farrakhan and Chavis Can Only Hurt Black Men," *The Tennessean* (October 13, 1995), p. 13A.

Chapter 12: History in the Remaking

1. Lynne V. Cheney, *Telling the Truth: Why Our Culture and Our Country Have Stopped Making Sense—and What We Can Do About It* (New York: Simon and Schuster, 1995), p. 23.
2. John Leo, "True Lies vs. Total Recall," *U.S. News and World Report* (August 7, 1995), p. 16.

3. Pete Winn, "What's New in School? Lesbians and Wizards," *Citizen* (June 18, 1990), p. 10.
4. Thomas Sowell, *Inside American Education: The Decline, the Deception, the Dogmas* (New York: The Free Press, 1993), p. 176.
5. Dinesh D'Souza, "The Visigoths in Tweed," in *Beyond PC: Toward a Politics of Understanding*, Patricia Aufderheide, ed. (Saint Paul, Minn.: Graywolf Press, 1992), p. 15.
6. D'Souza, p. 15.
7. D'Souza, p. 16.
8. Roger Kimball, *Tenured Radicals: How Politics Has Corrupted Our Higher Education* (New York: Harper and Row, 1991), p. xiii.
9. Gregory Wolfe, "The Humanities in Crisis: A Symposium," *The Intercollegiate Review* 23 (Fall 1987): 3.
10. Scott Turow, "Where Have All the Radicals Gone?" *Newsweek* (September 2, 1996), p. 47.
11. Two helpful collections of Marx's writings are *The Portable Karl Marx*, Eugene Kamenka, ed. (New York: Viking Penguin, 1983), and *Marx and Engels: Basic Writings on Politics and Philosophy*, Lewis S. Feuer, ed. (New York: Anchor Books, 1989). For a sympathetic explanation of Marxism, see John Somerville, *The Philosophy of Marxism* (New York: Random House, 1967). Some insightful critiques of Marxism are provided by Thomas Sowell, *Marxism: Philosophy and Economics* (New York: William Morrow and Co., 1985); Alexander Solzhenitsyn, Mikhail Agursky, A. B., Evgeny Barabanov, Vadim Borisov, F. Korsakov, and Igor Shafarevich, *From Under the Rubble*, A. M. Brock et al., trans. (Washington, D.C.: Regnery Gateway, 1981); *The God That Failed*, Richard H. Crossman, ed. (Washington, D.C.: Regnery Gateway, 1949); Norman L. Geisler, *Is Man the Measure? An Evaluation of Contemporary Humanism* (Grand Rapids, Mich.: Baker Book House, 1983), chap. 5; Nikolaus Lobkowicz, "Marxism As the Ideology of Our Age," *Truth* 1 (1985): 37–44.
12. For a sampling of the varieties of relativism by advocates and critics alike, see: *Relativism: Interpretation and Confrontation*, Michael Krausz, ed. (Notre Dame, In.: University of Notre Dame Press, 1989); *Rationality and Relativism*, Martin Hollis and Steven Lukes, eds. (Cambridge, Mass.: MIT Press, 1982); James F. Harris, *Against Relativism: A Philosophical Defense of Method* (LaSalle, Ill.: Open Court, 1992); Erwin W. Lutzer, *The Necessity of Ethical Absolutes* (Grand Rapids, Mich.: Zondervan, 1981); Norman L. Geisler, *Christian Ethics: Alternatives and Issues* (Grand Rapids, Mich.: Baker Book House, 1989), chaps. 2–4; Millard J. Erickson, *Relativism in Contemporary Christian Ethics* (Grand Rapids, Mich.: Baker Book House, 1974).
13. James Rachels, "Morality and Moral Philosophy," in *The Right Thing to Do: Basic Readings in Moral Philosophy*, James Rachels, ed. (New York: Random House, 1989), p. 5. I added the numbers that precede each statement.
14. Plato, *Theaetetus*, 167; A. H. Armstrong, *An Introduction to Ancient Philosophy* (Westminster, Md.: Newman Press, 1957), pp. 9–11, 22–24; Frederick Copleston, *A History of Philosophy: Volume 1, Greece and Rome* (New York: Doubleday,

1993), chaps. 5, 12, 13; Joseph Owens, *A History of Ancient Western Philosophy* (Englewood Cliffs, N.J.: Prentice-Hall, 1959), pp. 41–55, 155–165; John Mansley Robinson, *An Introduction to Early Greek Philosophy* (Boston: Houghton Mifflin, 1968), chaps. 5, 12.

15. William Graham Sumner, "Cultural Relativism," in *The Right Thing to Do*, pp. 52–53.
16. Sumner, p. 53.
17. Richard Hofstadter, *Social Darwinism in American Thought* (Boston, Mass.: Beacon Press, 1983), p. 193.
18. Henry H. Bagish, "Confessions of a Former Cultural Relativist," in *Anthropology 83/84*, Elvio Angeloni, ed. (Guilford, Conn.: Dushkin, 1983), p. 23.
19. Clifford Geertz, *The Interpretation of Cultures* (New York: Basic Books, 1973), p. 24.
20. For some helpful introductions to deconstructionism, see Danny J. Anderson, "Deconstruction: Critical Strategy/Strategic Criticism," in *Contemporary Literary Theory*, G. Douglas Atkins and Laura Morrow, eds. (Amherst, Mass.: University of Massachusetts Press, 1989), pp. 137–157; Walter Truett Anderson, *Reality Isn't What It Used to Be: Theatrical Politics, Ready-to-Wear Religion, Global Myths, Primitive Chic, and Other Wonders of the Postmodern World* (San Francisco, Calif.: HarperSanFrancisco, 1990), chap. 4; Jim Leffel, "Postmodern Impact: Literature," in *The Death of Truth: What's Wrong with Multiculturalism, the Rejection of Reason, and the New Postmodern Diversity*, Dennis McCallum, ed. (Minneapolis, Minn.: Bethany House, 1996), chap. 6; Gene Edward Veith, Jr., *Postmodern Times: A Christian Guide to Contemporary Thought and Culture* (Wheaton, Ill.: Crossway, 1994), chap. 3; J. Richard Middleton and Brian J. Walsh, "Facing the Postmodern Scalpel: Can the Christian Faith Withstand Deconstruction?" in *Christian Apologetics in the Postmodern World*, Timothy R. Phillips and Dennis L. Okholm, eds. (Downers Grove, Ill.: InterVarsity Press, 1995), chap. 7.
21. Kimball, p. 102. Derrida's writings tend to be obtuse, filled with paradoxes, technical jargon, and lengthy, meandering digressions. Even for professional philosophers, Derrida's work is often difficult to grasp. With this in mind, I suggest this source as a useful starting point for tackling his thought: "Jacques Derrida," in *Philosophy: End or Transformation?*, Kenneth Baynes, James Bohman, and Thomas McCarthy, eds. (Cambridge, Mass.: MIT Press, 1987), chap. 4.
22. Kimball, p. 102. During World War II de Man wrote dozens of anti-Semitic newspaper articles supporting the Nazi cause. (See Kimball, chapter 4.)
23. Several critical responses to deconstruction can be found in the following essays which occur in *European Philosophy and the American Academy*, Barry Smith, ed. (LaSalle, Ill.: Hegeler Institute, 1994): Dallas Willard, "The Unhinging of the American Mind: Derrida as Pretext," pp. 3–20; David Detmer, "Obstacles to Fruitful Discussion in the American Academy: The Case of Deconstruction," pp. 55–65; Ward Parks, "Textual Imperialism," pp. 67–79; J. Claude Evans, "The Rigors of Deconstruction," pp. 81–98. Two essays in this book which are more sympathetic to deconstruction are: Christopher Norris, "The 'Apocalyptic

Tone' in Philosophy: Kierkegaard, Derrida and the Rhetoric of Transcendence," pp. 145–193; Joseph Margolis, "Deferring to Derrida's Difference," pp. 195–226.

24. Cited in Ronald H. Nash, *The Closing of the American Heart: What's Really Wrong with America's Schools* (Dallas, Tex.: Probe Books, 1990), p. 70.
25. Kavita Varma, "New, Not-So Politically Correct, Goals for History," *USA Today* (April 3, 1996), p. 4D.
26. In 1992, Lynne Cheney (chairwoman of the National Endowment for the Humanities) and Lamar Alexander (the U.S. Secretary of Education) began portioning out a $2.2 million grant to UCLA to develop the project. The standards were largely written by a revisionist historian named Gary Nash. In the 1970s, he was the organizer of the Angela Davis Defense Committee. Angela Davis is a longtime communist, black political activist, and academian. In 1970, she was dismissed as a professor of philosophy from UCLA's faculty for her radical views. She was also accused, and eventually acquitted, of conspiracy and murder charges. In 1980 and 1984, she ran as the vice-presidential candidate on the Communist party ticket. (Ted Yanak and Pam Cornelison, *The Great American History Fact-Finder* [Boston, Mass.: Houghton Mifflin, 1993], p. 104.)
27. Lynne V. Cheney, *Telling the Truth: Why Our Culture and Our Country Have Stopped Making Sense—and What We Can Do About It* (New York: Simon and Schuster, 1995), pp. 26–27; Patrick Buchanan, "This Politically Correct Garbage Needs Trashing," *The Tennessean* (November 6, 1994), p. 5D; John Elson, "History, the Sequel," *Time* (November 7, 1994), p. 64.
28. Tip O'Neill, as cited in Buchanan, p. 5D.
29. Cheney, p. 27.
30. Cheney, p. 26.
31. Other historians, however, provide the fuller picture, which involved religious rituals where the Indian gods were fed with human blood. "One of the principal aims of war was to capture enemies alive who might be sacrificed later either on the altar or in a ritual ball game. Their hearts were cut out and offered to the gods of war and fertility. . . . The sheer quantity of blood needed was striking as well: tens of thousands were sacrificed, so far as we can tell, at great festivals and at the consecration of major temples from Mexico to Peru. . . . The Spaniards saw human beings dismembered, decapitated, and sacrificed amid sacred serpents. The priests performing the sacrifices were forbidden to cut their hair or nails, or wash the gore from their bodies." Robert Royal, *1492 and All That: Political Manipulations of History* (Washington, D.C.: Ethics and Public Policy Center, 1992), pp. 97–98.
32. Cheney, p. 28.
33. John Leo, "The Hijacking of American History," *U.S. News and World Report* (November 14, 1994), p. 36.
34. John Leo, "History Standards Are Bunk," *U.S. News and World Report* (February 6, 1995), p. 23. See also chapter 11 of this book, *The New Absolutes.*
35. Sumner, pp. 53–54; Dinesh D'Souza, *The End of Racism: Principles for a Multiracial Society* (New York: The Free Press, 1995), pp. 32–36.

36. Phyllis Schlafly, "Controversial History Standards Fight Back," *Conservative Chronicle* (March 29, 1995), p. 24.
37. Leo, "History Standards Are Bunk," p. 23.
38. Kavita Varma, "Revised History Standards Blunt 'Bias' Criticism," *USA Today* (April 3, 1996), p. 4D.
39. "School's Out to Lunch," *National Review* (May 6, 1996), p. 19.
40. See Kimberlee Whaley and Elizabeth Ble Swadener, "Multicultural Education in Infant and Toddler Settings," *Childhood Education* (Summer 1990): 238–242. They quote the following statement approvingly and seek to show how its call can be materialized: "Multicultural and nonsexist experiences, materials, and equipment should be provided for children of all ages" (p. 238).
41. Benjamin Hopkins, as cited in Dinesh D'Souza, *Illiberal Education: The Politics of Race and Sex on Campus* (New York: Vintage Books, 1992), p. 7.
42. Reed Way Dasenbrock makes this very point in his article "The Multicultural West," in *Beyond PC*, pp. 210–211.
43. Page Smith, *Rediscovering Christianity: A History of Modern Democracy and the Christian Ethic* (New York: St. Martin's Press, 1994), pp. 27–31. See also two essays by David Herlihy: "The Making of the Medieval Family: Symmetry, Structure, and Sentiment," *Journal of Family History* (Summer 1983): 116–130; and "The Family and Religious Ideologies in Medieval Europe," *Journal of Family History* 12:1–3 (1987): 3–17.

Chapter 13: The Politically Correct Life

1. The list is culled from an article by Dale Russakoff called "Driving a Point Home: The First Rule of Selling a House: Locution, Locution, Locution," *Washington Post National Weekly Edition* (June 6–12, 1994), p. 10.
2. Russakoff, p. 10.
3. Russakoff, p. 10.
4. Russakoff, p. 10.
5. Rosa Ehrenreich, "What Campus Radicals?" in *Beyond PC: Toward a Politics of Understanding*, Patricia Aufderheide, ed. (St. Paul, Minn.: Graywolf Press, 1992), p. 140.
6. Chester E. Finn, Jr., "The Campus: 'An Island of Repression in a Sea of Freedom,'" in *Are You Politically Correct? Debating America's Cultural Standards*, Francis J. Beckwith and Michael E. Bauman, eds. (Buffalo, N.Y.: Prometheus Books, 1993), pp. 57–58.
7. Some supporting and informative sources are: Walter Goodman, "Correctness vs. Content in Language," *New York Times* (January 5, 1994), p. B3; Anthony Lewis, "University Acts to Limit Free Speech," *The Tennessean* (November 29, 1995); Beckwith and Bauman, eds., *Are You Politically Correct?*; Aufderheide, ed., *Beyond PC*; Thomas Sowell, *Inside American Education: The Decline, the Deception, the Dogmas* (New York: The Free Press, 1993); Christian Hoff Sommers, *Who Stole Feminism? How Women Have Betrayed Women* (New York: Simon and Schuster, 1994); David O. Sacks and Peter A. Thiel, *The Diversity Myth: "Multicultur-*

alism" and the Politics of Intolerance at Stanford (Oakland, Calif.: The Independent Institute, 1995).

8. Hunter Havelin Adams III, "African and African-American Contributions to Science and Technology," as cited in Lynne V. Cheney, *Telling the Truth: Why Our Culture and Our Country Have Stopped Making Sense—and What We Can Do About It* (New York: Simon and Schuster, 1995), pp. 46–47. See also Arthur M. Schlesinger, Jr., *The Disuniting of America: Reflections on a Multicultural Society* (New York: W. W. Norton and Co., 1992), pp. 65, 69; Robert K. Landers, "Conflict Over Multicultural Education," *Editorial Research Reports* (November 30, 1990), pp. 683, 692.
9. Schlesinger, pp. 69–70, 78–79; Cheney, pp. 48–49; Mary Lefkowitz, "Not Out of Africa," *Chronicles* (September 1995), p. 17.
10. Schlesinger, p. 70.
11. Leonard Jeffries, as cited in Schlesinger, p. 71.
12. Zora Neale Hurston, *Dust Tracks on a Road,* as cited in Thomas Fleming, "Caliban in the Classroom," *Chronicles* (September 1995), pp. 10–11. She traced this story of black heritage back as far as 1829.
13. Some clearheaded and fair-minded refutations of Afrocentrism are provided by Schlesinger, chaps. 2–3; Lefkowitz's article, pp. 17–19, and her book *Not Out of Africa: How Afrocentrism Became an Excuse to Teach Myth As History* (New York: Basic Books, 1996); Dinesh D'Souza, *The End of Racism: Principles for a Multiracial Society* (New York: The Free Press, 1995), chap. 9.
14. Schlesinger, pp. 67–68; D'Souza, *Illiberal Education: The Politics of Race and Sex on Campus* (New York: Vintage Books, 1992), p. 7; John Taylor, "Are You Politically Correct?" in *Are You Politically Correct?,* p. 28.
15. The student's remarks are as reported and summarized by Taylor, pp. 28–29. In addition, Jeffries was reported to have attacked black males for succumbing to the "white pussy syndrome," that is, pursuing white women.
16. Schlesinger, p. 70.
17. Na'im Akbar, as cited in Schlesinger, p. 64. See also Nicholas Stix, "Black English," *Chronicles* (September 1995), pp. 25–27.
18. Taylor, p. 29.
19. Schlesinger, p. 94.
20. Editorial, "Cowardice, Racism Fuel Rash of Church Burnings," *USA Today* (June 11, 1996), p. 10A.
21. Charley Reese, "Arson Doesn't Justify Demagoguery," *Conservative Chronicle* (July 10, 1996); Roger G. Owens, "Racism's Imprint on Church Burnings," *USA Today* (July 1, 1996), p. 12A; Tom Morganthau with Ginny Carroll, Daniel Klaidman, Mark Miller, and Martha Brant, "Fires in the Night," *Newsweek* (June 24, 1996), pp. 29–32; "Black Church Burnings: Why They Did It," *USA Today* (July 1, 1996), p. 2A.
22. A thirteen-year-old white girl burned down one black church in North Carolina. Local authorities said she acted alone. They also described her as a troubled youth who was motivated by an anti-Christian bias, not racial bigotry. "Church Fires May Be More Faith-Based Than Race-Based," *Family Issues Alert*

(June 19, 1996), p. 1; Steve Marshall, "Group: Black Churches Are 'Endangered,'" *USA Today* (June 17, 1996), p. 1A; Gary Fields and Bob Twigg, "More Church Fires Set; Girl Is Arrested," *USA Today* (June 11, 1996), p. 1A.

23. In Texas, the suspect in two black-church burnings is an eighteen-year-old, mentally handicapped black man. At first he confessed to the fires, then later recanted. As of this writing, he is still being held by authorities for the crimes. Officials are saying that the fires were "acts of *local* vandalism." Earlier in their investigations, police arrested two whites and a Hispanic in connection with one of the church fires, but they were later released. Mark Miller and Marc Peyser, "'We Live in Daily Fear,'" *Newsweek* (September 2, 1996), p. 52; "Church Fires May Be More Faith-Based Than Race-Based," p. 2.

24. One church-burning arsonist was a white volunteer fire fighter who was charged with four arsons in 1994, one of which was a black church. He was trying "to divert suspicion from fire fighters charged with setting grass fires." His motive was not race. (Paul Leavitt, "Church Arson," *USA Today* [July 10, 1996], p. 3A.) Yet another arsonist was a black volunteer fire fighter. He set fire to the church of which he was a member. The church was predominantly black. (Paul Leavitt, "Church Arson," *USA Today* [July 11, 1996], p. 3A.) I could not find a report of his motive, but it certainly was not race.

    My brother is a part-time fire fighter and a reserve deputy sheriff with the arson-bomb detail in Southern California. California gets a number of brush fires every year, and its share of structure fires, too. I recently asked my brother to characterize the typical arsonist. His answer surprised me.

    "We often discover that the fires," he said, "were set by fire fighters."

    "Why would they do that?" I asked.

    "Well, in California many fire fighters only get paid for the time they spend actually fighting fires. When their money runs low, some of them will set fires intentionally. Many times the arsonist is the first person on the scene.

    "We have also discovered," he continued, "that sometimes arsonists will set a fire in one place to divert attention away from another fire they set. Multiple fires are sometimes the result of arsonists becoming worried that investigators are getting close to catching them."

    The conversation occurred in late July 1996.

25. Morganthau et al., p. 32.
26. Reese, p. 22; Hamblin, p. 23; Debbie Howlett, "Young, Poor, Uneducated Describe Most Arsonists," *USA Today* (July 1, 1996), p. 2A; "Church Fires May Be More Faith-Based Than Race-Based," p. 1.
27. Gary Fields and Tom Watson, "In Three Years, Twenty-three Churches Burned," *USA Today* (February 16, 1996), p. 3A; Howlett, p. 2A.
28. Howlett, p. 2A.
29. Morganthau et al, p. 31.
30. Reese, p. 22; Ken Hamblin, "Honest, Bill, It's Not So Bad Being Black," *Conservative Chronicle* (July 10, 1996), p. 23.
31. Morganthau et al., p. 30.
32. Gary Fields, "Church Has Been Heart of Black Life," *USA Today* (March 18, 1996), p. 3A.

33. "Church Fires May Be More Faith-Based Than Race-Based," p. 1.
34. Marshall, p. 1A.
35. The media took many opportunities to forge a link between the church burnings of the '90s with the race-motivated terrors of the '60s. They often did this by showing pictures of black churches burning in the South (especially in Mississippi) and setting them near pictures or headlines that harked back to the tumultuous years of the Civil Rights movement. Sometimes they reprinted photos of parents grieving over loved ones who had been killed in church bombings during the '50s and '60s. *USA Today* did this, showing black mourners in deep travail leaving a funeral service for "four girls killed in the bombing of a church in Birmingham, Alabama" in 1963. The subheading in the article on the left of the photo read "Throwback to the 1960s." The article to the right of the photo began, "Few people born before 1960 can hear of the latest wave of church burnings and not be taken back thirty-two years to a church in Birmingham, Alabama." (Fields, "Church Has Been Heart of Black Life," p. 2A.) The connection being made could not have been clearer than that unless the material had been set in neon lights. *Newsweek* accomplished the same end when it reprinted a photo showing some of the violence of the Civil Rights era and then placed an article title above it that made the connection to the acts of arson today. The title read, "The Fire the Last Time: The Civil Rights Movement Was Born Amid Blazes." (Melissa Fay Greene, "The Fire the Last Time: The Civil Rights Movement Was Born Amid Blazes," *Newsweek* (June 24, 1996), p. 34.)
36. Susan Page, "Clinton to Urge Healing in Visit to Site of Arson," *USA Today* (June 11, 1996), p. 3A.
37. Lori Sharn, "Churches Get Aid in Time of Need," *USA Today* (June 17, 1996), p. 3A; Gary Fields and Tom Watson, "'Decent Folks' Don't Accept Arsons, Hatred," *USA Today* (March 18, 1996), p. 2A.
38. Daniel Donaldson, as cited in Gary Fields, "Donors Boost Black Church Recovery Funds," *USA Today* (April 1, 1996), p. 3A.
39. Lois Anderson, as cited in Fields and Watson, "'Decent Folks' Don't Accept Arsons, Hatred," p. 2A.
40. Jesse Jackson, as cited in Samuel Francis, "Using Church Fires . . . ," *Conservative Chronicle* (June 26, 1996), p. 3.
41. Ronald Bayer, *Homosexuality and American Psychiatry: The Politics of Diagnosis*, as cited in William Dannemeyer, *Shadow in the Land: Homosexuality in America* (San Francisco, Calif.: Ignatius Press, 1989), pp. 25–26.
42. Stuart Reges, as cited in David O. Sacks and Peter A. Thiel, *The Diversity Myth: "Multiculturalism" and the Politics of Intolerance at Stanford* (Oakland, Calif.: The Independent Institute, 1995), pp. 147–148.
43. Sacks and Thiel, pp. 149–150.
44. Sacks and Thiel, pp. 100–101.
45. Sacks and Thiel, p. 101. For more on homosexuality in educational institutions nationwide, see Jerry Z. Muller, "Coming Out Ahead: The Homosexual Moment in the Academy," *First Things* (August/September 1993): 17–24.

46. Dennis Altman, *The Homosexualization of America* (Boston, Mass.: Beacon Press, 1982), pp. 6–9.
47. Jane Rule, *Lesbian Images* (New York, N.Y.: Doubleday, 1975), p. 5.
48. Bruce Voeller, "Stonewall Anniversary," *The Advocate* (July 12, 1979), as cited in Altman, p. 176. Voeller is recognized as a "conservative" homosexual.
49. For example, see Debbie Howlett, "Crusade Now Quieter, More Focused," *USA Today* February 14, 1994), p. 10A; also her article "Stonewall: Kicking the Closet Open," *USA Today* (June 24, 1994), p. 4A; Richard Bernstein, "When One Person's Civil Rights Are Another's Moral Outrage," *New York Times* (October 16, 1994), p. 6E; Joan Biskupic, "Taking Gay Rights Law to the Top," *Washington Post* (December 27, 1993–January 2, 1994), p. 33; Steven A. Holmes, "Gay Rights Groups Plot a Strategy in Ballot Fights," *New York Times* (January 12, 1994), p. A9; J. David Woodard, "Same-Sex Politics," *World* (October 30, 1993), p. 16; Evangelical Press, "Texas County Reverses Decision, Will Accept Firm's Gay Benefit Policy," *Dallas/Fort Worth Heritage* (January 1994), p. 6. Taking a lead in influencing public opinion to accept the homosexual agenda is an increasing number of vocal homosexual journalists. See William Glaberson, "Gay Journalists Leading a Revolution," *New York Times* (September 10, 1993), p. A13.
50. *Romer v. Evans,* No. 94–1039, 1996 WL 262293, at * 1, 3 (U.S. May 20, 1996).
51. *Romer v. Evans,* at * 6, 8.
52. *Romer v. Evans,* Scalia, dissenting opinion, at * 16. For other critical voices, see these editorials in the June 5, 1996 issue of the *Conservative Chronicle:* George Will, "To What Has Constitutional Law Come?," p. 5; Paul Craig Roberts, "Why We Should Tar and Feather the Supreme Court," p. 6; Mona Charen, "Vote for the Supreme Court of Your Choice," p. 4; Samuel Francis, "Court's Decision Twists Meaning of 'Rights,' " p. 9.

Chapter 14: When Worlds Collide

1. Randy Frame, "Baptist Church Becomes Target in the Culture Wars," *Christianity Today* (November 8, 1993), p. 57. See also Peter LaBarbera, "At the Gate: Homosexual Activists in San Francisco Besiege Church," *World* (October 9, 1993), pp. 14–15.
2. "Whee! the People," *Citizen* (July 22, 1996), p. 8.
3. Michele Patenaude, "On Not Having Children," in *Childless by Choice: A Feminist Anthology,* Irene Reti, ed. (Santa Cruz, Calif.: HerBooks, 1992), pp. 33–34.
4. Jyl Lynn Felman, "Mediation for My Sisters: On Choosing Not to Have Children," in *Childless by Choice,* pp. 80–81.
5. Mona Charen, "Welcome Honesty From a Pro-Choice Feminist" (Creator's Syndicate, 1995), retrieved off of the Internet.
6. Alex Witchel, "The Real Jane Roe, Unlikely Role Model," *New York Times* (July 28, 1994), p. B4.
7. Norma McCorvey, as cited in Jeannine Lee and Masud Khan, " 'Roe' Litigant's About-Face: 'I'm Pro-Life,' " *USA Today* (August 11, 1995), p. 3A.
8. McCorvey, as cited in Associated Press, "Roe vs. Wade Plaintiff Joins Anti-

Abortion Group," *The Tennessean* (August 11, 1995), p. 1A.

9. McCorvey, as cited in Cal Thomas, "There Is a Simple Explanation: She Had a Conversion," *The Tennessean* (August 16, 1995), p. 9A. See also Norma McCorvey with Andy Meisler, *I Am Roe: My Life, Roe v. Wade and Freedom of Choice* (New York: HarperCollins, 1994), pp. 2–4.
10. McCorvey, as cited in Michelle Mittelstadt, "Jane Roe Defection Another Thorn in Pro-Choice's Side," *The Tennessean* (August 13, 1995), p. 3D.
11. Sarah Weddington, as cited in Thomas, p. 9A.
12. See McCorvey with Meisler, chaps. 8, 11–14.
13. Thomas, p. 9A.
14. Richard Louv, *Childhood's Future* (New York: Anchor Books, 1990), pp. 46–47.
15. John Leo, "Yale Is Latest Casualty of Multicultural Mush," *Conservative Chronicle* (April 5, 1995), p. 13.
16. Leo, p. 13. See also William F. Buckley, Jr., "Faculty's Pride Costs Yale $20 Million," *Conservative Chronicle* (April 5, 1995), p. 23.
17. Deal W. Hudson, "Mortimer J. Adler and Multiculturalism," *Crisis* (January 1995), p. 4.
18. Patrick F. Fagan, "Why Religion Matters: The Impact of Religious Practice on Social Stability," The Cultural Policy Studies Project, The Heritage Foundation, Washington, D.C. (January 25, 1996), pp. 2–4.
19. Barry Lynn, "Defining American Culture: A Panel Discussion," *Liberty, Life and Family: A Journal of Interdisciplinary Concerns* 2:1 (1995): 150, 151.
20. Lynn, p. 186.

Chapter 15: A Plea for Intolerance

1. Richard M. Weaver, *Ideas Have Consequences* (Chicago: University of Chicago Press, 1948), p. 1.
2. Carle C. Zimmerman, *Family and Civilization* (New York: Harper & Brothers, 1947), pp. 760, 776–777.
3. See also Dick Keyes, "Lite Champions: Has Heroism Become a Trivial Pursuit?" *Christianity Today* (May 13, 1988), pp. 29–32.
4. See also *The Nine Lives of Population Control*, Michael Cromartie, ed. (Grand Rapids, Mich.: Wm. B. Eerdmans, 1995); E. Michael Jones, "Beijing's Revenge: How Population Control Creates Illegal Immigration," *Culture Wars* (September 1995), pp. 20–35; E. Michael Jones, "Bela Does Cairo: The Great Satan Swings and Misses at the Cairo Conference on Population and Development," *Liberty, Life, and Family* 2:1 (1995): 1–37; Jacqueline R. Kasun, "Cairo: A Second Opinion," *Culture Wars* (May 1995), pp. 23–41; George Weigel, "What Really Happened at Cairo," *First Things* (February 1995), pp. 24–31.
5. William J. Bennett, *The Index of Leading Cultural Indicators: Facts and Figures on the State of American Society* (New York: Simon and Schuster, 1994), p. 9.
6. Zimmerman, p. 778.
7. Zimmerman, p. 777, italics added to the last sentence.
8. Zimmerman, p. 782.
9. Zimmerman, pp. 777–783.

10. Zimmerman, p. 781.
11. Jonathan Chaves, "When West Meets East," *Chronicles* (September 1995), p. 16.
12. Mother Teresa, comments made before the National Prayer Breakfast gathering in Washington, D.C., on February 2, 1994.
13. For discussions of relativism, pro and con, see: *Relativism: Interpretation and Confrontation*, Michael Krausz, ed. (Notre Dame, Ind.: University of Notre Dame Press, 1989); *Rationality and Relativism*, Martin Hollis and Steven Lukes, eds. (Cambridge, Mass.: MIT Press, 1982); Frederick F. Schmitt, *Truth: A Primer* (Boulder, Colo.: Westview Press, 1995); James F. Harris, *Against Relativism: A Philosophical Defense of Method* (LaSalle, Ill.: Open Court, 1992); Erwin Lutzer, *The Necessity of Ethical Absolutes* (Grand Rapids, Mich.: Zondervan, 1981); Millard J. Erickson, *Relativism in Contemporary Christian Ethics* (Grand Rapids, Mich.: Baker Book House, 1974); Norman L. Geisler, *Christian Ethics: Options and Issues* (Grand Rapids, Mich.: Baker Book House, 1989), chaps. 2–4; Francis J. Beckwith, "Philosophical Problems With Moral Relativism," *Christian Research Journal* (Fall 1993), pp. 21–23, 39; James Rachels, "A Critique of Ethical Relativism," in *Philosophy: The Quest for Truth*, Louis P. Pojman, ed. (Belmont, Calif.: Wadsworth, 1989), pp. 317–25; *Relativism and the Study of Man*, Helmut Schoeck and James W. Higgins, eds. (Princeton, N.J.: D. Van Nostrand, 1961); *Cultural Relativism and Philosophy: North and Latin American Perspectives*, Marcelo Dascal, ed. (Leiden, Netherlands: E. J. Brill, 1991); Henry H. Bagish, "Confessions of a Former Cultural Relativist," in *Anthropology 83/84*, Elvio Angeloni, ed. (Guilford, Conn.: Dushkin, 1983), pp. 22–29.
14. Relativists have tried to overcome these criticisms by arguing that the claims "All morals are relative" and "All truth is relative" are exempt from their own criteria. They are, in other words, meta-statements. This means they are not statements made *within* a viewpoint (which would be first-order statements) but rather statements made *about* a viewpoint (which would be second-order statements). These respondents contend that language *within* a given perspective is relative to that perspective and so subject to its criteria, whereas language *about* a given perspective is nonrelative to that perspective and so is not subject to its criteria but serves to articulate by what criteria the given perspective is subject. So a relativist can rightly argue that the claim "All truth is relative" is a second-order statement and therefore exempt from its own criteria of judgment, thus not subject to the charge of self-refutation.

    One critical problem with this relativistic rejoinder is that it simply does not rescue either epistemological or moral relativism. On the epistemological side, even assuming "All truth is relative" is a second-order statement, it means that there is at least one second-order claim that is not relative. If that is the case, then there may be more. To find out, we will have to look at the evidence and reflect on it to discover if there are any other absolute truths. Christians would contend that some of these absolute truths are found in the Judeo-Christian worldview. A relativist could not rule out this claim *a priori*; she would have to consider the evidence for each truth claim before passing judgment. Hence, the possibility that there are other absolute truths must always be permitted, thereby making it impossible for a relativist to substantiate the universality of relativism.

Ethical relativism fares no better. If "All morals are relative" is viewed as a second-order statement, that is, a statement *about* ethics rather than a statement *of* ethics, then an absolutist could respond that this second-order epistemological statement entails the moral claim that one should order her life according to ethical relativism.

15. Romans 2:15, NIV.
16. C. S. Lewis develops these points about the natural moral law in two of his books: *Mere Christianity* (New York: Macmillan, 1952), and *The Abolition of Man* (New York: Macmillan, 1947).
17. John Adams, as cited in William J. Federer, *America's God and Country: Encyclopedia of Quotations* (Coppell, Tex.: Fame, 1994), pp. 10–11.
18. James Madison, as cited in David Barton, *The Myth of Separation* (Aledo, Tex.: WallBuilder Press, 1992), p. 120, italics added.
19. Madison, in Federer, pp. 411–412.

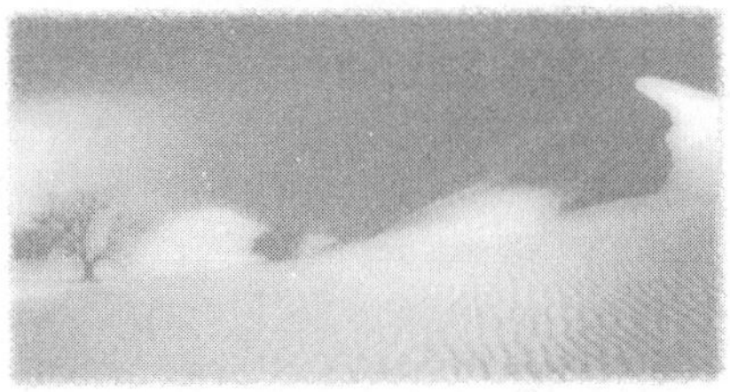

Bibliography

"A Lightning Rod Is Struck." *The Catholic World Report* (January 1995).

"Abortion Coverage Strategy: Use the Vote." *New York Times* (October 8, 1993).

Adams, Charles Francis, ed. *The Works of John Adams, Second President of the United States.* Freeport, N.Y.: Books for Libraries Press, 1969.

"Ads Rankle Planned Parenthood," *Christianity Today* (March 7, 1994).

Alcorn, Randy. *Pro-Life Answers to Pro-Choice Arguments.* Sisters, Ore.: Multnomah, 1992.

Allen, David G. "Critical Social Theory as a Model for Analyzing Ethical Issues in Family and Community Health." *Family and Community Health* 10 (May 1987).

Allen, Ronald B. *The Majesty of Man: The Dignity of Being Human.* Portland, Ore.: Multnomah, 1984.

Alter, Jonathan. "White and Blue." *Newsweek* (October 16, 1995).

Altman, Dennis. *The Homosexualization of America.* Boston, Mass.: Beacon Press, 1982.

American Home Economics Association. *A Force for Families.* Washington, D.C.: AHEA, n.d. [c. 1976].

Amos, Gary T. *Defending the Declaration: How the Bible and Christianity Influenced the Writing of the Declaration of Independence.* Brentwood, Tenn.: Wolgemuth & Hyatt, 1989.

Anderson, Danny J. "Deconstruction: Critical Strategy/Strategic Criticism," in *Contemporary Literary Theory.* G. Douglas Atkins and Laura Morrow, eds. Amherst, Mass.: University of Massachusetts Press, 1989.

Anderson, Walter Truett. *Reality Isn't What It Used to Be: Theatrical Politics, Ready-to-Wear Religion, Global Myths, Primitive Chic, and Other Wonders of the Postmodern World.* San Francisco, Calif.: HarperSanFrancisco, 1990.

Angeloni, Elvio, ed. *Anthropology 83/84* (Guilford, Conn.: Dushkin, 1983).

Appleby, Joyce, ed. *Liberalism and Republicanism in the Historical Imagination.* Cambridge: Harvard University Press, 1992.

Armstrong, A. H. *An Introduction to Ancient Philosophy.* Westminster, Md.: Newman Press, 1957.

Associated Press. "Roe vs. Wade Plaintiff Joins Anti-Abortion Group." *The Tennessean* (August 11, 1995).

Atkins, G. Douglas, and Laura Morrow, eds. *Contemporary Literary Theory.* Amherst, Mass.: University of Massachusetts Press, 1989.

"Attack on Rare Abortion Procedure Invites Misery." *USA Today* (November 3, 1995).

Aufderheide, Patricia, ed. *Beyond PC: Towards a Politics of Understanding.* St. Paul, Minn.: Graywolf Press, 1992.

Bagish, Henry H. "Confessions of a Former Cultural Relativist." *Anthropology 83/84.* Elvio Angeloni, ed. Guilford, Conn.: Dushkin, 1983.

Bailey, Kenneth E. "Paul's Theological Foundation for Human Sexuality." *Theological Review* 3:1 (1980).

Ball, William Bentley, ed. *In Search of a National Morality: A Manifesto for Evangelicals and Catholics.* Grand Rapids, Mich.: Baker Book House; San Francisco, Calif.: Ignatius Press, 1992.

Barker, Kenneth, gen. ed. *The NIV Study Bible.* Grand Rapids, Mich.: Zondervan, 1985.

Barna, George. *The Future of the American Family.* Chicago: Moody Press, 1993.

Barna, George. *Virtual America.* Ventura, Calif.: Regal Books, 1994.

Barndt, Joseph. *Dismantling Racism: The Continuing Challenge to White America.* Minneapolis, Minn.: Augsburg, 1991.

Barton, David. *The Myth of Separation.* Aledo, Tex.: WallBuilder Press, 1992.

Bayles, Fred. "Simpson—Racial Split." Associated Press (October 4, 1995).

Baynes, Kenneth, James Bohman, and Thomas McCarthy, eds. *Philosophy: End or Transformation?* Cambridge, Mass.: MIT Press, 1987.

Beckman, The Reverend John. "Kinsey's Gals." *Fidelity* (October 1993).

Beckwith, Francis J., and Michael E. Bauman, eds. *Are You Politically Correct? Debating America's Cultural Standards.* Buffalo, N.Y.: Prometheus Books, 1993.

Beckwith, Francis J. "Philosophical Problems with Moral Relativism." *Christian Research Journal* (Fall 1993).

Beckwith, Francis J., and Norman L. Geisler. *Matters of Life and Death: Calm Answers to Tough Questions About Abortion and Euthanasia.* Grand Rapids, Mich.: Baker 1991.

Beckwith, Francis J. *Politically Correct Death: Answering Arguments for Abortion Rights.* Grand Rapids, Mich.: Baker Book House, 1993.

Bennett, William J. *The De-Valuing of America: The Fight for Our Culture and Our Children.* New York: Summit Books, 1992.

Bennett, William J. *The Index of Leading Cultural Indicators: Facts and Figures on the State of American Society.* New York: Simon and Schuster, 1994.

Bergh, Albert E., ed. *The Writings of Thomas Jefferson.* Washington, D.C.: Thomas Jefferson Memorial Association, 1905.

Berkouwer, G. C. *Man: The Image of God*, Studies in Dogmatics. Grand Rapids, Mich.: William B. Eerdmans, 1981.

Berlin, Ira. *Slaves Without Masters: The Free Negro in the Antebellum South.* New York: Pantheon, 1974.

Bernstein, Richard. "When One Person's Civil Rights Are Another's Moral Outrage." *New York Times* (October 16, 1994).

Biskupic, Joan. "Taking Gay Rights Law to the Top." *Washington Post* (December 27, 1993–January 2, 1994).

Bizjak, Tony. "Family Images: Focusing in on New Definitions." *Sacramento Bee* (June 28, 1992).

"Black Church Burnings: Why They Did It." *USA Today* (July 1, 1996).

Black, Jim Nelson. *When Nations Die: Ten Warning Signs of a Culture in Crisis.* Wheaton, Ill.: Tyndale House, 1994.

Blocher, Henri. *In the Beginning: The Opening Chapters of Genesis.* Downers Grove, Ill.: InterVarsity, 1984.

Bloom, Allan. *The Closing of the American Mind.* New York: Simon & Schuster, 1987.

Boehm, Frank H. "Never Learn?" *The Tennessean* (January 11, 1994).

Bokenkotter, Thomas. *A Concise History of the Catholic Church*, rev. ed. New York: Image Books, 1990.

Bonavoglia, Angela, ed. *The Choices We Made: Twenty-Five Women and Men Speak Out About Abortion.* New York: Random House, 1991.

Bonomi, Patricia U. *Under the Cope of Heaven: Religion, Society, and Politics in Colonial America.* New York: Oxford University Press, 1986.

Bowler, Peter J. *The Non-Darwinian Revolution: Reinterpreting a Historical Myth.* Baltimore, Md.: Johns Hopkins University Press, 1988.

Brothers, Carter. "No Right Exists for Late-Term Abortion." *The Tennessean* (November 28, 1995).

Brown, Colin, ed. "Image, Idol, Imprint, Example." *The New International Dictionary of New Testament Theology.* Grand Rapids, Mich.: Zondervan, 1976, vol. 2.

Brown, DeNeen L. "The New Age of Innocence?" *Washington Post National Weekly Edition* (November 29–December 5, 1993).

Brown, Harold O. J. "The Decline of Morality." *In Search of a National Morality: A Manifesto for Evangelicals and Catholics.* William Bentley Ball, ed. Grand Rapids, Mich.: Baker Book House; San Francisco, Calif.: Ignatius Press, 1992.

Brown, Rita Mae. "Reflections of a Lavender Menace." *Ms.* (July/August 1995).

Buchanan, Patrick. "This Politically Correct Garbage Needs Trashing." *The Tennessean* (November 6, 1994).

Buckley, Jr., William F. "Faculty's Pride Costs Yale $20 Million." *Conservative Chronicle* (April 5, 1995).

Budiansky, Stephen. "Population Wars." *U.S. News and World Report* (September 12, 1994).

Buehrer, Eric. *The Public Orphanage: How Public Schools Are Making Parents Irrelevant.* Dallas, Tex.: Word, 1995.

Bull, Chris. "The Condom Queen Reigns." *The Advocate* (March 22, 1994).

Burtchaell, James T. *Rachel Weeping: The Case against Abortion.* San Francisco, Calif.: Harper and Row, 1982.

Buss, Dale. "Homosexual Rights Go to School." *Christianity Today* (May 17, 1993).

Butler, Larisha. "Thousands Reported Heeding Farrakhan's Call." *The Tennessean* (October 13, 1995).

Cameron, Nigel M. de S. *The New Medicine: Life and Death after Hippocrates.* Wheaton, Ill.: Crossway, 1991.

Cantor, Norman F. *The Civilization of the Middle Ages*, rev. ed. New York: HarperCollins, 1993.

Carlson, Allan C. "By the Decades: The Troubled Course of the Family, 1945–1990 . . . and Beyond." *The Family in America* 4:5 (1990).

Carlson, Allan C. *From Cottage to Work Station: The Family's Search for Social Harmony in the Industrial Age.* San Francisco, Calif.: Ignatius, 1993.

Carter, Gayle Jo. "Tipper Gore and Teens Talk Tough." *USA Weekend* (March 4–6, 1994).

Carter, Stephen L. *The Culture of Disbelief: How American Law and Politics Trivialize Religious Devotion.* New York: HarperCollins, 1993.

"Case Briefs," a pamphlet published by the Alliance Defense Fund, Scottsdale, Ariz., n.d.

Cass, Connie. "The Black Male Takes His Plight to the Streets of Washington." *The Tennessean* (October 15, 1995).

"Census Counts More Two-Parent Families." *The Tennessean* (October 16, 1995).

"Census Report on Children Paints a Diverse Picture of Family Life." *New York Times* (August 30, 1994).

Chadwick, Owen. *A History of Christianity.* New York: St. Martin's Press, 1995.

Charen, Mona. "Vote for the Supreme Court of Your Choice." *Conservative Chronicle* (June 5, 1996).

Charen, Mona. "Welcome Honesty From a Pro-Choice Feminist." Creators Syndicate, 1995.

Chartock, Roselle K., and Spencer, eds. *Can It Happen Again? Chronicles of the Holocaust.* New York: Black Dog and Leventhal, 1995.

Chaves, Jonathan. "When West Meets East." *Chronicles* (September 1995).

Cheney, Lynne V. *Telling the Truth: Why Our Culture and Our Country Have Stopped Making Sense—and What We Can Do About It.* New York: Simon and Schuster, 1995.

Chesler, Ellen. *Woman of Valor: Margaret Sanger and the Birth Control Movement.* New York: Doubleday, 1992.

Christensen, Bryce J. "The Definition of Family Should Remain Limited." *The Family in America: Opposing Viewpoints.* Viqi Wagner, ed. San Diego, Calif.: Greenhaven Press, 1992.

Christensen, Bryce J. *Utopia Against the Family: The Problems and Politics of the American Family.* San Francisco, Calif.: Ignatius Press, 1990.

Christenson, Cornelia. *Kinsey: A Biography.* Bloomington, Ind.: Indiana University Press, 1971.

"Church Fires May Be More Faith-Based Than Race-Based." *Family Issues Alert* (June 19, 1996).

Clark, Robert E. D. *Darwin: Before and After—An Examination and Assessment.* Grand Rapids, Mich.: Grand Rapids International, 1958.

Colson, Charles, with Ellen Santilli Vaughn. *Kingdoms in Conflict.* New York: William Morrow; Grand Rapids, Mich.: Zondervan, 1987.

Compton, Bill. "Trial Shows Juries Not Totally Objective." *The Tennessean* (October 13, 1995).

"Condom Controversy." *World* (July 1993).

Connery, John R. "The Ancients and the Medievals on Abortion: The Consensus the Court Ignored." *Abortion and the Constitution: Reversing Roe v. Wade Through the Courts.* Dennis J. Horan, Edward R. Grant, and Paige C. Cunningham, eds. Washington, D.C.: Georgetown University Press, 1987.

Cooper, Abraham, and Harold Brackman. "Given Track Record, Why Back Farrakhan?" *USA Today* (October 13, 1995).

Copleston, Frederick. *A History of Philosophy: Volume 1, Greece and Rome.* New York: Doubleday, 1993.

Corcoran, Chris. "A Church-Backed Sex-Ed Program Stirs Furor Among Parents, Clergy." *New York City Tribune* (July 18, 1988).

Cord, Robert L. *Separation of Church and State: Historical Fact and Current Fiction.* New York: Lambeth, 1982.

"Cowardice, Racism Fuel Rash of Church Burnings." *USA Today* (June 11, 1996).

Cranston, Maurice. "What Are Human Rights?" *The Human Rights Reader,* rev. ed., Walter Laqueur and Barry Rubin, eds. New York: New American Library, 1989.

Cromartie, Michael, ed. *The Nine Lives of Population Control.* Grand Rapids, Mich.: William B. Eerdmans, 1995.

Crossman, Richard H., ed. *The God That Failed.* Washington, D.C.: Regnery Gateway, 1949.

D'Elia, Donald J., and Stephen M. Krason, eds. *We Hold These Truths and More: Further Catholic Reflections on the American Proposition.* Steubenville, Ohio: Franciscan University Press, 1993.

D'Souza, Dinesh. "The New Feminist Revolt: This Time It's Against Feminism." *Policy Review* (Winter 1986).

D'Souza, Dinesh. "The Visigoths in Tweed." *Beyond PC: Toward a Politics of Understanding.* Patricia Aufderheide, ed. St. Paul, Minn.: Graywolf Press, 1992.

D'Souza, Dinesh. *The End of Racism: Principles for a Multiracial Society.* New York: The Free Press, 1995. p. 59.

Dannemeyer, William. *Shadow in the Land: Homosexuality in America.* San Francisco, Calif.: Ignatius Press, 1989.

Darwin, Charles. *On the Origin of Species.*

Dascal, Marcelo, ed. *Cultural Relativism and Philosophy: North and Latin American*

Perspectives. Leiden, Netherlands: E. J. Brill, 1991.

Davidheiser, Bolton. *Evolution and Christian Faith.* Grand Rapids, Mich.: Baker Book House, 1969.

Davidson, Nicholas. *The Failure of Feminism.* Buffalo, N.Y.: Prometheus, 1988.

De Gobineau, Arthur. *The Inequality of Human Races.* Adrian Collins, trans. New York: Howard Fertig, 1967.

Debold, Elizabeth, Marie Wilson, and Idelisse Malavé. *Mother/Daughter Revolution: From Betrayal to Power.* Reading, Mass.: Addison-Wesley, 1993.

"Decision . . . Division." *Newsweek* (October 16, 1995).

" 'Defense of Marriage Act' Sprints Toward Promised Presidential Nod." *Family Issues Alert* (May 29, 1996).

Delahoyde, Melinda. *Fighting for Life: Defending the Newborn's Right to Live.* Ann Arbor, Mich.: Servant, 1984.

Dellapenna, Joseph W. "Abortion and the Law: Blackmun's Distortion of the Historical Record." *Abortion and the Constitution: Reversing Roe v. Wade Through the Courts.* Dennis J. Horan, Edward R. Grant, and Paige C. Cunningham, eds. Washington, D.C.: Georgetown University Press, 1987.

Denfeld, Rene. *The New Victorians: A Young Woman's Challenge to the Old Feminist Order.* New York: Warner Books, 1995.

Desmond, Adrian, and James Moore. *Darwin: The Life of a Tormented Evolutionist.* New York: Warner, 1991.

Detmer, David. "Obstacles to Fruitful Discussion in the American Academy: The Case of Deconstruction." *European Philosophy and the American Academy.* Barry Smith, ed. LaSalle, Ill.: Hegeler Institute, 1994.

"Docket List." *Law & Justice* 1:4 (Summer 1992).

"Docket List." *Law & Justice* 1:3 (Winter 1993).

Donohue, William A. *The Politics of the American Civil Liberties Union.* New Brunswick, N.J.: Transaction, 1985.

Douglas, J. D. ed. *New Bible Dictionary.* Downers Grove, Ill.: InterVarsity Press, 1982.

Dreifus, Claudia. "Joycelyn Elders." *The New York Times Magazine* (January 30, 1994).

Dudley, William, ed. *Homosexuality: Opposing Views.* San Diego, Calif.: Greenhaven Press, 1993.

Duncan, Richard F. "Who Wants to Stop the Church: Homosexual Rights Legislation, Public Policy, and Religious Freedom." *Notre Dame Law Review* 69:3 (1994).

Duncan, Richard F., and Gary L Young. "Homosexual Rights and Citizen Initiatives: Is Constitutionalism Unconstitutional?" *Notre Dame Journal of Law, Ethics and Public Policy* 9:1 (1995).

Dunlap, David W. "Gay Survey Raises a New Question." *New York Times* (October 18, 1994).

Durant, Will. *Caesar and Christ: A History of Roman Civilization and of Christianity from Their Beginnings to A.D. 325.* New York: Simon and Schuster, 1972.

Duzak, Warren. "Commission Cites Bible in Gay Vote." *The Tennessean* (November 21, 1995).

Eastland, Terry, ed. *Religious Liberty in the Supreme Court: The Cases That Define the Debate over Church and State.* Grand Rapids, Mich.: William B. Eerdmans, 1993.

Ebert, Michael. "Pedophilia Steps into the Daylight." *Citizen* (November 16, 1992).

Editorial Research Reports on the Changing American Family. Washington, D.C.: Congressional Quarterly, 1979.

Ehrenreich, Barbara. "The Bright Side of Overpopulation." *Time* (September 26, 1994).

Ehrenreich, Rosa. "What Campus Radicals?" *Beyond PC: Toward a Politics of Understanding.* Patricia Aufderheide, ed. St. Paul, Minn.: Graywolf Press, 1992.

Ehrlich Paul R., and Anne H. Ehrlich. *The Population Explosion.* New York: Simon and Schuster, 1990.

Elders, M. Jocelyn. "Adolescent Health Issues: What Is Our Role?" *North Carolina Medical Journal* 52:5 (May 1991).

Elders, M. Joycelyn. "Schools and Health: A Natural Partnership." *Journal of School Health* 63:7 (September 1993).

Elders, M. Joycelyn. "The Future of U.S. Public Health." *Journal of the American Medical Association* 269:17 (May 1993).

"Elders Wants Sex Education for Two-Year-Old Children." *Dallas/Fort Worth Heritage* (January 1994).

Elias, Marilyn. "One in Four Kids Suffers Some Form of Abuse." *USA Today* (October 3, 1994).

Elliot, Gil. *Twentieth-Century Book of the Dead.* New York: Charles Scribner, 1972.

Elson, John. "History, the Sequel." *Time* (November 7, 1994).

Erickson, Millard J. *Relativism in Contemporary Christian Ethics.* Grand Rapids, Mich.: Baker Book House, 1974.

Evans, J. Claude. "The Rigors of Deconstruction." *European Philosophy and the American Academy.* Barry Smith, ed. LaSalle, Ill.: Hegeler Institute, 1994.

Fagan, Patrick F. "Why Religion Matters: The Impact of Religious Practice on Social Stability." The Cultural Policy Studies Project. The Heritage Foundation, Washington, D.C. (January 25, 1996).

"Farrakhan's Critics Look at Million Man March." *Family Issues Alert* (October 25, 1995).

Farrakhan, Louis. " 'My Duty Is to Point Out the Wrong and the Evil.' " *Newsweek* (October 30, 1995).

Federer, William J., ed. *America's God and Country: Encyclopedia of Quotations.* Coppell, Tex.: Fame, 1994.

Felman, Jyl Lynn. "Mediation for My Sisters: On Choosing Not to Have Children." *Childless by Choice: A Feminist Anthology.* Irene Reti, ed. Santa Cruz, Calif.: HerBooks, 1992.

Ferguson, Carrie. "A Union of Fidelity, Honor, Respect." *The Tennessean* (February 21, 1994).

Fesperman, Francis I. "Jefferson's Bible." *Ohio Journal of Religious Studies* 4:2 (October 1976).

Feuer, Lewis S., ed. *Marx and Engels: Basic Writings on Politics and Philosophy.* New York: Anchor Books, 1989.

Fields, Gary, and Bob Twigg. "More Church Fires Set; Girl Is Arrested." *USA Today* (June 11, 1996).

Fields, Gary, and Tom Watson. "In Three Years, Twenty-Three Churches Burned." *USA Today* (February 16, 1996).

Fields, Gary, and Tom Watson. " 'Decent Folks' Don't Accept Arsons, Hatred." *USA Today* (March 18, 1996).

Fields, Gary. "Church Has Been Heart of Black Life." *USA Today* (March 18, 1996).

Fields, Gary. "Donors Boost Black Church Recovery Funds." *USA Today* (April 1, 1996).

Fineman, Howard and Vern E. Smith. "An Angry 'Charmer.' " *Newsweek* (October 30, 1995).

Finn, Jr., Chester E. "The Campus: 'An Island of Repression in a Sea of Freedom.' " *Are You Politically Correct? Debating America's Cultural Standards.* Francis J. Beckwith and Michael E. Bauman, eds. Buffalo, N.Y.: Prometheus Books, 1993.

Fleming, Thomas. "Caliban in the Classroom." *Chronicles* (September 1995).

Foote, Henry Wilder. *Thomas Jefferson: Champion of Religious Freedom, Advocate of Christian Morals.* Boston, Mass.: Beacon, 1947.

Fournier, Keith A. "In Defense of Liberty." *Law & Justice* 2:2 (Spring 1993).

Fournier, Keith A. and William D. Watkins. *In Defense of Life.* Colorado Springs, Colo.: NavPress, 1996.

Fournier, Keith A.. *Religious Cleansing in the American Republic.* Virginia Beach, Va.: Liberty, Life and Family, 1993.

Fournier, Keith A., with William D. Watkins. *A House United? Evangelicals and Catholics Together—A Winning Alliance for the Twenty-First Century.* Colorado Springs, Colo.: NavPress, 1994.

Fournier, Keith. "Not Just Speaking for Catholics." *Washington Times.* May 5, 1996.

Fox, Robin Lane. *Pagans and Christians.* San Francisco: HarperSanFrancisco, 1986.

Fox-Genovese, Elizabeth. "Better or Worse, Mostly Worse." *National Review* (May 6, 1996).

Fox-Genovese, Elizabeth. *Feminism without Illusions: A Critique of Individualism.* Chapel Hill, N.C.: University of North Carolina Press, 1991.

Frame, Randy. "Ad Campaign Filled With Life." *Christianity Today* (April 27, 1992).

Frame, Randy. "Baptist Church Becomes Target in the Culture Wars." *Christianity Today* (November 8, 1993).

Francis, Samuel. "Court's Decision Twists Meaning of 'Rights.' " *Conservative Chronicle* (June 5, 1996).

Francis, Samuel. "Using Church Fires . . . ." *Conservative Chronicle* (June 26, 1996).

Francke, Linda Bird. *The Ambivalence of Abortion.* New York: Random House, 1978.

Franklin, John Hope. *Race and History.* Baton Rouge, La.: Louisiana State University Press, 1989.

French, Marilyn. *The War Against Women.* New York: Ballantine, 1992.

Frerking, Beth. "Americans Clinging to the Family Style of 'Ozzie & Harriet.'" *Patriot* (May 24, 1992).

Gaede, S. D. *When Tolerance Is No Virtue: Political Correctness, Multiculturalism and the Future of Truth and Justice.* Downers Grove, Ill.: InterVarsity Press, 1993.

Gangelhoff, Bonnie. "Gloria Steinem Fights a Women's Revolution Within." *Houston Post* (December 6, 1992).

Gannon, James P. "Christian Speech Only One to Face Discrimination Ax." *The Tennessean* (November 6, 1994).

Garcia, Laura. "Can Marriage Be Saved?" *Catholic Dossier* 1:4 (November-December 1995).

Garrow, David J. *Bearing the Cross: Martin Luther King, Jr., and the Southern Christian Leadership Conference.* New York: William Morrow and Co., 1986.

Garrow, David J. *The FBI and Martin Luther King, Jr.: From "Solo" to Memphis.* New York: W. W. Norton and Co., 1981.

Gaustad, Edwin S. *Faith of Our Fathers: Religion and the New Nation.* San Francisco, Calif.: Harper & Row, 1987.

"Gay Students Have a Safe Haven in Oregon." *USA Today* (July 10, 1996).

Geertz, Clifford. *Local Knowledge: Further Essays in Interpretive Anthropology.* New York: Basic Books, 1983.

Geertz, Clifford. *The Interpretation of Cultures.* New York: Basic Books, 1973.

Geisler, Norman L. "The Hermeneutics of Natural Law." pp. 10–11. Unpublished paper delivered at the Evangelical Theological Society annual meeting in Lisle, Chicago, on November 19, 1994.

Geisler, Norman L., and William D. Watkins. *Worlds Apart: A Handbook on World Views.* Grand Rapids, Mich.: Baker Book House, 1989.

Geisler, Norman L. *Christian Ethics: Options and Issues.* Grand Rapids, Mich.: Baker Book House, 1989.

Geisler, Norman L. *Is Man the Measure? An Evaluation of Contemporary Humanism.* Grand Rapids, Mich.: Baker Book House, 1983.

Gelman, David, with Debra Rosenberg, Vicki Quade, Elizabeth Roberts, and Danzy Senna. "Tune In, Come Out." *Newsweek* (November 8, 1993).

Geraci, Joseph, and Donald Mader. "Interview: John Money." *Paidika* (Spring 1991).

Gillespie, Ed, and Bob Schellhas, eds. *Contract with America.* New York: Times Books, 1994.

Gimlin, Hoyt, ed. *Editorial Research Reports on the Changing American Family.* Washington, D.C.: Congressional Quarterly, 1979.

Glaberson, William. "Gay Journalists Leading a Revolution." *New York Times* (September 10, 1993).

Glasser, Ira. *Visions of Liberty: The Bill of Rights for All Americans.* New York: Arcade, 1991.

Gleick, Elizabeth. "Should This Marriage Be Saved?" *Time* (February 27, 1995).

Glendon, Mary Ann. *A Nation Under Lawyers: How the Crisis in the Legal Profession Is Transforming American Society.* New York: Farrar, Straus and Giroux, 1994.

Goodman, Walter. "Correctness vs. Content in Language." *New York Times* (January 5, 1994).

Grant, Michael. *The World of Rome.* New York: Meridian, 1960.

Greene, Melissa Fay. "The Fire Last Time: The Civil Rights Movement Was Born Amid Blazes." *Newsweek* (June 24, 1996).

Gregory, Joseph R. "African Slavery 1996." *First Things* 63 (May 1996).

Gross, Jane. "In School." *New York Times* (July 27, 1994).

Grossman, Cathy Lynn. "Season Fuels Debate Over Church, State." *USA Today* (December 15, 1993).

Gudel, Joseph P. "That Which Is Unnatural: Homosexuality in Society, the Church, and Scripture." *Christian Research Journal* 15:3 (Winter 1993).

Hall, Kermit L., ed. *The Oxford Companion to the Supreme Court of the United States.* New York: Oxford University Press, 1992.

Hall, Mimi. " 'Differences' Are Surgeon General's Downfall." *USA Today* (December 12, 1994).

Hall, Mimi. " 'Partial Birth' Abortions Face House Vote." *USA Today* (November 1, 1995).

Hall, Mimi. "Drumbeat Growing Against Elders." *USA Today* (June 29, 1994).

Hall, Mimi. "House Approves Ban on 'Partial Birth' Abortions." *USA Today* (November 2, 1995).

Hamblin, Ken. "Honest, Bill, It's Not So Bad Being Black." *Conservative Chronicle* (July 10, 1996).

Hardy, W. G. *The Greek and Roman World*, rev. ed. Cambridge, Mass.: Schenkman, 1970.

Harris, Abram. *The Negro as Capitalist.* New York: Arno Press, 1936.

Harris, James F. *Against Relativism: A Philosophical Defense of Method.* LaSalle, Ill.: Open Court, 1992.

Hart, Benjamin. *Faith and Freedom: The Christian Roots of American Liberty.* San Bernardino, Calif.: Here's Life Publishers, 1988.

Hart, Johnny. "B.C." *The Tennessean* (July 17, 1994).

Heilbrun, Carolyn G. *The Education of a Woman: The Life of Gloria Steinem.* New York: Dial Press, 1995.

Herbert, Bob. "The Crowd Was There, But Where the Leader?" *The Tennessean* (October 23, 1995).

Herlihy, David. "The Family and Religious Ideologies in Medieval Europe." *Journal of Family History* 12:1–3 (1987).

Herlihy, David. "The Making of the Medieval Family: Symmetry, Structure, and Sentiment." *Journal of Family History* (Summer 1983).

Hern, Warren M. "Is Pregnancy Normal?" *Family Planning Perspectives* 3:1 (January 1971).

Heth, William A., and Gordon J. Wenham. *Jesus and Divorce: The Problem With the*

Evangelical Consensus. Nashville, Tenn.: Thomas Nelson, 1984.

Higginbotham, Jr., A. Leon. *In the Matter of Color: Race and the American Legal Process: The Colonial Period.* New York: Oxford University Press, 1978.

Hilts, Philip J. "Blunt Style on Teen Sex and Health." *New York Times* (September 14, 1993).

Himmelfarb, Gertrude. *Victorian Minds: A Study of Intellectuals in Crisis and Ideologies in Transition.* Chicago, Ill.: Elephant, 1968.

Hofstadter, Richard. *Social Darwinism in American Thought.* Boston, Mass.: Beacon Press, 1983.

Hollis, Martin, and Steven Lukes, eds. *Rationality and Relativism.* Cambridge, Mass.: MIT Press, 1982.

Holmes, Steven A. "Gay Rights Groups Plot a Strategy in Ballot Fights." *New York Times* (January 12, 1994).

Holt, Thomas. *Black Over White: Negro Political Leadership in South Carolina During Reconstruction.* Urbana, Ill.: University of Illinois Press, 1977.

Horan Dennis J., and Thomas J. Balch. "*Roe v. Wade:* No Justification in History, Law, or Logic." *Abortion and the Constitution: Reversing* Roe v. Wade *Through the Courts.* Dennis J. Horan, Edward R. Grant, and Paige C. Cunningham, eds. Washington, D.C.: Georgetown University Press, 1987.

Horan, Dennis J., Edward R. Grant, and Paige C. Cunningham, eds. *Abortion and the Constitution: Reversing* Roe v. Wade *Through the Courts.* Washington, D.C.: Georgetown University Press, 1987.

Howlett, Debbie. "Clark Says Verdict Was Based on Race." *USA Today* (October 6, 1995).

Howlett, Debbie. "Crusade Now Quieter, More Focused." *USA Today* (February 14, 1994).

Howlett, Debbie. "Stonewall: Kicking the Closet Open." *USA Today* (June 24, 1994).

Howlett, Debbie. "Young, Poor, Uneducated Describe Most Arsonists." *USA Today* (July 1, 1996).

Hudson, Deal W. "Mortimer J. Adler and Multiculturalism." *Crisis* (January 1995).

Hull, Jon D. "The State of the Union." *Time* (January 30, 1995).

Hunter, James Davison. *Culture Wars: The Struggle to Define America.* New York: HarperCollins, 1991.

Hutchinson, Dennis J. "Brown v. Board of Education." *The Oxford Companion to the Supreme Court of the United States.* Kermit L. Hall, ed. (New York: Oxford University Press, 1992).

Iannone, Carol. "What Moderate Feminists?" *Commentary* (June 1995).

Irons, Peter, and Stephanie Guitton, eds. *May It Please the Court: The Most Significant Oral Arguments Before the Supreme Court Since 1955.* New York: New Press, 1993.

Isikoff, Michael. "The Silly Season." *Newsweek* (October 16, 1995).

James Otis. "Rights of the British Colonies" (1764).

James, Kay Coles. "A Condom for Every Kid." *World* (July 31, 1993).

Jastrow, Robert. "The Background to Darwin's Theory." *The Essential Darwin*, Masters of Modern Science Series. Robert Jastrow, gen. ed. Commentary and selections by Kenneth Korey. Boston, Mass.: Little, Brown and Co., 1984.

Jehl, Douglas. "Surgeon General Forced to Resign by White House." *New York Times* (December 10, 1994).

Johnson, Paul. *A History of Christianity.* New York: Atheneum, 1976.

Johnson, Paul. *The Birth of the Modern: World Society 1815–1830.* New York: HarperCollins, 1991.

Johnson, Phillip E. *Reason in the Balance: The Case Against Naturalism in Science, Law and Education.* Downers Grove, Ill.: InterVarsity Press, 1995.

Jones, E. Michael. "Beijing's Revenge: How Population Control Creates Illegal Immigration." *Culture Wars* (September 1995).

Jones, E. Michael. "Bela Does Cairo: The Great Satan Swings and Misses at the Cairo Conference on Population and Development." *Liberty, Life, and Family* 2:1 (1995).

Jones, E. Michael. "Dionysos Goes Free Again: The Cultural Scenario That Let O. J. Walk, *Culture Wars* (November 1995).

Jones, E. Michael. "The Beloved Community Gets Down: How the Civil Rights Movement Destroyed the Black Family. *Culture Wars* (October 1995).

Jones, E. Michael. *Degenerate Moderns: Modernity as Rationalized Sexual Misbehavior.* San Francisco, Calif.: Ignatius Press, 1993.

Jordan, Winthrop. *The White Man's Burden.* New York: Oxford University Press, 1974.

Kamenka, Eugene, ed. *The Portable Karl Marx.* New York: Viking Penguin, 1983.

Kaminer, Wendy. "Feminism's Identity Crisis." *The Atlantic Monthly* (October 1993).

Kanamine, Linda. "Number of Two-Parent Families Up." *USA Today* (October 16, 1995).

Kasun, Jacqueline R. "Cairo: A Second Opinion." *Culture Wars* (May 1995).

Keen, Judy. "March Affirms Farrakhan's Clout." *USA Today* (October 17, 1995).

Kennedy, D. James, and Jerry Newcombe. *What If Jesus Had Never Been Born?* Nashville, Tenn.: Thomas Nelson, 1994.

Kersten, Katherine. "What Do Women Want? A Conservative Manifesto." *Policy Review* (Spring 1991).

Kevles, Daniel J. *In the Name of Eugenics: Genetics and the Uses of Human Heredity.* Cambridge, Mass.: Harvard University Press, 1995.

Keyes, Alan. "Defining American Culture: A Panel Discussion." *Liberty, Life and Family* 2:1 (1995).

Keyes, Dick. "Lite Champions: Has Heroism Become a Trivial Pursuit?" *Christianity Today* (May 13, 1988).

Kimball, Roger. *Tenured Radicals: How Politics Has Corrupted Our Higher Education* (New York: Harper and Row, 1991).

King, Jr., Martin Luther. "I Have a Dream." *A Testament of Hope: The Essential*

Writings of Martin Luther King, Jr. James Melvin Washington, ed. San Francisco, Calif.: Harper and Row, 1986.

Kinsey, Alfred C., Wardell B. Pomeroy, and Clyde E. Martin. *Sexual Behavior in the Human Male.* Philadelphia, Pa.: W. B. Saunders, 1948.

Kinsey, Alfred C., Wardell B. Pomeroy, Clyde E. Martin, and Paul H. Gebhard. *Sexual Behavior in the Human Female.* Philadelphia, Pa.: W. B. Saunders, 1953.

Koerbel, Pam. *Does Anyone Else Feel Like I Do?: And Other Questions Women Ask Following an Abortion.* New York: Doubleday, 1990.

Kolchin, Peter. *American Slavery, 1619–1877.* New York: Hill and Wang, 1993.

Kourany, Janet A. et al., eds. *Feminist Philosophies: Problems, Theories, and Applications.* Englewood Cliffs, N.J.: Prentice-Hall, 1992.

Krausz, Michael, ed. *Relativism: Interpretation and Confrontation.* Notre Dame, Ind.: University of Notre Dame Press, 1989.

LaBarbera, Peter. "At the Gate: Homosexual Activists in San Francisco Besiege Church." *World* (October 9, 1993).

Lackey, Patrick K. "DMV OKs 'God' on License Plates." *Virginia Pilot* (January 14, 1994).

LaFollette, Hugh, and George Graham, eds. *Person to Person.* Philadelphia, Pa.: Temple University Press, 1987.

Landers, Robert K. "Conflict Over Multicultural Education." *Editorial Research Reports* (November 30, 1990).

Lawton, Kim A. " 'No Fault' Divorce Under Assault." *Christianity Today* (April 8, 1996).

Leach, Penelope. *Children First: What Our Society Must Do—and Is Not Doing—for Our Children Today.* New York: Alfred A. Knopf, 1994.

Leavitt, Paul. " 'Dr. Death' Case." *USA Today* (July 11, 1996).

Leavitt, Paul. "Church Arson." *USA Today* (July 10, 1996).

Lee, Jeannine, and Masud Khan. " 'Roe' Litigant's About-Face: 'I'm Pro-Life.' " *USA Today* (August 11, 1995).

Leffel, Jim. "Postmodern Impact: Literature." *The Death of Truth: What's Wrong with Multiculturalism, the Rejection of Reason, and the New Postmodern Diversity.* Dennis McCallum, ed. Minneapolis, Minn.: Bethany House, 1996.

Lefkowitz, Mary. *Not Out of Africa: How Afrocentrism Became an Excuse to Teach Myth As History.* New York: Basic Books, 1996.

Lefkowitz, Mary. "Not Out of Africa." *Chronicles* (September 1995).

Lehrman, Karen. "The Feminist Mystique." *The New Republic* (March 16, 1992).

Lejeune, Jerome. *The Concentration Can: When Does Human Life Begin? An Eminent Geneticist Testifies.* San Francisco, Calif.: Ignatius, 1992.

Leo, John. "Cradle-to-Grave Intimacy." *Time* (September 7, 1981).

Leo, John. "History Standards Are Bunk." *U.S. News and World Report* (February 6, 1995).

Leo, John. "The Hijacking of American History." *U.S. News and World Report* (November 14, 1994).

Leo, John. "The Trouble With Feminism." *U.S. News and World Report* (February 10, 1992).

Leo, John. "True Lies vs. Total Recall." *U.S. News and World Report* (August 7, 1995).

Leo, John. "Yale Is Latest Casualty of Multicultural Mush." *Conservative Chronicle* (April 5, 1995).

Leone, Bruno, and M. Teresa O'Neill, eds. *Sexual Values: Opposing Viewpoints.* St. Paul, Minn. Greenhaven Press, 1983.

Lewis, Anthony. "University Acts to Limit Free Speech." *The Tennessean* (November 29, 1995).

Lewis, C. S. *Mere Christianity.* New York: Macmillan, 1952.

Lewis, C. S. *The Abolition of Man.* New York: Macmillan, 1947.

Lewis, Dwight. "Hopefully, a Million Men Will Walk for Responsibility." *The Tennessean* (September 17, 1995).

Lobkowicz, Nikolaus. "Marxism As the Ideology of Our Age." *Truth* 1 (1985).

"Look at the Stats." *The Tennessean* (October 12, 1995).

Louv, Richard. *Childhood's Future.* New York: Anchor Books, 1990.

Luce, Clare Boothe. *Is the New Morality Destroying America?* Washington, D.C.: Ethics and Public Policy Center, 1979.

Lukes, Steven. "Five Fables About Human Rights," in *On Human Rights: The Oxford Amnesty Lectures, 1993.* Stephen Shute and Susan Hurley, eds. New York: Basic Books, 1993.

Lutzer, Erwin W. *The Necessity of Ethical Absolutes.* Grand Rapids, Mich.: Zondervan, 1981.

Lyall, Francis. *Slaves, Citizens, Sons: Legal Metaphors in the Epistles.* Grand Rapids, Mich.: Zondervan, 1984.

Lynn, Barry. "Defining American Culture: A Panel Discussion." *Liberty, Life, and Family* 2:1 (1995).

Mack, Kurt. "O. J. Is Not a Black Hero." *Newsweek* (October 30, 1995).

Madison, James. *Annals of the Congress,* vol. 1.

Madvig, D. H. "Corinth." *The International Standard Bible Encyclopedia,* rev. ed. Grand Rapids, Mich.: William B. Eerdmans, 1979.

Malthus, T. R. *A Summary View of the Principle of Population.* Reprinted in Thomas Robert Malthus. *An Essay on the Principle of Population* and *A Summary View of the Principle of Population.* Antony Flew, ed. New York: Penguin, 1970.

Manney, James, and John C. Blattner. *Death in the Nursery: The Secret Crime of Infanticide.* Ann Arbor, Mich.: Servant, 1984.

Margolis, Joseph. "Deferring to Derrida's Difference." *European Philosophy and the American Academy.* Barry Smith, ed. LaSalle, Ill.: Hegeler Institute, 1994.

Marshall, Robert G., and Charles A. Donovan. *Blessed Are the Barren: The Social Policy of Planned Parenthood.* San Francisco: Ignatius, 1991.

Marshall, Steve. "Group: Black Churches Are 'Endangered.'" *USA Today* (June 17, 1996).

Maslow, Abraham, and James M. Sakoda. "Volunteer Error in the Kinsey Study."

The Journal of Abnormal and Social Psychology 42:2 (April 1952).

Mason, Mike. *The Mystery of Marriage.* Portland, Ore.: Multnomah Press, 1985.

Mathewes-Green, Frederica. *Real Choices: Offering Practical, Life-Affirming Alternatives to Abortion.* Sisters, Ore.: Multnomah, 1994.

Mauro, Tony. "Court Mulls Aid for Christian Magazine." *USA Today* (November 1, 1994).

Mauro, Tony. "Court Rules Against Jewish School District." *USA Today* (June 28, 1994).

Maynard, Roy. "Non-Sexual Revolution." *World* (December 11, 1993).

McCallum, Dennis, ed. *The Death of Truth: What's Wrong with Multiculturalism, the Rejection of Reason, and the New Postmodern Diversity.* Minneapolis, Minn.: Bethany House, 1996.

McCormick, John, Mark Starr, Vern E. Smith, and Howard Fineman. "Whites v. Blacks." *Newsweek* (October 16, 1995).

McCorvey, Norma, with Andy Meisler. *I Am Roe: My Life,* Roe v. *Wade, and Freedom of Choice.* New York: HarperCollins, 1994.

McDonald, H. *The Christian View of Man.* Westchester, Ill.: Crossway, 1981.

McGowan, Jo. "In India, They Abort Females." *Newsweek* (January 30, 1989).

McIlhaney, Jr., Joe S. *Why Condoms Aren't Safe.* Colorado Springs, Colo.: Focus on the Family, 1993.

McManus, Michael J. *Marriage Savers: Helping Your Friends and Family Stay Married.* Grand Rapids, Mich.: Zondervan, 1993.

Means, Marianne. "What Planet Were Those Women On?" *The Tennessean* (October 14, 1995).

"Message of Today's March Is Self-Help, Not Racism." *USA Today* (October 16, 1995).

Mestel, Rosie. "Sex by the Numbers." *Discover* (January 1994).

Michael, Robert T., John H. Gagnon, Edward O. Laumann, and Gina Kolata. *Sex in America: A Definitive Survey.* Boston, Mass.: Little, Brown and Co., 1994.

Middleton, J. Richard, and Brian J. Walsh. "Facing the Postmodern Scalpel: Can the Christian Faith Withstand Deconstruction?" *Christian Apologetics in the Postmodern World.* Timothy R. Phillips and Dennis L. Okholm, eds. Downers Grove, Ill.: InterVarsity Press, 1995.

Miller, Mark and Marc Peyser. " 'We Live in Daily Fear.' " *Newsweek* (September 2, 1996).

Miller, William Lee. *Arguing About Slavery: The Great Battle in the United States Congress.* New York: Alfred A. Knopf, 1996.

Mills, Gary B. *The Forgotten People: Cane River's Creoles of Color.* Baton Rouge, La.: Louisiana State University Press, 1977.

Mills, Nicolaus, ed. *Debating Affirmative Action: Race, Gender, Ethnicity, and the Politics of Inclusion.* New York: Dell, 1994.

Mirken, Bruce. "School Programs Should Stress Acceptance of Homosexuality." *Homosexuality: Opposing Views.* William Dudley, ed. (San Diego, Calif.: Greenhaven Press, 1993.

Mittelstadt, Michelle. "Jane Roe Defection Another Thorn in Pro-Choice's Side." *The Tennessean* (August 13, 1995).

Monaghan, Thomas Patrick. "Misusing the Constitution." *Law & Justice* 2:3 (May/June 1993).

Monaghan, Thomas Patrick. "The Abiding Unconstitutionality and Illegitimacy of *Roe v. Wade.*" *Liberty, Life, and Family* 1 (1994).

Moreland, J. P., and David M. Ciocchi, eds. *Christian Perspectives on Being Human: A Multidisciplinary Approach to Integration.* Grand Rapids, Mich.: Baker Book House, 1993.

Moreland, J. P. "James Rachels and the Active Euthanasia Debate." *Journal of the Evangelical Theological Society* 31:1 (March 1988).

Morganthau, Tom, with Ginny Carroll, Daniel Klaidman, Mark Miller, and Martha Brant. "Fires in the Night." *Newsweek* (June 24, 1996).

Moss, Desda, and Gary Fields. "Men Ready for Rally Today." *USA Today* (October 16, 1995).

Moss, Desda. "Islam March Is Tapping Into Mainstream." *USA Today* (September 25, 1995).

Moss, Desda, and Gary Fields. "Jackson Finds He's in Tight Spot." *USA Today* (October 16, 1995).

Moss, Desda, and Gary Fields. "Mobilizing One Million." *USA Today* (October 13–15, 1995).

Mount, Ferdinand. *The Subversive Family: An Alternative History of Love and Marriage.* New York: The Free Press, 1992.

Muller, Jerry Z. "Coming Out Ahead: The Homosexual Moment in the Academy." *First Things* (August/September 1993).

Murphy-O-Connor, Jerome. "Corinthian Slogans in 1 Corinthians 6:12–20." *The Catholic Biblical Quarterly* 40:3 (July 1978).

Muschamp, Herbert. "A Sanctuary, Yes, but This Is Not a Place to Hide." *New York Times* (November 28, 1994).

Nash, Ronald H. *The Closing of the American Heart: What's Really Wrong with America's Schools.* Dallas, Tex.: Probe Books, 1990.

Neuhaus, Richard John. "The Feminist Revelation." *First Things* (December 1991).

Newman, Leslea, and Diana Souza. *Heather Has Two Mommies.* Boston, Mass.: Alyson Publications, 1989.

Ney, Philip G. "Is Elective Abortion a Cause of Child Abuse?" *Sexual Medicine Today* 40:6 (June 1980).

Noll, Mark A. *A History of Christianity in the United States and Canada.* Grand Rapids, Mich.: William B. Eerdmans, 1992.

"Nontraditional Families Gaining." *The Tennessean* (July 30, 1994).

Norris, Christopher. "The 'Apocalyptic Tone' in Philosophy: Kierkegaard, Derrida and the Rhetoric of Transcendence." *European Philosophy and the American Academy,* Barry Smith, ed.. LaSalle, Ill: Hegeler Institute, 1994.

Nuechterlein, James. "O. J. Simpson and the American Dilemma." *First Things* (December 1995).

Nuland, Sherwin B. *How We Die: Reflections on Life's Final Chapter.* New York: Alfred A. Knopf, 1993.

O'Beirne, Kate. "Bread & Circuses." *National Review* (May 6, 1996).

Offen, Karen. "Defining Feminism: A Comparative Historical Approach." *Signs: Journal of Women in Culture and Society* 14:1 (1988).

"Ongoing Legal Activities." *Law & Justice* 3:1 (1994).

"One Verdict, Clashing Voices." *Newsweek* (October 16, 1995).

Ostling, Richard N. "In So Many Gods We Trust." *Time* (January 30, 1995).

Owens, Joseph. *A History of Ancient Western Philosophy.* Englewood Cliffs, N.J.: Prentice-Hall, 1959.

Owens, Roger G. "Racism's Imprint on Church Burnings." *USA Today* (July 1, 1996).

Padover, Saul K. *Thomas Jefferson and the Foundations of American Freedom.* New York: Van Nostrand Reinhold, 1965.

Page, Susan. "Clinton to Urge Healing in Visit to Site of Arson." *USA Today* (June 11, 1996).

Page, Susan. "Clinton Urges Both Races to 'Clean House.'" *USA Today* (October 17, 1995).

Page, Susan. "Late-Term Abortion Bill Vetoed." *USA Today* (April 11, 1996).

Paine, Thomas. *Rights of Man, Part Second* (1792).

Painter, Kim. "More Figures on Homosexuality." *USA Today* (October 7, 1994).

Painter, Kim. "Teens and Sex a Fact of American Life." *USA Today* (June 7, 1994).

Parks, Ward. "Textual Imperialism." *European Philosophy and the American Academy.* Barry Smith, ed. LaSalle, Ill.: Hegeler Institute, 1994.

Parshall, Gerald. "Hanging Offenses." *U.S. News and World Report* (March 6, 1995).

Patenaude, Michele. "On Not Having Children." *Childless by Choice: A Feminist Anthology.* Irene Reti, ed. Santa Cruz, Calif.: HerBooks, 1992.

Patterson, James, and Peter Kim. *The Day America Told the Truth: What People Really Believe About Everything That Really Matters.* New York: Plume, 1991.

Patterson, James, and Peter Kim. *The Second American Revolution.* New York: William Morrow and Co., 1994.

Payne, J. Barton. *The Theology of the Older Testament.* Grand Rapids, Mich.: Zondervan, 1962.

Peterson, Karen S. "A Million Men, a Single Message." *USA Today* (October 13, 1995).

Peterson, Karen S. "Cohabiting First Doesn't Secure Knot." *USA Today* (May 10, 1995).

Peterson, Merrill D., ed. *The Portable Thomas Jefferson.* New York: Penguin Books, 1975.

Phillips, Timothy R., and Dennis L. Okholm, eds. *Christian Apologetics in the Postmodern World.* Downers Grove, Ill.: InterVarsity Press, 1995.

Plato, *Theaetetus.*

Pogrebin, Letty Cottin. *Family Politics: Love and Power on an Intimate Frontier.* New York: McGraw-Hill, 1983.

Pojman, Louis P., ed. *Philosophy: The Quest for Truth.* Belmont, Calif.: Wadsworth, 1989.

Pollock, John C. "William Wilberforce and the Abolition of Slavery." in *Great Leaders of the Christian Church,* John D. Woodbridge, ed. Chicago: Moody Press, 1988.

Pomeroy, Wardell B. *Dr. Kinsey and the Institute for Sex Research.* New York: Harper and Row, 1972.

Popenoe, David. "American Family Decline, 1960–1990: A Review and Appraisal." *Journal of Marriage and the Family* 55 (August 1993).

Price, Richard. "For the Public, Deliberations Go On." *USA Today* (October 6, 1995).

Quinn, Sally. "The Feminist Betrayal." *Reader's Digest* (June 1992).

"Quoting Bible Wins New Trial." *The Tennessean* (October 17, 1993).

Rachels, James. "A Critique of Ethical Relativism." *Philosophy: The Quest for Truth,* Louis P. Pojman, ed. Belmont, Calif.: Wadsworth, 1989.

Rachels, James, ed. *The Right Thing to Do: Basic Readings in Moral Philosophy.* New York: Random House, 1989.

Rakove, Jack N. *Original Meanings: Politics and Ideas in the Making of the Constitution.* New York: Alfred A. Knopf, 1996.

Rawson, Beryl. "Family Life Among the Lower Classes at Rome in the First Two Centuries of the Empire." *Classical Philology* 61:2 (April 1966).

"Recent Victories and Other Legal Activities." *Law & Justice* 2:3 (May/June 1993).

Reese, Charley. "Arson Doesn't Justify Demagoguery." *Conservative Chronicle* (July 10, 1996).

Reilly, John J. "The Fish Rots First at the Head." *Culture Wars* (March 1996).

Reilly, Robert R. "The Truths They Held: The Christian and Natural Law Background to the American Constitution." *We Hold These Truths and More: Further Catholic Reflections on the American Proposition.* Donald J. D'Elia and Stephen M. Krason, eds. Steubenville, Ohio: Franciscan University Press, 1993.

Reisman, Judith A., and Edward W. Eichel. *Kinsey, Sex, and Fraud: The Doctrination of a People.* Lafayette, La.: Huntington House, 1990.

Rensberger, Boyce. "Damping the World's Population." *Washington Post National Weekly Edition* (September 12–18, 1994).

Reti, Irene, ed. *Childless by Choice: A Feminist Anthology.* Santa Cruz, Calif.: Her-Books, 1992.

Reynolds, Barbara. "Guilty Get Away, Innocents Die When Justice Fails." *USA Today* (October 6, 1995).

Rice, Charles. *Fifty Questions on the Natural Law: What It Is and Why We Need It.* San Francisco, Calif.: Ignatius Press, 1993.

Richert, Christine. "Sex Education Encourages Promiscuity." *Sexual Values: Opposing Viewpoints.* Bruno Leone and M. Teresa O'Neill, eds. St. Paul, Minn.: Greenhaven Press, 1983.

Rimer, Sara. "Trip to History for Boston Teenagers: To the South of the Civil Rights Fight." *New York Times* (July 29, 1994).

Roberge, Lawrence F. *The Cost of Abortion: An Analysis of the Social, Economic, and Demographic Effects of Abortion on the United States.* LaGrange, Ga.: Four Winds, 1995.

Roberts, Paul Craig. "Why We Should Tar and Feather the Supreme Court." *Conservative Chronicle* (June 5, 1996).

Robinson, John Mansley. *An Introduction to Early Greek Philosophy.* Boston: Houghton Mifflin, 1968.

Rosenblatt, Roger. "A Nation of Pained Hearts." *Time* (October 16, 1995).

Rowan, Carl. "Farrakhan and Chavis Can Only Hurt Black Men." *The Tennessean* (October 13, 1995).

Royal, Robert. *1492 and All That: Political Manipulations of History.* Washington, D.C.: Ethics and Public Policy Center, 1992.

Rule, Jane. *Lesbian Images.* New York: Doubleday, 1975.

Russakoff, Dale. "Driving a Point Home: The First Rule of Selling a House: Locution, Locution, Locution." *Washington Post National Weekly Edition* (June 6–12, 1994).

Russell, Bertrand. *Why I Am Not a Christian.* New York: Simon and Schuster, 1957.

Sacks, David O., and Peter A. Thiel. *The Diversity Myth: "Multiculturalism" and the Politics of Intolerance at Stanford.* Oakland, Calif.: The Independent Institute, 1995.

Salholz, Eloise, with Pamela Ambramson, Shawn Doherty, Renee Michael, and Diane Weathers. "Feminism's Identity Crisis." *Newsweek* (March 31, 1986).

Sanger, Margaret. "A Parents' Problem or Woman's?" *The Birth Control Review* (March 1919).

Sanger, Margaret. "Birth Control and Racial Betterment." *The Birth Control Review* (February 1919).

Sanger, Margaret. "Birth Control or Abortion?" *The Birth Control Review* (December 1918).

Sanger, Margaret. "Birth Control." *State Government/American Legislator* (September 7, 1934).

Sanger, Margaret. "Birth Control—Past, Present and Future." *The Birth Control Review* (August 1921).

Sanger, Margaret. "Morality and Birth Control." *The Birth Control Review* (March 1919).

Sanger, Margaret. "No Healthy Race without Birth Control." *Physical Culture* (March 1921).

Sanger, Margaret. "Preparing for the World Crisis." *The Birth Control Review* (April 1920).

Sanger, Margaret. "The Case for Birth Control." *The Crisis* 4:6 (1934).

Sanger, Margaret. "The Case for Birth Control." *The Woman Citizen* (February 23, 1924).

Sanger, Margaret. "The Eugenic Value of Birth Control Propaganda." *The Birth Control Review* (October 1921).

Sanger, Margaret. "The Function of Sterilization." *The Birth Control Review* (October 1926).

Sanger, Margaret. "The Need for Birth Control." *The Birth Control Review* (August 1928).

Sanger, Margaret. "The Pope's Position on Birth Control." *The Nation* (January 27, 1932).

Sanger, Margaret. "The Tragedy of the Accidental Child." *The Birth Control Review* (April 1919).

Sanger, Margaret. "The War Against Birth Control." *The American Mercury* 2:6 (July 1924).

Sanger, Margaret. "War and Population." *The Birth Control Review* (June 1922).

Sanger, Margaret. "Wasting Our Human Resources." *The Birth Control Review* (March 1920).

Sanger, Margaret. "When Should a Woman Avoid Having Children?" *The Birth Control Review* (November 1918).

Sanger, Margaret. "Why Not Birth Control in America?" *The Birth Control Review* (May 1919).

Sanger, Margaret. "Women and Birth Control." *The North American Review* (May 1929).

Sanger, Margaret. *Woman and the New Race.* New York: Brentano's, 1920.

Saucy, Robert L. "Theology of Human Nature," in *Christian Perspectives on Being Human: A Multidisciplinary Approach to Integration.* J. P. Moreland and David M. Ciocchi, eds. Grand Rapids, Mich.: Baker Book House, 1993.

Schlafly, Phyllis. "Controversial History Standards Fight Back." *Conservative Chronicle* (March 29, 1995).

Schlesinger, Jr., Arthur M. *The Disuniting of America: Reflections on a Multicultural Society.* New York: W. W. Norton and Co., 1992.

Schmidt, Thomas E. *Straight and Narrow? Compassion and Clarity in the Homosexuality Debate.* Downers Grove, Ill.: InterVarsity Press, 1995.

Schmitt, Frederick F. *Truth: A Primer.* Boulder, Colo.: Westview Press, 1995.

Schoeck, Helmut, and James W. Higgins, eds. *Relativism and the Study of Man,* Princeton, N.J.: D. Van Nostrand, 1961.

"School's Out to Lunch." *National Review* (May 6, 1996).

Sekulow, Jay Alan. "A Reason for Hope." *CaseNote* (February 1994).

Sekulow, Jay Alan. "Quick Action Provides Avenue for Gospel!" *CaseNote* (September 1994).

Sekulow, Jay Alan. "Religious Speech and the First Amendment," *Law & Justice* 2:3 (May/June 1993).

Sekulow, Jay Alan. "Second-Grader Formally Disciplined for Typing 'Jesus' on School Computer." *CaseNote* 2:5 (1995).

Sekulow, Jay Alan. "The Abortion Distortion." *Law & Justice* 2:1 (Fall 1992).

Sekulow, Jay Alan. "We Still Have a Prayer." *Law & Justice* 4:3 (1995).

Shaffern, Robert W. "Christianity and the Rise of the Nuclear Family." *America* (May 7, 1994).

Shain, Barry Alan. *The Myth of American Individualism: The Protestant Origins of American Political Thought.* Princeton, N.J.: Princeton University Press, 1994.

Sharn, Lori. "Churches Get Aid in Time of Need." *USA Today* (June 17, 1996).

"She Won a License to Pray." *Woman's World* (May 31, 1994).

Sheffield, K. "Wrong to Categorize All 'Blacks' As One." *The Tennessean* (October 15, 1995).

Sheler, Jeffery L. "Spiritual America." *U.S. News and World Report* (April 4, 1994).

Shettles, Landrum, and David Rorvik. *Rites of Life: The Scientific Evidence for Life Before Birth.* Grand Rapids, Mich.: Zondervan, 1983.

Shinkoskey, Robert Kimball. "Without Law." *The Family in America* 7:1 (January 1993).

Shipman, Pat. *The Evolution of Racism: Human Differences and the Use and Abuse of Science.* New York: Simon and Schuster, 1994.

Singer, Peter, and Helga Kuhse. "On Letting Handicapped Babies Die." *The Right Thing to Do: Basic Readings in Moral Philosophy,* 1st ed., James Rachels, ed. New York: Random House, 1989.

Smedley, Audrey. *Race in North America.* Boulder, Colo.: Westview Press, 1993.

Smith, Barry, ed. *European Philosophy and the American Academy.* LaSalle, Ill.: Hegeler Institute, 1994.

Smith, Page. *Rediscovering Christianity: A History of Modern Democracy and the Christian Ethic.* New York: St. Martin's Press, 1994.

Smith, Patricia. "School Programs Should Not Stress Acceptance of Homosexuality." *Homosexuality: Opposing Views.* William Dudley, ed. San Diego, Calif.: Greenhaven Press, 1993.

Solzhenitsyn, Alexandr, Mikhail Agursky, A. B., Evgeny Barabanov, Vadim Borisov, F. Korsakov, and Igor Shafarevich. *From Under the Rubble.* A. M. Brock et al., trans. Washington, D.C.: Regnery Gateway, 1981.

Somerville, John. *The Philosophy of Marxism.* New York: Random House, 1967.

Sommers, Christina Hoff. "Hard-Line Feminists Guilty of Ms.-Representation." *Wall Street Journal* (November 7, 1991).

Sommers, Christina Hoff. "Philosophers Against the Family." *Person to Person,* Hugh LaFollette and George Graham, eds. Philadelphia, Pa.: Temple University Press, 1987.

Sommers, Christina Hoff. *Who Stole Feminism? How Women Have Betrayed Women.* New York: Simon and Schuster, 1994.

Sowell, Thomas. *Civil Rights: Rhetoric or Reality?* New York: William Morrow, 1984.

Sowell, Thomas. *Ethnic America: A History.* New York: Basic Books, 1981.

Sowell, Thomas. *Inside American Education: The Decline, the Deception, the Dogmas.* New York: The Free Press, 1993.

Sowell, Thomas. *Marxism: Philosophy and Economics.* New York: William Morrow and Co., 1985.

Sowell, Thomas. *Preferential Policies: An International Perspective.* New York: William Morrow, 1990.

Sowell, Thomas. *Race and Culture: A World View.* New York: Basic Books, 1994.

Sowell, Thomas. *The Economics and Politics of Race: An International Perspective.* New York: Quill, 1983.

Stacey, Judith. "Good Riddance to 'The Family': A Response to David Popenoe." *Journal of Marriage and the Family* (August 1993).

Stacey, Julie. "Children Bearing Children." *USA Today* (February 22, 1994).

Stafford, Tim. "Are People the Problem?" *Christianity Today* (October 3, 1994).

Stampp, Kenneth. *The Peculiar Institution: Slavery in the Antebellum South.* New York: Vintage, 1956.

Steinem, Gloria. "Foreword." *The Choices We Made.* Angela Bonavoglia, ed. New York: Random House, 1991.

Steinem, Gloria. *Outrageous Acts and Everyday Rebellions,* 2d ed. New York: Henry Holt and Co., 1995.

Steward, Samuel A. "Remembering Dr. Kinsey: Sexual Scientist and Investigator." *The Advocate* (November 13, 1980).

"Still Fuming Over the O. J. Verdict." *Newsweek* (October 30, 1995).

Stix, Nicholas. "Black English." *Chronicles* (September 1995).

Sullivan, Christopher. "Simpson—Blacks Reflect." Associated Press (October 3, 1995).

Sweet, William W. *The Story of Religion in America.* Grand Rapids, Mich.: Baker Book House, 1973.

Taylor, E. L. Hebden. *The Reformational Understanding of Family and Marriage.* Nutley, N.J.: Craig Press, 1975.

Taylor, Jared. *Paved With Good Intentions: The Failure of Race Relations in Contemporary America.* New York: Carroll and Graf, 1992.

Taylor, John. "Are You Politically Correct?" *Are You Politically Correct? Debating America's Cultural Standards.* Francis J. Beckwith and Michael E. Bauman, eds. Buffalo, N.Y.: Prometheus Books, 1993.

"Teens Talk About Sexuality." *USA Weekend* (September 22–24, 1995).

"Texas County Reverses Decision, Will Accept Firm's Gay Benefit Policy." *Dallas/Fort Worth Heritage* (January 1994).

Thomas, Cal. "There Is a Simple Explanation: She Had a Conversion." *The Tennessean* (August 16, 1995).

Thompson, Anne. "Simpson—Money or Race?" Associated Press (October 4, 1995).

Thornton, Jeannye. " 'I'm Not Going to Ride the Bus.' " *U.S. News and World Report* (December 11, 1995).

Tidball, Derek. *The Social Context of the New Testament: A Sociological Analysis.* Grand Rapids, Mich.: Zondervan, 1984.

Turow, Scott. "Where Have All the Radicals Gone?" *Newsweek* (September 2, 1996).

"Two Major Court Decisions and Other Recent Victories and Activities." *Law & Justice* 2:2 (Spring 1993).

U.S. Bureau of the Census. *Negro Population of the United States: 1790–1915.* Washington, D.C.

Usdansky, Margaret L. " 'Blended,' 'Extended' Now All in the Family." *USA Today* (August 30, 1994).

Varma, Kavita. "New, Not-So Politically Correct, Goals for History." *USA Today* (April 3, 1996).

Varma, Kavita. "Revised History Standards Blunt 'Bias' Criticism." *USA Today* (April 3, 1996).

Veith, Jr., Gene Edward. *Postmodern Times: A Christian Guide to Contemporary Thought and Culture.* Wheaton, Ill.: Crossway, 1994.

Vitz, Paul C. "An American Disaster: Moral Relativism," in *In Search of a National Morality: A Manifesto for Evangelicals and Catholics.* William Bentley Ball, ed. Grand Rapids, Mich.: Baker Book House; San Francisco, Calif.: Ignatius Press, 1992.

Voeller, Bruce. "Stonewall Anniversary." *The Advocate* (July 12, 1979).

Wallis, Claudia. "The Nuclear Family Goes Boom!" *Time* (Fall 1992).

Waltke, Bruce K. "Reflections from the Old Testament on Abortion." *Journal of the Evangelical Theological Society* 19:1 (Winter 1976).

Washington, James Melvin, ed. *A Testament of Hope: The Essential Writings of Martin Luther King, Jr.* San Francisco, Calif.: Harper and Row, 1986.

Watkins, Jr., William J. "*Plessy* v. *Ferguson*—One Hundred Years Later." *Chronicles* (August 1996).

Weatherhead, Leslie D. *It Happened in Palestine.* London: Hodder and Stoughton, 1936.

Weaver, Richard M. *Ideas Have Consequences.* Chicago: University of Chicago Press, 1948.

Weigel, George. "What Really Happened at Cairo." *First Things* (February 1995).

Westermann, Claus. *Genesis 1–11: A Commentary.* John J. Scullion, trans. Minneapolis, Minn.: Augsburg, 1984.

Westfall, Bruce. "The Sex Revolution's Phony Foundation." *Citizen* (September 16, 1991).

Whaley, Kimberlee, and Elizabeth Blue Swadener. "Multicultural Education in Infant and Toddler Settings." *Childhood Education* (Summer 1990).

"Whee! the People." *Citizen* (July 22, 1996).

Whitehead, Barbara Dafoe. "The Failure of Sex Education." *The Atlantic Monthly* (October 1994).

Whitehead, Barbara Dafoe. "The Moral State of Marriage." *The Atlantic Monthly* (September 1995).

Whitehead, K. D. "Is It Time to Get Rid of the Surgeon General? Part I: The Rise and Fall of Joycelyn Elders." *Culture Wars* (July/August 1995).

Will, George. "To What Has Constitutional Law Come?" *Conservative Chronicle* (June 5, 1996).

Willard, Dallas. "The Unhinging of the American Mind: Derrida as Pretext." *European Philosophy and the American Academy.* Barry Smith, ed. LaSalle, Ill.: Hegeler Institute, 1994.

Willhoite, Michael. *Daddy's Roommate.* Boston, Mass.: Alyson Wonderland, 1990.

Williams, Walter. "Why Do We Listen to Fools?" *Conservative Chronicle* (March 1, 1995).

Willis, Ellen. "Abortion: Is a Woman a Person?" in *Feminist Philosophies: Problems, Theories, and Applications.* Janet A. Kourany et al., eds. Englewood Cliffs, N.J.: Prentice-Hall, 1992.

Winn, Pete. "What's New in School? Lesbians and Wizards." *Citizen* (June 18, 1990).

Wirt, Sherwood Eliot. *The Social Conscience of the Evangelical.* New York: Harper and Row, 1968.

Witchel, Alex. "The Real Jane Roe, Unlikely Role Model." *New York Times* (July 28, 1994).

"Witness Abortion, Senators Urged." *USA Today* (November 3, 1995).

"Witness Abortion, Senators Urged." *The Tennessean* (November 18, 1995).

Wolfe, Gregory. "The Humanities in Crisis: A Symposium." *The Intercollegiate Review* 23 (Fall 1987).

Woodard, J. David. "Same-Sex Politics." *World* (October 30, 1993).

Woodbridge, John D., ed. *Great Leaders of the Christian Church.* Chicago: Moody Press, 1988.

Yanak, Ted, and Pam Cornelison. *The Great American History Fact-Finder.* Boston, Mass.: Houghton Mifflin, 1993.

Zimmerman, Carle C. *Family and Civilization.* New York: Harper and Brothers, 1947.

Index of Proper Names